CHAUCER AND THE JEWS

THE MULTICULTURAL MIDDLE AGES
Sheila Delany, Series Editor

CHAUCER AND THE JEWS
Sources, Contexts, Meanings
edited by Sheila Delany

CHAUCER AND THE JEWS
SOURCES, CONTEXTS, MEANINGS

EDITED BY SHEILA DELANY

ROUTLEDGE
NEW YORK AND LONDON

Published in 2002 by
Routledge
29 West 35th Street
New York, NY 10001

Published in Great Britain by
Routledge
11 New Fetter Lane
London EC4P 4EE

Routledge is an imprint of the Taylor & Francis Group.

Printed in the United States of America on acid-free paper.

10 9 8 7 6 5 4 3 2 1

Library of Congress Cataloging-in-Publication Data is available from the Library of Congress.
Chaucer and the Jews/edited by Sheila Delany

ISBN 0-415-93882-1

Contents

v

Acknowledgments

First and foremost I want to thank the contributors to this volume, especially the authors of new essays, who rose heroically to the several challenges of early deadlines, editorial exigency, and press requirements. At Routledge, Anne Davidson has been warmly supportive of this project, and before the volume was transferred to Routledge via its parent company's purchase of Garland, Paul Szarmach, director of the Medieval Institute at Western Michigan University, and Chris Zacher, of Ohio State University, welcomed the volume into a Garland series.

Preparation of the manuscript could not have proceeded smoothly without the invaluable aid of my techie research assistants, Margot Kaminski and Blair Leggett; I fervently thank them for their time, effort, perfectionism, and electronic wizardry. Aeron Carre and Ken Kaminski provided technical support and advice at crucial moments. Also essential were the marvelously helpful staff at Simon Fraser University's Bennett Library, especially Mark Bodnar and Emily Sheldon.

Acknowledgment is due to Mary Hamel at the *Chaucer Review* for permission to reprint Elisa Narin van Court's essay from vol. 29 (1995); to St. Martin's Press for Sylvia Tomasch's chapter from The *Postcolonial Middle Ages,* ed. Jeffrey J. Cohen (2000); to Maud McInerney and Routledge for Christine Rose's chapter in *Hildegard of Bingen* . . . (Garland, 1998); to Brill Publishers for my article from *Medieval Encounters* (vol. 5, 1999); and to Frank Cass Company for Colin Richmond's chapter in *The Jewish Heritage in British History: Englishness and Jewishness*, ed. Tony Kushner (1992).

Editor's Introduction

SHEILA DELANY

When Sir Edmund Hillary was asked why he climbed Mount Everest, he replied, "Because it's there." My impulse for this project was the opposite: because it isn't there. Such a book, whether in collection or monograph format, hasn't existed, but is needed for many reasons. In part, this project grows out of the same realization that inspired a previous one, my guest-edited book-length issue of *Exemplaria* (12.1, 2000), titled *"Turn it again": Medieval Jewish Studies and Literary Theory*. My then-recently developed attention to medieval Jewish culture had indicated little mutual awareness between conventionally trained medievalists and their Jewish studies colleagues. The *Exemplaria* issue was meant to help bridge that gap by publishing the work of a group of theoretically informed Jewish studies medievalists. The present volume does something similar with a canonical English author: to recuperate a side of his work and culture that has usually been occluded.

In a real sense it was Chaucer that turned me to Jewish studies—more precisely, teaching Chaucer's poetry—because of the impatience I increasingly felt when, of necessity, ventriloquizing Catholic doctrine in order to render his work accessible and comprehensible to my (mostly Christian secular) students. The problematic that Gillian Steinberg and Judith Neaman address in their discussions of teaching this material to Jewish students is not limited to the Orthodox. A secular, even atheistic Jew might well feel just as troubled by the ethico-theological underpinnings of Chaucer's or other medieval Catholic poetry as an observant rabbi-to-be. I wonder how many readers bridled at the phrase "Catholic poetry" in the previous sentence: Do we think of Chaucer as exemplifying *Catholic* poetry? Do we offer courses in "Renaissance Christian drama" when teaching Shakespeare and others; in "the Anglo-Catholic sonnet sequence"; in "medieval Catholic lyric," or "European Catholic romance in translation"? That we generally do not— despite an abundance of Jewish or indeed Islamic material in all these genres—is precisely the point. We would probably be asked, or feel compelled, to specify if teaching a course in medieval Jewish literature (an exhilarating experience that I strongly recommend to any medievalist), but the other label is invisible because—as Colin Richmond's essay documents—it is culturally normative, hence requires no specification. This has been the case even when, as Richmond argues, the Jews, whether present or absent, were crucial to the formation of Anglo-Saxon attitudes and the concept of "Englishness" itself.

"Tell it like it is": a difficult imperative for historians or historicists, especially those working in medieval studies. "Alterity" and "presentism" come to mind as signals of the shoals: do we dare to impose our sense of things on a much earlier period, which may have been irredeemably different from our own? Yet if there is one thing that hasn't changed down the ages, surely it is the attempt to manufacture consent (in Noam Chomsky's phrase). David Aers has reminded us how very manufactured is the consent, the consensus, around religious matters, how demanding of the powers not only of the holy but of the state, its armed forces, its judiciary, its cooperating intellectuals.[1]

Those are the sorts of powers examined here, as the writers collected in this volume contemplate the paradox of what Gloria Cigman some time ago called "an absent presence."[2] She meant the absence and presence of Jews, expelled from England in 1290 by royal mandate (though no official document has been found, any more than for the French expulsion of 1394). The English expulsion occurred only about a half century before Chaucer's birth, so that during his early lifetime there might still have been a few converted Jews in England,[3] and certainly old folk who, as children, had lived alongside them and who remembered them—much as middle-aged or elderly Hungarians today remember the Jews who were taken from their villages during World War II and who never returned. Only late in the seventeenth century, after years of inconclusive national debate, did Jews begin to enter England in significant numbers (although a few had emigrated there earlier, whether after the Spanish expulsion of 1492 or as employees at court).[4]

Despite their physical absence, the literary, theological, and visual representation of Jews continued; hence the questions animating this volume are "How?" and "Why?" By what channels were late medieval English writers enabled to represent Jews, and for what motives—personal, political, or cultural—did they wish to do so? Timothy Jones and Mary Dove examine the legacy of Hebrew scripture as reinterpreted and retranslated during the fourteenth century. Denise Despres explores the significance of the late-fourteenth-century Vernon manuscript, produced during Chaucer's lifetime, as a vehicle for ambivalent attitudes toward Jews; a similar approach is taken in Elisa Narin van Court's contextualized study of the late-fourteenth-century alliterative historical romance *The Siege of Jerusalem.* The peculiarity of the

English experience is reflected, Nancy Turner argues, in theologian Robert Holcot's representation of Jews in his "Wisdom Commentary," a work known to Chaucer. Anthony Bale pushes beyond Chaucer into the fifteenth century with his illuminating history of the production and consumption of material on the cult of little Robert of Bury, drawing on materials in the Chaucerian and post-Chaucerian cultural environment.

Some readers may respond to this volume by observing that it doesn't fit the mandate expressed in its title: not through insufficiency (though surely a few will have a Chaucerian work or phrase in mind that could have been written about), but rather through excess, for the volume considers much more than Chaucer per se. That is because I have sought to challenge the idea of "author per se": an exercise we can learn from various sources—for me, Marxian dialectic, which always investigates source, context, and trajectory, has been primary; for others, the work of Michel Foucault, interdisciplinary scholars, or new historicists whether renaissance or medieval will loom larger. There are many roads into the Middle Ages, each leading to or producing a different Middle Ages. Chaucer is neither the only nor invariably the best road in, and one way to show this is to dissolve his canonically, at least partially, produced uniqueness, blurring its edges into the surrounding milieu. Hence I've taken a running leap into the period, starting earlier in his century and ending in the next, in order to embed the author in a network of practices and discourses constitutive of his own. One hopes that this is construed as good news by medievalists and Chaucerians, who worry about the fate of their—our—field, often quite publicly (as at the 1999 Modern Language Association forum, "Millennial Chaucer," at which I was a panelist). Beside making the field more fun with films, music, ribald jokes, and student performances of *The Canterbury Tales* (need we guess which ones?) at the expense of texts, it seems to me that the strategy recently dubbed "alterdisciplinarity" by R. A. Shoaf holds out more hope in offering new ways of looking at canonicity, new issues to engage students with, new texts to use in pedagogy and scholarship.

It is one of the planned features (virtues, I would say) of this volume that *The Prioress's Tale*—the only one of Chaucer's works to animate Jews directly—is the subject of only one essay, and that several other Chaucer texts are treated as hitherto unconsidered sources of Jewish-oriented material. Christine Rose establishes a hitherto ignored cultural matrix and visual semiotic for *The Man of Law's Tale* with her investigation of the figure of Synagoga; Jerome Mandel looks at ironies in *The Tale of Sir Thopas*; historian William Chester Jordan's first foray into literary criticism explores Christian ideas about Jewish magic in connection with *The Pardoner's Tale*; Sylvia Tomasch offers a theoretically inflected overview of the Chaucerian corpus. The subject remains, of course, far from exhausted; should a second volume appear under someone else's editorship, that would be the best index of success.

Notes

1. David Aers, "The Humanity of Christ: Reflections on Orthodox Late Medieval Representations," and "The Humanity of Christ: Representation in Wycliffite Texts and *Piers Plowman*," in *The Powers of the Holy*, ed. David Aers and Lynn Staley (University Park: Pennsylvania State University Press, 1996), chapters 1 and 2.
2. Gloria Cigman, "The Jew as an Absent-Presence in Late Medieval England." The seventeenth Sacks lecture of the Oxford Centre for Postgraduate Hebrew Studies, delivered May 29, 1991.
3. On the *Domus Conversorum*, founded by Henry III in 1232 for converted Jews, see Michael Adler, "The History of the Domus Conversorum" [1903] in his collected essays, *The Jews of Medieval England* (London: Jewish Historical Society, 1939). Conversion guaranteed a place in the *domus* and a stipend. By 1353, only one woman remained in the *domus*, Claricia of Exeter; she died in 1356. Records from 1359 to 1386 are lost; thereafter, a few Spanish, French, and Sicilian converts were admitted.
4. James Shapiro, *Shakespeare and the Jews* (New York: Columbia University Press, 1996), 55–62. Shapiro observes that, as with the expulsion, no decree or legislation of "readmittance" exists.

PART I

Chaucer Texts

1

The Jewish Mother-in-Law

Synagoga and the *Man of Law's Tale*

CHRISTINE M. ROSE

I. The Synagogue as Mother-in-Law

Hildegard of Bingen's fifth vision personifies the people of the covenant in the form of a woman, Synagoga (see fig. 1), who is "mother of the incarnation" and thus the mother-in-law of the Christian Church, Ecclesia, who is the bride (*sponsa*) of Christ. Hildegard adopts the terms of Biblical exegesis of the Song of Solomon along with medieval iconography in which the two female figures are rivals: Synagoga because of her unbelief, and supplanted in favor of Ecclesia. She begins with what she sees:

> After this, I saw the image of a woman, pale from her head to her navel and black from her navel to her feet; her feet were red and around her feet was a cloud of purest whiteness. She had no eyes, and had put her hands in her armpits; she stood next to the altar that is before the eyes of God, but she did not touch it. And in her heart stood Abraham, and in her breast Moses, and in her womb the rest of the prophets, each displaying his symbols and admiring the beauty of the Church. She was of great size, like the tower of a city, and had on her head a circlet like the dawn.[1]

Next Hildegard tells us what she hears:

> And again I heard the voice from Heaven saying to me: "On the people of the Old Testament God placed the austerity of the Law in enjoining circumcision on Abraham; which He then turned into sweet Grace when He gave His Son to those who believed in the truth of the Gospel, and anointed with the oil of mercy those who had been wounded by the yoke of the Law.

Last comes Hildegard's interpretation of her vision:

3

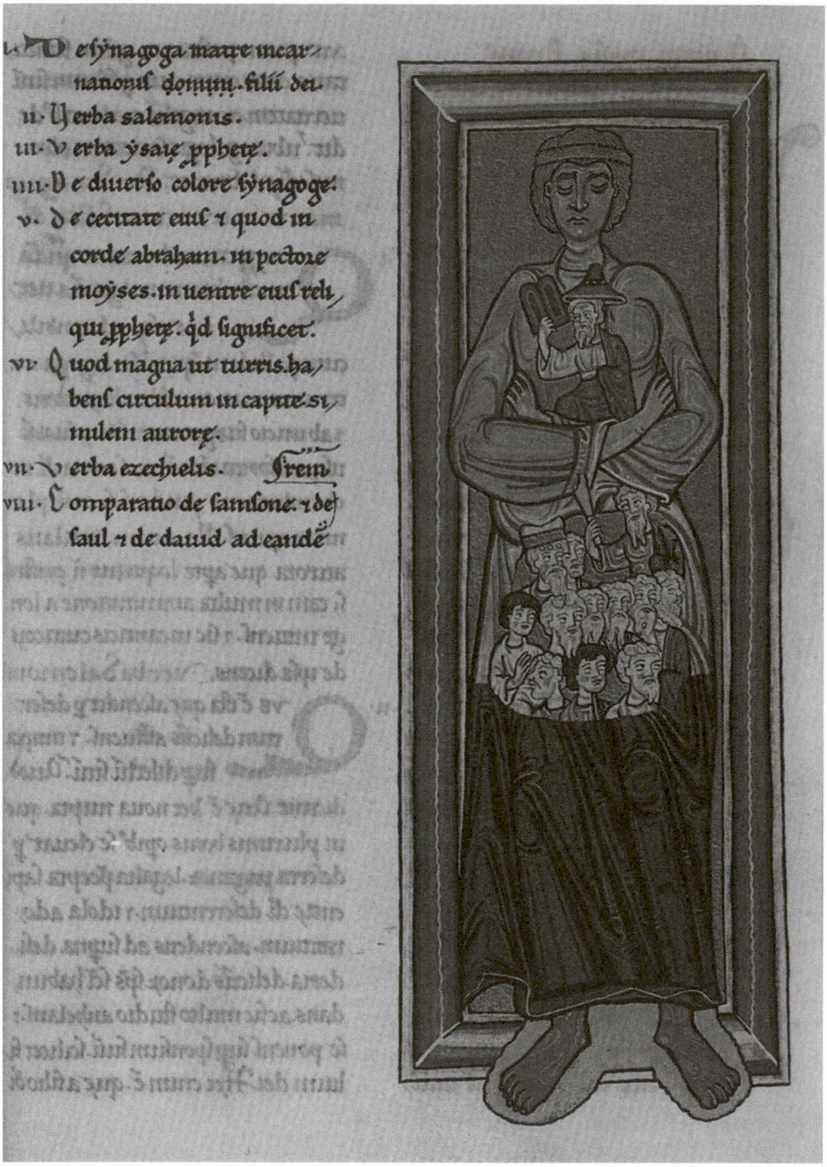

Figure 1. Synagoga. Hildegard of Bingen's *Scivias* 1.4; southern Germany, c. 1165. Formerly Wiesbaden, Hessiche Landesbibliothek MS. Cod. minor Hildegardis, folio 35, recto. Present whereabouts unknown. Permission to reproduce image from facsimile courtesy of Brepols Publishing.

> Therefore you see the image of a woman. . . . She is the synagogue, which
> is the mother of the Incarnation of the Son of God. From the time her chil-
> dren began to be born until their full strength she foresaw in the shadows
> the secrets of God, but did not fully reveal them. For she was not the glow-
> ing dawn who speaks openly [i.e., Ecclesia], but gazed on the latter from
> afar with great admiration and alluded to her thus in the Song of
> Songs: . . . Who is this who comes up from the desert, flowing with delights
> and leaning upon her beloved [Song of Solomon 3:6, 8:5] . . .

Hildegard goes on to explain that Synagoga, deserted by God in favor of
Ecclesia, "lies in vice" (134). The parti-colored figure of Synagoga is pale
above, but "black from her navel to her feet," which are red for she is "soiled
by deviation from the Law and by transgressions of the heritage of her
fathers . . . for she disregarded the divine precepts in many ways and followed the pleasures of the flesh" (134) and waded in the blood of Christ.

Still, despite these negative features, the outcome Hildegard foresaw
for Synagoga was ultimately positive, representing an early position in the
evolving Jewish-Christian polemic: "So too the Synagogue, stirred up by
Divine clemency, will before the last day abandon her unbelief and truly
attain the knowledge of God." Far from being everlastingly condemned for
her unbelief, Synagoga will in the final days be enfolded into the Church of
Christ: "Here the old precepts have not passed away but are transformed
into better ones" (135). Hildegard's vision of Synagoga "stresses the saving
interrelationships" between the Church and the community of the Jews, and
represents a dignified, if melancholy, Synagoga, her body enfolding the
Old Testament prophets, relinquishing her sway to Ecclesia. Eckert suggests that from this meditation it is evident that Hildegard recognized "the
intrinsic solidarity of Church and Synagogue; she knew of the ultimate gift
of salvation for all Israel" and thus reflected, or even surpassed in forbearance, the twelfth-century attitude of relative tolerance for contemporary
Jewry.[2]

Hildegard's vision and its accompanying explanation have their roots in
traditional exegetical and typological commentaries on the Song of Solomon,
which figure the Church as the Bride of Christ. Such readings were "univer-
sally familiar" by the twelfth century.[3] Imagistically, in medieval art the Synagogue's literalistic interpretation of Hebrew Scripture was often represented
as darkness or the moon's half-light, while the Church corresponded to the
light of the fulfillment of the prophecies and the sun's radiance.[4] I want to
suggest here that Hildegard's ambivalent representation of Synagoga—blind
and vicious, the murderer of Christ, yet simultaneously the genesis and pre-
figuration of the new Church, in fact the agent of its transformation—might
profitably be seen as part of the complex code underlying two episodes in
Chaucer's *Man of Law's Tale*. There, two wicked and non-Christian mothers-
in-law of the heroine, Custance, interfere with her marriage to their sons,

banish her from their realms, and, most importantly, try to prevent her from procreating and thus usurping their rule and the rule of their religions. Chaucer's depiction of the evil mothers-in-law evokes the longstanding tradition of the supplanted rule of the Old Law by the New; the mother replaced by her son's new bride.

What I will attempt to set forth here, using Hildegard's vision as my touchstone (but with no suggestion of direct influence on Chaucer), is a notion of the cultural matrix into which we might place Chaucer's rendition of this tale and our reading of it. The tale of the Man of Law, when coupled with some exploration of its sources, gestures towards an identification of the evil pagan mothers-in-law with Jewry and the allegorical figure of Synagoga. Further, I would argue that the method by which Chaucer composes his tale, selects his source material, and adds some original touches, highlights the association of the repudiated and vicious mothers-in-law with the feminized, marginalized Synagoga of an entire medieval iconographic and intellectual tradition of opposition between Synagoga and Ecclesia. Thus, what has generally been recognized by critics of the tale as Custance's poetic opposition to the pagan and demonized feminine Eastern/Muslim Other, should be extended to include her opposition to that equally threatening Other, the Synagogue. I hope to show that Chaucer's two mothers-in-law are not merely Orientalized villains, but are depicted in such a way as to render them reminiscent of Synagoga, with her traditional opponent, Ecclesia, represented by the tale's heroine, Custance. Chaucer's allegorizing, furthermore, is not purely exegetical, but informed by historically current constructs. It is my contention that this tradition of *disputatio*, of Jewish-Christian polemic about the place of Synagoga, was central to a medieval visual semiotics, which as literary critics we have ignored. The powerful impact of such images enables Chaucer's tale to work on levels we have hitherto left unexplored.

At its thematic heart, the tale of the Man of Law is about families and pedigree. Custance, Christian daughter of the Roman Emperor, becomes a mother through her second husband Alla of Northumberland, who has converted to Christianity; her son, Maurice, returns with his mother to Rome from England and by dynastic right becomes the next Roman Emperor. Carolyn Dinshaw has demonstrated that the narrator Chaucer assigns to the tale, the Man of Law, is adept at *family* law, including "marriage gift, legitimacy of offspring, rules of descent, the establishment of the household, and succession to property."[5] So it comes as no surprise that family, in this tale, forms a locus of anxiety. Dinshaw elegantly argues that the lawyer tells a tale which represses the story of incest and gender asymmetry which the patriarchal code within the tale must not articulate. I would add to Dinshaw's analysis of familial dynamics the notion that in a large sense the tale demonstrates a kind of Oedipal hostility towards the mother (Synagogue, orientalized as Other) and old ways of matriarchy, turning to embrace the patriarchy which in the tale is aligned with (despite the feminine noun) Ecclesia.[6] The tale might also be construed as a repudiation of sinful mother Eve in favor of her redeemed descendant, the Virgin Mary,[7] for the mothers-in-law do in fact become poetically associated with Eve in the tale, as Custance does with the Virgin. The endogamy which the evil mothers-in-law wish for their sons is replaced by the exogamy of their marriages to Custance, marriages which doom the pedigree of those pagan empires and their religions. Likewise, exhortation to endogamy is a marked feature of many Old Testament books; exogamy and proselytizing a feature of the New. Christianity's descendants, as well as its ancestors, are depicted in the families at the center of *The Man of Law's Tale*. I propose that Chaucer's poem can be seen to allude to, although it does not name, the central mother-in-law/daughter-in-law conflict perceived by the Middle Ages: that between Synagoga and Ecclesia.

In medieval law and medieval imagination, the Jew and the Muslim "were inextricably linked together in the consciousness of Christians."[8] The two idolatrous creeds were conflated in the object of the Crusades—the retrieval of the Holy Land—and the xenophobia of the Crusaders was directed at the undifferentiated infidel who hindered that quest. If we attempt a cultural reading of *The Man of Law's Tale*—one which considers art-historical monuments and which historicizes images—we find that the Jewish Other irrupts from its repression in the text, through its abundant availability in the medieval context of art, history, and theological debate. This repression is symptomatic of the Jew as the essential Other to the medieval Christian West, despite their textual absence from the tale, and indeed their physical absence from England.

What kind of cultural work such a tale might perform, and why Chaucer's version identifies the pagan women with Synagoga more specifically than does his immediate source in Trevet,[9] are topics worth pondering. In her work on anti-Semitism in *The Prioress's Tale*, Louise O. Fradenburg sees representations of the Other as revealing an important perspective on Western Christian self-representations. Fradenburg maintains that *The Prioress's Tale* is shaped by the fear of being cut off from language and community.[10] Such concerns permeate *The Man of Law's Tale* as well, where the mothers-in-law, who fear for their communities, are silenced. Bereft of her community early on and sent off by her parents to appease political exigencies, Custance journeys through the tale generally silent except to pray, and at several points (1. 525, ff., 981–82) even refusing to speak to reveal her own identity. The narrator's voice—that of the Man of Law—dominates and bloviates as the victorious Christian voice, refusing to validate the consciousness of those who are outside the community. As both Fradenburg and Susan Schibanoff contend, this silencing of the evil Other serves to strengthen social structures against a common enemy. Sheila Delany, noting the Orientalism in Chaucer's *Legend of Good Women*, suggests that anxiety about

Ottoman expansion in the fourteenth century, fueled by threats and actual confrontations in the 1390s, would have been of real concern to an English diplomat like Chaucer, and thus sees nothing untypical in the pervasive use of the essentialized Oriental Other in Chaucer's work.[11] Still, no one has yet recognized the conventional anti-Semitic elements in *The Man Of Law's Tale*, veiled and muddled as they are with the generalized pagan and Saracen threat. It is conceivable that anxiety about the recurrent Muslim was threat combined with the age-old yet vacillating Jewish anxiety that *The Man of Law's Tale* encodes. Chaucer here appropriates from his sources a tale about appropriation, making it "new," much like the New Law that Custance propagates and which reigns at the end of the tale.

II. Medieval Images of Synagoga

I turn now to images in order to contextualize in terms of the visual semiotics of the pervasive images of Synagoga both *The Man of Law's Tale* and Hildegard's allegorical vision of the Synagogue, which first alerted me to this potent strand of contrast between Synagoga and Ecclesia implicit in Chaucer's tale. Traditional medieval iconographic representations of the Synagogue reflect the notions which inform Hildegard's vision: the Synagogue is blind to the event of the Incarnation; thus, pictorial or sculptural representations often show her veiled, blindfolded, with eyes downcast, averted, or in some position in which she cannot see what is manifestly there. But she is not demonized in Hildegard's vision, as she will appear in later images. Blindness is a constant theme in the tale of the Man of Law, too: the mothers-in-law are "blind" to the truth of Custance's God; Custance cures a blind Briton in Northumberland, and this miracle causes the constable of the realm to be converted (ll. 572–74). Some medieval art depicts Synagoga's eyes covered by a serpent wound about her head. Hildegard allows that her Synagoga "had no eyes," yet, interestingly, the image in the now-lost manuscript of her *Scivias* has the eyes painted as closed. The notable discrepancy between written vision and painted image renders Synagoga able to see but refusing to in the latter, whereas Hildegard's words imply that she could not see, even if she tried, since she has not the capacity (eyes) to do so—a conundrum which might lead one to believe that the artist did not comprehend exactly the delicacy of Hildegard's forgiveness of Synagoga's lack of recognition of her errors.

Synagoga as the personification of the old Jewish Temple was superseded in its rule when the veil which hid the Holy of Holies in the Temple at Jerusalem tore as Christ died: "And, behold, the veil of the temple was rent in twain from the top to the bottom; and the earth did quake and the rocks rent" (Matt. 27:51). Traditional exegesis of this event decodes it as the end of the rule of the Synagogue and the illumination, through the death of Christ, of a law that had been hitherto hidden in darkness (Schiller, 110–12). Light came to previously dark prophecies, yet the Temple itself remained benighted in its continued unbelief. From the time of the early medieval Church, this triumph of light over darkness, of Ecclesia over Synagoga, has been interpreted iconographically in a variety of images, most notably crucifixion images. Synagoga traditionally occupies the position on the crucified Christ's left hand, with Ecclesia on his right, the one turning away, the other facing and welcomed by the figure on the cross. Often, Synagoga is depicted as standing off balance or as falling. Such images carry out the theme of the replacement of the Old Law by the New, of the Old Synagoga/mother, by the New Ecclesia/bride of Christ and daughter-in-law. The pictorial opposition of Synagoga/Ecclesia became an important part of crucifixion images, and Gertrude Schiller traces in such medieval artistic productions a growing hostility between the figures of Ecclesia and Synagoga. Seifirth describes an illustration from the Sacramentary of Bishop Drogo (ca. 850, Metz), which represents "the first ascertainable portrait of Ecclesia at the foot of the cross."[12] In a crucifixion scene within the historiated initial "O" in this early medieval prayer book, a haloed female Ecclesia stands at the foot of the cross, carrying a banner, holding aloft a chalice to receive the blood from Christ's wound: "The Christian Church receives her mission and authority from Christ at the hour of his death" (Seifirth, 1). Opposite Ecclesia, and apart from the cross, sits a white-haired male figure who raises his right hand to the cross, seemingly grasping a symbol of his authority in his left. Probably, as Seifirth and Schiller agree, the artist meant this figure to represent the Old Covenant of the Jews. This early *mise-en-page* arrangement of the three figures formed a powerful iconic statement, which both connected Old and New Law through the cross and separated them by it. Over time and varying from location to location, this theme was transformed, becoming less temperate and more virulent. Later crucifixion scenes show in place of the old man a female allegorical figure, "Hierusalem," which subsequently becomes "Synagoga" (Seifirth, 3). The allegorical opposition between these two female figures of Ecclesia and Synagoga, like that of Eve and the Virgin, becomes a fixture of medieval representation in varied mediums over many centuries throughout Western Europe.

What seems, then, to begin as the representation of a partnership between Synagoga and Ecclesia in birthing the New Law changes to an adversarial position beneath the cross, representing contention between the Christian Church and the hostile Jews. Hildegard, however, seems to partake of the earlier, more tolerant image of Synagoga in transition, not as terminally evil: Synagoga "gazed on the latter [Ecclesia] from afar with great admiration . . ." (*Scivias*, 133). Nevertheless, as Schiller demonstrates, stern scenes of the "deposition of Synagoga" became increasingly common (110). In such scenes, Ecclesia demands of Synagoga that she surrender the symbols of her sovereignty: the lance (*basta*) or sceptre (*baculus*) to which a three-tongued standard (*flammula*) is attached, the globe (ty*mpanum*), and the crown.[13] According to Schiller, such an image typifies a growing attitude demonizing the Jews in the ninth century and later. This demonization, as Seiferth indicates, fluctuated with political vicissitudes, Jews being more and less reviled according to the economic and political tenor of the times, and according to how optimistic the Church was at any given moment about their imminent conversion and about their kinship to the New Testament Law.

Scenes of the deposition of the Synagogue in early medieval art display Ecclesia appropriating the insignia of power from Synagoga, and have been read exegetically to mean that Christ has given her power that had, until his death, belonged to Synagoga and the people of the Old Covenant. Tellingly, in crucifixion scenes and other images, Synagoga acquires new attributes which emphasize her defeat and that of Jewry, stressing the contrast between the Jewish cult of sacrifice and Christ's sacrificial death: the veiled, defeated Synagoga droops, grasping a broken staff or lance with a banner, sometimes displaying a scorpion on it; the tablets of the Law slip from her hands; a crown falls from her head; a blindfold or veil may display her failure to recognize the Messiah and his New Law—a much harsher picture than the one Hildegard's vision provides. On some depictions, the Lamentations of Jeremiah are put into the mouth of Synagoga, or alluded to: "The Crown is fallen from our head: Woe unto us, that we have sinned! For this our heart is faint; for these things our eyes are dim" (Lamentations, 5:16–17).

A crucifixion miniature such as appears in the thirteenth-century Psalter of Robert de Lindesey represents a fairly typical rendering of the Synagoga/Ecclesia bifurcation, showing the moment of transfer of power from Synagogue to Church.[14] Above the cross are the sun, open-eyed, gazing at Christ on the cross, and the moon with its eyes closed. In rondels on the borders are Ecclesia and Synagoga, with the two rondels at the bottom of the frame showing St. Peter and Moses, a parallel to the two top figures, representing the New and Old Law. Synagoga, in this miniature, is crowned and veiled, carrying the tablets of the law of Moses. Her staff is broken; her head hangs in despondency.

In other artistic representations, she might wear the symbols of Christ's sufferings as the mark of her sins: the crown of thorns, the rod with the sponge attached, the lance. A he-goat may accompany her, as a symbol of the Old Testament sacrifice, but also a symbol of lust and demonization (Seifirth, figs. 29, 40). She occasionally rides an ass that may be shown collapsing on its knees before the cross. She may hold the knife of the circumcision figuring the Old Testament baptism, but also calling to mind the medieval legendary association of the Jews with ritual murder and blood libel. She may be shown being driven away by an angel, like Adam and Eve from the Garden of Eden. She may be leading the Jews into hell, a serpent wrapped about her head, or with a devil shooting into her eyes. Synagoga is even on occasion a masculine figure, or a man costumed womanishly, figuring the Jew as of ambiguous gender, thus debasing Jews by associating them with feminization, gender reversal, and the "virago."[15] Images showing the fall of Synagoga and generally associated with crucifixion scenes, persist into the fifteenth century, providing an important source of iconic notions of Ecclesia and Synagoga and their relationship, at times familial, at times hostile.

I believe that Chaucer could not have helped coming into contact with such images contrasting Synagoga and Ecclesia, whether in his reading, in the art and drama around him, or in his travels. In fact, at Canterbury Cathedral, destination of Chaucer's pilgrims, the stained glass shows Synagoga and Ecclesia facing each other across the northeast/southeast transept. The late-twelfth-century glass of a rose window in the northeast transept features Moses and Synagoga sitting at the center surrounded by prophets. They face the Blessed Virgin and Ecclesia (in a reconstructed window) in the southeast transept, representing the New Law, thus allowing the viewer to contemplate "themes of light and dark, old and new."[16] A growing hostility to the Jews in England had resulted in their expulsion in 1290; the denigration conveyed in the artistic images of Synagoga at Canterbury becomes a part of this general antagonism to the Jews in England and in the rest of Europe. Iconographic depictions grew more reprehensible during the later Middle Ages; Synagoga was no longer passing the torch as an ancestor or even sad bystander, but was envisioned as the enemy of Ecclesia, standing in league with sin, death, and damnation. She may be shown wearing a Jew's pointed hat, generally a negative attribute. The color yellow, which Mellinkoff demonstrates as iconographically associated with the unpleasant (treachery, heresy, greed, jealousy, spittle, and urine) often amplifies the negative connotations of her figure.[17] While the artists' choices about her attributes varied, common to all the later portraits of Synagoga is the "resounding note of her defeat" (Mellinkoff, 1:49). Mellinkoff designates c. 1100 as the point after which Synagoga is rarely represented as the fulfillment of the Old Testament by the New, who will ultimately embrace the New Law of Christ, the Synagogue that will ultimately become the Church. Instead, Synagoga is rendered symbolic of contemporary Jewry in each era's portraiture, despised for denying Christ and rejecting Christianity. The fierce opposition between Ecclesia and Synagoga evinced in many images represents the struggle between life and death, good and evil, dark and light. Like Cain, whose Jew's hat she sometimes wears, Synagoga may be figured as a murderer of kin. Here lies another likeness with the Sultaness in *The Man of Law's Tale*, to which I will return: she murders her son, the Sultan, at a welcoming feast for Custance; thus the marriage of Old Law and New never takes place.

Latin replaces Hebrew as the official sacred language of the Law, as the Church replaces the Synagogue. Further artistic evidence of the Ecclesia/Synagoga opposition is orientalized pseudo-Hebrew lettering often found on

Synagoga's clothing or on something she carries. This lettering figures the typological argument that Moses' writing of the Torah in Hebrew *concealed* the mysteries of God until the world was ready to receive them (Mellinkoff, 1:97).[18] The diptych of the tablets of the Law which Synagoga often carries as one of her attributes recalls her blind obedience to the letter rather than the spirit of the law. She is iconographically associated with Satan, who may also be pictured holding a scroll on which pseudo-Hebrew writing appears. I note here that the second mother-in-law of Chaucer's tale, Donegild, has this duplicitous connection with writing and with Satan (see lines 778–84 quoted on page 19). In an illustration in the psalter of Amesbury Abbey (c. 1250–55), Christ has Latin on his scroll, but Satan has Hebrew.[19] This tradition thus depicts the Jews and Satan united in a common language (Mellinkoff, 104).

By far the most distressing iconography of the opposition between Ecclesia and Synagoga is the late medieval group of images of the "Living Cross" (see fig. 2).While these images are, strictly speaking, contemporary to neither Hildegard nor Chaucer, they are important to my study in that they embody the lengths to which the Synagoga/Ecclesia bifurcation was taken in popular theology. When contrasted with Hildegard's early explanation of Synagoga's fallen yet redeemable state, these later images manifest the demonization of Jewish law that is also reflected in Chaucer's work. In these images of the "Living Cross," the cross's extremities terminate in hands that do not belong to the figure of Christ. Synagoga, represented as riding an ass, is killed with a sword held in the left hand of the cross, so that the tree of Life (the cross) becomes a tree of Death for the infidel Synagogue. In this image of harshly violent judgment, the scene is divided in four, with Ecclesia and Synagoga separated by the shaft of the cross and by the body of Christ, whose face turns towards Ecclesia, as the cross stabs Synagoga. The viewer is reminded of the two who were crucified with Christ: one thief damned, one saved. As further reminder of Old Law, Eve stands near Synagoga.

Other medieval iconography of the Synagoga/Ecclesia opposition, in addition to the Canterbury windows, which Chaucer himself may have seen, is found in Seifirth's plates: Chartres (fig. 20); St. Denis in Paris (fig. 31); possibly the work of the Limbourg brothers, c. 1402 to 1416, Paris (figs. 52 and 54); and a late-twelfth-century medallion from the cross at Bury St. Edmunds (fig. 65), now at the Metropolitan Museum of Art (the Cloisters). Notre Dame de Paris's main portal, where a devil in the form of a serpent coils itself around Synagoga's head covering her eyes, built during the twelfth-century reign of Philip Augustus who drove the Jews out of France in 1182, was in place for Chaucer to have seen it on his diplomatic missions, and later readers of his tale would no doubt have experienced the continued currency of this iconographic representation in such a public site (Seifirth, 99).[20]

Medieval dramatic records, scanty as they unfortunately are, do contain scenes of Synagoga and Ecclesia approximating the representations we see

Figure 2. Crucifixion miniature in historiated letter. Codex Monachensis 23041, f. 3v, late fifteenth century. Staatsbibliothek Munich. Note Eve and Synagoga on Jesus's left.

in medieval art. For example, the Bavarian *Play of Antichrist* (c. 1150), an ambitious Latin drama about the end of the world, roughly contemporary in time and proximate in geography to Hildegard, portrays Jews and the Synagogue, together on the stage with Ecclesia, evoking some sympathy and respect for the Old Law and some optimism for the conversion of the Jews, as Hildegard's vision does.[21] When the Jews fall to Antichrist, the prophets

Enoch and Elijah arrive and reveal the word of God to them; the Jews are instantly converted and denounce Antichrist: "Our error shames us, but now our faith is sure / Despite all persecution we shall endure" (Wright, 59, and lines 399–400, p. 97). In contrast, the staging directions for a fourteenth-century presentation play of Phillip de Mézières (c.1372) calls for "a most beautiful woman, aged about twenty, who shall be called *Ecclesia* and who shall represent the Church. Then there shall be a woman of advanced age who shall be called *Synagoga*, and who shall represent the law of Moses and the Old Testament."[22] Records from this play also describe Synagoga's costume: she has a veil, a broken banner, stone tablets with writing "like Hebrew" tilted downwards, and her demeanor is to have her "face inclined to the left . . . as if sorrowful" (219) (see fig. 3). She weeps and complains, and

Figure 3. *Synagoga,* from altarpiece by Conrad Witz, about 1435. Basel, Öffentliche Kunstsammlung, Basel Kunstmuseum. Photo by Martin Buhler.

is driven out of the playing space to the west by angels. Here surely the scene was construed as comedic, since the stage directions prescribe that "the instruments shall play for a short while and until the people have quietened their laughter at the expulsion of Synagoga" (220). The tablets of the law are destroyed by hostile actors in the play.

Typological interest in the *Concordia Veteris et Novi Testamenti* occupied theologians who wrote about Jewish matters in the early Middle Ages. Scriptural figuralism was a dominant discursive theme, as well as a major compositional principle in art (Seifirth, 16). Hildegard's vision, at once theology and art (since she had her visions painted) partakes of this tradition. Writings of Paul, Augustine, Prudentius, even Dante, articulate the new as obviating the old, while arising out of it.[23] Two influential early works attributed to Augustine, although unlikely to be his, *Altercatio Ecclesiae et Synagogae and Sermo Contra Judeos, Paganos et Arianos, de Symbolo,* exacerbate the conflict between the two rules, denying the memory of *concordia*, and instead teeming with accusations against the Jews who must surrender to Ecclesia (Seifirth, 33–37). The confrontational nature of the *altercatio* marks the Synagogue's "transformation into a living and suffering creature [in art]" . . . and "coincided with the growing conflict between Christian society and the Jewish minorities." Synagoga was "subjected to the fate of medieval Jewry" (41).

III. The Mothers-in-Law

The first of Custance's two mothers-in-law is a "Sowdanesse" from "Surrye" (Syria), belonging to a "barbre nacion" (l. 281) and loyal to the "creance" of "Makomete" or "Mahoun." The second mother-in-law, Donegild, whom Custance acquires three years after the murder of her first husband by his Sultaness-mother and her subsequent casting of Custance adrift in a rudderless and oarless boat, is the mother of Alla, king of "Northhumberlond" in England, where everyone is pagan (l. 534). Nonetheless, the kingdom seems to have some relic of a Christian past, for "A Britoun book, written with Evaungiles" (l. 666), is produced during a murder inquiry, on which a man who accuses Custance of murder is made to swear. This Donegild, from the marginalized north of England, will be the genetic link to Christianity, since she is the grandmother of Custance's son Maurice, who becomes Holy Roman Emperor. Both non-Christian women are tarred with the brush of violence and jealousy towards Custance, who as a kind of lone crusader has managed to convert their sons through their love for her. Both matriarchs are repudiated by their sons when each man embraces the new Word.

What Chaucer says about the duo of evil women demonstrates in his language and his narrator's tone an affiliation between these women and the figure of Synagoga. Both mothers-in-law are portrayed as desirous of political power, thus challenging the patriarchal rule represented by their sons and the wife whom they fear will bear Christian heirs to usurp them. The first mother-in law,

> This olde Sowdanesse, cursed krone,
> Hath with hir freendes doon this cursed dede,
> For she hirself wolde al the contree lede. (432–34)

and later, Donegild:

> But who was woful, if I shal not lye,
> Of this weddyng but Donegild, and namo,
> The kynges mooder, ful of tirannye? (694–96)

The Sultaness worries about the abandonment of the "olde sacrifices" (l. 325)—an inherently Jewish/Old Testament term—by her son, and declares her intent to remain faithful to her "law," whether her people are forced to convert or not. In discussing with her council Custance's upcoming marriage to the Sultan, who has converted in order to marry her, the Sultaness fumes:

> "Lordes," quod she, "ye knowen everichon,
> How that my sone in point is for to lete
> The hooly lawes of our Alkaron,
> Yeven by Goddes message Makomete.
> But oon avow to grete God I heete,
> The lyfe shal rather out of my body sterte
> Or Makometes lawe out of myn herte!
>
> What sholde us tyden of this newe lawe
> But thraldom to oure bodies and penance,
> And afterward in helle to be drawe,
> For we reneyed Mahoun our creance?" (330–40)[24]

She plots with her retinue to convert, to take baptism as a ruse, trading its "coold water" for the "rede" of Christian blood. It is hard not to find this clever and blasphemous speech humorous:[25]

> "We shul first feyne us cristendom to take—
> Coold water shal nat greve us but a lite!—
> And I shal swich a feeste and revel make
> That, as I trowe, I shal the Sowdan quite.
> For thogh his wyf be cristned never so white,
> She shal have nede to wasshe awey the rede,
> Thogh she a font-ful water with her lede." (351–57)

At this point, in a tirade of invective, Chaucer's Man of Law accuses the Sultaness, worried about her kingdom's and her religion's future, and concerned for her own disempowerment, of being in league with Satan who has confounded Eve and now makes the Sultaness serve him too:

> O Sowdanesse, roote of iniquitee!
> Virago, thou Semyrame the secounde!
> O serpent under femynymytee,
> Lik to the serpent depe in helle ybounde!
> O feyned womman, al that may confounde
> Vertu and innocence, thurgh thy malice,
> Is bred in thee, as nest of every vice!
>
> O Sathan, envious syn thilke day
> That thou were chaced from our heritage,
> Wel knowestow to wommen the olde way!
> Thou madest Eva brynge us in servage;
> Thou wolt fordoon this Cristen mariage.
> Thyn instrument so—weylawey the while!—
> Makestow of wommen, whan thou wolt bigile. (358–71)

But the most telling invective the Man of Law hurls at the Sultaness comes just before she throws a welcoming feast for Custance and her Christian retinue at which she has her son and the Christians killed:

> But this scorpioun, this wikked goost,
> The Sowdanesse, for al hire flaterynge,
> Caste under this [i.e., the appearance of welcome] ful mortally
> to stynge.
>
> (404–406)

The scorpion, a detail not found in Chaucer's sources, is iconographically associated with the figure of Synagoga from the early times of her allegorical depiction, and can be seen in many extant medieval artistic representations of Synagoga and Jews which Chaucer himself might have also seen.[26] So, this believer in "Mahoun's" law is a kind of hybrid threat to Christendom— "feyned womman," serpent-like, a "scorpioun," connected explicitly with Satan and imagistically with Synagoga. After killing her son, Custance's retinue, and all the new Christians in her own retinue, the Sultaness casts out Custance to wander the seas in a rudderless boat. But Custance's God takes care of her just as Jahweh cared for the Jews in their desert wanderings. As V. A. Kolve suggests, the boat as an emblem of the Church has a long history.[27] *Naves* is Latin for "ship" and the church building's central space is called a "nave" following this allegorical mindset of the ship of the Church, while a cathedral's triangular ceiling sections bisected by ribbed vaulting are called *veles*, sails Custance's ship is launched by the wicked Mohammedan mother-in-law, but God is its navigator ("He that is lord of Fortune be thy steere!" [1. 448]) and will save her as He saved Daniel, Jonah, and the Jews in their exodus (470–90). Allegorically, it is the Old Testament figure of Synagoga who launches the ship of the Church, carrying Ecclesia away from the East to proselytize and convert the Western world, where she finds more fertile ground.

One sinister mother-in-law is traded for another when Custance, trusting only in God, miraculously lands in the north of England, where she weds Alla, its ruler. Donegild, the second mother-in-law, when confronted with the birth of a Christian grandchild, waylays the messenger who bears this news to Alla, who is warring on the Scottish front, and herself forges a substitute message accusing Queen Custance of having borne a "feendly creature," a monster-child. Interestingly, the monster-child motif is also encountered in many of the folktale analogues of Custance's story, with its most salient representation in the various versions of the early-fourteenth-century Middle English romance the *King of Tars*.[28] The malformed child transformed to beauty upon his baptism or that of his parents is often represented as a child half-black/half-white, who thence changes entirely to white after baptism. Hornstein notes, "It was also generally believed that the union of a white with a Moor (a Christian with a heathen) would produce offspring partly black and white," such as Feirfis, Parzival's half-brother (85). The "miracle" enacted by the child becoming entirely white was symbolic evidence of the "complete spiritual acceptance of the true faith" (87). This black-and-white child, part Christian, part Moor is relevant to the context of the tale of Custance because of the parti-colored picture of Synagoga Hildegard has provided, incompletely accepting spiritual truth, "pale from her head to her navel and black from her navel to her feet." Absent or repressed in Chaucer's version (and in his immediate source) is the piebald nature of the monster-child, but when read against its analogue, the pagan/Christian child Maurice is indeed reminiscent of the medieval religious symbolism of the black-and-white Synagoga which Hildegard explicates. Here again, the tale's cultural context asks us to consider the occluded Jewishness of the mothers-in-law, as well as the struggle for the acceptance of Christian faith that the tale explicitly inscribes.

Upon the return of the messenger with Alla's admonition to "keepe this child, al be it foul or feir / And eek my wyf, unto myn hoom-comynge" (774–75), Donegild again befuddles the messenger with drink, and writes a missive to the court purporting to be from Alla, saying that Custance and her son are once more to be exiled in the rudderless boat. The wicked mother-in-law Donegild usurps male hegemony in her jealous political and religious (and suggestively incestuous) desire for power in her kingdom. Chaucer omits from his tale Trevet's painstaking description of Constaunce as an educated woman, one who receives letters in her own right and was known for her scholarship. That Donegild writes, and Custance does not, helps to further polarize the two kinds of women, evil and good, writing and non-writing, duplicitous and honest, letter and spirit, infidel and Christian. Like the Synagogue who cannot correctly interpret the prophecies and thereby misuses the letter of the law, Donegild uses words corruptly: "ful subtilly . . . ful synfully" (746–47). The narrator berates her in another passage of venom, but demurs that he has

> noon Englissh digne
> Unto thy malice and thy tirannye!
> And therfore to the feend I thee resigne;
> Lat him enditen of thy traitorie!
> Fy, mannysh, fy!—o nay, by God, I lye—
> Fy, feendlych spirit, for I dar wel telle,
> Thogh thou heere walke, thy spirit is in helle! (778–84)

Her "mannysh" "feendlych" nature is poetically akin to that of the Sultaness—"Virago, thou Semyrame the secounde"—and opposed to the pure, passive, Christian Custance. Alla, upon his return, kills his mother for her duplicity and wickedness (an act which he later repents and confesses at Rome, a move which neatly brings him to a reunion with his wife, who has found her way there in her boat). Meanwhile, the Sultaness and her "Surryens" have all been slaughtered by Custance's father, the Emperor of Rome, when he gets wind of the massacre in Syria. Thus the two female exotic threats are quashed by Christian male rulers.

Significantly, both the orientalized Other *and* the agency of Custance are annihilated at the end of the tale: the mothers-in-law are marginalized and defanged by the triumph of the Church, and especially by the example of the good woman, Custance, whose faith in the law of her God is the force for conversion and change in this tale. But at the tale's conclusion, Custance returns to her father's house and the "governance" and "thralldom" from which she had originally been sent out as a kind of treaty-gift to the Sultan—her first husband—in order to secure certain rights for the Christian empire and to guarantee the conversion of that Muslim empire. Her famous line on setting out for that first marriage: "Wommen are born to thraldom and penance / And to been under mannes governance" (ll. 286–87), becomes eerily fulfilled from first to last.

The point I have tried to make here is that Chaucer's perplexing and intricate tale of the Man of Law, while overtly decrying the "law" of the pagans and "Saracens," represents a veiled evocation of that other threat to Christian hegemony, the Jew. What initially may seem a tenuous connection between the mothers-in-law and the Synagogue, and even between Chaucer

and Hildegard, can now be seen as securely coupled to our reading of the
tale. When one unpacks and destabilizes the unified Eastern Other, which at
first demarcates the mothers-in-law, one allows that figure of the mother-in-
law, related to, yet different from Custance, to suggest the ubiquitous
medieval icon of the blind, reviled, and deposed Synagoga against Custance's triumphant Ecclesia, the image which Hildegard's mystical theology
reaffirms as crucial to the understanding of Christianity. Chaucer's reinscrip-
tion—conscious or not—of this central and paradoxical allegorical image for
Christianity allows us to perceive within the poem a recognition of both the
kinship and the necessity of repudiation of the Jewish origins of Western
Christianity, demonstrating the continued potency of the vexed dyad of
Ecclesia/Synagoga for the Western imagination.

Notes

Especial thanks to Professor Denise L. Despres for reading a draft of this
essay and offering valuable suggestions, for reminding me of the usefulness
of Mellinkoff's work for this study, for allowing me to read her unpublished
work on anti-Semitism in English manuscripts, and for the benefits her
friendship and stimulating conversations about medieval literature have
brought to me.

1. All Hildegard quotations are from *Scivias*, trans. Mother Columba Hart and
   Jane Bishop (New York: Paulist Press, 1990); hereafter cited in text.

2. Willehard Paul Eckert, "The Vision of Synagoga in the *Scivias* of Hildegarde
   of Bingen," trans. from the German by N. L. Quigley and L. Frizell, in *Standing Before God: Studies on Prayer in Scriptures and in Tradition with Essays*,
   eds. Asher Finkel and Lawrence Frizell (New York: Ktav Pub. House, 1981),
   310. Eckert does allow that Hildegard probably did not have a Jewish mentor
   with whom to discuss her conception of Synagoga because of some misunderstandings of Jewish law she conveys in *Scivias* (306, 310).

3. Gertrude Schiller, *Iconography of Christian Art*, trans. Janet Seligman, 2
   vols., (Greenwich, Conn.: New York Graphic Society, 1971–72) vol. 1, 24;
   hereafter cited in text. Schiller notes that such commentaries were composed
   by Rupert von Deutz, Honorius Augustodunensis, Anselm of Canterbury, and
   others; gradually, the place of Ecclesia/Sponsa is taken over by the Virgin in
   allegorical and iconographic interpretations of the scene.

4. See, for example, Hassell's commentary to *The Holkum Bible Picture Book* (66,
   79, 135), where Synagogue is associated with Cain, the owl who prefers darkness to light, and the moon as seen opposed to the sun in Crucifixion portrayals.

5. Carolyn Dinshaw, "The Law of Man and Its 'Abhomynacions,' " Chap. 3,
   Chaucer's Sexual Politics (Madison: University of Wisconsin Press, 1989), 90.

6. I do not, of course, argue here for Judaism as essentially matriarchal, but for
   its being conceptualized in the tale and in representational art as generally
   feminine, despite its occasional portrayal in late-medieval art, drama, and in
   the tale as transgendered or mannish. Synagoga, the allegorical figure, like all

proper nouns describing abstract concepts in Latin (e.g., Fortuna, Fama, Ecclesia), is feminine in gender, and this feminization is carried out in iconographic programs.

7. Chaucer suggests the identification of his Custance with the Virgin when she prays to the Virgin for delivery from her travails and the Virgin answers her prayers (*The Man of Law's Tale*, ll. 841–54; 920–24; 977–78).

8. Michael Camille, *The Gothic Idol: Ideology and Image-Making in Medieval Art*, (Cambridge: Cambridge University Press, 1989), 164. Camille notes that Canon 69 of the Fourth Lateran Council prevented both Muslims and Jews from holding office; Innocent III's dress codes and "badge of shame" were laws against both Muslims and Jews at once. See, for further development of this theme, Sheila Delany's essay in this volume; also Stephen Kruger "Medieval Christian (Dis)identifications: Muslims and Jews in Guibert of Nogent," *New Literary History* 28, 1997), 185–203.

9. The section of Nicholas Trevet's *Les Cronicles* pertaining to the tale of "Constaunce," is found in British Library MS Arundel 56, and printed in *Originals and Analogues of Some of Chaucer's Canterbury Tales,* eds. F. J. Furnivall, Edmund Brock, and W. A. Clouston (1872; rpt. London: Trubner, 1887), 1–53. The Constaunce selection from Oxford Magdalen 45, edited by Margaret Schlauch, is printed in *Sources and Analogues of Chaucer's Canterbury Tales*, eds. W. F. Bryan and Germaine Dempster (1941; rpt. New York: Humanities Press, 1958), 165–81. This work also identifies numerous other works related to the *MLT*. Also see my edition of the c. 1440 Middle English version of Trevet's Anglo-Norman chronicle, *Trevet's Englished Chronicle*: Houghton Library Harvard University fMS Eng 938 (forthcoming). The Middle English translator follows the Anglo-Norman fairly closely in the section that contains the tale of Constaunce. See also Christine M. Rose, "The Provenance of the Trevet Chronicle (fMS Eng 938)" *Harvard Library Bulletin* 3 no. 4, (New Series, Winter 1992/93), 38–55. See also Margaret Schlauch, *Chaucer's Constance and Accused Queens* (1927; rpt. New York: Gordian Press, 1969) for the folktale background. Ruth J. Dean's studies of Trevet's work and milieu is invaluable; see especially her "Nicholas Trevet, Historian," in *Medieval Learning and Literature*: *Essays Presented to R.W. Hunt,* ed. J. J. G. Alexander and M. T. Gibson (Oxford, 1976), 339–46, and "The Manuscripts of Nicholas Trevet's Anglo-Norman Cronicles," *Mediaevalia et Humanistica* 14 (1962), 95–105. Robert Correale is currently preparing an edition of Trevet's French *Les Cronicles,* based on a study of all nine extant Anglo-Norman manuscripts, for the *Chaucer Library* project. His "Chaucer's Manuscripts of Nicholas Trevet's *Les Cronicles,*" *Chaucer Review* 25 (1991), 238–265, previews some of his findings about Chaucer's source manuscript, and concludes it was probably one related to Paris, Bibliothèque Nationale, franç. 9687, fols. 1va–114va (c. 1340–50).

10. Louise O. Fradenburg, "Criticism, Anti-Semitism, and *The Prioress's Tale,*" *Exemplaria* 1 (1989), 82. See also Denise Despres, "Cultic Anti-Judaism and Chaucer's Litel Clergeon," *Modern Philology* (1994), 413–27 for further insight into medieval anti-Semitism as it is encoded in the tale of Chaucer's Prioress.

11. Delany argues that Orientalism identified against the Ottoman Empire and
     Muslim incursions into fourteenth-century Europe would have affected the
     courtier/diplomat Chaucer, and that "Orientalism becomes a rhetorical
     device enabling Chaucer to do two things: to create a moral structure in the
     poem and to offer a veiled commentary on some aspects of English foreign
     policy": *The Naked Text: Chaucer's* Legend of Good Women (Berkeley: Uni-
     versity of California Press, 1994), especially "Geographies of Desire: Orien-
     talism in the *Legend,*" 164–86. On the *MLT* in this connection, see Delany,
     " 'Loi' and 'foi' in the Man of Law's Introduction, Prologue, and Tale,"
     Mediaevalia 8 (1985 for 1982), as well as her seminal "Womanliness in the
     Man of Law's Tale," Chaucer Review 9 (1974), 63–71. Also see Susan
     Schibanoff's insightful essay, "Worlds Apart: Orientalism, Antifeminism and
     Heresy in Chaucer's *Man of Law's Tale," Exemplaria* 8 (1996), 59–96. On
     gender and Orientalism in Chaucer's tales of the Squire and the Franklin, see
     Kathryn Lynch, "East Meets West in Chaucer's Squire's and Franklin's
     Tales," *Speculum* 70 (1995), 530–51.
12. Wolfgang S. Seiferth, *Synagogue and Church in the Middle Ages: Two Symbols
     in Art and Literature,* trans. Lee Chadeayne and Paul Gottwald (New York:
     Frederick Unger, 1970), 1; hereafter cited in text. See Seifirth's plate I, 171.
13. Schiller explains that the scenes in early-medieval art showing such a deposition
     of the synagogue are likely based on the work by Pseudo-Isidore, *De alterca-
     tione ecclesiae et synagoga dialogus,* of the mid-ninth century. See *Patrologia
     Latina,* ed. J. Migne (Paris, 1878–90), vol. 42, col. 1131ff. But Schiller also clar-
     ifies that "the theme is older, particularly in Syrian tradition" (111).
14. Reproduced in *The Golden Age of English Manuscript Painting, 1200–1500,*
     eds. Richard Marks and Nigel Morgan (New York: Brazillier, 1981), pl. 3, p.
     44. Folio 35v of MS, c. 1220–22.
15. In "The Bodies of Jews in the Late Middle Ages," *The Idea of Medieval Lit-
     erature,* eds. James Dean and Christian Zacher (Newark: University of
     Delaware Press, 1992), 301–23, Steven F. Kruger demonstrates the perva-
     siveness in the late Middle Ages of the notion of the Jews as having disgust-
     ing bodies. Jewish bodies were likened to the bodies of women, traditionally
     repudiated as contaminated and foul. Myth had it that Jewish men menstru-
     ated as a symbol of their foulness and gender ambiguity (303). See also
     Sander L. Gilman, *The Jew's Body* (London: Routledge, 1991).
16. Sarah Brown, *Stained Glass of Canterbury Cathedral* (Cathedral Gifts, Ltd.,
     1991), 13.
17. Ruth Mellinkoff, *Outcasts: Signs of Otherness in Northern European Art of
     the Late Middle Ages,* 2 vols. (Berkeley: University of California Press,
     1993), 1: 35–36; hereafter cited in text.
18. See also Irven M. Resnick, "Lingua Dei, Lingua Hominis: Sacred Language
     and Medieval Texts," *Viator* 21 (1990), 51–74.
19. This book (c. 1250–55), now Oxford All Souls College Library MS 6, might
     have been seen by Nicholas Trevet or his patroness, a nun at Amesbury; the
     scene is on fol. 64v.
20. See "Chaucer's Life," by Martin M. Crowe and Virginia E. Leland, in the
     Riverside Chaucer, xv–xxvi, gen. ed. Larry D. Benson (Boston: Houghton

Mifflin Co., 1987), for some of the salient details of Chaucer's diplomatic career and travels on the continent.

21. The play is Munich MS 19411. See the English edition by Wright, who accounts for the sympathetic portrait of Jews with reference to the twelfth century being "generally regarded as a relatively peaceful and tolerant period in Jewish-Christian relations" (57). The protective attitude of monarchs towards Jewry was "expedient" and "paternal" (58) at best, claims Wright, and the official position of the Church as of Pope Calixtus II's *Sicut Iudeis non* (c. 1120) was "physical toleration coupled with doctrinal opposition": J. Wright, *The Play of Anti-Christ*, trans. and intro. J. Wright, (Toronto: Pontifical Institute of Mediaeval Studies, 1967), 57; hereafter cited in text.

22. Peter Meredith and John Tailby, eds. *The Staging of Religious Drama in Europe in the Later Middle Ages: Texts and Documents in English Translation,* trans. Raffaella Ferrari, Early Drama, Art and Music Monograph Series, 4, (Kalamazoo: Medieval Institute Publications, Western Michigan University, 1983).

23. Seifirth's chapters 2 and 3 detail much of this discussion of the intellectual history of the images of *concordia* and *altercatio* between the Church and Synagogue, as does Margaret Schlauch, "The Allegory of Church and Synagogue," *Speculum* 14 (1939), 448–64.

24. See Delany, " 'Loi' and 'foi.' " The word "tyranny" does not appear in Trevet's version of this scene.

25. See Robert C. Stacey, "The Conversion of Jews to Christianity in Thirteenth-Century England," *Speculum* 67 (1992), 263–83. Some Jews may have pretended to convert in order to stay in England and conduct their business.

26. See the plates in Mellinkoff, Schiller, Seifirth. Although the plates are not always large enough to adequately identify the scorpions, they appear on some of the banners Synagoga holds. Crucifixion scenes often have Roman/Jewish soldiers carrying banners decorated with scorpions.

27. V. A. Kolve, in his classic *Chaucer and the Imagery of Narrative: The First Five Canterbury Tales* (Stanford: Stanford University Press, 1984), 297–358, approaches the tale of the Man of Law iconographically through the use of the images of the rudderless boat and the sea. Traces of other iconographic, allegorical motifs such as that of the blind and outcast Synagoga, reinforce Kolve's reading of the Christian imagery in the tale, while suggesting political and gender issues not overtly focussed on by the tale or by Kolve's reading.

28. Lillian Herlands Hornstein, "A Folklore Theme in *The King of Tars*," *Philology Quarterly* 20 (1941), 82–87. See Schlauch, *Chaucer's Constance and Accused Queens* for further material on folk motifs in the tale.

2

The Pardoner's "Holy Jew"

WILLIAM CHESTER JORDAN

Chaucer's *Pardoner's Tale* is divided into four parts.[1] The first of these, an Introduction that serves as transition from the *Physician's Tale,* gives the circumstances in which the Host asks the Pardoner, one of the strangest of the Canterbury pilgrims, to tell a story. The second part is the Prologue. In it the Pardoner, an ecclesiastic licensed to give absolution and indulgences, describes himself, his tools, and his mode of operation. The story that he recounts to the other pilgrims is the third and longest element of the sequence. Here the Pardoner narrates the tale of three vicious ne'er-do-wells whose lust for wealth leads them all to pathetic, exemplary, and well-deserved deaths. The storyline is not original with Chaucer, although the manner of telling, the subtle characterizations, and the linguistic play are his alone. The last section in the sequence is a brief "Epilogue," not explicitly marked as such by either Chaucer or his various editors, in which the Pardoner reprises some of the themes first given expression in the Prologue.

This essay looks principally at the Introduction, Prologue, and Epilogue, the framing narratives of the tale, rather than at the tale itself, in order to explicate the Pardoner's character and the dramatic thrust of his performance. To do so, I pay attention to the tools of the Pardoner's vocation, in particular the relics he carries with him, and to the means by which he attempts to authenticate their wonder-working potential. Any effort to understand the Pardoner and the ramifications of his dramatic encounter with the other pilgrims, seems to me, as it has seemed to many other interpreters, to have a great deal to do with making sense of the most surprising relic in his arsenal (the shoulder bone of a sheep) and the equally surprising claim of its potency (its pedigree from an ancient Jew's sheep).

The *Pardoner's Tale* is a masterwork of dramatic and narrative art. Its army of interpreters has profoundly enriched readers' appreciation, although no attempt to plumb the depths of its meaning has been or perhaps can be entirely successful. This essay attempts to move the discussion forward by offering a critique of some earlier interpretations, providing some new data, and putting forward a number of suggestions for further consideration.

The Pardoner's Predicament

The Host asks the Pardoner, whom he addresses as good fellow ("beel amy," l. 318), to tell a light-hearted story in order to lift his and the pilgrims' spirits following the Physician's sad tale of the virtuous and beautiful Virginia, only fourteen years old, slain by her father in order to protect her from slavery and sexual exploitation. With the prospect of a tankard of new ale for lubrication, the Pardoner agrees, but the other pilgrims insist on a morally uplifting rather than a ribald tale. As a preliminary to his story, the Pardoner launches into an extended description of himself as a deceiver and hypocrite who preaches on avarice as a means of shaming his listeners, most of whom are unlettered peasants ("lewed people," ll. 392, 437), into making oblations to him with which he purchases, among other things, the sexual favors of prostitutes. He does not intend his description as a step toward reconciliation with God or his fellow pilgrims. Instead, he wants to dazzle his audience with how successful he has been in his scam.

Chaucer describes the Pardoner in the General Prologue unflatteringly (GP, ll. 675–91). He has stringy, thin, long yellow hair, cares too much about fashion, and has glassy staring eyes. He sings well but in a thin goaty voice, and "No berd hadde he, ne nevere sholde have; / As smoothe it was as it were late shave. / I trowe he were a gelding or a mare." Influenced by this description as well as the Pardoner's avarice, generations of learned commentators have characterized the deceitful pilgrim in a variety of ways: physical eunuch, spiritual eunuch, homosexual, and, because of his self-professed spending habits and appetite for ale, a drunken lecher.[2] His confession of hypocrisy and his long-winded prologue which manages to mock everything from voluntary poverty to the nurturing of widows and orphans in famine times have seemed to certain commentators to suggest that his propensity for overindulging in drink is evident in the monologue itself. This interpretation, among them all, is least likely, however, since the Pardoner, quite unlike a drunken man, quickly realizes that his dismissive remarks about widows and orphans in particular (ll. 449–51) bring the company up short. As an experienced preacher he knows from his companions' mumbling that he is at the boundary of complete estrangement from the group, and finds it necessary to distract his listeners from his own sordid biography, which is no longer very funny, and tell his tale. He immediately tries to recapture his audience and escape his predicament by a pointed outburst of distracting, mirthful talk, and a hasty segue into the morally uplifting tale of the three ne'er-do-wells who get their just deserts. In the Epilogue, Chaucer recalls to the reader's mind certain of these aspects of the Prologue, especially the storyteller's initially friendly relationship with the Host and the falsity of his relics, but also the Pardoner's avarice and his nearly incessant and sometimes perilously uncontrolled speech. They provide him with the motifs to construct an ending for the tale that achieves dramatic and moral closure.

Relics

One of the richest fields for interpretation of the Pardoner's character is his discourse on his pseudo-relics, which are of various sorts. According to the Prologue, they include bits of cloth and bone, a presumably large shoulder bone of a sheep, as well as a glove (ll. 348, 372). The General Prologue mentions a pillowcase that the Pardoner passes off as the Virgin's veil and a piece of canvas sail from the boat Saint Peter sailed the night he tried to walk on water, only to require Jesus's rescue. He also has stones and pig bones (GP, ll. 694–700). Most of these objects the Pardoner displays in what his listeners would regard as standard reliquaries. At least, they have the semblance of reliquaries. The raglets and bone shards are stuffed inside clear containers ("longe cristal stones, / Ycrammed ful of cloutes and of bones," [ll. 347–48]; "in a glas he hadde pigges bones," [GP, l. 700]). The ovine shoulder bone is covered "in latoun" (l. 350), imitation gold leaf of a brassy color. It would glint impressively in the sunlight. The General Prologue adds that the latoun container is made in the form of a cross (GP, l. 699).

The Pardoner, the self-styled preacher against avarice, has described his style of preaching for the other pilgrims in the following way. He tells them that when he finds a suitable audience, he appeals in part to his listeners' greed in making his relics attractive. He will tell a peasant (a potential victim of his scam) to have him, the Pardoner—for a price—lave the sheep's shoulder bone in a well. Then once a week, after a fast and before dawn, the gullible rustic should quaff some of the water. As a result, his herd will grow in number, and he will be blessed with a general increase of all his other goods: "If that good-man that the beestes oweth / Wol every wyke, er that the cok hym croweth, / Fastynge, drynken of this well a draughte, / . . . His beestes and his stoor shal multiplie" (ll. 361–63, 365). Or, there is a simpler method. A peasant could give his oblations ("offre pens, or elles grotes," [l. 376]) to the Pardoner for permission to place his hand in the holy glove, perhaps a sower's glove. The promised result is not a big herd (simplicity of ritual has its drawbacks), but superabundant harvests—no matter what the crop. "He that his hand wol putte in this mitayn, / He shal have multipliyng of his grayn, / Whan he it had worked, both parties would benefit, the avaricious Pardoner and the greedy peasant hath sowen, be it whete or otes" (ll. 373–75).[3] In this "economy," if it had worked, both parties would benefit, the avaricious Pardoner and the greedy peasant.

Despite the prominence given to the mutual cupidity of the Pardoner and his audience, Chaucer's preacher spends more time in describing and extolling the healing miracles of his ovine shoulder bone. Peasants, the Pardoner intones, should listen carefully and take him at his word. If he laves his bone in a well, the water will take on other miraculous properties than those associated with the fasting goodman who wants to increase the size of his herd. The water will help truly desperate peasants, too, those whose vermin-infested beasts lie sick with distended bellies. The Pardoner instructs the gloomy men to rinse their animals' mouths with the sanctified water to bring about their recovery: "If that this boon be wasshe in any welle, / If cow, or calf, or sheep, or oxe swelle / That any worm hath ete, or worm ystonge, / Taak water of that welle and wassh his tonge, / And it is hool anon" (ll. 353–57). Other common ovine diseases also vanish after the ingestion of the holy water: "Of pokkes and of scabbe, and every soore / Shal every sheep be hool that of this welle / Drynketh a draughte" (ll. 358–60).

More curiously, the healing properties of the shoulder-bone-blessed well water extend to male jealousy. Here the Pardoner, who is careful in various instances to specify the sex of his listeners (cf. "Goode men and women," l. 377; "Or any woman," l. 381), addresses only men: "And, sires, also it heeleth jalousie" (l. 366). The cure for a case of "jalous rage" (l. 367) is the consumption of soup made with the holy water: "Lat maken with this water his potage" (l. 368). The effect of the cure is more curious still. A reader might be misled into thinking the word "rage" (madness) suggests an unreasonable jealousy, the implication being that the husband has no legitimate cause to suspect his wife of infidelity. The relic-generated miracle would then be the restoration of the husband's reason, his capacity to give a rational, that is to say, true interpretation of his wife's entirely faithful behavior.

But the sequel brings the reader up short. The absurdity of the relic is matched by the absurdity—the madness, one is tempted to say—of the outcome. The well water-laced potage actually kills the husband's enfeebled rational faculties; it does not heal them. The sated husband will no longer suspect his wife, even if he knows the truth (*soothe*) of her sins of the flesh with any number of churchmen: "And nevere shal he moore his wyf mystriste, / Though he the soothe of hir defaute wiste, / Al had she taken prestes two or thre" (ll. 369–71)—a result reminiscent of January's fate in the *Merchant's Tale*.

On closer reading, therefore, only the healing miracles of the sick animals seem to conform to medieval Catholics' legitimate expectations (hopes for, faith in) authentic relics.[4] Genuinely hard-pressed peasants (not just greedy ones) interested principally in making ends meet and concerned to heal their disease-stricken herds, want divine help. A man of God appears with a sheep's shoulder bone which, when used properly and accompanied by scarcely affordable oblations, is alleged to be able to bring the animals to health. But should not even a desperate peasant have gagged at a sheep's shoulder bone as a Christian relic? Chaucer, our guide, makes clear that the answer is, Yes. Consequently, he tells us, and the Pardoner tells the farmers who supposedly listen to him, that the sheep's shoulder bone is a *Jewish* relic: "a sholder-boon / Which that was of an hooly Jewes sheep" (ll. 350–51).

There is a long tradition in scholarship of a certain anthropological bent to root among folklore and atavistic rustic customs for the origins of strange ritual practices described in medieval fictions. Our sheep's shoulder bone has enjoyed this treatment. Drawing on the pioneering work of the brothers Grimm and, in the English tradition, of Sir James Frazer in *The Golden Bough*, generations of scholars have pointed out that scapulamancy, the use of (usually sheep) shoulder or collar bones to predict the future, was a venerable practice from early recorded times.[5] The heartland of medieval Europe does not in fact provide rich evidence of the practice. It is found instead among the steppe peoples of Central Asia, in the pre-Islamic and Islamic Near East and in the so-called Celtic fringe.[6] The argument is that Chaucer was evoking scapulamancy, a black art practiced beyond Christendom—beyond civilization—or in its geographical and conceptual borderlands, by choosing a sheep's shoulder bone as the Pardoner's principal relic (Anderson, 630–39). This interpretation finds a good deal of support in a passage in the *Parson's Tale* denouncing "false enchantours or nigromanciens" who employ "a shulderboon of a sheep" (l. 602). The Pardoner's audience of peasants could have heard that sheep shoulder bones, strangely handled in faraway and savage lands or by their "half-savage" Celtic neighbors, were magical, potent, divinatory; maybe, under certain circumstances, they could cure.

There remain a few problems. The Pardoner's relic does not offer hope of predicting the future, the function of scapulamancy in the folkloric sources and that which is condemned in the *Parson's Tale*. And, if there were space to list the full array of divinatory practices associated with sheep shoulder bones in these same folkloric sources, it could be shown that none of them quite evokes the laving of the bone in well water, the rinsing of animals' mouths with the water, the ingestion of the water by men and women, or the preparation of soup from it. Typically, the shoulder bones employed in scapulamancy are scraped of meat and "read," or scraped, cooked and read, or scraped, cooked, broken, and read by a shaman (Burnett, 35–36). Moreover, any "unpolluted" sheep's shoulder bone will do in scapulamancy, whereas the Pardoner's bone is almost unique.[7] His is an ancient bone. There may be one more in existence, since sheep have two shoulders, but that is all.

The authentication of the sheep's shoulder bone in the Prologue to the *Pardoner's Tale* rests more firmly and centrally in its alleged place in ancient Jewish relic lore, transmitted down the generations to early Christians, and thence to the Middle Ages ("As thilke hooly Jew oure eldres taughte," l. 364). In late-fourteenth-century England, Jews were strange by what was known of their dietary restrictions, among other customs, and stranger still by their absence since the expulsion of 1290. But did Jews uncritically incorporate the practice of relic veneration in their religious devotions? The answer, as one might expect, is, No.

Indeed, medieval rabbis forbade relic gathering and relic veneration, in the face of a few popular practices, precisely because relics smacked of idolatry and, thus, the base influence of Christianity. The rabbis were, it follows, fundamentally hostile to the Christian cult of relics.

> This is how the heretics [Christians] should be refuted with regard to their practice of taking the bones of the dead as holy relics: The fact is that God has declared them impure, as it is written, "Whoever in the open field touches one who is slain with a sword, or a dead body, or a bone of a man, or a grave, shall be impure seven days" (Num. 19:16). Thus, they are themselves impure and they also impart impurity to others; indeed even the bones of Abraham, Isaac, Jacob, and all righteous men convey impurity just like those of other men, for Scripture makes no qualifications here.[8]

The rabbis further cautioned Jews about turning to Christian relics for healing purposes, going so far as to condemn explicitly the drinking of allegedly therapeutic water that had been treated with a relic. The following parable from a medieval Hebrew collection of the wisdom of the pious (*hasidim*) illustrates the point nicely.

> The son of a Jewish woman became ill. A Gentile woman came and said to her: "Give your son to drink upon this stone and he will be cured." The Jewish woman said: "What is the nature of this stone?" The Gentile woman said that the stone was brought from the pit [the storyteller's pejorative for the Holy Sepulchre] and it is part of the stone in which (Jesus) was buried, and indeed some Gentiles were given to drink and were cured. The Jewish woman said: "Because she said that it is of (Jesus), I do not wish my son to drink upon this stone": And this (is what is meant by) "With all thy soul . . . thou shalt love the Lord thy God."[9]

Nonetheless, Christians believed or at least circulated stories alleging that Jews had information, which they kept to themselves, about relics that would contribute to belief in Christianity. Miracles and force, so the stories went, had compelled them to give up some of their secrets. These included the location of the True Cross, of Saint Stephen the Protomartyr's bones, of Jesus' robe and shroud, and of the Virgin Mary's mantle.[10] "The role of the Jew," writes Ora Limor, "as the preserver and revealer of the Christian truth, or, in other words, the relationship of the Jewish authority to the things sacred to Christianity—text and space—are repeatedly illustrated in . . . [the] Holy Land traditions dealing with Christian holy sites and holy relics." (63)

Chaucer, therefore, chose to make the sheep's shoulder bone a once-Jewish relic precisely because it was absurd and yet resonated with the idea of the Jew as alien and as a purveyor of sacred information, especially about powerful relics. His Pardoner, it goes without saying, knows that his own attempt at authentication is absurd but just seductive enough; that is why it is funny in context. The Pardoner has faith that poor desperate peasants, "lewed peple," can be swayed to believe in the sheep shoulder bone's thaumaturgic properties, and that the other pilgrims will laugh at their alleged gullibility. Moreover, several other medieval circumstances, besides scapulamancy, would have helped "persuade" the rustics of the power of a relic dipped in well water. Legends of miraculous wells in the Holy Land had entered England through returned crusaders, and the details of their supernatural powers paralleled indigenous insular legends of therapeutic wells. All of these Chaucer could have expected his audience to be familiar with. Moreover, the legends of miraculous wells in the Holy Land were all associated with "holy" Jews.

The Holy Jew

High- and late-medieval Christian commentators make a sharp distinction between scriptural and post-scriptural Jews. The former, although inclined to repeated outbursts of rebellion against God and His holy ordinances, were a chosen people, peculiarly beloved by the Almighty. A few of these Jews were paragons and, even if marred by sin, like David's adultery and Solomon's idolatry, were regarded by Christians as exemplary figures. The patriarchs and the prophets, the judges (men and women), a few of the Israelite kings, and a small number of other figures (Mordechai and Esther, Ruth, Susannah, Judith, Judas Maccabaeus, among others) were holy Jews.[11] They were saints, as their visual iconography in medieval Christian manuscripts attests.[12] And they had figuratively handed down the Hebrew Scriptures to the Christian community for its more perfect reception and interpretation.

Post-scriptural Jews, with rare exceptions, (e.g., gospel figures, like Nicodemus, who became Christians), were different. They authorized the killing of Jesus. They were those to whom the Pardoner compares the malign protagonists of the tale he finally tells. The characters of the tale are men who so violate Christian norms of decency by cursing—that is, swearing by Christ's body—that, in effect, they dismember the God-man, as though believing that the Jews had done an inadequate job of tormenting him: "Hem thoughte that Jewes rente hym noght ynogh" (l. 475).[13] Contemporary Jews, descendants of the crucifiers and heirs of their sin, were in rebellion against the truth of Christianity. In the course of the high Middle Ages, they came to be considered willful deniers of the divinity of Jesus, even in the face of "rational," that is, scholastic, proofs that would persuade, so it was implied, true human beings graced with reason. Contemporary Jews were thereby likened to beasts.[14] It took no great effort for many Christians to believe that Jews were also capable of virtually inhuman crimes, like the crucifixion or ritual murder of Christian children and the desecration of the sanctified Host.[15] Finally, medieval Jews in the high- and late-medieval Christian imagination indulged their avarice mercilessly, as their principal vocation, moneylending, and their allegedly usurious rates of interest (though often inferior to those of Christian moneylenders) made plain.[16]

The sheep whose shoulder bone the Pardoner offered as a thaumaturgic relic had been owned by a *holy* Jew, therefore, a scriptural Jew. Chaucer signals the fact, plausibly, by noting that the proper use of the shoulder bone is sanctioned by a tradition from the Jewish elders (l. 364). Who was the holy Jew? Does Chaucer's failure to name him signify anything? Early Chaucerians, following Skeat, decided that the reference was particular and had to be to Jacob the Patriarch.[17] Jacob did miracles to cattle; he made them increase (Genesis 30.37–43). Unfortunately he used rods, not a bone; and as one quaint dissenter from Skeat's position pointed out, the Pardoner's miracles were "watery ones."[18] Jacob did dip his rods in trough water, but this evidently was not watery enough for the commentator. His alternative suggestion, that the judge, Gideon, "surely a holy Jew," was the referent, is, however, more implausible, being based as it is on the capacity of Gideon's fleece to become soaked with dew in an otherwise dry environment (Judges 6.36–40).

Jacob is better than Gideon as a referent, but Chaucer's failure to name the Jew is suggestive.[19] Jacob is one of several holy Jews who would make the Pardoner's claims seem somewhat less absurd than they might otherwise appear to his audience. Not that there is some obvious allusion to Jewish-owned sheep with miraculous shoulder bones that supercharge well water. The key here is rather the cluster of ancient and medieval traditions of wells associated with holy Jews, of which one set concerns Jacob's well. The well is not explicitly mentioned in the Hebrew Bible, but in the Gospel (John 4.6). In this case, the text incorporates a traditional belief in the location and origin of the well, a belief that non-Christian sources attest was also authentically Jewish.[20] The gospel scene is Jesus' lonely encounter with the Samaritan woman coming to draw water from the well in the midday heat (John 4.1–42). She wants water. He is thirsty. She has the means to draw water from the well. He asks her to draw some for him. But why should she? She is a Samaritan, to the Jews a heretic. Jews and Samaritans have nothing to do with each other. Jesus' rebuke is strange: he says he has "living water," water that gives eternal life (John 4.10). His water is superior to the water from Jacob's well.

The first point relevant here is that the offer of "living water" takes on particular significance because Jacob's well and the water from it have such potent force in the imagery of the passage. "Art thou," the woman asks, "greater than our father Jacob, who gave us the well, and drank thereof himself, and his children, and his cattle?" (John 4.12, Douay Version) Jesus implies that he *is* greater than Jacob, and that his power exceeds anything the waters from Jacob's well can accomplish. It should come as no surprise that this is a story in which Jesus explicitly declares his messiahship (John 4.26). Nor should it be surprising that medieval commentators, like the influential versifier of biblical interpretations, Petrus Riga, draws on the story to make Jesus into the "sacred well."[21]

Jews and native Christians in the Holy Land in the time of the Crusades told of Jacob's well and a number of other wells associated with holy Jews. Jacob's well became an important pilgrimage site, and a church was built at the site.[22] There was also Job's well, in Jerusalem, which was reputed to be the well created by God specifically to provide the water with which the righteous man miraculously washed himself clean of his afflictions. It too became a pilgrimage site, and legends told of the waters overflowing the well as a sign of "plentiful crops."[23] Medieval pilgrims also visited and heard fabulous tales of Abraham's well and the water in it, which was said to have risen to the surface for the patriarch's sheep. And they knew of David's well in Bethlehem. When that well was once in hostile Philistine hands, David had craved aloud for water from it and, by doing so, had inspired his troops to break through the Philistine lines.[24] Tales of the miraculous healing powers of the well of Miriam (Moses' sister) were also circulated.[25] In other words, it was no strange thing for medieval Christians to have heard of holy Jews and the holy, thaumaturgic waters of their wells. Nearly contemporary with Chaucer is an elaborate Middle English tract on the cultivation of Christian virtue, which is cast as an extended meditation on the spiritually rejuvenating powers of Jacob's well, and goes by that name.[26]

Christians in England would have assimilated the legends and miracle stories of Jacob's and other holy Jews' wells (often pilgrimage sites) with their own indigenous beliefs about holy wells and holy water.[27] There were wells whose water cured stiffness of joints, blindness and any number of other diseases of the eye, as well as dullness of the mental faculties. Some cured human skin diseases and were also good for sick animals. A modern enumeration attaches legends of miracles of this sort to at least one hundred and thirty-five "ancient, holy and healing wells" in just a single English county. And while some of these legends are of modern origin, many have been traced back in texts to the medieval or immediate post-medieval period.[28] The Church, of course, contributed to help maintain the belief that blessed water could effect miraculous cures (although most high churchmen certainly disapproved of the well water lore). In ecclesiastical ceremonies animals were aspersed with holy water to protect them from the pox and the scab, the conventional formula for describing sheep diseases, and the formula used by the Pardoner to describe the diseases of his listeners' sheep (1. 358).[29] At Becket's tomb, the Canterbury pilgrims themselves would have encountered a well with miraculous water, said to have become holy through the reception of the martyr's blood.[30] Moreover, there was a long tradition of using the "water of St. Thomas" (water supposedly mixed with drops of his blood) as a curative by drinking it or dabbing it on an injured part of the body.[31]

All of this made plausible to the Pardoner's putative listeners— peasants—the miraculous properties of well water "sanctified" by a sheep's shoulder bone. And it was meant, I believe, to make their gullibility all the funnier to the pilgrims listening to the Pardoner. It appealed to their cultural superiority, for, though they were familiar with the same legends and practices as the "lewed" rustics, they could critically distance themselves from the Pardoner's willfully outlandish claims and share the joke with him. That, at least, was presumably the Pardoner's hope.

The Pardoner's Relics Revisited

The tale of three greedy youths that the Pardoner finally tells is an exemplum (1. 435), a moralized history meant to be recounted in a sermon intended to inspire sinners to amend their lives.[32] It comes as no surprise, therefore, that the coda of the story (ll. 904–19) is addressed to an imagined audience of congregants. The Pardoner urges them to seek forgiveness for their own greed, whose likely dire consequences he has foreshadowed in describing the ugly deaths of the protagonists of the exemplum ("ware yow for the synne of avarice," l. 905). As in the Prologue, he makes plain that he preaches against usury while relishing his own. He offers his "hooly pardoun," "his hooly bulle" of indulgence, his "heigh power" to forgive (ll. 906, 909, 913) the imagined congregants. In return he receives their oblations of coin ("nobles or sterlynges," l. 907), precious goods ("silver broches, spoones, rynges," l. 908), or more homely women's goods like woolen cloth ("ye wyves . . . youre wolle," l. 910). He promises nothing less than to enroll the supplicants' names on the book of everlasting life ("Youre names I entre heer in my rolle anon; / Into the blisse of hevene shul ye gon," ll. 911–12). They shall pass over, absolved, into Paradise like newborn babes—if they pay up: "I yow assoile . . . / Yow that wol offre, as clene and eek as cleer / As ye were born" (ll. 914–15).

Then, curiously, the Pardoner speaks as though the pilgrims themselves were his congregants. The transition to what I am calling the Epilogue is abrupt, merely a short sentence about what he has just said, "And lo, sires, thus I preche" (l. 915). Thereupon, he appeals to the pilgrims to receive Christ the Physician's absolution: "And Jhesu Crist, that is oure soules leche, /

So graunte yow his pardoun to receyve, / For that is best; I wol yow nat deceyve" (ll. 916–18).

What comes next has been a source of what seems like infinite debate. The Pardoner urges the other pilgrims to come forward and be absolved. He has relics and indulgences; they are as good as any anywhere in England (ll. 920–21). Instead of the tradition of the holy Jew as authentication, this time he claims to have the indulgences and, presumably, the relics direct from the hands of the supreme pontiff (l. 922). The Jewish pedigree, we have already seen, would not persuade these more sophisticated listeners, as it might the rustics in the imagined audience of the Prologue. "Relikes and pardoun"; "myn absolucioun"; "mekely receyveth my pardoun" (ll. 920, 924, 926)— the spewing of the phrases threatens to become interminable. Fortune is with the pilgrims, the Pardoner insists, in having him along. "It is an honour to everich that is heer / That ye mowe have a suffisant pardoner / T'assoile yow in contree as ye ryde" (ll. 931–33). Or, again, what wonderful protection it is to have him near: "Look which a seuretee is it to yow alle / That I am in youre felawshipe yfalle, / That may assoile yow" (ll. 937–39).

Travelers are always at risk ("aventures . . . may bityde. / Paraventure ther may fallen oon or two / Doun of his hors and breke his nekke atwo," ll. 934–36). Why not be pardoned every mile to be on the safe side ("Or elles taketh pardoun as ye wende, / Al newe and fressh at every miles end," ll. 927–28)? Turning to the Host, the Pardoner urges him, as a sinner through and through, to undergo the preacher's rites, beginning with an oblation (first things first!) and then kissing each of the (false) relics.

> I rede that oure Hoost heere shal bigynne,
> For he is moost envoluped in synne.
> Com forth, sire Hoost, and offre first anon,
> And thou shalt kisse the relikes everychon.

And, of course, once more, he mentions the oblation. "Ye, for a grote! Unbokele anon thy purs" (l. 945).

Are these passages meant to evoke Becket's shrine, the pilgrims' goal? If so, as several scholars have intimated, the Pardoner's spiritual deviance is deeper and more transgressive than one might otherwise suspect.[33] He would be suggesting that venerating the relics in his possession is equivalent to venerating Becket's.[34] Kissing his would relieve the pilgrims of the necessity to kiss Becket's, which was the traditional way, besides offering alms, of honoring the saint at the shrine.[35] This interpretation draws on the Host's response to the Pardoner's entreaty. Harry Bailey not only berates the storyteller, but he imagines aloud that such a vile man might even offer his own befouled breeches to be kissed as a relic.

Indeed, another allusion to Becket's shrine may be the Host's reference to the Pardoner's "olde breech," which he (the Pardoner) would willingly avow "a relyk of a seint" (ll. 948–49), if it were at hand. Since Becket's breeches (the counterpart of his hairshirt) were venerated at Canterbury, the reference is suggestive (Storm, 815). Indeed, it seemed to Knapp "impossible that the Chaucer we know could have written such a passage without recognizing what he had done. Certainly it must be conceded," he continued, "that 'Kisse myn olde breech' is . . . a poetic figure . . . but would such a poet be likely to have fallen into such a figure unconsciously?"[36] It hardly matters that the genuine martyr's breeches were suspended above his tomb and do not seem to have been kissed or perhaps even touched by ordinary pilgrims who might otherwise have stealthily snipped off portions for themselves. Yet, the problem with this interpretation is that it is incomplete. The seriousness of the Pardoner's sin, manifest in the Host's evident allusion in his response, needs to be set beside the initial lightheartedness of Harry Bailey's response—a lightheartedness, to be sure, that the Pardoner and many commentators fail to recognize or, paradoxically perhaps, fail to take seriously enough.

Do the passages under discussion, then, constitute "an elaborate joke," one that fortuitously gives "a gross insult to the pilgrims"? (*Riverside* commentary, 906). This seems true to the dramatic situation.[37] Moreover, it helps justify my calling the passage the Epilogue, for it is the dramatic completion of the Prologue. Let us recall how the Prologue ends. The Pardoner overspeaks, much as he overspeaks in the Epilogue. He says too many and too deeply cynical things. The monologue ceases to be funny, and he realizes that he is alienating his audience. In a vain attempt to win them back, he starts joking, but even this fails. Now, in the Epilogue, he wants his comrades to be glad that he is in their fellowship, and he resumes his jocular persona. The proof is that he joshes with the one person who in the Introduction characterized him as a "beel amy": the Host. The Host, the Pardoner must believe, is much like him. He can take a joke. He will get into the spirit of the occasion.

Unfortunately, the Host, like the pilgrims in general, although they may have appreciated the Pardoner's exemplum, still seems to be out of sorts. He has heard enough of these false relics. He projects disgust, if not all of the other myriad emotions attributed to him by commentators.[38] The Pardoner, Harry Bailey asserts (ll. 948–50), has so little propriety that he would make his shit-stained drawers a relic and have men kiss them. By the True Cross, he swears—not by the phony cross-shaped latoun reliquary in the Pardoner's hoard—he would rather cut off the Pardoner's balls (not proof, by the way, that the Pardoner actually has any) and encase them in pig crap than do obeisance to the raglets, shards, glove, and shoulder bone of a holy Jew's sheep (ll. 951–55).[39] This rejection and the utter failure to redeem himself that the rejection implies, despite his well-told exemplum and his portrayal of himself as a jocular fellow, can only result in one reaction from the Pardoner: an intensity of anger that literally throttles his speechifying. "So wrooth he was, no word ne wolde he seye" (l. 957).

The Host, on the contrary, is anything but speechless. In fact, *he* was just joking. It is the Pardoner who cannot take a joke; it is the Pardoner on whom the humor of the Host's reply is lost. The Host makes it plain at this point that he has no desire to have anything to do with—to "pleye with"—a man who grows wrathful at this kind of humor, a man who can dish it out but not take it: " 'Now,' quod oure Hoost, "I wol no lenger pleye / With thee, ne with noon oother angry man' " (ll. 958–59). And everybody *laughs* (l. 961). The Pardoner's alienation is complete.[40]

Or nearly so. Fortunately, all these folk are pilgrims, whatever else they are. It is the "worthy Knyght" (l. 960) among their number who seeks to salvage the situation. Whether he is effective or not is immaterial. He tries, and his words are replete with significance. He urges the Pardoner to return to his good spirits ("be glad and myrie of cheere"); he urges both Host and Pardoner to reconcile with the kiss of peace (ll. 965–68), a more efficacious kiss, it is hoped, than one on a sheep's shoulder bone or on shit-stained drawers. With equally exquisite care at the choice of words, the Knight bids the fellowship to *laugh* and *play* as they once had (l. 967), that is, before the troubling interval during which the Pardoner held center stage.

Conclusion

More than anything else this reading of the framing narratives of the *Pardoner's Tale* suggests that Chaucer was trying to and did achieve dramatic closure in the Epilogue. The pilgrims, like late-medieval readers, would have understood the implicit and multiple allusions to sheep's shoulder bones, holy Jews, holy wells, and so forth. They would also have recognized the Pardoner's impudence, his corrupt ascription of holy tradition to the authentication of his relics. Holy Jews gave the Christian community the prophetic Old Testament, not knowledge of a sheep's shoulder bone. Medieval anticlericalism notwithstanding, the Pope represented the continuity of living Christian traditions rooted in the life and teachings of Jesus and the apostles, not the authentication of pig bones as relics, as the Pardoner asserts.

The counterfeit, in the modern sense of the term, is the Pardoner. He mocks revelation and tradition equally. One thing interpreters have often missed is the point in the *Pardoner's Tale* at which the other pilgrims cease tolerating his cynical humor and come to realize how thoroughly accurate the Pardoner's description of himself as a "ful vicious man" is. The Pardoner's downward spiral is near its nadir already in the last section of the Prologue.[41] The magnificent telling of his story of three youthful miscreants is part of his attempt to recuperate his standing in the pilgrims' fellowship. He believes he has done so by what all scholars regard as his bravura performance in telling the tale, and he therefore resumes the manner of speechifying that he had earlier adopted—and abandoned—in the Prologue. The disaster of this choice is patent: dishonoring of the Host as the greatest sinner and the insistence on kissing false relics, which mocks the ritual of veneration at Becket's tomb. There are limits to what even the most accomplished performances can accomplish. Would such a sinner even refrain from offering his own soiled breeches to kiss as the relics of a saint, when the genuine relics, also breeches, of an authentic saint were the goal of the pilgrimage? The grim and ugly repartee here, though overlaid with a sardonic kind of humor and temporarily effaced by the worthy Knight's intervention, remains emotionally troubling, yet morally correct. In a wonderful irony—what fate could be worse for a preacher?—the Pardoner is speechless before this truth.

Notes

1. All references are to the *Riverside Chaucer*, ed. Larry Benson (Boston: Houghton Mifflin, 1987); hereafter cited in text as *Riverside.*
2. Robert Miller, "Chaucer's Pardoner, the Scriptural Eunuch, and the *Pardoner's Tale*," in *Twentieth-Century Interpretations of the Pardoner's Tale*, ed. Dewey Faulkner (Englewood Cliffs, NJ: Prentice Hall, 1973), 43–69; Carolyn Dinshaw, "Eunuch Hermeneutics," in *Chaucer's Sexual Politics* (Madison, WI: University of Wisconsin Press, 1989), 156–84; Robert Sturges, *Chaucer's Pardoner and Gender Theory: Bodies of Discourse* (New York: St. Martin's Press, 2000). The volume in the Chaucer Bibliographies, *Chaucer's Pardoner's Prologue and Tale*, comp. Marilyn Sutton (Toronto: University of Toronto Press, 2000), 149–54, lists many other relevant recent works on the Pardoner's alleged status as eunuch and/or homosexual. For a rigorous critique of this approach, see Lee Patterson, "Chaucer's Pardoner on the Couch: Psyche and Clio in Medieval Literary Studies," *Speculum* 76 (2001), 638–80. Terence McVeigh, "Chaucer's Portraits of the Pardoner and Summoner and Wyclif's *Tractatus de Simonia*," *Classical Folia* 29 (1975), 54–58, argues that one of the Pardoner's sins is simony, and that simony is linked figuratively with sodomy. In fact, for this opinion McVeigh draws on Wyclif's treatise on simony, but, as McVeigh was aware (56–57), Wyclif quotes Guillaume de Perault, who made the linkage not with simony but (as was conventional) with avarice, the Pardoner's explicit vice.
3. The *mitayn*'s possible evocation of a sower's glove was first suggested (according to the Riverside commentary, 907) by Carleton Brown in the *critica* to his edition of the Pardoner's Tale (*Chaucer: The Pardoner's Tale* [Oxford: Clarendon Press, 1835/recte 1935], 28 n. 44). It is probably the case that the evidence he cited for doing so is insufficient. Consequently, most scholars, like David Andersen, "The Pardoner's True Profession," *Neuphilologische Mitteilungen* 75 (1974), 637–38, hereafter cited in text, view the glove as merely one more absurdity. He writes, "Where did the 'miteyn' come

from? Did some saint wear mittens? How did the mitten gain such wonderful power? No one is likely to ask such questions about the 'miteyn,' coming as it does from the same bag as the Virgin's veil and the fragment of St. Peter's sail." Brown's suggestion, however, at least points in the direction of why farming people might see some relevance to an agricultural miracle in the glove. Gullibility requires some rational level of believability as a precondition. In the case of the Pardoner's glove, I would suggest that more was needed than mere association with the other relics.

4. R. N. Swanson, "Letters of Confraternity and Indulgence in Late Medieval England," *Archives* 25 (2000), 40–57, describes the canonical view of indulgences and relic veneration, while placing satires like the *Pardoner's Tale* in context.

5. Jacob Grimm, *Teutonic Mythology*, 4th ed., trans. James Stallybrass, III (London: W. Swan Sonnenschein and Allen, 1883), 1113; James Frazer, *The Golden Bough*, part II: *Taboo and the Perils of the Soul*, 3rd ed. (London: Macmillan, 1936), 229.

6. Charles Burnett, "Arabic Divinatory Texts and Celtic Folklore: A Comment on the Theory and Practice of Scapulamancy in Western Europe," *Cambridge Medieval Celtic Studies* 6 (1983), 31–42; hereafter cited in text.

7. By "unpolluted" I mean "bought from an honest merchant," "decapitated in a clean place," not perceiving "the sword by which it is slain," and so forth; Burnett, "Arabic Divinatory Texts," 35.

8. The quotation is from the *Nizzahon Vetus*, a Jewish polemical text of the thirteenth century which conveniently summarizes hostile rabbinic attitudes towards Christianity: *The Jewish-Christian Debate in the High Middle Ages: A Critical Edition of the Nizzahon Vetus*, ed. and trans. David Berger (Northvale, NJ, and London: 1996), 225.

9. *Sefer Hasidim* (twelfth century), quoted in William Jordan, *The French Monarchy and the Jews from Philip Augustus to the Last Capetians* (Philadelphia: University of Pennsylvania Press, 1989), 25.

10. Ora Limor, "Christian Sacred Space and the Jew," in *From Witness to Witchcraft: Jews and Judaism in Medieval Christian Thought*, ed. Jeremy Cohen (Wiesbaden: Harrassowitz Verlag, 1996), 55–72; hereafter cited in text.

11. Aquinas represents the dominant view here, that is expressed in the text; he, like other medieval Christian commentators, would have seen a decisive falling away from virtue, however, in the course of early Jewish history, the era when the prophets repeatedly had to call the chosen back to virtue. See John Hood, *Aquinas and the Jews* (Philadelphia: University of Pennsylvania Press, 1995), 6.

12. Which is not to say that the presence of such halos would have persuaded viewers necessarily of the thoroughgoing virtue of the Jews so depicted; cf. Ruth Mellinkoff, *Outcasts: Signs of Otherness in Northern European Art of the Late Middle Ages*, 2 vols. (Berkeley: University of California Press, 1993), I, 73.

13. My gratitude to Sheila Delany for making this point clear to me. In her *Impolitic Bodies: Poetry, Saints, and Society in Fifteenth-Century England* (Oxford, 1998), 113, she notes that the dismemberment motif is a "widespread topos in late-medieval sermons and pious art, both literary and visual."

14. For exhaustive statements of this scholarly point of view, see Anna Sapir Abulafia, *Christians and Jews in the Twelfth-Century Renaissance* (New York: Routledge, 1995), and Jeremy Cohen, *Living Letters of the Law: Ideas of the Jew in Medieval Christianity* (Berkeley: University of California Press, 1999), 147–312.

15. Three articles by Gavin Langmuir in his collected essays, *Toward a Definition of Antisemitism* (Berkeley: University of California Press, 1990), constitute the now classic studies of ritual murder accusations, "Thomas of Monmouth: Detector of Ritual Murder," "The Knight's Tale of Young Hugh of Lincoln," and "Ritual Cannibalism" (209–81). On the desecration of the Host, see Miri Rubin, *Gentile Tales: The Narrative Assault on Late Medieval Jews* (New Haven, CT, and London: Yale University Press, 1999).

16. Langmuir, *Toward a Definition of Antisemitism* 60; Shlomo Simonsohn, *The Apostolic See and the Jews: History* (Toronto: Pontifical Institute of Mediaeval Studies, 1991), 190–95.

17. *Riverside* commentary, 906–907, without endorsement of Skeat's opinion, but it was endorsed, with a typical "probably" or "most probably" by others, such as John Koch, ed., *The Pardoner's Prologue and Tale* (Berlin: Verlag von Emil Felber, 1902), 106.

18. G. M. Rutter, "An Holy Jewes Shepe," *Modern Language Notes* 43 (1928), 536.

19. A fact noted by Leo Henkin, "Jacob and the Holy Jew," *Modern Language Notes* 55 (1940), 256. See also Brown, *Chaucer: The Pardoner's Tale*, 27.

20. *Anchor Bible Dictionary*, III (New York and elsewhere: Doubleday, 1992), 608, with reference to agreement on the existence and, indeed, location of the well in "all traditions—Jewish, Samaritan, Christian, and Muslim."

21. *Aurora*, 2 vols., ed. Paul Beichner (Notre Dame, IN: University of Notre Dame Press, 1965), II, 508. For the use of the metaphor in poetic sources roughly contemporary with Chaucer, see, e.g., *Late Medieval English Lyrics and Carols, 1400–1530*, ed. Thomas Duncan (Harmondsworth U.K.: Penguin, 2000), 227.

22. *The Sacred Land*, comp. Zev Vilnay, II: *Legends of Judea and Samaria* (Philadelphia: Jewish Publication Society, 1975), 270; *Dictionnaire de la Bible*, ed. F. Vigouroux, III (Paris: Letouzey et Ané, 1903), 1076–81.

23. *Sacred Land*, I: *Legends of Jerusalem* (Philadelphia: Jewish Publication Society, 1973), 283, and II: *Legends of Judea and Samaria*, 272–73.

24. On Abraham's well, *Sacred Land*, II: *Legends of Judea and Samaria*, 217, 247–48; on David's, 12–13 of the same volume.

25. *Sacred Land*, III: *Legends of Galilee, Jordan, and Sinai* (Philadelphia: Jewish Publication Society, 1978), 128–29.

26. *Jacob's Well: An English Treatise on the Cleansing of Man's Conscience*, ed. Arthur Brandeis (Early English Text Society 115; London: Kegan Paul, Trench, Trübner and Co., 1900). Brandeis dates the manuscript to the first quarter of the fifteenth century, xiii.

27. The most comprehensive treatment of this lore for England is James Rattue's *The Living Stream: Holy Wells in Historical Context* (Woodbridge, Suffolk: Boydell Press, 1995), but a brief informed survey that goes beyond England

may be found in the article "Wells and Springs" in *Medieval Folklore: An Encyclopedia of Myths, Legends, Tales, Beliefs, and Customs*, 2 vols., ed. Carl Lindahl and others (Santa Barbara, CA: ABC-CLIO Books, 2000), II, 1028–30. The only locatable medieval *mikva* (ritual bath) in England (in Bristol) came to be known as "Jacob's well"; R. R. Emanuel and M. W. Ponsford, "Jacob's Well, Bristol, Britain's Only Known Medieval Jewish Ritual Bath (*Mikveh*)," *Transactions of the Bristol and Gloucestershire Archaeological Society* 112 (1994), 73–86.

28. James Rattue, "An Inventory of Ancient, Holy and Healing Wells in Leicestershire," *Transactions of the Leicestershire Archaeological and Historical Society* 67 (1993), 59–69.

29. Cf. the formula found in a thirteenth-century Anglo-French linguistic charm of English provenance the *Cartulary of Eynsham*, ed. H. E. Salter, 2 vols. (Oxford: Oxford Historical Society, 1907–1908), I, 18 no. xx ("de la u[er]ole et de la Clousicke"= "of the pox and the scab"). David Andersen is likely correct to see such formulas and thaumaturgic practices as going back at least to the Anglo-Saxons; Andersen, "Pardoner's True Profession," 635–36.

30. A. P. Stanley, *Historical Memorials of Canterbury* (New York: A. D. F. Randolph, 1888), 272.

31. Pierre Sigal, "Naissance et premier développement d'un vinage exceptionnel: l'eau de saint Thomas," *Cahiers de Civilisation Médiévale* 44 (2001), 35–44.

32. Claude Bremond et al., *L'Exemplum* (Typologie des sources du moyen âge 40; Turnhout, Brepols, 1982).

33. Daniel Knapp, "The Relyk of a Seint: A Gloss on Chaucer's Pilgrimage," *English Literary History* 39 (1972) 13–18; John Fleming, "Chaucer and Erasmus on the Pilgrimage to Canterbury: An Iconographical Speculation," in *The Popular Literature of Medieval England* [*Tennessee Studies in Literature*, 28], ed. Thomas Heffernan (Knoxville: University of Tennessee Press, 1985), 148–66. I wish to thank Professor Fleming for his help with the bibliography on the relics of the Becket cult, and for generously critiquing an early draft of this paper.

34. Melvin Storm, "The Pardoner's Invitation: Questor's Bag or Becket's Shrine," *Publications of the Modern Language Association* 97 (1982), 810–18; hereafter cited in text.

35. On the relics at Canterbury and their veneration, see W. A. Scott Robertson, "The Crypt of Canterbury Cathedral (II)," *Archaeologia Cantiana* 13 (1880), 500–23; and Stanley, *Historical Memorials*, 261–62.

36. Knapp, "Relyk of a Seint," 14. Like Storm ("Pardoner's Invitation," 816 n. 5), however, and in opposition to Knapp (15–16 n. 20), I remain unpersuaded that the presence of Saint Simeon's humerus (shoulder or upper arm) at Becket's shrine resonates with the sheep shoulder bone in the Pardoner's hoard. (H)umerus was used for a human bone, not typically for a quadruped's.

37. Cf. Spearing, *Pardoner's Prologue and Tale*, 48–49. H. Marshall Leicester, Jr., " 'Synne Horrible': The Pardoner's Exegesis of His Tale and Chaucer's," in *Geoffrey Chaucer's The Pardoner's Tale*, ed. Harold Bloom (New York and elsewhere: Chelsea House Publishers, 1988), 99, makes a similar point, but

his creative elaboration of it seems to go far beyond what the text can bear.

38. Spearing, *Pardoner's Prologue and Tale*, 48–49. Cf. *Riverside* commentary, 906.
39. Storm ("Pardoner's Invitation," 815) has recognized the importance of the Host's swearing by the cross Saint Helen found, that is, the *True Cross*.
40. For a somewhat different reading of this scene, see Patterson, "Chaucer's Pardoner on the Couch," 676.
41. Despite some similarities in our views, therefore, I obviously dissent from Ralph Elliott's conclusion that "the Pardoner is completely in control of his 'performance' until at the very end the Host's unexpected reaction renders him speechless"; *The Nun's Priest's Tale / The Pardoner's Tale* (Oxford: Basil Blackwell, 1965), 42. The Pardoner's "control" was never complete, and what power he had had over his audience was rendered fragile long before the host's reply to him in the Epilogue.

3

Chaucer's Prioress, the Jews, and the Muslims

SHEILA DELANY

On the road to Canterbury, Chaucer's Prioress, Madame Eglantine, tells a shocking tale. This romantically named, exquisitely mannered nun relates the story of the torment and killing by Christians of a group of Jews in retaliation for the Jews' alleged complicity in the murder of a Christian child. Much has been written about what this narrative means, but few scholars have addressed the curious detail of geographical setting. The opening line of the tale sets the events "in Asye in a greet citee," and it is this setting that I will interrogate to see what it can yield for interpretation of a particularly challenging late-medieval poem.

First: where, for Chaucer, is "Asia"? According to Magoun's *Gazetteer*, it could mean Lydia or Asia Minor—the areas we now call Turkey, Syria, Iran, and Iraq—and Asia Minor would be distinct from Asia Major.[1] For other sources, though, there is no such distinction between major and minor, but only a tripartite division of the known world into Europe, Asia, and Africa. Chaucer evidently accepted this more extensive sense of "Asia," for the only other use of the word in his entire oeuvre reads "In Auffrike, Europe, and Asye" (*House of Fame*, 3:249). Thus Chaucer's "Asia" most likely includes the vast sweep of Central Asia as well as Turkey and the Arab regions.

Besides being an unusual word for Chaucer, the Asia setting is unique to Chaucer among the thirty-three extant versions of this story, which are set in various European cities: Carcassonne, Paris, Toledo, or Lincoln.[2] Chaucer's is the only one to locate the tale in Asia. Obviously, then, this was a deliberate authorial choice, and I will suggest that the choice of setting played a role in the poet's construction of meaning. I have argued elsewhere that the east-west dialectic in the *Legend of Good Women* enabled Chaucer to produce a sexual-geographic morality in that poem, and we could adduce a similar dynamic in the *Man of Law's Tale*.[3] Sex is clearly not the point in the *Prioress's Tale*, but political geography certainly is, because in the late fourteenth century virtually all of Chaucer's "Asia" was under Islamic rule. Despite the pioneering efforts of scholars like Dorothée Metlitzki and Maria Menocal, it is still all too easy for Eurocentric and Christian-centric medievalists to ignore the immense cultural and physical presence of Islam both within and surrounding Europe.[4] The same can, of course, be said of the (less immense) Jewish presence: another and connected story.

This essay, then, may serve as a small effort to redress the balance in favor of history, and history of a particular kind. André Gunder-Frank observes that "very few write international history; almost nobody writes *world* history."[5] The kind of historicism I want to practice here is an internationalist one, based on what Gunder-Frank calls "world system history"; I specify in order to distinguish this from other, more parochial or pseudo-historicisms that have sometimes arisen in medieval studies.

Now it is not strictly true that no one has commented on the Asian setting of the *Prioress's Tale*. In 1964, Sherman Hawkins wrote an exegetical analysis of the poem that he claimed

> belongs to a world of the allegorical and supernatural rather than the world of literal reality. Its very setting in far-off Asia places the action midway between fourteenth-century England and miraculous events of Biblical history.[6]

Accordingly, Hawkins interpreted the Jews as figurative Jews, not real ones: they represent the ideological "enemy," or anyone of any religion "whose wisdom is without faith" (606). Their slaughter by Christians is the triumph of spirituality over mere historicity or literality. It is a victory over a "Jewish" way of reading—a literalistic way—which we moderns would presumably not want to duplicate when we read Scripture or when we read Chaucerian narrative.[7] Thus in this view we have figurative Jews, figurative Christians, and evidently a figurative Asia. As Daniel Boyarin has observed, "One consequence of . . . the post-Pauline Christian adoption of dualist notions was to allegorize the reality of Israel quite out of corporeal existence."[8]

Twenty-five years later, in a bold and complex 1989 article, Louise Fradenburg critiqued Hawkins's view.[9] She reread his reading as an essentially anti-Semitic gesture, precisely on account of its refusal to confront the literal historicity of Jews and of pogroms, which were, after all, the real ritual murders in late-medieval and early modern European culture. Yet despite Fradenburg's insistence on historicity, even she, curiously, does not engage the reality of Asia. She emphasizes strangeness, distance, and exoticism, coming uncomfortably close to an allegorized Asia: "The emptiness of the Prioress's characterization of urban 'asye' is . . . an emptying-out of the city for the purposes of the staging of belief " (99). This is surely right, but it nearly reads the setting as an Asia of the mind; a space that can only be read as empty, can only serve as one term in the rhetorical structure of narrowing focus which opens the tale: we move from exotic continent to unnamed city to ghetto to group and finally to an individual body, that of the murdered boy.

Moreover, to the extent that Fradenburg historicizes the Jews, it is with reference to a twelfth-century German Hebrew martyrology. This enables her to make an eloquent point about the Jews' own voicing of loss and pain, but it is of little help in contextualizing a late-fourteenth-century English representation. Lastly, when Fradenburg explains her point as being "how Christian culture abuses its [own] children" (i.e., the murdered boy, who had been beaten at his Christian school), and interprets the tale as a Freudian projection onto Jews of intra-Christian violence, she undercuts her demand for history, recoils from the literal, and winds up once again in the embrace of allegory, albeit a distinctively modern version of allegory (110–11, n. 28). What I propose here is a really Jewish reading of Asia: a fully literal, contemporary, and historicized reading of it, I call this a Jewish reading—without quotation marks—for much the same reasons that Christian polemicists always have, starting with St. Paul: namely that in defending their religion theoretically, and their right to practice it, Jews have in fact traditionally relied on historicist exegesis of Scripture. Joseph Kimhi's *Book of the Covenant* is a twelfth-century instance that can stand for many over two millennia. Like other polemicists and commentators, Kimhi historicizes Scripture in order to argue against concepts such as Jesus the Messiah, the virgin birth, and other points of Christian doctrine that rely on the figural or spiritualized interpretation of Scripture.[10]

In this essay I want to fill in that emptied-out Asian city and show its relevance to the Chaucerian story. My argument is that the setting introduces a third component into the Jewish-Christian polarity that forms the axis of both the medieval narrative and its modern criticism. It brings in the Muslims, who—as Chaucer well knew—not only ruled "Asia," but also were present in and further encroaching upon Europe. Islam had occupied Spain for nearly seven centuries when Chaucer wrote, albeit diminished from the glory days of Muslim dominion in al-Andalus. Northern Africa was also Islamic, as were Asia Minor, Arabia, and Central Asia. The Ottoman Empire was already, in the mid-fourteenth century, expanding westward into Europe with conquests in Bulgaria and Hungary. Thus Islamic society was by no means as distant as some Chaucerians have suggested, or as many late-medieval Christians might have wished it to be.

Accordingly, European politicians had to incorporate Islam into their plans. England and France competed for influence in Islamic Iberia from the 1330s; both John of Gaunt and Edmund Langley married Castilian princesses, thus acquiring dynastic claims in Spain. John undertook a personal crusade to further his claim. He was "in constant contact with Muhammad V of Granada, even offering the Muslims a portion of the Castilian kingdom if they would aid him in his conquest."[11] This so-called crusade occupied the English Parliament and national financial resources for several years during the 1380s. The Islamic presence in Spain, although lessened by Chaucer's day, clearly played a significant role in English foreign policy of the period.

As a courtier, diplomat, customs official, and member of Parliament, Chaucer not only had to follow such major developments closely but also would be involved in them. Indeed, the impact of Islam was felt in England in very direct and personal ways. There was the presence at the English court of rulers displaced by the Ottoman advance. There were constant appeals to the English government for support of anti-Islamic crusades, to which appeals English knights and nobles flocked in response, despite the reservations of their government. There was the rehearsal of crusade history in the famous Scrope-Grosvenor trial of 1385 and 1386, in which Chaucer testified.[12] In short, for Chaucer, Asia was no exotic fairy-tale dreamscape. Rather, it was the political terrain of a powerful and expanding empire, terrain to which many of his acquaintance had traveled; moreover, this empire possessed a high intellectual culture of its own which was well known to English intellectuals and scholars, as Metlitzki and others have shown.

One important aspect of Islamic society was its treatment of Jews, something Chaucer as a well-traveled English diplomat would likely be aware of and have an opinion on. Many medieval Jews did not, after all, inhabit Christian Europe but Islamic territory, whether in Spain, Egypt, Morocco, Algeria, Iran, Iraq, Armenia, Turkey, or Syria, where they formed part of the *ahl al-dhimma*, or protected non-Islamic population, along with Christians, Sabeans, Zoroastrians, and others. Given this heterogeneity, Jews were not unusually distinctive in Islamic society. Like others, they were governed by *dhimma* law, which offered a range of protections, as well as some financial obligations and social restrictions. Though not entirely free of insecurity, harassment, or symbolic humiliation, Jews in Islamic lands had civil status. They worked in many different trades, from dyer, butcher, and tanner up to banker, merchant, doctor, or government official, and they participated in the public affairs of the multicultural communities they inhabited.

Ideologically, Islam was more positively disposed to Judaism than Catholicism was. Like Christianity, Islam was an offshoot of Judaism: not in the direct Christian mode of the founders being Jews, but in more mediated fashion. Abraham is considered not a Jew but a proto-Muslim.[13] The Jews were originally Muslims until they deviated from Allah's will by demanding a king and establishing the Davidic dynasty. Muhammad considered Moses his precursor and model.[14] Large portions of the Qur'ān contain Hebrew Scriptural stories fleshed out with rabbinic commentary and other Jewish legend. In some sense, then, Islam positioned itself as a Jewish fundamentalism, returning to the foundational patriarchal period of Jewish history: it saw itself as the true Judaism, early Judaism as a true Islam.

Christianity also appropriated Judaism in other ways, but the theorists of Islam apparently felt no need to depreciate the precursor to the extent that Christianity did. Partly this was because Islam lacked a myth of Jewish deicide—or rather the reverse: it developed no myth of inherent Jewish criminality because the animus was lacking. Muhammad, the founder of Islam, did demand the conversion of Jews in gratitude for Allah saving them from Firwa (Pharaoh). Some Jews obliged, for to them, the rapid and massive political success of Islam against Rome, Persia, and Byzantium "seemed to presage the imminent fulfillment of the Jewish prophecies and the coming of the Messianic age."[15] The resistance of other Jews had both practical and literary consequences: warfare and massacre, Qur'ānic commentary, and several anti-Jewish tales showing Jewish disrespect for Muhammad and the new religion. Nonetheless these hostilities did not evolve into a full-fledged anti-Judaic tradition in either the civil or the cultural sphere; as Stillman observes, "Once subdued and made tribute bearers, they [Jews and Christians] were to be shown tolerance."[16]

Let us now turn to Chaucer's narrative with the Muslim information in mind. Here is its heavily laden first stanza:

> Ther was in Asye, in a greet citee,
> Amonges Cristene folk a Jewerye
> Sustened by a lord of that contree
> For foule usure and lucre of vileyne
> Hateful to Crist and to his compagnye;
> And thurgh the strete men myghte ride or wende,
> For it was free and open at eyther ende.

First, in an Islamic society the Christians would not be in charge, but would themselves be governed by *dhimma* law. An intracommunal dispute among different *dhimmi* populations would be referred to the central Islamic authority.[17] Next, there would be no "Jewry" in the sense of a compulsory and exclusive residential ghetto, for normative *dhimma* law encouraged co-residentiality so that nonbelievers might be exposed to Islam. Propinquity was not uncommon, in the same quarter and in the same apartment block or compound.[18] There might be Jewish or Christian or Samaritan areas in a city, particularly around a synagogue or a church, but this was voluntary and carried no stigma. There would be no Jewish monopoly on moneylending because many other occupations were open to Jews, and because Islam openly valued mercantilism and profit. And, though we may imagine the little Christian boy and his mother as European in appearance, they would far more likely be Christian Arabs.

At the end of Chaucer's tale there is no legal procedure: no interrogation, investigation, or trial. Instead, the Jews are condemned, tortured, and executed on circumstantial evidence supported by a miracle. There is no confession; the actual murderer is not caught; and those who are hanged are punished not for any action but for knowing about the murder (l.630). Islamic civil law, however, would normally have required a rigorous court proceeding, in which the Jews would probably have won—as they did in documented cases, including one false murder accusation made by an Islamic nobleman, the son of a vizier (Stillman, *Jews,* 254, 189–90). Lastly, the Prioress associates her tale with the distinctively European discourse of ritual murder when she mentions little Hugh of Lincoln, but in Asia there was no discourse of Jewish ritual murder.[19]

Thus the tale told by Chaucer's Prioress makes little sense in its setting. In its ensemble, the narrative would be virtually impossible in a great Asian city. What the Prioress does is to make a calque of negative European attitudes and impose it on Asia.[20] Why does Chaucer have her do so? Perhaps it is part of her social aspiration, for "Asia" was a fashionable topic among the nobility with which she identifies. Perhaps it is the sign of her superficial education, along with her English-accented French. Or perhaps this politically minded poet has his own reasons, speculation on which necessarily leads us into interpretation.

It is fair, then, to argue that Islam is conspicuous by its absence from this tale, and that the Asia setting is precisely the tell-tale sign of that effacement, a sign of a specter haunting the background of the tale, just as it haunted the borders of Europe and the minds of European and English politicians. There is, moreover, another tradition in politics, theology, canon law, and the arts which brings Islam even more fully into play in medieval literature than the political realities I have just adduced. This tradition is the linkage of Jews and Muslims ("Saracens") that became a common trope from the thirteenth century on, especially in northern Europe, so common that by Chaucer's day it would be difficult to name the one group without conjuring up the other.

What enabled this linkage? Its material base was surely the real economic, political, and military relations of Jews and Muslims in Spain, Arabia, and North Africa—relations that Epstein describes as "commonality of interests," and Levy, more strikingly, as "symbiosis."[21] On the ideological level, an important role was played by the flexible Catholic concept of Antichrist, which could incorporate any and all heretics and pagans, but especially Muslims and Jews, simultaneously and with no sense of contradiction. As Richard Emmerson observes, "All those who persecute or otherwise undermine the true Christian church are Antichrist's supporters . . . In the Middle Ages, the most important supporters of Antichrist are the Jews."[22] Scriptural passages were glossed to yield the belief that Antichrist would be born of Jewish parents from the tribe of Dan; he would be circumcised, he would rebuild the Temple in Jerusalem, and he would be diabolical. At the same time, Mohammad was seen as "the anti-messiah of the Saracens and Jews." Islam loomed large in apocalyptic thought, hence in commentaries on Scriptural books such as Revelation, Daniel, John, and others; these commentaries—some of them by English ecclesiastical scholars—formed a transmission belt between elite and popular cultures in providing a rich source for sermons and encyclopedic compilations. In this commentary tradition, Jews and Muslims were partners in "the great anti-Christian coalition."[23]

This tradition of Muslim-Jewish linkage appears in English and continental drama and other literature, in treatises, in canon law, and in the visual arts. A very few instances will have to suffice for the many that could be adduced. I will begin with ecclesiastical discourse.[24]

Catholic clergy resented the Jews' supposed alliance with Islamic invaders against Christian regimes and armies, starting as early as Visigothic Spain and the Byzantine Empire.[25] In 640, Maximus the Confessor wrote of the Arabs as "a Jewish people,"[26] and at the Council of Toledo in 694, "Iberian Jews were accused of conspiring with North African co-religionists to hand over Spain to the Muslims" (Stillman, "Jewish Life," 53). Such accusations continued on the popular level, as when, in 1010, the Jews of Orléans were massacred because of rumors that Palestinian Jews had helped the Islamic regime destroy a famous church in Jerusalem. Catholic clergy also resented the frequent prominence of Jews as government officials in Islamic regimes both in Spain and abroad. Canon law usually made similar rules for Muslims and Jews, especially regarding questions of property and conversion, but also in arguments for and against crusade;[27] Lomax notes the "increasing linkage of Jews and Saracens that occurred in canon law during [the thirteenth century]."[28] During the same period, Pope Innocent III—who had already sponsored a crusade against the Albigensians and the disastrous Fourth Crusade—planned a fifth crusade against the Islamic East, to be launched at the Fourth Lateran Council of 1215. Recovery of the Holy Land had been an urgent priority since the loss of Jerusalem in 1187, and as recently as 1212, "the Patriarch of Alexandria was imprisoned by the Sultan of Egypt and several Christian strongholds were lost to the infidel."[29] In his crusade appeals of 1213, Innocent identified Muhammad as the Beast of the Apocalypse, or as Antichrist, whose 666 years were nearly fulfilled (Muhammad's dates being c. 570–632).[30] In this apocalyptic theoretical framing, the crusade would be a means of conversion of Muslims and Jews alike, preparatory to a glorious era of renewed Christian peace and influence. The visual identification by clothing required for the first time at this council for European Jews was also to be imposed on Muslims ("Iudaeos seu Saracenos") so that neither Jews nor Muslims would be mistaken for Christians by Christian women. Likewise, public office was forbidden to Jews and this exclusion was extended "ad paganos."[31] I doubt we presume too far in thinking that Innocent expected these rules to be exported beyond Europe after a victorious crusade. Returning to Chaucer: it is surely no coincidence that the very poem which uses Innocent's work as a source should be precisely the one that most starkly polarizes east and west, Syria and Rome, Muslim and Christian: I mean, of course, the Man of Law material.[32] Chaucer was evidently well aware of ecclesiastical international politics in the preceding century, and in his own.

Literary texts known to Chaucer make the same connection. In the *Inferno*, Dante has a soul—that of Guido da Montefeltro—who brings Jews and Muslims together as those against whom Pope Boniface VIII should wage a crusade (Inf. 27:85 ff.); he even Jew baits the pope as a "new Pharisee." Although Guido is in the *bolgia* of those who gave bad advice, it is doubtful that every medieval reader would grasp the possible irony. Guido da Pisa, writing a few years after Dante's death, apparently saw nothing odd, but simply accepted the logic of a crusade against Italian Jews in his commentary on this line.[33] Muhammad is tormented in the ninth *bolgia* of hell (Canto 28), and in the last canto, the mythic geography of earth's spiritualized interior makes "la Giudecca" (the Jewish quarter) the location of the giant triple-faced Lucifer.[34] In short, there is a thorough imbrication of Judaism, Islam, and the satanic in a work that was one of Chaucer's important sources.[35]

In England, this equation was common in the popular drama.[36] Chaucer refers explicitly to Noah and Herod plays in his *Miller's Tale* (lines 3384, 3538–43, 3559–61, 3582). The Croxton *Play of the Sacrament* has Jewish characters pray to Machomet; the York *Passion* has Pilate swear by Mahound and soldiers by "Mahoundes blood"; in the Digby *Mary Magdalene*, Herod, a Jew, does likewise (lines 142–43), as do minor characters in the Digby *Killing of the Children*. Similarly, in Italian and French passion plays, Pilate, Herod, and the Jewish high priest Annias address Muhammad as their deity.

The Cutlers marshal a range of evidence for the Jewish-Muslim exchangeability in Christian writing and painting from the eleventh through sixteenth centuries.[37] As in some passion plays, Muslims are anachronistically associated with the Crucifixion in paintings of that event. Some of the Muslims are dark-skinned with Negroid features, others appear as turbaned Arabs; still others have Mongoloid slit eyes, long braids, and drooping mustaches, so that the cultural and ethnic variety within Islam is accurately portrayed. Conversely, the Islamic crescent is shown on flags carried by Jews at the Crucifixion, and martyred Jews are represented in some Christian chronicles as calling on Mahomet as they die. A German woodcut (1508) shows the figure of Synagoga with an Islamic flag and, conversely, Mahomet with a Jewish banner. It is an irony of history that only a couple of decades later, Catholicism itself would be classified with Islam under the label of heretical "Turkopapalism"—by Luther and other Protestant polemicists in England and on the continent.[38]

What, then, are the implications for interpretation? First, it seems legitimate to suggest that even if the Prioress is mainly concerned with Jews,

Chaucer is at least equally interested in Muslims, who were a real political-military threat, and whom he and his audience were taught to see as equivalent to, perhaps represented by, Jews. The Prioress's Jews, I propose, are no less "real" than any other fictional characters—and real Jews were often seen as partners with real Muslims, as were fictional Jews with fictional Muslims.

Some scholars assume that Chaucer never saw or met a Jew because Jews were expelled from England in 1290.[39] This is an excessively narrow view. Chaucer was a government official, and in this capacity he traveled to many major European cities that had Jewish communities. He is likely to have encountered the Jewish physicians, merchants, booksellers, illumina-tors, scribes, musicians, actors, moneylenders, or scholars who lived and worked at some of the courts and cities he visited, and above all in Spain—specifically Navarre and Castile, where Chaucer is known to have been in February 1366, and probably for some months afterward. Navarre, England's ally in the ongoing war—the so-called Hundred Years War—against France, welcomed both Jews and Muslims and treated both groups fairly well.[40] Pedro of Castile, John of Gaunt's father-in-law, celebrated by Chaucer in the *Monk's Tale*, had good relations with both Muslims and Jews, and employed many of both in important posts. Baer observes that Pedro "was then gener-ally called the 'king of the Jews.' " There were nonetheless numerous inci-dents, and just at the time when Chaucer was travelling through the region on a safe-conduct from the King of Navarre (Charles II, known as "the bad"), an entire community at Briviesca, about two hundred families, was massacred by French mercenaries and the troops of Henry of Trastamara.[41] The Lancas-trian settlement in Castile some years later imposed new measures for segre-gating Jews and Muslims from Christians (Russell, 497). Chaucer cannot have been ignorant of any of this: the closeness, the incident, the change—or, still later, the massive persecutions that began in Castile and spread to Andalusia and Navarre during 1391.

Similarly, there is no way Chaucer could have been unaware of the expulsion of the Jews from France in 1394 by Charles VI, or failed to follow the well-publicized events leading up to it.[42] Since this is the country with which England was at war and at truce, thus in constant communication, it seems obvious that Chaucer, even in post-1290 *Judenrein* England, had to be just as aware of the continental Jewish presence, and its vicissitudes, as he was of the Islamic.

It is dismaying to notice the provinciality with which authoritative schol-arship has ignored the Jewish and Islamic facts. In the *Variorum* edition of the *Prioress's Tale*, Beverly Boyd supplies ample information about the treatment of Jews in London (where there were none), Rome, and Regensburg, but not a word about Paris (where there was a significant community in which a notori-ous incident occurred in 1394), much less Baghdad, Aleppo, Samarkand, Damascus, or Aden (which are in "Asia" and had large Jewish populations).

She comments that the forced vulnerability of the ghetto in the *Prioress's Tale*, with its free access at either end, demonstrates how harmoniously the Christians are living with "their" [*sic*] Jews.[43] In the *Riverside* edition, Florence Ridley describes the tale as a celebration of "the triumph of the innocent and weak." By this she does not mean the slandered, exploited, marginalized, and demonized Jews of medieval Europe or of the tale itself, but the little Christian boy: implicitly she accepts the ideological structure of the narrative. Thus two of the most "authoritative" treatments of this tale simply take for granted a traditional and outdated northern European- and Christian-centered perspective.[44] This selective blindness is certainly not confined to medieval studies. As James Shapiro observes in his groundbreaking study of Jews in early modern England, "Jewish questions . . . almost never appear in modern Jewish histories of Shakespeare's England, though virtually every major writer, theologian, and political figure of that period had at some point dealt with one or more of them."[45]

I return now to the question of interpretation. To restore the effaced Islamic presence to the *Prioress's Tale* does not drastically alter the tale's problematic, but does intensify it. There are still two possible views. One is the rigorist approach: the Prioress is a reliable narrator despite her foibles (much like the Monk). With Catholic rigor and Anglo-European patriotism she chastises both the well-known Islamic tolerance of Christ's other enemies, and European Christians inclined to a liberal treatment of such enemies at home or abroad. Who might such soft-minded Christians be? Chaucer's friend John Gower was notoriously pacifistic toward pagans in his *Confessio Amantis* (3: 2487–89, 2513; 4: 1679–81). John of Gaunt had allied himself with pro-Jewish Muslims in Spain, and many English, particularly those in government, had moral or political scruples about a hardnosed crusade or even a conversion perspective for Jews and Muslims. There were plenty of candidates for chastisement. This perspective tends to align the *Prioress's Tale* with the *Parson's Tale*, whose apparently exemplary teller refers more than once to "cursede Jewes" (X [1], 590–99). It would also bring in the *Man of Law's Tale,* with which the *Prioress's Tale* shares a verse form, an exotic— indeed "Asian"—setting, a polarized religious structure, and the plot of a Christian victim persecuted by diabolical non-Christian opponents, but vindicated by miracles. Someone arguing this view might also point out that Chaucer could have chosen to portray a virtuous Jew somewhere in his work, as Boccaccio, for instance, had already done in the *Decameron*.[46]

The other view—we might call it the "liberal" view—would take the Prioress as an ignoramus and a sentimental bigot, hopelessly obsolete with her reference to the 1175 Hugh of Lincoln episode as "just a little while ago." The obvious excess of her tale would suggest ironically that neither Jews nor Muslims are the devil's spawn, that both may be rational or virtuous individuals even if not enlightened by Christian grace. This was, after all, a perfectly respectable position held by various scholars of the day, especially the *moderni* or nominalists so influential in English and European universities of the fourteenth and fifteenth centuries. We are meant to reject the xenophobic jingoism and ultraorthodoxy exposed in the narrative, and instead we are meant to consider a more civil, more humane attitude toward both "people of the book" than was currently displayed in Christian Europe. This perspective tends to relate the *Prioress's Tale* to the *Legend of Good Women*, which shows a moral equivalency between Roman and Egyptian, Athenian and barbarian, Trojan and Carthaginian. Anyone can be good or bad, and the *Legend* shows military adventurers in no good light; thus a subtle critique of the crusade ideal may inform this "liberal" model of Chaucerian ethical politics.

Of course it is possible that Chaucer occupied both positions during his lifetime, but imprecision of dating makes it difficult to say in which direction he might have changed. In this sense, the present paper, like the Chaucerian Jewry, is open at either end. Whichever Chaucer we choose, one thing is clear and certain: that for him the Islamic East was no merely figurative realm, but was pressing its intellectual and political claims as literally as it does today. The presence of Muslims and Jews in any artwork of the period could not have had exclusively or even primarily allegorical meaning for a late-medieval courtly writer; it was, quite simply, too important empirically. A merely exegetical reading of this or any poem effaces history both medieval and modern.

Notes

Versions of this paper were given in Robert Hanning's informal discussion group at Columbia University, and as the R. H. Robbins annual lecture for the New York Medieval Club in 1998. I am indebted to both audiences for thoughtful comments, especially to Chris Baswell, Peter Travis, and Sylvia Tomasch.

1. F. P. Magoun, *A Chaucer Gazetteer* (Chicago: University of Chicago Press, 1961).
2. Other Marian miracles—not analogues to the *Prioress's Tale*—are set in various places both "Asian" and European, indeed so many of the latter that the eastern or "exotic" setting cannot be considered a convention of the genre as some critics have claimed. Eastern settings include Byzantium, Caesarea, lesser Armenia, Alexandria, Lydda, and Jerusalem; European sites include Bourges, Rome, Pisa, Hungary, Toledo, England, Lincoln, Cluny, Chartres, St. Ouen, Cambrai, Orléans, Rheims, and Denmark. See, for example, items in Evelyn Faye Wilson, ed., *The Stella Maris of John of Garland* (Cambridge, MA.: Wellesley College and Medieval Academy of America, 1946).
3. See my *The Naked Text: Chaucer's Legend of Good Women* (Berkeley and Los Angeles: University of California Press: 1994), 164–86; "Womanliness in the *Man of Law's Tale*" in S. Delany, *Writing Woman* (New York: Schocken, 1983), 36–46; " 'Loi' and 'Foi' in the Man of Law's Introduction, Prologue and Tale," *Mediaevalia* 8 (1985 for 1982), 135–49.

4. See Maria Menocal, *The Arabic Role in Medieval Literary History: A Forgotten Heritage* (Philadelphia: University of Pennsylvania Press, 1987); and Dorothée Metlitzki, *The Matter of Araby in Medieval England* (New Haven, CT: Yale University Press, 1977).

5. André Gunder-Frank, *The Centrality of Central Asia* (Amsterdam: Vrije Universiteit Press, 1992), 2 (emphasis in original).

6. Sherman Hawkins, "Chaucer's Prioress and the Sacrifice of Praise," *Journal of English and Germanic Philology* 63 (1964), 599–624; citation to 599.

7. Edward H. Kelly agreed with Hawkins's remark that "anti-Semitism . . . is quite beside the point": " 'By mouth of innocentz': the Prioress Vindicated," *Publications in Language and Literature* 5 (1969), 362–74 on 368 n. 9. Kelly acknowledged the Asian setting, saying that the Christians do not punish the Jews but the provost of the land does. This observation may imply that the provost is not Christian. Yet the text plainly specifies that the provost "herieth Crist . . . And eek his mooder" (618–19) before imprisoning the Jews, so obviously he is imagined as a Christian.

8. Daniel Boyarin, *Carnal Israel: Reading Sex in Talmudic Culture* (Berkeley and Los Angeles: University of California Press, 1993), 6.

9. Louise O. Fradenburg, "Criticism, Anti-Semitism, and the Prioress's Tale," *Exemplaria* 1 (1989), 69–115.

10. Of course Jewish exegetes also used non-literal methods, whether numerical or allegorical. Their effort, though, was to avoid violating the literal sense, and when their aim was anti-Christian polemic they were often best served by historicist literality. See Esra Sherevsky, *Rashi: The Man and His World* (New York: Sepher-Harmon Press, 1982; Northvale, NJ, and London: Jason Aronson, 1996), 61–66, 122–29. For Kimhi: *The Book of the Covenant*, trans. Frank Talmage (Toronto: Pontifical Institute of Mediaeval Studies, 1972).

11. P. E. Russell, *The English Intervention in Spain and Portugal in the Time of Edward III and Richard II* (Oxford: Clarendon, 1955), 444.

12. For a more detailed presentation of these data, see my *The Naked Text*, 164–86.

13. Helmut Götje, *The Qur'an and Its Exegesis* (Oxford: Oneworld, 1971); repr. Routledge, 1997), 98–100, 135, 245.

14. Marie-Rose Séguy, introduction and commentary to *The Miraculous Journey of Mahomet* (New York: Braziller, 1977), commentary to Plate 23.

15. Bernard Lewis, *The Jews of Islam* (Princeton NJ: Princeton University Press, 1984), 93; see also Norman Stillman, "Jewish Life in Islamic Spain," in *Aspects of Jewish Culture in the Middle Ages,* ed. Paul Szarmach (Albany, NY: SUNY Press, 1979), 51–84.

16. Norman Stillman, *The Jews of Arab Lands: A History and Source Book* (Philadelphia: Jewish Publication Society, 1979), 18.

17. Bat Ye'or, *The Decline of Eastern Christianity under Islam* (Madison, NJ: Fairleigh Dickinson University Press, 1996), 151.

18. Mark R. Cohen, *Under Crescent and Cross: The Jews in the Middle Ages* (Princeton, NJ: Princeton University Press, 1994), chapter 7. I am indebted to Cohen's book for other details in this section as well.

19. I do not wish to suggest an image of utopia here. There was occasional or intermittent persecution of Jews and other *dhimmi* by Islamic regimes, but

this was not the norm. Cohen's introduction offers a clear and balanced exposition of evolving views and agendas on this question. There were some
blood libels by Christians against Jews in fifteenth- and sixteenth-century
Anatolia, but the accusers were brought to Istanbul and punished for slander:
see Aryeh Shmuelevitz, *Jews of the Ottoman Empire in the Late Fifteenth and
the Sixteenth Century* (Leiden, Brill, 1984), 3, and Mark Alan Epstein, *The
Ottoman Jewish Communities and Their Role in Fifteenth- and Sixteenth-
Century Turkey* (Freiburg, Klaus Schwatrz Verlag, 1980), 38.

20. I am indebted to Chris Baswell for this image.

21. Epstein, *Ottoman Jewish Communities*, 42–44; Avigdor Levy, *The Jews of the
Ottoman Empire* (Princeton, NJ: Darwin Press, 1994).

22. Richard Emmerson, *Antichrist in the Middle Ages* (Seattle: University of
Washington Press, 1981), 216. Other citations in this paragraph to 91 and
197.

23. David Burr, "Antichrist and Islam in Medieval Franciscan Exegesis," in
Medieval Perceptions of Islam, ed. J. V. Tolan (New York: Garland, 1996),
citation to 152 n. 50.

24. The attitudes brought forward here were not standard everywhere or at every
time; there was variability, with Jews often being invited, accepted, and protected by Catholic rulers and populations. In 1387, for example—to use a
ruler Chaucer would have been familiar with—Gian Galeazzo Visconti guaranteed to Jews the "enjoyment of civil rights," tax exemptions, and the right
to work as moneylenders among other occupations, thus bringing to an end
over a century of exclusion; the charter is printed in Shlomo Simonsohn, *The
Jews in the Duchy of Milan* (Jerusalem: Israel Academy of Sciences and
Humanities, 1982), vol. 1, 1387–1477. In 1394, when the Jews were expelled
from France by Charles VI, some regional lords protested and did not comply.

25. Bernard Lewis, "An Apocalyptic Vision of Islamic History," *Bulletin of the
School of Oriental and African Studies*, University of London, 13, part 2
(1950), 308–38; citation to 321–22.

26. John C. Lamoreaux, "Early Eastern Christian Responses to Islam," in Tolan,
Medieval Perceptions, 14.

27. Benjamin Z. Kedar, *Crusade and Mission: European Approaches toward the
Muslims* (Princeton, NJ: Princeton University Press, 1984), 137, 175, 187.

28. John Philip Lomax, "Frederick II, his Saracens, and the Papacy," in Tolan,
Medieval Perceptions, 191 n. 6.

29. Brenda Bolton, "A Show with a Meaning: Innocent III's Approach to the
Fourth Lateran Council," *Medieval History* 1 (1991), 53–67, and reprinted in
Innocent III: Studies on Papal Authority and Pastoral Care (Aldershot, Vari-
orum, 1995), citation to 58.

30. See documents #27 and 44, dated November 1199 and April 1213, in *Cris-
tianità-Islam: Cattività e Liberazione in Nome di Dio* (Rome: Editrice Ponti-
ficia Università Gregoriana, 1992), 508, 537–38.

31. See *constitutiones* 68 and 69 of the Fourth Lateran Council in *Conciliorum
Oecumenicorum Decreta*, ed. Joseph Alberigo et al. (Basil: Herder, 1962),
242–43. Jews and "Saracens" are brought together again in the last ruling
(#71) in connection with the complex finances of the planned crusade: Many

supporters will either have their options limited by debt to Jews, or have to borrow from Jews, while some traitor Christians will sell arms and ships to the enemy Saracens; they are excommunicated and anathematized in advance.

32. See my "Womanliness" in *Writing Woman* and " 'Loi' and 'foi'; " also Christine Rose, "The Jewish Mother-in-Law: Synagoga and the *Man of Law's Tale*," in this volume.

33. Vincenzo Cioffari, ed., *Guido da Pisa, Expositiones et glose super comediam Dantis . . .* (Albany, NY: SUNY Press, 1974), 559.

34. See Sylvia Tomasch, "Judecca, Dante's Satan, and the *Dis*-placed Jew," in *Text and Territory: Geographical Imagination in the European Middle Ages*, ed. Sylvia Tomasch and Sealy Gilles (Philadelphia: University of Pennsylvania Press, 1998), 247–67; reference to 248; 265 n. 2.

35. This is despite the likelihood of Dante's having been influenced by Islamic literature—particularly Muslim visions of heaven and hell—which he could have learned about from many sources, including his beloved teacher Brunetto Latini, who had resided at the court of Alfonso the Wise in Spain, and whose work is full of Islamic material; see Miguel Palacios Asin, *Islam and the Divine Comedy* (Lahore: Quasain, 1977). We should remember that Chaucer is likely to have read an annotated version of the *Commedia*, or perhaps only a commentary, much as with other monumental "authoritative" texts such as Ovid's *Metamorphoses*.

36. Some plays are of post-Chaucerian date but clearly draw on preexisting tradition. Rosemary Woolf writes that York had a cycle by 1376, though no details are known of it: *The English Mystery Plays* (Berkeley and Los Angeles: University of California Press, 1972), 305. The extant passion sequence and other plays in the cycle were rewritten after 1415. John Ganim suggests that supervision of plays might well have been one of Chaucer's official responsibilities: *Chaucerian Theatricality* (Princeton, NJ: Princeton University Press, 1990), 38.

37. Allan H. Cutler and Helen E. Cutler, *The Jew as Ally of the Muslim: Medieval Roots of Anti-Semitism* (Notre Dame, IN: University of Notre Dame Press, 1986). I am well aware of scholarly criticisms made of the Cutlers' controversial thesis in reviews of this book, but they do not apply to the empirical visual arts and literary material I adduce here.

38. S. Fischer-Galati, "The Protestant Reformation and Islam," in *The Mutual Effects of the Islamic and Judaeo-Christian Worlds,* ed. A. Ascher et al. (Brooklyn: Brooklyn College Press, 1979), 53–64.

39. See, for example, Florence Ridley's comment in *The Riverside Chaucer*: "The tale has little connection with English life of the time; Jews had been banished from England since 1290" (913–14).

40. See Beatrice Leroy, "Le Royaume de Navarre et les Juifs aux XIVe et Xve Siècles: Entre l'Accueil et la Tolérance," *Sefarad* 38 (1978), 263–92; and Leroy, "Dans le royaume de Navarre à la fin du XIVe siècle: les Juifs, la Cour et la diplomatie," in *Les Juifs au regard de l'histoire*, ed. Gilbert Dahan (Paris: Picard, 1985).

41. Yitzhak Baer, *A History of the Jews in Christian Spain*, 2 vols. (Philadelphia: Jewish Publication Society of America, 1966), 1: 364–65.

42. For a study of these events and their possible relation to the *Prioress's Tale*,
     see my forthcoming "The Jewish Connection: Chaucer and the Paris Jews,
     1394," given as a lecture at Hebrew University, Jerusalem in 1998. I thank
     Larry Besserman for inviting me to offer it there, and for his warm support of
     the project. The paper was also given at Green College at the University of
     British Columbia in 1998; my thanks to Paul Yachnin, director of the
     Medieval-Renaissance program at Green College. The most recent version
     was given at Kalamazoo, in 1999, and at the Association for Jewish Studies
     conference, in 2001.

43. Beverly Boyd, ed., *The Canterbury Tales: Part 20, "The Prioress's Tale"*
     (Norman, OK: University of Oklahoma Press, 1987).

44. To give a flavor of the tenacity of attitudes similar to those displayed in the
     Prioress's Tale, consider the following: (1) In the *Concise Biographical Dic-
     tionary of Saints* by John Coulson (London: Hawthorn Books, 1958), 47, we
     read, concerning the alleged ritual murders of Simon of Trent and William of
     Norwich: "Blood was used in certain magical rites and the children could have
     been killed by magicians who may have happened to be Jews. Another expla-
     nation is that, as Christian persecution of the Jews reached a climax at Easter
     (the time of the Jewish pasch) [evidently this author cannot bear to pronounce
     the name Passover], some Jews may have been goaded [goaded by whom, one
     wonders! Satan, perhaps?] to take retaliation upon the only defenceless Chris-
     tians they could find, children like Simon of Trent and William of Norwich!"
     (2) John J. Delaney, *Dictionary of Saints* (New York: Doubleday, 1980), s.v.
     Hugh the Little, "one of the most tragic stories of the Middle Ages," in which
     "the murderer confessed" after torture! The writer continues: "That a Christian
     child may have been killed by a Jew or Jews may have taken place, but it was
     never proven."

     It is bizarre how desperately these authors cling to the myth of the blood
     libel. Of course, and more importantly, the existence of a demonizing anti-
     Semitism continues outside of scholarship as well, as newspaper notices of
     various incidents remind us. Among them is a short notice in *The Chronicle of
     Higher Education* (December 6, 1996), headlined "Alleged Exorcism Results
     in a Beating." The victim, a student at Mississippi College, a Baptist institu-
     tion, was Jewish; two classmates wanted to "exorcise her of demonic spirits."

45. James Shapiro, *Shakespeare and the Jews* (New York: Columbia University
     Press, 1996), 2–3.

46. As Stephen Spector observes in "Empathy and Enmity in the *Prioress's Tale*,"
     in *The Olde Daunce: Love, Friendship, Sex and Marriage in the Medieval
     World*, ed. Robert Edwards and Stephen Spector (Albany, NY: SUNY Press,
     1991), 211–28.

4

"Jewes werk" in *Sir Thopas*

JEROME MANDEL

> He dide next his white leere,
> Of cloth of lake fyn and cleere,
> A breech and eek a sherte;
> And next his sherte an aketoun,
> And over that an haubergeoun
> For percynge of his herte;
>
> And over that a fyn hawberk,
> Was al ywroght of Jewes werk,
> Ful strong it was of plate;
> And over that his cote-armour
> As whit as is a lilye flour,
> In which he wol debate.
> SIR THOPAS, LINES 857–68

One piece of Sir Thopas' armor—the "fyn hauberk," "ful strong . . . of plate," and "al ywroght of Jewes werk"—has long been a puzzle. We know, for example, that both a hauberk and its derivative, the haubergeoun, are short coats or tunics, first of chain and later of plate mail worn over a padded, often quilted undergarment, the aketoun.[1] From the middle of the fourteenth century, a plate was often affixed or worked into the hauberk to provide greater protection to the chest, and then to the back and thighs. Is Thopas wearing a haubergeoun of chain mail, and over that a hauberk of plate or of chain with "strong" plate attached? Ambiguity attends other words. Is "fyn" used judgmentally to mean "well-made" or descriptively to mean "closely linked"? Is the hauberk "fyn" because the plate is strong or is it "fyn" because it is "Jewes werk"? Does the word "ywroght" mean that the hauberk itself is "decorated," that the strong plate is damascened, engraved,

59

painted, niello-work (or some other form of ornamentation), or merely that the hauberk has been worked or made by Jews? Is the reference positive and admiring, or negative and ironic? It is the purpose of this essay to assess the reputation of Jews as makers of fine armor in the Middle Ages and so elucidate the phrase in both a social and literary context.[2]

Chaucer's first modern editor, W. W. Skeat, dismissed Tyrwhitt's gloss on Jew as "magician" and Jephson's etymologically faulty connection of Jew with "jewel," and concluded that "the phrase still remains unexplained."[3] He suspected that "it means no more than wrought with rich or expensive work, such as Jews could best find the money for. It is notorious that they were the chief capitalists, and they must often have had to find money for paying armourers" (Skeat, 5: 196). Since Jews were generally forbidden to bear weapons in Chaucer's day,[4] we may well wonder why they would decorate armor they could not wear, and though some in England and elsewhere were rich merchants or moneylenders, the vast majority of medieval Jews were marginal pawnbrokers, shopkeepers, and artisans, hence far from being the chief capitalists of European or even North African economies.[5]

The publication of H. Graetz's six-volume *History of the Jews* in 1891 to 1898, and of *The Jewish Encyclopedia* in an English language edition allowed H. S. Ficke, in an article on this passage, to update Skeat's gloss. Not only does "skill in metal working [date] from the beginning of Jewish history," but "there is an unbroken record of the development of this industry from the first century down to the fourteenth," and "wherever the Mohammedan power was established, we find Jewish armorers."[6] He concludes that the phrase "Jewes werk" means simply "Jews' work."

But what does that mean? Does Chaucer acknowledge superior workmanship or denigrate the shabby work of a despised religion long banished from England? The answer to this question depends upon how the satire works in *Sir Thopas* and what Chaucer's perception of Jews' work was. In coming to terms with ridicule and absurdity in the tale, J. M. Manly focused on the object of satire, which he takes to be "the ridiculous pretentiousness of these Flemings," and comments at one point on the topos of "arming the knight."

> It was therefore an absurdity that the knight should don an aketon [i.e., when made of leather, the defensive armor of a common foot soldier; in Chaucer's time, a quilted cotton coat]; a double absurdity that he should put on over it a haubergeon; a triple absurdity that over these should be worn a fine hauberk; and a final touch of perfection that the cote armour which should display the armorial bearings of the knight was blank.[7]

Herben, on the other hand, saw the arming passage as "a fairly realistic description of the successive stages of arming," and located the satire in "the over-elaboration of detail and in the emphasis upon the obvious." Linn found

Chaucer's satire in "the significant omission of any reference to Sir Thopas's sword or spurs."[8] Derek Brewer has most recently evaluated this scene:

> The arming of Sir Thopas contains a very usual selection of usual elements, with the quite reasonable and realistic addition of breeches and shirt beneath. Even the coat-armor and bridle can be found elsewhere. The greaves are present, but they indeed are in a wrong and silly place. What is ridiculous is the presentation of the details with certain modifications, exaggerations, and oddities such as, possibly, the white surcoat; certainly the shield of *gold*, so soft and heavy; the leathern, not steel, greaves; the sword-sheath of ivory yet no sword mentioned; the helmet of the cheap soft metal, latten; the shining bridle; the mild horse; etc. The placing and pomposity of the arming, the prelude of the wine (of which I have noticed no precedent), Sir Thopas's swearing on ale and bread, are all splendidly absurd, and even more so when read against the long tradition of solemn splendor.[9]

Since all view the arming scene as ironic, how then does Chaucer's reference to "Jewes werk" fit in? If "Jewes werk" was splendid, we have a silly, physically amusing man in excellent armor. If "Jewes werk" was shoddy, the armor is appropriate and the term expands Thopas's silliness. Two similarly antithetical attitudes toward the Jews themselves were current in the Middle Ages. Jews were configured both in positive and in negative terms, as Christ crucifiers, in other words, historical Jews, whom Chaucer's Prioress refers to as "cursed Jewes" *(PrT,* 599, 685), and as Scriptural Jews, whom the Pardoner refers to as "hooly Jewes" *(PardT,* 351), presented from pulpit and in text as worthy of admiration and emulation. Recent scholarship argues for "the strong conceptual presence of Jews in England in the fourteenth century"[10] long after their expulsion from England. Jews, in both of these medieval configurations, were in the air even if they were not on the ground. What, then, was the reputation of "Jewes werk" in Chaucer's time?

Although documentary sources describe medieval English Jews almost exclusively as moneylenders, "it is almost inconceivable that any medieval man and *a fortiori* any medieval community, Jewish or Christian, could live by moneylending alone. Moneylending and trade went together."[11] Evidence indicates that English Jews were vintners, cheesemongers, fishmongers, ironmongers, physicians, goldsmiths, soldiers, and pawnbrokers.[12] Pawnbroking "necessarily implies skill in the repair and refurbishing of jewellery and plate, clothing and armour, to make them readily saleable" (Richardson, 26–27), but this sort of occasional skill can hardly support a reputation for fine artistry. Only metalworking would be relevant to making or decorating armor. In 1290, the Jews were expelled from England.[13] Whatever residual reputation for armor making the Jews might have had a hundred years later, Chaucer would have had little opportunity to evaluate firsthand the quality of Jewish workmanship in England, even if evidence suggested that Jews engaged in that profession. No such English evidence exists. We must look to the continent for the reputation of Jews as artisans and workers in metal.

Jews in northern European towns were far less restricted in their occupations than Jews in England. They played no role of any importance in the great industrial and commercial centers of Flanders and northern Italy, where Chaucer might have come upon them in his diplomatic missions to the continent.[14] "Among the Jews of Germany and north France in the thirteenth and fourteenth centuries are found masons, tanners, card-painters, armorers, stone-engravers, glaziers, and even makers of mouse-traps."[15] A surprising number of Jewish sword makers are recorded in Bohemia and Moravia, though the references date from the fifteenth and sixteenth centuries.[16] Even if they were active earlier, we have no evidence Chaucer was ever in the area. In Italy, too, Jews were active in metalworking. A Jewish ironmonger supplied material to repair the roof of the Church of Saint Francis in Assisi in 1436, and Gabriele di Angelo was blacksmithing in Assisi in the second half of the fifteenth century,[17] but competence in ironmongery and blacksmithery (or locksmithing and mousetrappery) does not bespeak a reputation for excellence in making hauberks—even if the men or their workshops existed when Chaucer was Italy half a century earlier. On the other hand, Italian metalworkers were noted sword makers. Among the most famous in the fifteenth century was Ercole de' Fideli (born Salomone da Sesso) who worked for the court of Ferrara, decorated swords with etched figures, and made the "Queen of Swords" for Cesare Borgia (Wischnitzer, 144). Since the secrets of medieval manufacturing were jealously guarded and communicated only within a family of artisans, it is possible that the da Sesso family or some other group of notable Jewish metalworkers were making swords or decorating armor in northern Italy when Chaucer was there on several occasions between 1368 and 1378.

But it was in Spain under the Moors and the Christians that the Jews were most free to follow their economic endeavors from the eighth to the fifteenth century.[18]

> Since the Jewish inhabitants of Spain were never restricted to being bankers, tax-collectors, or merchants, they became a petty bourgeoisie of shopkeepers, artisans, and craftsmen in a great variety of occupations for which artistic taste and manual skill were required. Indeed, from the time of Muhammad, Jews were masters of all the crafts necessary to support their community and were especially renowned throughout the Arab world for the quality of their arms and armor.[19]

It was said, with only slight exaggeration, that following the Arab conquest of North Africa in the seventh and eighth centuries, Jews were the only locksmiths, goldsmiths, metal founders, and minters.[20] By the thirteenth century,

Jewish life in Spain was concentrated in the north, to which many Jews had fled from the persecution of the fanatical Almohade Berbers, and many Jewish communities sprang up in Castile, Aragon, and Navarre, especially in Burgos, Logroño, Soria, Segovia, and Toledo. Since so many of the Spanish towns inhabited by the Jews are along the pilgrimage route to San Juan de Compostella (which, together with Rome and Jerusalem, was one of the three most important pilgrimage sites in Christendom, the closest to England, and the easiest for the English to access), the Spanish reputation for fine Jewish artistry in metal and other media may have returned to England with pilgrims.

And Chaucer himself was, of course, in Navarre. Pedro the Cruel granted Chaucer a safe-conduct to travel with three companions, their servants, horses, and luggage through Navarre from February 22 to May 24, 1366. We do not know whether he was on pilgrimage to San Juan de Compostela, on a mission from the king to quell the activity of English mercenaries, or scouting the territory for the Black Prince with whom he may or may not have been at the battle of Nájera the following year (March 28, 1367), but we can be certain he kept his eyes and ears open.[21] The royal household in Pamplona, the capital of Navarre, employed Jewish seamsters, tailors, and goldsmiths, and Jewish artisans occupied their own rows of shops in Tudela, Pamplona, and the other larger northern cities (Wischnitzer, 104). The Aragonese royal court in Saragossa "markedly favored Jewish artisans and appointed some of them [including armorers] as master craftsmen of the court" (Wischnitzer, 100–101). Chaucer's conception of Jewish artistry may well have been determined by the general reputation for superior Jewish workmanship originating in and current throughout northern Spain.

> In Segovia in the late 14th century, out of 55 Jewish earners "23 were artisans—weavers, shoemakers, tailors, furriers, blacksmiths, saddlers, potters, and dyers" (Baer, *Spain*, I [1961], 198). "There was a street known as Shoemakers' Lane in the *juder'a* of Toledo in the 14th century" (*ibid.*, 197). "Conspicuous in Aragon are Jewish bookbinders, scientists who devise scientific instruments, and gold- and silversmiths" (*ibid.,* 426). Baer assumes that in the 14th century "at least half of the Jews of Barcelona . . . were artisans: weavers, dyers, tailors, shoemakers, engravers, blacksmiths, silversmiths (including some highly esteemed craftsmen who made Christian religious objects), bookbinders (who bound the registers of the royal chancery), workers in coral and porters" (*ibid.*, 2 [1966], 37). The same holds more or less true for Saragossa (*ibid.*, 55–56).[22]

Jewish handiwork in a variety of media was well-known and highly praised. Jews were prominent in textiles, "the number one item of commerce in both general and luxury goods" (Goitein, 16). In Sicily, for example, Jews controlled the manufacture of silk which they exported to Italy and France

(Abrahams, 238). Andalusia, too, was "especially renowned" for the manufacture of silk. Jews "excelled" in working gold embroidery. The lace made by the Jews in the Balearics was interwoven with gold and silver (called *redecillas* or *tellilas*) and restricted in the sumptuary legislation of Castile, Aragon, and Navarre (Wischnitzer, 102). Jews were reputed to possess professional secrets associated with the chemical processes involved in dying fabric, for which they almost had a monopoly in Moslem countries (Goitein, 17). Because of that mastery of chemistry, the most popular professions for Jews in the Geniza correspondence appear to be druggist, pharmacist, and perfumer. Spanish leather was excellent and Jews were "renowned throughout other countries" for tanning and dying. Similarly, "The jewelry and other gold objects manufactured in Cordova and Seville—rings, bracelets, goblets, and other table articles—all acquired a reputation in the neighboring countries."[23] That reputation remained throughout Chaucer's lifetime, enduring under Moslem and Christian rule and beyond the expulsion of the Jews from Spain.

The chemical processes involved in the refining and drawing of gold and silver led Jews to be active, if not dominant, in the Moslem world as gold- and silversmiths and, indeed, in all kinds of metal work. Jewish goldsmiths occupied every sizable town in Christian Spain and produced Christian religious artifacts such as reliquaries, goblets, and crucifixes (*Encyclopaedia Judaica*, s.v. "Goldsmiths and Silversmiths"). "Their methods of refining and wire-drawing metals, especially silver, were noted for their excellence" (Abrahams, 239).[24] There were three Jewish smithies in Toledo in 1365 and others in Avila, Valladolid, Valdeolivas near Cuenca, and Talavera de la Reina. There were many Jewish smiths, engravers, and goldsmiths in Barcelona before 1391, and a register of 1401 lists "many Jewish engravers and artisans in copper and iron" in Saragossa (*Encyclopaedia Judaica*, s.v. "Metals and Mining"). On the one hand, the gold and silver work produced by the Jews of Spain was sold individually and not traded wholesale (Goitein, 18), which suggests limited or localized fame for the kind of beautifully produced work that can create a reputation. On the other hand, "the Jewish smiths in Spain . . . were the only ones who knew how to work in accordance with Arabic taste. They developed this profession in Spain until in the tenth century it reached a standard that brought its products great fame in lands far and near" (Ashtor, 274). That reputation endured throughout the Middle Ages.

Although a few specific mentions of Jewish armorers (mostly sword makers) exist and though medieval Jews were skilled in ironmongery and in gold-, silver-, black-, and coppersmithing, I have found no evidence before 1400 that they possessed a reputation in western Europe for making splendid armor in general or hauberks in particular. But the reputation of Spanish Jews for fine craftsmanship in other areas, and especially in the decorative arts of gold- and silversmithing, could easily spill over to affect the general appreciation of "hooly Jewes" work. In this atmosphere, then, it is plausible that Chaucer could attribute to Thopas's armor the fine quality of Jewish workmanship which was reputed throughout Europe. Whether or not this attitude arrived in England with pilgrims returning from San Juan de Compostela or whether Chaucer arrived at this appreciation from what he saw and heard in Navarre in 1366, I believe that the general and very positive reputation for fine Jewish artistry which existed in Chaucer's lifetime affected Chaucer's decision to give Sir Thopas a "fyn hawberk," "strong . . . of plate," that was "Jewes werk."

His having done so contributes additional amusements to the tale. For one, our knowing the provenance of Thopas's hauberk adds to the comedy by complicating rather than clarifying. The disparity between the despicable and the admirable Jews (i.e., historical and scriptural) necessarily ambiguates any audience's response to the quality of Thopas's armor. Moreover, if the name Sir Oliphant—Thopas's opponent—suggests "Elephant," and hence some eastern association, then Thopas's armor should bear a crusader's cross or otherwise be connected to the Christian faith and not be the work of the hated Jews. This leads to the final comic absurdity, to continue the point made by Derek Brewer: part of the fun in Chaucer's *Tale of Sir Thopas* is that Thopas' armor is made of the wrong stuff. The hauberk, an important piece of defensive body armor, is "Jewes werk" when Jews were known for silk, lace, gold embroidery, leatherwork, fine tableware, jewelry, and decorative swords, but not for making hauberks. Sir Thopas can win no honor with which to impress the elf-queen if he sallies forth against the giant Sir Oliphant overdressed in beautiful armor produced by Jews best known for fine and dainty work.

Notes

1. See *The Oxford English Dictionary,* 2nd ed., and the *Middle English Dictionary,* s.v. "hauberk" and "habergeon," as well as Claude Blair, *European Armor circa 1066 to circa 1700* (London: Batsford, 1958). By Chaucer's time, the mailed tunic often extended to the knees and the fingertips.

2. J. A. Burrow's note to "Jewes werk" in *The Riverside Chaucer,* ed. Larry D. Benson, 3rd ed. (Oxford: Oxford University Press, 1987), 921, refers to "Ysak de Barceloigne," presumably a Jew, as the maker of a fine hauberk in one French chanson. No one has been able to trace this figure. Although one French literary reference to a Jewish hauberk maker does not justify a reputation of fine Jewish armorers in the Middle Ages, it does suggest that such a reputation may have existed.

3. *The Complete Works of Geoffrey Chaucer*, ed. W. W. Skeat, 7 vols. (Oxford: Clarendon Press, 1904–07), 5:196; hereafter cited in text. Skeat refers to nineteenth-century editions of Chaucer prepared by Thomas Tyrwhitt, *The Poetical Works of Geoffrey Chaucer* (London: Edward Moxon, 1843), 200, n.

to v. 13793, and Robert Bell [assisted by John H. Jephson], *Poetical Works of Geoffrey Chaucer* (London: Parker and Son, 1854–56), 3: 123–24, n. 2.

4. "[I]n most places the Jews were not allowed to bear arms even in their own quarters and for self-defence. In 1181 it was enacted in England that 'no Jew shall keep with him mail or hauberk, but let him sell or give them away, or in some other way remove them from him.' " In Spain, however, Jews fought as warriors under the Christian kings and especially during the period of the Reconquest. "Jews highly prized the privilege of wearing arms, styling them-selves knights, and bearing stately names. Frequent attempts were made to prevent this, especially towards the end of the fourteenth century. In 1390 the Jews of Majorca were forbidden to carry arms in their ghetto; in 1412 the King of Castile resolved that no Jews might 'carry swords, daggers, or simi-lar arms in the cities, towns and places of my kingdom' " (Israel Abrahams, *Jewish Life in the Middle Ages*. New edition revised and enlarged by Cecil Roth [London: Edward Goldston, 1932], 401–402; hereafter cited in text. This edition significantly supersedes the original edition published in London by Macmillan in 1896 and reprinted without Roth's revisions in 1962. See especially the lists of Jewish trades and occupations on pp. 265–70.). See also Yitzhak Baer, *A History of the Jews in Christian Spain,* trans. Louis Schoff-man et al., 2nd ed. 2 vols. (Philadelphia and Jerusalem: Jewish Publication Society, 1992 [orig. 1961–66]), 1: 113; hereafter cited in text. And the *Jewish Encyclopedia*, s.v. "Army."

5. "The vast majority of English Jewry eked out a meagre livelihood, while many lived in dismal poverty" (Salo Baron, *A Social and Religious History of the Jews*, 2nd ed., 18 vols. [New York: Columbia University Press, 1952–83], 12: 141). "The trade in money rarely profited the Jews, who remained mostly poor or possessed of very moderate wealth; the real gainers were the kings, the aristocracy, and the towns" (Abrahams, 270).

6. H. S. Ficke, "Iewes Werk," *Philological Quarterly* 7 (1928), 82–85; hereafter cited in text.

7. J. M. Manly, "Sir Thopas: A Satire," *Essays and Studies* 13 (1928), 60, 70.

8. Steven J. Herben, Jr., "Arms and Armor in Chaucer," *Speculum* 12 (1937), 481; and Irving Linn, "The Arming of Sir Thopas," *Modern Language Notes* 51 (1936), 310.

9. Derek Brewer, "The Arming of the Warrior in European Literature and Chaucer," in *Chaucerian Problems and Perspectives: Essays Presented to Paul E. Beichner*, eds. Edward Vasta and Zacharias P. Thundy (Notre Dame, IN: University of Notre Dame Press, 1979), 237–38.

10. Elisa Narin van Court, "Socially Marginal, Culturally Central: Representing Jews in Late Medieval English Literature," *Exemplaria* 12 (October 2000), 293–326.

11. H. G. Richardson, *The English Jewry under Angevin Kings* (London: Methuen, 1960), 25; hereafter cited in text.

12. V. D. Lipman, *The Jews of Medieval Norwich* (London: Jewish Historical Society, 1967), 79–80.

13. For the condition of English Jewry in the three decades before expulsion and their restriction to limited, mostly financial occupations, see Robin R. Mundill,

England's Jewish Solution: Experiment and Expulsion, 1262–1290 (Cambridge, England: Cambridge University Press, 1998); and Zefira Entin Rokeah, "The State, the Church, and the Jews in Medieval England," in *Anti-Semitism Through the Ages,* ed. Shmuel Almog, trans. Nathan H. Reisner (Oxford: Pergamon Press, 1988), 99–125.

14. James Parkes, *The Jew in the Medieval Community* (London: Soncino Press, 1938), 332. See also Sheila Delany, "Chaucer's Prioress, the Jews, and the Muslims," in this volume. Chaucer's continental journeys were to and through France to Spain and Italy. We have no evidence of his having been in northern or eastern Europe where some Jews worked metal.

15. *The Jewish Encyclopedia,* s.v. "Artisans—Medieval." The source cited is Joseph Jacobs, *An Inquiry into the Sources of the History of the Jews in Spain* (London: D. Nutt, 1894), xv, xxiii.

16. Mark Wischnitzer, *A History of Jewish Crafts and Guilds* (New York: Jonathan David, 1965), 155–156, 160; hereafter cited in text.

17. Ariel Toaff, *Love, Work, and Death: Jewish Life in Medieval Umbria* (London: Littmann Library of Jewish Civilization, 1996), 167, 205.

18. Jews and Moors held "the dominant position in the arts and crafts down to the expulsions of 1492, 1501, and 1609" (Wischnitzer, 108). See Wischnitzer, chapter 10, "Jewish Arts and Crafts in the Iberian Peninsula until 1391: Spain, Navarre, Portugal."

19. Muhammad declared war on the Beni Cainucaa, a Jewish tribe living near Medina and famed for the quality of their armor and goldsmithing. When they surrendered after a siege of fifteen days, he took three bows, three swords, and two coats of mail as his share of the spoils (Ficke, 83–84). Citing William Muir, *The Life of Mahomet,* 4 vols. (London: 1858–61), 3: 137, and Muhammad's "Arab biographer" (quoted in J. Wellhausen, *Muhammed in Medina das is Valkidi's Kitab al Maghazi* [Berlin, 1882], 278), Ficke refers to other occasions of Muhammad's appreciation for Jewish armor and his military methods of acquiring them. Indeed, the fame of Jewish workmanship among the Moslems appears in the Koran (Surat al-anbiyā' [xxi], verse 80): "It was We [Allah] who taught him (David [i.e., the Jews or, perhaps, a specific Jewish smith]) the making of coats of mail for your benefit [i.e., that of the Moslems], to guard you from each other's violence: Will ye then be grateful?" (quoted in David Alexander, *The Arts of War: Arms and Armour of the 7th to 19th Centuries* [Oxford: Oxford University Press, 1992], 11). When Mohammad conquered Medina, "many of the weapons he obtained for his army were manufactured by local Jewish artisans" (*Encyclopaedia Judaica,* s.v. "Metals and Mining"). See also Michael Lecker, "Wāqidī's Account of the Status of the Jews of Medina: A Study of a Combined Report," in *The Life of Muhammad,* ed. Uri Rubin (Aldershot, England: Ashgate, 1998), 23–40.

20. *The Jewish Encyclopedia,* s.v. "Metals." See also *Encyclopaedia Judaica,* s.v. "Goldsmiths and Silversmiths," "Crafts," "Guilds," and the attendant bibliographies.

21. See the biographical information in Benson, xviii, and cf. Donald R. Howard, *Chaucer, His Life, His Works, His World* (New York: Dutton, 1987), 115.

22. *Encyclopaedia Judaica,* s.v. "Crafts." See also Wischnitzer, 96–97; Baer,

1:113, 179; Vivian B. Mann, Thomas F. Glick, and Jerrilynn D. Dodds, eds. *Convivencia Jews, Muslims, and Christians in Medieval Spain* (New York: George Braziller, 1992), 166; and J. Doñate Sebastia and J. R. Magdalena Nom de Deu, *Three Jewish Communities in Medieval Valencia* (Jerusalem: Magnes Press, 1990), 281–83.

23. Eliyahu Ashtor, *The Jews of Moslem Spain,* trans. Aaron Klein and Jenny Machlowitz Klein, 3 vols. in 2 (Philadelphia: Jewish Publication Society, 1992 [orig. pub. 3 vols., 1973–84]), 272; hereafter cited in text.

24. Abrahams goes on to note that when the Jews were expelled from Lyons in 1446, "they established a silver industry in Trévoux which was unrivalled," and which they continued to practice in the first half of the nineteenth century. See Wischnitzer, 86.

5

Postcolonial Chaucer and the Virtual Jew

SYLVIA TOMASCH

In the *Canterbury Tales,* Geoffrey Chaucer alludes to Jews more frequently
and more explicitly than the almost exclusive critical attention paid to the
Prioress's Tale would indicate.[1] Chaucer's allusions, ranging from the faintly
positive to the explicitly negative, present Jews as proto-Christian prophets,
wandering exiles, blasphemers and torturers, and anti-Christian murderers—
all familiar depictions in his time. Some medievalists have found Chaucer's
reiteration of the sign "the Jew" puzzling, Jews having been expelled from
England one hundred years earlier. In fact, it is perfectly consonant with the
late-medieval circumstances that perpetuated the presence of the "virtual
Jew" in the absence of actual Jews. Denise Despres puts the case for such
simultaneous "absent presence"[2] most cogently when she writes: "Despite
the fact that no practicing Jews were permitted to reside in fourteenth- and
fifteenth-century England, late-medieval English devotional culture is rife
with images of Jews, from the Old Testament patriarchs in the Corpus Christi
Plays to the blasphemous, terrifying Host desecrators dramatized in the
Croxton Play of the Sacrament and legitimized in Middle English sermons."[3]
Although some scholars have tried to explain away "the paradoxical centrality of Jews to late-medieval English literature and art" by "asserting that Jews
function in this literature to represent a generic 'Other,' or as a displacement
for the Lollard sect," Despres concludes that, to the contrary, "Jews were not
merely symbols of alterity in English culture, whether generic or specific, but
rather . . . their presence was a necessary element in the devotional world of
the later medieval English laity."[4]

Following Despres, and along with Colin Richmond and James Shapiro,
I argue in this chapter that "the Jew" was central not only to medieval English Christian devotion but to the construction of Englishness itself. As
Shapiro writes, "The desire on the part of the English to define themselves as
different from, indeed free of, that which was Jewish, operated not only on

an individual level but on a national level as well: that is, between 1290 and 1656 the English came to see their country defined in part by the fact that Jews had been banished from it" (Shapiro, 42). The centrality of Jews to English religious devotion and national identity certainly helps explain the persistence of "the Jew," both pre- and post-expulsion. But in addition, we can understand this enduring sign as marking the persistence of colonialism in England from the thirteenth into the fourteenth century. For although the expulsion signaled the exile of the Jews, it did not entail an utter break with England's colonial past. That is to say, the English colonialist program did not end in 1290, and its pernicious effects continued to be felt, postcolonially, by the colonizing subjects, the English themselves.[5]

Some scholars have insisted on using "colonial" and "postcolonial" only in reference to the modern period. And indeed, if we define these notions exclusively in terms of European imperialism or the rise of capitalism or the birth of nationalism,[6] then they will not serve to delineate conditions in the Middle Ages. But if we attend to Kathleen Biddick's assertion that "[t]he periodization of colonialism . . . begins to look very different if one includes Jews,"[7] then it is possible to employ these terms to explore certain very troubling aspects of late-medieval culture. To that end, recent theorizations of the relationship between colonialism and postcolonialism provide a critical grammar for describing the mentality of Chaucer's England. In addition, recent theorizations of the idea of the virtual contribute to a more nuanced understanding of late-medieval representations of "the Jew." Considering Chaucer's poetry through the double lens of the colonial and the virtual provides grounds for refuting those who would either save him from charges of anti-Semitism or damn him accordingly. Rather than try to do either, I intend here to explore the complexities of medieval representations of Jews so as to understand the ways in which post/colonial English conditions fostered the creation of virtuality and the paradox of Jewish absent presence.

The acme of English depiction of Jews occurred in the thirteenth century as prelude to and, no doubt, stimulus for the 1290 expulsion.[8] In thirteenth-century England, Jews served all sorts of theological, political, social, and economic purposes, being alternately commended or condemned according to the interests of their observers. For example, Matthew Paris, in his *Chronica majora,* extended "his condemnation when the Jews advanced royal power and, conversely, his unconditional support whenever the Jews either obstructed the centralising aims of the king or became the victims of royal policy."[9] Similarly, other monastic chronicles, such as the *Annals of Burton,* distinguished between blameworthy contemporary English Jews (thought to be demonic descendants of Judas) and their praiseworthy ancestors.[10] Such inconsistent, even contradictory, attitudes are common, and, according to Jeremy Cohen, correlate with contemporary theological shifts in conceptions of the "hermeneutical Jew."[11] This shift followed from the "traumatic encounters" of Christian Europeans with Muslims; encounters that led to a new perception of Jews as allied to external adversaries such as Tartars, Saracens, and Turks. Perceiving Jews as aligned with many threatening Others helped justify violence against them on the "assumption," in Sophia Menache's words, "that they constituted an actual danger to the physical survival of Christendom" (Menache, "Matthew Paris," 144). This new perception of Jews was thus one crucial part of religio-political trends that led not only to the 1290 expulsion from England and Aquitania but also to subsequent expulsions throughout Europe. This new perception also led to the paradox of English post/colonialism: For the sake of security, Jews had to be removed; for the sake of self-definition, "the Jew" had to remain. The English shift from colonialism to postcolonialism is thus marked both by the expulsion of the actual and by the persistence of the virtual.

It is not surprising, therefore, that artistic productions of the period depict Jews in a striking variety of roles. Thirteenth-century English apocalypse manuscripts, for example, portray Jews in a wide variety of guises, some positive, such as Old Testament prophets or the allegorical personification of the Old Testament itself, and some negative, such as beast worshippers, resistant listeners to Franciscan sermons, or captives of demons.[12] As Suzanne Lewis's magisterial study shows, these manuscripts also depict various others as Jews, including John, the author of Revelation, the Four Horsemen of the Apocalypse, the sponge wielder at the crucifixion, and two figures from Canticles used to symbolize the nation of Israel—the Bridal Soul and the Shulamite. In these manuscripts a single visual panel often contains more than one Jewish representation or allusion. For example, in the illustration showing John consoled by the Elder (Lewis fig. 33), the Old Testament patriarchs are embodied three times, by the angel, the Elder, and John. The angel represents those who prophesied Christ as the redeemer, while the Elder and the weeping John symbolize those who, believing only literally, "held the Old Testament but did not see it" (Lewis, 72). Thus throughout the thirteenth century, "the Jew" appears in multiple, sometimes contradictory variations that are repeatedly reinscribed—even after the expulsion.

The persistence of Jewish representation in fourteenth-century cultural productions is well illustrated, albeit often with a diminution in intensity. For example, according to Michael Camille, although the *Luttrell Psalter* still contains "distorted hook-nosed semitic stereotypes of Christ's torturers:" such images are "notably less emphatic" than their counterparts in thirteenth-century psalters (Camille, 282). Similarly, as Martin Walsh shows, the *Holkham Bible Picture Book* only intermittently employs stereotypical Jewish characteristics; often it does so to emphasize basic theological distinctions. For example, one four-paneled illustration (see fig. 4) shows the course of Joseph's conversion from incredulous Jew to believing Christian

Figure 4. Four-panel image of Joseph, Ms. Add. 46780, f.12. By permission of the British Library.

by setting out a series of contrasting actions and attributes. In the first panel, Joseph is fully denoted as a Jew, first by his placement among others of his kind, and second by his hold on Old Adam's spade; however, in the second panel, as he lays his hand on Mary's womb, he is unmarked. In the third panel, during his encounter with Gabriel, Joseph wears the *pileus cornutus,* one of the sartorial signs of difference enjoined by the Fourth Lateran Council in 1215. But in the fourth panel, as he is reconciled with Christian truth, both "the Jewish hat and Adam's spade are now put behind him."[13] Lying as he does on the typological "fault line between the Old and New Testaments" (Walsh, 297), Joseph thus attests not only to the multiple Jewish figurations available to Christian artists of the time but also to the continuing centrality of Jews to Christian self-definition. In these ways, both of these early fourteenth-century illustrated texts, the *Luttrell Psalter* and the *Holkham Bible Picture Book,* are typically post-expulsion, for despite a diminishment in frequency and negative intensity, Jews remain what "they had already become in the thirteenth century: a ubiquitous presence in the English imagination established largely (and after 1290, entirely) through words, texts, and images."[14] Or as Camille says of Robert Mannyng's *Handlyng Synne,* its "minimal detraction of Jews . . . as been ascribed to the fact that there were no Jews [in England in the fourteenth century]. . . . But their nonpresence in English society does not mean that they cannot still be attacked in the realm of the imaginary . . . as part of the very definition of a good society—that is, as excluded from it" (Camille, 284). Turning to the words, texts, and images of Geoffrey Chaucer, we can see the continuing postcolonial construction of the good society and of its negative exemplum, the virtual Jew.

In the *Canterbury Tales,* one crucial component of the fabrication of the good society is the construction of Englishness, both geographically and characterologically. We see this construction in the tales of the Prioress and the Pardoner. In the *Prioress's Tale,* a polluted Asia—polluted through Jewish presence and actions—is implicitly contrasted with a purified England, whose sanitized state is founded on the displacement of the Jews.[15] The geographical removal of the Jews to Asia echoes their prior territorial expulsion. On one hand, it *removes* the narrative from the context of English land, English people, English acts, and, especially, English Jews. On the other hand, it *requires* that forbidden identification and reasserts Englishness by including the coda recalling Hugh of Lincoln's martyrdom at the hands of the—now-expelled—Jews. This dislocation also enables an unremitting replay of perpetual Jewish crimes by containing Jews in an eternal, orientalized present. Because "translating Jews from time into space was a way in which medieval Christians could colonize—[by imagining that they exercised dominion albeit in] phantasmatic space" (Biddick, 270), the Prioress's "Asye" can be understood not only as the medieval orientalized East that replaces the familiar English home ground, but also as the "phantasmatic space" that supplants in the English imaginary the actual, contested Asia of losing crusades. This is also an Asia, therefore, not only of subjugated Jews, but also of triumphant Christians; here actual victorious Saracens are displaced by virtual vanquished Jews.

If the Prioress's Asia substitutes for England as purified space, the Pardoner's Flanders stands for England as corrupted place. The *Pardoner's Tale* speaks to the vice-ridden conditions of English life that were blamed, at least in part, for the ravages of the plague. Representing the wicked English populace, the rioters are responsible for bringing Death upon themselves by seeking out its agent, the Old Man. In the tale, the Old Man emblematizes many of the most popular and pernicious anti-Judaic fantasies of the Middle Ages. Linked to the Wandering Jew,[16] the legendary figure punished for his mocking of Christ, the Old Man personifies not only Jews in general (nonbelieving exiles wandering through Christian time and space), but medieval European Jews in particular. Like them, he is intimately connected with gold—the unearned profits of avarice and usury—as well as with the massive population decimations of the mid-fourteenth century within which the Pardoner sets his tale. The evil nature that supposedly caused New Testament Jews to revile Christ, and induced their Norwich and Asian coreligionists to kill innocent Christian boys, also was believed to lead contemporary Jews to poison wells and spread the Black Death.[17] Precisely because he is undenoted as a Jew, the Old Man performs a perfect displacement of them.

A corollary component of the fashioning of the good society is the construction of Christianness, particularly as manifested in the material bodies of believers.[18] We see this dynamic in the tales of the Parson and the Monk. In order to dissociate good Christians from evil Jews, the *Parson's Tale* (like the chronicle of Burton) must first dissociate Jews from their own religion. Through traditional typological strategies, laudable Old Testament Hebrew prophets are distinguished from blameworthy New Testament, or contemporary Jews. Solomon, Moses, David, and others are cited with approbation, while post-scriptural Jews appear in the context of deicide. The tale makes clear that medieval Jews are abominations to the sacred, embodied community their ancestors are used to authenticate. By linking words and bodies, the Parson specifically admonishes Christians not to swear and thereby emulate Jews: "For certes, it semeth that ye thynke that the cursede Jewes ne dismembred nat ynough the preciouse persone of Crist, but ye dismembre hym moore" (X [I].591). Such a focus on bodily dismemberment recalls not just the blood crimes of which contemporary Jews were accused (as in the *Prioress's Tale)*, but also hints at their perverse physicality, voluntarily enacted in the continued self-dismemberment accomplished through the superseded ritual of circumcision.

As the *Parson's Tale* dissociates Jews from their own religion, the *Monk's Tale* dissociates them from their own bodies. The Prioress's murderous dismemberment of the Christian boy is countered in this tale by the salvific self-destruction of Samson. The Monk presents Samson, simultaneously the christianized proto-martyr and the judaized self-mutilator, in a number of ways, all of which dissociate Jews from their own bodies as well as from their own religion. First, the fact that he is an exemplary Israelite judge—or, as the tale puts it, "fully twenty winter . . . / He hadde of Israel the governaunce" (VII.2059–60)—is almost completely elided. His generalized loss of power is specifically carnalized in his physical blindness, a blindness (like that of the allegorical figure of Synagoga) that symbolizes Jewish spiritual lack. Moreover, when Delilah cuts Samson's hair, the action makes visible—by metaphorical displacement—the self-castrating (i.e., the circumcising) impotence of Jews. What is particularly interesting, however, is that at the same time that the Monk presents Samson as a thoroughly impotent Jew, he also dejudaizes him. The very first lines of the episode—"Loo Sampsoun, which that was annunciat / By th'angel longe er his nativitee, / And was to God Almyghty consecrat" (VII.2015–17)—serve to reposition Samson within a famously Christian context.

In these tales, drawing on well-established representational conventions, Chaucer continues the post-expulsion English practice of reiterating the sign "the Jew." As is typical in medieval postcolonial cultural productions, he assumes the factuality of blood guilt and bodily difference, without, however, ever matching pre-expulsion artists and writers in their relish for portraying Jewish perfidy and perversity. As we have seen in other post/colonial texts, in the *Canterbury Tales* "the Jew" is never entirely or solely negative; in certain instances the sign can be understood, at least superficially, as philo-Semitic. The Man of Law, for example, speaks merely descriptively when he cites the "peple Ebrayk" (II [B].489), and the Pardoner himself mentions "hooly" Jews (VI [C].364). (In similar fashion, Bromyard praises Jews for their piety; Langland, for their kindness; and Brunton, for their compassion for their poor.[19]) However, it should be obvious, especially when we remember patriarchy's complementary valorization of Mary and denigration of Eve, that all stereotypical assertions, both positive and negative, are merely isotopic variants. Like phonemes, they have no base term. The two sides—Jews as wicked murderers/Jews as generous alms-givers—are not merely conjoined, but, as with Mary and Eve, they are the same. By the late Middle Ages, every Jew is both evil and good, murderous and charitable; for all Jews can be characterized as "the Jew." Following Zygmunt Bauman, therefore, we may find that a better term to describe such indivisible, isotopic variation is "allosemitism."[20] What is important for appraising a writer such as Chaucer, therefore, is not whether he is anti- or philo-Semitic—he was, I believe, inevitably both—but rather that, given his Englishness and his Christianness, Chaucer could not help but contribute to the ongoing allosemitic construction of the virtual Jew.

What does it mean for an entire people to be virtual? And how does that virtuality correlate with their actuality? We can begin to address these questions by contextualizing medieval Jewish virtuality within the shift in England from a condition of colonialism to one of postcolonialism. Anne McClintock's definitions of "colonization" and "internal colonization" are helpful here:

Colonization involves direct territorial appropriation of another geo-political entity, combined with forthright exploitation of its resources and labor, and systematic interference in the capacity of the appropriated culture (itself not necessarily a homogeneous entity) to organize its dispensations of power. *Internal colonization* occurs where the dominant part of a country treats a group as it might a foreign colony.[21]

The case for understanding pre-expulsion medieval English Jews as an "internally colonized" people is a complex one.[22] On one hand, although Jews were not, strictly speaking, a separate "geo-political entity" within England, they were a distinct religious entity, with separate political and social responsibilities, privileges, and liabilities.[23] There is no question that their Christian overlords "systematic[ally] interfer[ed] in [the Jews'] capacity . . . to organize [their own] dispensations of power." Neither is there any question that in their use and abuse of Jews, the English did their best to "forthright[ly] exploit . . . [Jewish] resources and labor"—until, that is, such exploitation no longer suited their needs. Finally, "direct territorial appropriation" occurred, most vividly, although not uniquely, at the expulsion itself. Thus, while this case is not one McClintock considers, the situation of thirteenth-century English Jews fits her definition of internal colonization all too well.

On the other hand, the internal colonization of medieval English Jews was not territorial in any simple fashion. Three paradoxical aspects are important for understanding not only the decolonization of the Jews but also postcolonialism itself. First, however long Jews had been in residence in England (and most scholars agree that it closely followed within one hundred years of the conquest of 1066), they were by no means the indigenous inhabitants. The nonnative nature of their English habitation was important to monastic chroniclers of the expulsion. Whereas some accounts (e.g., the *Annals of Waverley*) stressed the continuity of Jewish residence, others (e.g., the *Annals of Dunstable*) stressed the justness of such punishment because of their sins (especially that of blasphemy). One consequence of their second-order status, therefore, was that during the troubles of the thirteenth century, Jewish resources could more easily be appropriated by the very same Christians who expressed pity for their plight. The post-expulsion image of the Jews is thus the familiar double one: ancient inhabitants, whose exile after their long sojourn is to be pitied (according to the Cistercians of Waverley) versus threatening interlopers, enemies of Christ whose exile is deserved (according to the *Annals of Osney*).[24] Creatures of such unresolvable duality are obvious dangers to, and therefore must be rent from, the body of Christian society.

This state of inassimilable difference leads to the second paradox: At the very same time that Jews were understood as secondary in terms of territorial occupation, in more important ways—important, that is, in terms of Christian supersessionist theology—they also were perceived as necessarily prior.[25] While domination in the medieval English case involved the exploitation of land, resources, and labor, even more fundamentally it involved the appropriation of religious truth and the true religion, for the ultimate territory at stake in medieval English post/colonialism was theological. Although the expulsion was unarguably a consequence of a multitude of economic, political, and social factors, underlying all was the fact that the Jews were reviled, massacred, and expelled because they were not Christians, because they were not (truly) English, and because Christians/English were not (could not be, must not be) Jews. Although Judaism provided the foundations for Christianity, Jews threatened the definitions of Christian society. Jews were expelled not merely because they first possessed (English) lands and goods from which they needed to be displaced, but because they first possessed the (Christian) book—from which they needed to be displaced. In their priority lay the rationale for their alterity, the justification for their abuse, and the roots of their destruction. The Christian dilemma set the stage for English action: the "dreadful secondariness" (to use Edward Said's phrase)[26] of medieval Jews was thus a consequence of their intolerable primariness.

Third, and contrary to the usual modern postcolonial scenario, in medieval England it was the dominant group (the Christian English) that expelled the subordinate group (the English Jews), and not the other way around. It was the dominant group that then suffered from inevitably disappointed utopian fantasies of a purified and liberated state. It was the dominant group that exhibited the "pathology" resulting from "persisting colonial hierarchies of knowledge and value" (Gandhi, 7). In a word, it was the Christian English, not the English Jews, who suffered from the postcolonial condition. When Leela Gandhi asserts that "[t]he postcolonial dream of discontinuity is ultimately vulnerable to the infectious residue of its own unconsidered and unresolved past" (ibid., 7), she is referring to the condition of the formerly colonized. In the case of medieval England, however, the "postcolonial dream of discontinuity" was that of the colonizers, the English. As ever, that dream failed. In their attempts to liberate themselves from intrusive foreign elements, thereby purging their country of religious difference, the English expelled the Jews. Yet, as our examination of the *Canterbury Tales* and other texts has shown, while the English may have eliminated the Jews, they never eradicated "the Jew."

Terms proliferate to describe this reiterated sign: "hermeneutical," "theological," and "notional Jew" have all been proffered.[27] Yet none of these speaks directly to the postcolonial condition; for that purpose, I am proposing the term "virtual Jew." Although I derive "virtual" from cyberspace studies, "virtual Jew" is meant to foreground the condition of historically specific oppression, as well as the concomitant illusion of liberation from history that is postcolonialism at its most pernicious. "Virtual Jew" stresses the integral connections between imaginary constructions and actual people, even when they exist only in a fabricated past or a phantasmatic future. In cyberspace studies, "virtual" is used most often to modify "worlds" or "narratives."[28] Marie-Laure Ryan explains the usual "two senses of the term":

> One is the philosophical meaning, which invokes the idea of potentiality. The virtual is the field of unrealized possibilities that surround the realm of the actual in a system of reality. . . . [Within a narrative universe] the potential type of virtuality is represented in two ways: in the as-yet unrealized representations formed by the [text's] characters, such as wishes, goals and plans, and in the horizon of possible events surrounding the textual actual world. . . . The other sense of "virtual" describes an optical phenomenon. According to Webster's dictionary, a virtual image is one formed of virtual foci; that is, of points "from which divergent rays of light seem to emanate but do not actually do so." This meaning can be metaphorically transferred to a type of narrative discourse that evokes states and events indirectly as they are captured in a reflecting device that exists as a material object in the textual actual world. This reflecting device could be a mirror, text, photograph, movie, or television show.[29]

Building on Ryan's definitions, we see that the virtual does not actually refer to the actual, although this is what it claims to do. Rather, the virtual "surround[s] the realm of the actual in a system of reality," thereby creating a simulation that, by seeming to be more authentic than the actual, may be mistaken for it. When we examine the virtual Jew, for example, we see that it does not refer directly to any actual Jew, nor present an accurate depiction of one, nor even a faulty fiction of one; instead it "surrounds" Jews with a "reality" that displaces and supplants their actuality. In fact, following the trail of the virtual guarantees that one will never arrive at the actual, for the referent of any virtual is always irretrievable. Thus, rather than being surprised at or having to explain the continuation of English reference to Jews after the expulsion, we might better acknowledge that Jewish absence is likely the best precondition for virtual presence. For wherever in Western culture actual Jews come to reside, they encounter the phantom that follows and precedes them. By virtue of its virtuality, therefore, "the Jew" maintains its frightful power.

To further understand the subtle workings of this medieval phantasm, it will help to situate the virtual Jew within Homi Bhabha's discussion of colonial truth production. In his well-known essay, "Signs Taken for Wonders," Bhabha writes that

> the field of the "true" emerges as a visible effect of knowledge/power only after the regulatory and displacing division of the true and the false. From this point of view, discursive "transparency" is best read in the photo-

graphic sense in which a transparency is also always a negative, processed into visibility through the technologies of reversal, enlargement, lighting, editing, projection, not a source but a re-source of light. Such a bringing to light is never a prevision; it is always a question of the provision of visibility as a capacity, a strategy, an agency.[30]

In Bhabha's terms, the virtual Jew is a "transparency," "processed into visibility through [various] technologies." More than simply a projection of the Christian gaze in the psychological sense, the sign is a projection in the optical sense: an image that is necessarily an illusion. The virtual Jew is not a source of emanations of the actual in itself but a "re-source," a reflection constructed by means of such processes as "reversal, enlargement, editing," and so on. "The Jew" reflects not any actual Jews but the "capacity, strategy, agency" of the observer. In this sense, we do not start with the actual existence of actual Jews, then consider how the depiction of Jews in various forms of discourse in the Christian Middle Ages matched or distorted the actuality. Rather, we understand from the start that the virtual Jew is an invented "reality" that does not depend on actual medieval Jews for its connotations, let alone its denotation. For even if we were to observe actual medieval Jews, we could only come to the conclusion that they do not, in themselves, possess the "true." The widespread medieval use of phrases such as *"verus Israel"* and *"Hebraica veritas"* confirms Bhabha's assertion that the determination of true and false has been made *prior to* the reading of the true, for having determined that Jews are not the "true Israel," Christians then could claim to be those who, truly, possess "Hebrew truth."[31] When Christians become the true Hebrews and Jews the false, the need for Jews as Augustinian "bearers of the book" is superseded. And, as we have seen, such dispossession of Jews is actualized in colonial displacement, particularly, in England, in the expulsion of 1290.

Despite—or because of—its a priori determination of the real, the virtual contains almost unlimited potential for proliferation. Bhabha argues that such proliferation is an essential aspect of the stereotype, which functions in a "continual and repetitive chain . . . [so that] the *same old* stories of the Negro's animality, the Coolie's inscrutability, or the stupidity of the Irish *must* be told (compulsively) again and afresh, and are differently gratifying and terrifying each time."[32] To these compulsive retellings we can add the multiple medieval reiterations of "the Jew" that recur in the *Canterbury Tales*, as well as in apocalypse manuscripts, the *Luttrell Psalter,* and the *Holkham Bible Picture Book.* Reiterating the sign, "the Jew," is thus an act that releases possibilities of image—but also of event, with actual consequences for actual Jews. When Jews (whose basic religious tenets forbid blood contamination) are accused of blood crimes, or when Jews (who place little or no emphasis on proselytizing) are denounced for judaizing, the resulting persecutions are "effects of knowledge/power" of the virtual Jew upon actual Jews. The sign is thus the equivalent of an optical "reflecting device" ("not a source but a re-source of light"), by means of which the post/colonial "system of reality surrounding the actual" is constructed. According to this system, it is actual Jews who must suffer for the sins of the virtual Jew, and their punishments arise, in Louise Fradenburg's words, "from the very need to substantiate an irreality populated by hallucinations" (83).

However irreal, however phantasmatic, the power of the virtual is with us still. In thirteenth- and fourteenth-century England, social, political, and religious conditions ensured that artists, writers, and theologians participated in the paradox of continually ridding England of Jews while continually repatriating them. But, as we have seen, the ongoing colonial construction of the virtual Jew did not end with the expulsion of 1290; rather, it began to gather steam so that by the sixteenth century, "[m]ost European kingdoms had expelled their Jews. . . . [as the] idea of a Europe *Judenrein* began to take its place in the mentality of Western Christendom."[33] When Despres notes that "[l]ike the Canterbury pilgrims, Chaucer's audience lived in a post-expulsion world" ("Cultic Anti-Judaism," 427), she is alluding to the after-effects of colonialism on Chaucer and his English contemporaries. But modern medievalists also live in a postexpulsion world, and the England we construct for Chaucer is most often as *Judenrein* as the England of the *Canterbury Tales*. In light of the history that followed the expulsion—the history of European Jews as well as the history of Western imperialism—it therefore becomes imperative to consider the Middle Ages from the perspective of postcolonial studies as well as to consider postcolonialism from the perspective of medieval studies.

When Ella Shohat famously asks, "When exactly does the 'post-colonial' begin?" nowhere in her answer does she indicate that a reconfigured, non-hegemonic "notion of the past" might include the European Middle Ages.[34] I am not suggesting here that the Middle Ages is that origin; medievalists such as Allan Frantzen already have pointed out the dangers inherent in such a position.[35] Rather, I am suggesting that we need to recognize the many connections between medieval English Christians and Jews that constituted a colonial, then postcolonial, relation: The English acted as colonizers, using their power to exploit and deterritorialize; the Jews were an internally colonized people, achieving release from English colonialism only at the cost of exile; the English/Christians constructed "the Jew" as part of their fabrication of national/religious identity; and English artists and writers, such as Geoffrey Chaucer, participated in the ongoing, postcolonial, allosemitic production of the virtual Jew. When we consider all of these connections, then we also must recognize that the 1290 expulsion, while marking a turning point in English Christian and Jewish relations, constitutes but one episode within a postcolonial continuum whose tragic effects persist to the present day.

Notes

1. Surveys of the critical literature on Chaucer and the Jews are included in Florence Ridley, *The Prioress and the Critics,* University of California Publications, English Studies 30 (Berkeley: University of California Press, 1965); and Louise O. Fradenburg, "Criticism, Anti-Semitism, and the *Prioress's Tale,*" *Exemplaria* 1 (1989), 69–115; hereafter cited in text. Most notable among the articles written on the subject in the 1990s is Denise L. Despres, "Cultic Anti-Judaism and Chaucer's Litel Clergeon," *Modern Philology* 91 (1994), 413–27; hereafter cited in text. All references to and citations from the *Canterbury Tales* are from Geoffrey Chaucer, *The Riverside Chaucer,* 3rd ed., gen. ed. Larry D. Benson (Boston: Houghton Mifflin, 1987).

2. On Jewish absent presence in the *Divine Comedy,* see Sylvia Tomasch, "Judecca, Dante's Satan, and the Dis-placed Jew," in *Text and Territory: Geographical Imagination in the European Middle Ages,* eds. Sylvia Tomasch and Sealy Gilles (Philadelphia: University of Pennsylvania Press, 1998), 247–67. For the case in medieval England, see Michael Camille, *The Luttrell Psalter and the Making of Medieval England* (Chicago: University of Chicago Press, 1998), 284; Christine Chism, "*The Siege of Jerusalem:* Liquidating Assets," *Journal of Medieval and Early Modern Studies* 28 (1998), 319; Despres, "Cultic Anti-Judaism," 414; and Colin Richmond, "Englishness and Medieval Anglo-Jewry," reprinted in this volume; hereafter cited in text. For the case in early modern England, see James Shapiro, *Shakespeare and the Jews* (New York: Columbia University Press, 1996); hereafter cited in text. For a modern instance that reverses the usual sequence of absence following presence, see Leo Spitzer, *Hotel Bolivia: The Culture of Memory in a Refuge from Nazism* (New York: Hill and Wang, 1998), 166.

3. Denise L. Despres, "Immaculate Flesh and the Social Body: Mary and the Jews," *Jewish History* 12 (1998), 47. See also her "Cultic Anti-Judaism"; and "Mary of the Eucharist: Cultic Anti-Judaism in Some Fourteenth-Century English Devotional Manuscripts," in *From Witness to Witchcraft: Jews and Judaism in Medieval Christian Thought,* ed. Jeremy Cohen (Wiesbaden, Germany: Harrassowitz Verlag, 1997), 375–401.

4. Despres, "Cultic Anti-Judaism," 427. See also Thomas Bestul, *Texts of the Passion: Latin Devotional Literature and Medieval Society* (Philadelphia: University of Pennsylvania Press, 1996), especially chapter 3.

5. Postcolonial theorists agree that since the effects of colonialism are ongoing, the "post-" cannot be taken to mean a simple "after"; as Ania Loomba, *Colonialism/Postcolonialism* (London: Routledge, 1998), writes, "a country may be both postcolonial (in the sense of being formally independent) and neo-colonial (in the sense of remaining economically and/or culturally dependent) at the same time" (7). But since England was not colonized from without, was colonizing the Jews within, and was therefore not neocolonial in the ways Loomba indicates, I use "postcolonial" here to link both the shift in chronology and the continuation of colonial culture that inhered in England during Chaucer's lifetime. On occasion, I use "post/colonial" as shorthand for "colonial and postcolonial."

6. On these widely held positions, see Loomba, *Colonialism/Postcolonialism*, chapter 1.
7. Kathleen Biddick, "The ABC of Ptolemy: Mapping the World with the Alphabet," in *Text and Territory*, ed. Tomasch and Gilles, 291 n 2; hereafter cited in text.
8. On causes of the expulsion, see Shapiro, *Shakespeare*, 46–55.
9. Sophia Menache, "Matthew Paris's Attitudes toward Anglo-Jewry," *Journal of Medieval History* 23 (1997), 158; hereafter cited in text; on Henry's policy, see 160–61. Kenneth L. Stow, "The Avignonese Papacy or, After the Expulsion," in *From Witness to Witchcraft*, ed. Jeremy Cohen, cites a parallel case of papal pragmatism (what Zygmunt Bauman calls allosemitism, see below) when he describes the "precarious situation" of Jews under the Avignonese papacy as resulting not from "the alternation of repression with toleration or kindness, but of an integral policy in which all principles operated simultaneously" (277).
10. Sophia Menache, "Faith, Myth, and Politics—The Stereotype of the Jews and Their expulsion from England and France," *Jewish Quarterly Review* 75 (1985), 360.
11. Jeremy Cohen, "The Muslim Connection or On the Changing Role of the Jew in High Medieval Theology," in *From Witness to Witchcraft*, ed. Cohen, 159. David Nirenberg, *Communities of Violence: Persecution of Minorities in the Middle Ages* (Princeton, NJ: Princeton University Press, 1996), has countered the emphasis of Cohen and other historians on the perceived shift from toleration to persecution.
12. Suzanne Lewis, *Reading Images: Narrative Discourse and Reception in the Thirteenth-Century Illuminated Apocalypse* (Cambridge: Cambridge University Press, 1995); the illustrations cited in this paragraph are, in order, Lewis's figures 48, 83, 117, 177, 231, 9 (plus 17, 21, 33, etc.), 42 (plus 45, 48), 224, 233, 251, and 33.
13. Martin W. Walsh, "Divine Cuckold/Holy Fool: The Comic Image of Joseph in the English 'Troubles' Play," in *England in the Fourteenth Century: Proceedings of the 1985 Harlaxton Symposium*, ed. W. M. Ormond (Woodbridge, Suffolk: Boydell Press, 1986), 284. We should note that Joseph also wears the *pileus cornutus* in subsequent scenes (e.g., the Nativity). Other figures (e.g., Pharisees, torturers) are presented as grotesque, sometimes wearing peaked caps suggestive of the Jewish hat, but none is as explicitly marked as "a Jew" as is Joseph. Four-panel image of Joseph used by permission of the British Library (ADD46780F12).
14. Robert C. Stacey, "From Ritual Crucifixion to Host Desecration: Jews and the Body of Christ," *Jewish History* 12 (1998), 25.
15. On the locational politics of "Asye," see Fradenburg, "Criticism, Anti-Semitism," 98, and Sheila Delany's essay in this volume. Both Fradenburg and Despres, "Cultic Anti-Judaism," stress the importance in this tale of a purified England.
16. Nelson Sherwin Bushnell, "The Wandering Jew and the *Pardoner's Tale*," *North Carolina Studies in Philology* 28 (1931), 450–60, argues that only since the seventeenth century is the wanderer understood as Jewish; but

Despres, "Mary of the Eucharist," cites an example from the thirteenth-century *de Brailes Hours* (384).

17. On Jews and the plague, see Seraphiné Guerchberg, "The Controversy over the Alleged Sowers of the Black Death in the Contemporary Treatises on Plague," in *Change in Medieval Society: Europe North of the Alps, 1050–1500,* ed. Sylvia Thrupp (New York: Appleton-Century-Crofts, 1984), 208–24. See also Anna Foa, *Ebrei in Europa: Dalla peste nera all' emancipazione* (Rome: Laterza, 1992); and Nirenberg, *Communities of Violence,* especially "Epilogue."

18. On Christian and Jewish bodies, see Steven Kruger, "The Bodies of Jews in the Late Middle Ages," in *The Idea of Medieval Literature: New Essays on Chaucer and Medieval Culture in Honor of Donald R. Howard,* eds. James M. Dean and Christian Zacher (Newark, NJ: University of Delaware Press, 1992), 301–23. See also the articles in Sarah Kay and Miri Rubin, eds., *Framing Medieval Bodies* (Manchester, U.K.: Manchester University Press, 1994).

19. Philo-Semitic examples are cited by Stephen Spector, "Empathy and Enmity in the *Prioress's Tale*," in *The Olde Daunce: Love, Friendship, Sex, and Marriage in the Medieval World,* Robert R. Edwards and Stephen Spector (Albany, NY: SUNY Press, 1991), 211–28. On Brunton, also see Sister Mary Aquinas Devlin, "Bishop Thomas Brunton and His Sermons," *Speculum* 14 (1939), 324–44. For another view of Langland's citation of Jews, see Elisa Narin van Court, "The Hermeneutics of Supersession: The Revision of the Jews from the B to the C Text of *Piers Plowman*," *The Yearbook of Langland Studies* 10 (1996), 43–87.

20. Zygmunt Bauman, "Allosemitism: Premodern, Modern, Postmodern," in *Modernity, Culture, and "the Jew,"* eds. Bryan Cheyette and Laura Marcus (Stanford, CA: Stanford University Press, 1998), 143–56. See also Bryan Cheyette, "Introduction: Unanswered Questions," in *Between "Race" and Culture: Representations of "the Jew" in English and American Literature,* ed. Bryan Cheyette (Stanford, CA: Stanford University Press, 1996), 1–15. Although, strictly speaking, "allosemitism" is anachronistic in reference to the Middle Ages, I believe it is useful for encompassing the contradictions inherent in medieval Christian European attitudes toward and representations of Jews.

21. Anne McClintock, "The Angels of Progress: Pitfalls of the Term 'Post-Colonialism,' " *Social Text* 31/32 (1992), 88 (her italics).

22. For another discussion of premodern Jews as internally colonized, see Jonathan Boyarin, "The Other Within and the Other Without," *Storm from Paradise: The Politics of Jewish Memory* (Minneapolis: University of Minnesota Press, 1992), 77–98.

23. On thirteenth-century English anti-Jewish measures, see Jonathan A. Bush, " 'You're Gonna Miss Me When I'm Gone': Early Modern Common Law Discourse and the Case of the Jews," *Wisconsin Law Review* 5 (1993), 1264, on the statutes of 1233, 1253,1271, and 1275; Lewis, *Reading Images,* 216, the synods of Oxford (1222), Worcester (1240), Chichester (1246), Salisbury (1256), Merton (1258), and Lambeth (1261). On medieval Anglo-Jewry see Menache, "Faith, Myth, and Politics" and "Matthew Paris's Attitudes"; Richmond, "Englishness"; Shapiro, *Shakespeare,* 43–55; Robert C. Stacey, "The

Conversion of Jews to Christianity in Thirteenth-Century England," *Speculum* 67 (1992), 263–83; and "Recent Work in Medieval English Jewish History," *Jewish History* 2 (1987), 61–72. On Jewish-Christian relations in medieval Europe, see Anna Sapir Abulafia, "From Northern Europe to Southern Europe and from the General to the Particular: Recent Research on Jewish-Christian Coexistence in Medieval Europe," *Journal of Medieval History* 23 (1997), 179–90.

24. Throughout this paragraph, I rely on the discussion of monastic accounts in Menache, "Faith, Myth, and Politics."

25. On Christian supersessionism, see Daniel Boyarin, "The Subversion of the Jews: Moses's Veil and the Hermeneutics of Supersession," *Diacritics* 23 (1993), 16–35; also Narin van Court, "Hermeneutics of Supersession."

26. Edward Said, "Representing the Colonized: Anthropology's Interlocutors," *Critical Inquiry* 15 (1989), 207; quoted by Leela Gandhi, *Postcolonial Theory: A Critical Introduction* (New York: Columbia University Press), 7; hereafter cited in text.

27. "Hermeneutical Jew": Jeremy Cohen, "Introduction" in *From Witness to Witchcraft,* ed. Cohen, 9; "theological Jew": Gilbert Dahan, *Les intellectuels chrétiens et les Juifs au Moyen Age* (Paris: Cerf, 1990), 586; "notional Jew": Bush, " 'You're Gonna Miss Me When I'm Gone.' "

28. I know of only one other linking of medieval and cyberspace studies: Jeffrey Fisher, "The Postmodern Paradiso: Dante, Cyberpunk, and the Technology of Cyberspace," in *Internet Culture,* ed. David Porter (New York: Routledge, 1997), 111–28, who speaks of a body-transcending "will to virtuality" shared by medieval and cyberspatial texts.

29. Marie-Laure Ryan, "Allegories of Immersion: Virtual Narration in Postmodern Fiction," *Style* 29 (1995): 262–64.

30. Homi K. Bhabha, "Signs Taken for Wonders," in *The Post-Colonial Studies Reader,* eds. Bill Ashcroft, Gareth Griffiths, and Helen Tiffin (London: Routledge, 1995), 32.

31. On *verus Israel,* see Friedrich Lotter, "The Position of the Jews in Early Cistercian Exegesis and Preaching," in *From Witness to Witchcraft,* ed. Cohen, 163–85; also Marcel Simon, *Verus Israel: A Study of the Relations between the Christians and Jews in the Roman Empire (135–425)* (1948; 1964; reprinted Oxford University Press, 1986).

32. Homi K. Bhabha, "The Other Question," in *Contemporary Postcolonial Theory: A Reader,* ed. Padmini Mongia (London: Arnold, 1996), 47 (his emphases). I distinguish "virtual" from "stereotype" in that although "virtual" also has a psychological component, it is not tied narrowly to the construction of the individual colonial subject; see also Robert Chazan, *Medieval Stereotypes and Modern Antisemitism* (Berkeley: University of California Press, 1997). I also distinguish "virtual" from "simulacrum," for although they share a technological component, "virtual" does not depend on the globalization of capital, nor is it tied directly to the post-textual, commodified postmodern; see Jean Baudrillard, *Simulacra and Simulation,* trans. Sheila Faria Glaser (Ann Arbor: University of Michigan Press, 1994). Most important perhaps, I use "virtual Jew" in contradistinction to Jean-François

Lyotard's undifferentiated, universalized, lower-case "jew" as standing for the ultimate postmodern intellectual predicament—what Max Silverman, "Re-figuring 'the Jew' in France," in *Modernity, Culture, and "the Jew,"* eds. Cheyette and Marcus, calls "the judaizing of alterity in postmodern theory" (199); see Lyotard, *Heidegger and "the jews,"* trans. Andreas Michel and Mark S. Roberts (Minneapolis: University of Minnesota Press, 1990).

33. Jeremy Cohen, "Traditional Prejudice and Religious Reform: The Theological and Historical Foundation of Luther's Anti-Judaism," in *Anti-Semitism in Times of Crisis,* eds. Sander L. Gilman and Steven T. Katz (New York: New York University Press, 1991), 97.

34. Ella Shohat, "Notes on the 'Post-Colonial,' " in *Contemporary Postcolonial Theory,* ed. Mongia, 325, 330. Shohat shares an assumption of the necessarily post-Columbian origins of colonialism with other postcolonial theorists; see, for example, Ashcroft, Griffiths, and Tiffin, eds., *Post-Colonial Studies Reader,* 2.

35. Allan J. Frantzen, *Desire for Origins: New Language, Old English, and Teaching the Tradition* (New Brunswick, NJ: Rutgers University Press, 1990).

PART II

Chaucerian Contexts

6

Chaucer and the Translation of the Jewish Scriptures

MARY DOVE

The Jewish Scriptures in their entirety were translated into English for the first time in the Middle English or "Wycliffite" Bible, by associates and followers of John Wyclif between about 1370 and 1390.[1] Although the Jewish Scriptures were considered by Christians an integral part of the Christian Bible, Christian dominion posited an historical endpoint to the validity of Judaism: the advent of the Messiah.[2] What were the consequences of this for the translation of Jewish Scripture made during Chaucer's lifetime? Did the Wycliffite translators believe that the ways in which Jews read their Scriptures had been superseded by Christian interpretation, or do the reading practices of Jews, as the translators represent them, live on in the Wycliffite Bible to influence the reading practices of English Christians, including Chaucer?

The Wycliffite translators did far more than turn the Latin Bible into English. They paid more exact attention to the text and meaning of Jewish Scripture than did any other scholars in England in Chaucer's lifetime, for their project involved editorial, hermeneutic, and linguistic biblical scholarship. The man who represents himself as director of the project, customarily identified as John Purvey,[3] explains in the prologue prefixed to Genesis in the Later Version of the translation[4] that "þis symple creature [his periphrasis for himself] hadde myche trauaile wiþ diuerse felawis and helperis" to perform several tasks. First, the translators had to establish an authoritative Latin text of the Bible from what Anne Hudson nicely terms "the welter of variants in contemporary manuscripts of the Vulgate"; second, to study this authoritative text with the aid of commentaries and glosses, "and speciali Lire [the Franciscan biblical scholar Nicholas of Lyra, 1270–1349] on þe elde [old] testament"; third, to consult linguistic authorities in order to elucidate "harde wordis and harde sentencis"; and, fourth, to produce a clear and accurate English translation (*Wycliffite Bible,* i. 57/7–15).[5] As Hudson argues, the fourth stage, the work of translation itself, encompasses both the Earlier and the Later Versions of the translation, and work on all four stages must have proceeded simultaneously.[6]

For the first time, the biblical canon in its entirety was made accessible to the non-Latinate English reader, but also to the English reader literate in Latin, for whom this literal rendering of a carefully edited original would defamiliarize the well-known but often erroneous Latin, and sharpen awareness that the Latin was a translation, too. Chaucer, translating *A Treatise on the Astrolabe* for his son, who was in the preliminary stages of Latin literacy in 1391, writes this awareness into the prologue: "Latyn folk had [the contents of this treatise] first out of othere dyverse langages, and writen hem in her owne tunge, that is to seyn, in Latyn." Language is only a means to an end, Chaucer seems to suggest: "diverse pathes leden diverse folk the righte way to Rome,"[7] and even Latin itself was once a vernacular.

Whether the Bible should be translated into English became a matter for debate as a consequence of the Wycliffite Bible project. In the 1380s, contributions to this debate are typically found in prologues to various translated works, and consist of arguments justifying translation into English. John Trevisa's prologue to his translation of Ranulf Higden's *Polychronicon* (1387), and the final chapter of the prologue to the Wycliffite Bible (which I date 1388) make the most persuasive cases.[8] Not until the Oxford debate of 1401 did proponents of the Englishing of Scripture such as Richard Ullerston, author of the anti-Wycliffite *Defensorium Dotacionis Ecclesie*, find themselves in public academic conflict with scholars who were fearful of the consequences.[9] Glending Olson is right, I think, in suggesting that the *Astrolabe* prologue is Chaucer's characteristically allusive contribution to the early phase of the debate on biblical translation.[10]

Lewis Chaucer may have first encountered the Bible as well as the *Treatise on the Astrolabe* in English, if his father's advocacy extended to buying or borrowing a Wycliffite Bible, or some part of it. A copy of the Psalms, the first biblical book studied by schoolchildren, would have met Lewis's needs in 1391, and there are seven surviving copies of the Psalms alone, all in the Later Version.[11] Even English readers who, like Chaucer, were literate in Latin and who had access to institutional or private libraries were less likely to have access to Hebrew Scripture in English than to Christian. The Old Testament in its entirety is contained in twenty-three manuscripts, twenty of these being pandects, while 170 of the 250-odd surviving manuscripts contain only New Testament books.[12] This is in accordance with the first recommendation made in the prologue to the Wycliffite Bible: "Cristen men and wymmen, olde and ȝonge, shulden studie fast [intently] in þe newe testament, for it is of ful autorité and opyn to vndirstonding of simple men" (*Wycliffite Bible*, i. 2/31–32). Nonetheless, John Purvey, director of the project, is far from wanting to confine "simple" readers to the New Testament. He writes that the reader who maintains meekness and charity truly understands "al holi writ"

(i. 2/36), according to Augustine, and should not be too frightened to study it (2/38); the *clerk* who reads scripture blinded by pride and covetousness will, as Augustine promises, "go quyk [alive] in to helle" (3/1).[13]

The context in which the New Testament is recommended as being "of ful autorité" is a discussion of the biblical canon. The Earlier Version of the Wycliffite Bible includes Jerome's prologues to Old Testament books (as far as Baruch), and the prologue to the Wycliffite Bible reproduces Jerome's distinction[14] between the twenty-five books of Hebrew Scripture that for Christians "ben bookis of feiþ and fulli bookis of holy writ" (i. 1/1), because Jews themselves accept their canonicity, and, on the other hand, the books that are "set among apocrifa, þat is wiþouten autorité of bileue" (1/17–18): Wisdom, Ecclesiasticus, Judith, Tobit and 1 and 2 Maccabees.[15] Hudson claims that there would seem to be "a logical inconsistency" here, as Thomas Netter pointed out *contra Wyclevistos*, since the selection of canonical texts depended upon the Church's authority, an authority that the Wycliffites disputed.[16] Yet the prologue to the Wycliffite Bible appeals at every point not to the authority of an institution, but to the authority of the scholar-translator Jerome. Because Jerome makes Jewish canonicity the *reule* of what Christians should consider authoritative Hebrew Scripture, the Wycliffite translators do so too.

Nevertheless, seven manuscripts containing the whole of the Old Testament in the Later Version lack the prologue, and therefore lack any discussion of the canon;[17] moral or spiritual instruction seems to have mattered to the translators at least as much as canonicity, even against Jerome. Jerome thought highly of the non-canonical Wisdom and Ecclesiasticus, but not of Tobit. His prologue to Tobit (*Repertorium Biblicum*, no. 332) expresses polite surprise that bishops Cromatius and Heliodorus should desire him to translate a tale with no historical basis that the Jews themselves sever from "godis scripturis" (*Wycliffite Bible*, EV, ii. 376/8–9). The Later Version of the Wycliffite Bible counters Jerome's opinion with a marginal gloss on the first verse of Tobit, in effect a mini-prologue, offering readers the conclusion of a more recent consideration—that of Nicholas of Lyra—of the book's factuality: "þis storie of Tobie bifelde in þe sixte ʒeer of king Ezechie, Lire here [Lyra on Tob 1: 1]."[18] The prologue to the Wycliffite Bible says nothing about this, and prefaces its discussion of the book with a reminder that it is "not of bileeue" (*Wycliffite Bible*, i. 35/31),[19] but commends it as

> profitable to þe symple puple to maken hem to kepe patience and goddis heestis, to do werkis of mercy and teche wel hire children and to take wyues in þe drede of god, for loue of children and not al for foul lust of body, neiþer for coueitise of goodis of þis world; and also children moun lerne heere bi ʒunge Tobie to be meke and obedient and redi to serue fadir and modir in her nede; þerfore amonge alle þe bookis of þe elde testament symple men of wit schulden rede and here ofte þis book of Tobie. (35/31–37)

For people of all ages who cannot read, or who are not literate in Latin and never (unlike Lewis Chaucer) will be, this noncanonical book is recommended ahead of any canonical book of Hebrew Scripture, even Psalms. This astonishingly high view of Tobit demonstrates that, for the author of the prologue to the Wycliffite Bible, unambiguous moral lessons were what "symple puple" most needed: "be trewe to god," "eschewe idolatrie, glotenye and coueitise," "be pacient in tribulacioun" (35/37–39).[20] One copy of Tobit alone, with a particularly fine initial, calls Tobit a "blessid book."[21]

The synopsis of Hebrew Scripture that occupies chapters 3 to 11 of the prologue begins with the claim that "symple men of wit moun be edified mych to heuenly lyuyng bi redyng and knowyng of þe olde testament" (3/33–34), and for each book in turn the writer defines the nature of the edification offered. "Al þis proces[22] [series of events] of Genesis," for example, "shulde stire Cristen men to be feiþful and for to drede and loue god and in alle þingis to do his wille" (4/3–4). The implied audience would seem to be the "simple" reader of lowly estate, except for Kings and Chronicles. 1 Kings "schulde stire prestis to be not necligent in her offis, neiþer to be coueytous, and styre seculer lordis to be meke and iust to god and men" (10/3–5). And if "kingis and lordis" (29/40), he writes at the end of the synopsis of Chronicles, were to know no more holy Scripture than the stories of kings Jehoshaphat, Hezekiah and Josiah, "þei myȝte lerne sufficiently to lyue wel and gouerne wel hire puple bi goddis lawe, and eschewe al pride and ydolatrie and coueitise and oþer synnes" (29/43–4). Instead, they take their lesson from the wicked king Manasseh, placing idols (that is, unworthy clerics) in God's house (31/1–2), with the result that

> a fewe pore men and idiotis, in comparisoun of clerkis of scole, mown haue þe treuþe of holy scripture aȝens many þousinde prelatis and religiouse þat ben ȝouen to worldly pride and coueitise, symonie, ypocrisie and oþer fleschly synnes. (30/27–30)

Although educated men are clearly the intended audience here, nonetheless the writer aligns himself with the "pore men and idiotis," not with those who speak the same academic language as himself, for outside the schools God's law is found in holy Scripture, not in "synful mennis statutis" (30/33–34).

Indeed, so determined is Purvey in this passage to place as wide a gap as possible between true lovers of Scripture like himself and "clerkis of scole," that he associates himself with the all but unteachable *illiterati*, the "lewed pepel þat ben iclepid ydiotis," who can be taught only the bare elements of Christianity.[23] At the end of the prologue Purvey imagines "worldli clerkis" taking him at his word, sneeringly asking "what spiryt makiþ idiotis hardi to translate now þe bible into English?" (59/3–4). Yet, as he sees it, if "idiotis" translate Scripture into English and understand Scripture in English better than priests, prelates, lords, and schoolmen do in Latin, God's grace is all the more evident, and the English Bible is all the more transparently the Word of God.

The conflation of translators and readers cannot, however, be sustained, since (as we have seen) Purvey spells out the moral lessons of Jewish Scripture for simple Christian readers, privileging the moral sense over the literal sense, or rather providing the literal sense with a concluding *moralitas*. In the case of Proverbs, Ecclesiastes, and the Song of Songs, the moral lessons come first (40/2–8), and for the simple reader stand in place of the subsequent exposition of the subtleties of these three books. The elucidation of the moral sense of Jewish Scripture in the prologue's synopsis of the Pentateuch and the historical books takes it for granted that the summary of each book's literal content can be seamlessly matched with a Christian *moralitas*, as though Jewish Scriptural interpretation had indeed been superseded and as though their Bible were not, for Jews, the whole of *sacra scriptura*. Only very occasionally does the writer interrupt his synopsis to warn against the simple literal sense—when, for instance, he points out that the husband's legal right to give his wife a bill of divorcement (Deut. 24: 1) is "forbedun of crist" (7/14), reminding the reader that this is one of the Mosaic judgments which "was ended in þe tyme of cristis passioun" (3/11–12).

When he comes to the Psalms, though, Purvey laments the lack of attention that scholars have paid to the literal sense. Perhaps because the Psalms involve exceptional textual difficulties, "for oure [Latin] lettre discordiþ myche fro þe Ebreu" (38/4), *clerici* have preferred "þe goostly [spiritual] vndirstonding" (38/5). "Wel were him," he exclaims, recalling *Beatus vir*, the opening words of the first psalm, "þat koude wel vndirstonde þe Sautir [psalter], and kepe it in his lyuyng and seie it deuoutly and conuicte [persuade] Jewis þerbi" (38/5–39/2). Writer and simple reader seem momentarily united in the endeavour to make good literal-moral Christian sense of the psalter, "which is reed comynly in chirchis" (*Wycliffite Bible*, ii. 729),[24] and to live in charity. But apparently the writer has clergy in mind instead, for he asks God's grace "to teche [the Psalms] opinly to Cristen men and Jewis, and bringe hem þerby to oure Cristen feiþ and brennynge charité" (40/1–2).[25] Christians and Jews are equally in need of instruction, and if Jews are bad literal readers of their own Psalms, failing to recognize their Christological content, Christian clerics, let alone laypeople, are by no means good enough literal readers either. Certainly there is the expressed hope that Jews will repudiate their faith, but only at the end of a lengthy process of learning how to read *ad litteram*.

This may seem paradoxical, for the traditional Christian complaint was that the Jews were blinded by reading their Scriptures *too* literally and failing to recognize spiritual senses; as Bartholomew of Exeter puts it in his *Dialogue against the Jews* (c. 1170–1180), "[T]he chief cause of disagreement between ourselves and the Jews seems to be this: they take all the Old

Testament literally . . . They will never accept allegory, except when they have
no other way out."[26] But for Nicholas Lyra, the commentator on whose work
the Wycliffite translators importantly relied, the opposite was true. Lyra held
that the Jews were blinded by failing to read literally enough, for, as Frans von
Liere argues, Lyra was convinced that "if correctly interpreted, everything in
the Old Testament pointed irrefutably to Christ," and not only the Old Testament but the Talmud and the Targumim as well.[27] For Lyra, a Hebrew scholar
whose understanding of Jewish Scripture owed a great deal to the great Jewish
scholar Rabbi Solomon ben Isaac of Troyes (Rashi, 1045–1105), Jewish
hermeneutic was alive and well, albeit profoundly mistaken. As Karlfried
Froehlich puts it, defining the state of late-medieval biblical hermeneutics,
"The spiritual senses in their totality were subsumed under one principal
sense and appeared under the designation of 'true literal.' "[28]

Besides its revisionary notion of literality, Purvey's hermeneutic recom-
mendations for the reader of Psalms accomplish another purpose. We see
here, in the writer's awareness of the difficulty *for everyone* of reading literally, the outlines of a new pedagogical model, which refuses to acknowledge
a symbolic boundary between simple people and "those assumed to be
endowed with reason and hermeneutical perspicacity (men, clergy, *litterati*)."[29] Lewis Chaucer was one of those who, according to the traditional
pedagogical model, might have been expected to progress from childish elucidation of the grammar and rhetoric of texts to adult academic hermeneutics.[30] The fifth of Archbishop Arundel's *Constitutiones* (promulgated in
1409), described by Copeland as "a comprehensive response to the new ideological formations of the Lollard classroom," aimed to shore up the barrier
between simple readers and males literate in Latin, preserving for the latter
"the exposition of holy scripture."[31] In the Oxford debate of 1401, both opponents of translation "invoke the literal sense," as Rita Copeland says, "in relation to the Bible's accessibility to *vulgari*, as if by an established collocation"
(142). The Dominican Thomas Palmer, who identifies advocates of translation as Lollards, cites against the translators the text at the heart of Gregory
the Great's advocacy of spiritual senses, "littera occidit, spiritus autem vivifi-
cat" (2 Cor. 3:6), and expounds the Mosaic judgment "[i]f you happen upon
a bird's nest in a tree or on the ground, and the dam is sitting on her young,
you shall not take her along with the young, but you shall let her go" (Deut.
22:6), as meaning that "the literal sense . . . ought to be left behind, and its
offspring, that is the allegorical and anagogical [mystical] senses, retained."[32]
Kantik Ghosh notes that Palmer questions whether there can in any case be a
single literal sense in English Scripture, given "the inevitability of interpretation in translation."[33]

In the Wycliffite prologue to Isaiah, Purvey in effect reverses Gregory's
core text, implying instead that "the letter brings to life, whereas the spirit
kills." When the translators preparing the Later Version reached the begin-

ning of Isaiah, having omitted all prefatory materials in the Earlier Version to that point, they included a new prologue, to serve as "þe prologe of Ysaie and of oþere profetis" (*Wycliffite Bible*, iii. 323). This prologue, which accompanies the text of Isaiah in all Later Version manuscripts containing this book,[34] was written before the prologue to the Wycliffite Bible, for the writer of both mentions it when he comes to Isaiah in his synopsis of the Old Testament: "þe prophetis han a general prologe for alle" (i. 41/37–38). At the time the prologue to Isaiah was written, the intention to write a prologue prefixed to Genesis had already been formed, and a part of its content had already been planned, for Purvey says he will give a fuller account of the four senses of Scripture "if God wole, on þe bigynnyng of Genesis" (iii. 226/24–25; i.e., cc 12–14 of the prologue to the Wycliffite Bible). At that very late stage in the translation project, when a general prologue was already planned, the translators felt the need to alert the reader to the way the Jewish prophets should be read, and, more particularly, to the way in which they should *not* be read. The translators were influenced, I suspect, by Jerome's account of Philip's meeting with the Ethiopian eunuch (Acts 8:35) in his *Epistola ad Paulinum* (prefixed to the Latin Bible and to the Earlier Version of the Wycliffite Bible), where Philip's evangelism is the culminating example in Jerome's argument that "þou maist not entre in hooly scripturis withoute a forgoere and shewynge þe weie þerof."[35]

Although the Isaiah prologue begins "[a]s seynt Jerom seiþ," Purvey cannot accept Jerome's praise of Isaiah's elegant and urbane Hebrew rhetoric, calculated to appeal to the *litterati* and bemuse others. Wyclif had already countered Jerome, in the prologue to Isaiah in his *Postilla super totam Bibliam* (c. 1375), insisting that biblical rhetoric is different in kind from pagan rhetoric.[36] Lyra claims in his prologue to Isaiah that the book's *forma tractandi* is "lucidus et ornatus," and the writer of the Middle English Isaiah prologue mingles Lyra's text with Jerome's: "Isaie is ful witti and ful opyn in his writyng in Ebreu, þouȝ þe translacioun in to Latyn miȝte not kepe þe fairnesse of speche"(iii. 225/7–8). Not said, but understood, is the corollary that a translation *can* retain Isaiah's openness. The writer again terms Isaiah "opyn" in translating Jerome's claim that Isaiah is not so much prophet as evangelist: Isaiah is "a gospellere, for he declariþ so opynli þe mysteries of crist and of hooli chirche" (225/10–11).[37] Discussing the dimensions of the word "openness" in Lollard writings, Rita Copeland makes the point that "[i]mplicit in the idea of 'openness' is anti-elitism . . . 'Simple men's wit' becomes the abiding standard, the 'open' measure, for who should be allowed to read Scripture."[38]

The insistence upon the openness of the text is momentarily subverted when the writer proffers three rules, derived from Lyra, by which "þe derk places of þe profetis moun be vndurstondun liȝtli" (225/30–31), his little pun on "liȝt" (not dark; easy) being calculated to avert readerly alarm. The first rule is "þat þe principal entent of þe profetis is to declare þe mysterie" (225/31–32) of Christ and the whole history of the Church. The second is that the prophets meant also to "warnen þe puple of Jewis of her grete synnes, and exciten [incite] hem to do penaunce" (225/36–226/1) in order to achieve grace in this world and glory hereafter, and in order to avoid "tribulacioun in þis lijf and peyn wiþouten ende" (226/2–3). The third rule is that the prophets recall benefits previously given by God to the Jews, in order to exhort the Jews to believe their prophecies (226/4–5). The prophetical books should therefore be interpreted in relation to the "stories of Moises lawe" [the Pentateuch] (226/5), and the historical books of the Old Testament, or else in relation to the New Testament—but this only as a last resort, for from the time of Abelard onwards, as Theresa Gross-Diaz has recently reminded us in her discussion of Lyra's postills on the Psalms, it had been accepted that "[t]he New Testament is inadmissible as evidence in the context of a Jewish-Christian debate."[39]

These three rules for interpreting the prophets are rules *contra Judaeos*, intended to subvert Jewish interpretation of Hebrew prophecies. They are rooted in the assumption that the Jews would understand the christological content of their own scriptures if only they would read them "literally" in the Lyran sense of literality. The demand for a literal-christological interpretation of the prophets leads the writer of the Isaiah prologue into an emphatic assertion of the centrality of the literal sense. No allegorical, moral, or anagogical interpretation has authority, unless it is clearly founded upon the text, or is manifestly reasonable in accordance with principles or rules of faith, "as seynt Austin witnessiþ opynli" (226/9–13). Any sense other than the literal must be plainly, clearly, evidently warranted, on the authority of Augustine and Jerome, Lyra and Richard FitzRalph, who developed Lyra's ideas on authorial intention and the literal sense.[40] Ghosh has shown how the Wycliffite emphasis on reason as a hermeneutic tool "points towards the positivist vision of scriptural meaning as accessible and determinate," not subject to "ymaginacioun,"[41] and the author of the Isaiah prologue finds his own authentic Wycliffite voice as he warns the reader against a spiritual sense rooted not in the words of Scripture or in plain reason, but in "fantasie," make-believe:

> men moten seke þe treuþe of þe text and be war of goostli vndurstondynge eþer moral fantasie, and ȝyue not ful credence þerto, no but [unless] it be groundid opynly in þe text of hooli writ in o place or oþer, eþer in opyn resoun þat may not be avoided, for ellis it wole as likyngli be applied to falsnesse as to treuþe, and it haþ disseyued grete men in oure daies bi ouer greet trist to her fantasies. (226/15–20)

Here, at the climax of his argument, the writer acknowledges the reader as his contemporary, inviting him to agree that powerful men have been deceived by preferring their own imaginings to the open sense of the Bible. Who these men are, and what the consequences of their self-deception are, is too dangerous at the time to be specified, but this clause reveals the writer's awareness that the debate about biblical interpretation is also a debate about the exercise of control in church and state, and about persecution. In what for the Wycliffites are dark days, the open Lollard sense turns both writer and implied reader into potential victims.[42]

There are two categories of bad reader in the prologue to Isaiah, Jews and "grete men in oure daies," neither of whom read literally enough, but whereas Jews fail to understand the fully theologized "literal" sense of obscure passages of prophecy, men of power obfuscate the literal sense of open parts of Scripture. Purvey seems more anxious to convince his contemporaries of the perverse biblical interpretation practiced by men of power in England at the end of the fourteenth century than he is to correct Jewish misreading of the prophets. Indeed, he is so concerned to provide his readers with the very words of Hebrew Scripture and the Jewish interpretation of them that, as he says in the final chapter of the prologue to the Wycliffite Bible, where scholars have shown that the Hebrew text differs from the Latin "I haue set in þe margyn, bi maner of a glose, what þe Ebru haþ, and hou it is vndurstondun in sum place; and I dide þis most in þe Sauter, þat of alle oure bookis discordiþ most fro Ebru" (i. 58/5–7).[43]

Hudson has asked whether "any form of marginal glossing was ever put out with any authority," noting that Forshall and Madden's edition of the glosses is an inadequate basis for an answer.[44] Wyclif and the Wycliffites' profound unease with glossing, their often-expressed desire for a "naked" biblical text, might lead us to expect the translators to forgo glosses entirely.[45] One of the chief causes of their unease, the self-justifying glossing of the friars,[46] is famously satirized in Chaucer's *Summoner's Tale*, where the Friar lays bare to the wealthy layman Thomas his interpretive strategy:

> I ne have no text of it, as I suppose,
> But I shal fynde it in a maner glose,
> That specially oure sweete Lord Jhesus
> Spak this by freres, whan he seyde thus:
> "Blessed be they that povere in spirit been."
> (*Canterbury Tales*, III: 1919–23)

A "glose" on the biblical text (Latin *glossa*) had been understood, since the eleventh century, to mean an authoritative comment. When Purvey says that the Wycliffite translators studied "the text," their newly-corrected Latin Bible, "wiþ þe glose" (*Wycliffite Bible*, i. 57/10), he means the *Glossa Ordinaria*, the set of marginal and interlinear glosses derived from patristic and Carolingian exegetes to which the later Middle Ages assigned especial authority.[47] The Friar of the *Summoner's Tale*, on the other hand, uses the word "text" for an authoritative comment on the biblical text ("I ne have no text of it"), and drives a wedge between "text" and "glose," under cover of which friars can make the biblical text mean anything they want it to mean ("I *shal* fynde it in a maner glose": my italics).

The suspicion that glossing was characteristically tendentious and without any authoritative textual basis is inscribed in the Middle English verb *glosen*, meaning "interpret," but also, and more commonly, "flatter" or "deceive." When the Friar of the *Summoner's Tale* insists that "Glosynge is a glorious thing, certeyn, / For lettre sleeth, so we clerkes seyn" (1793–94), his gerund hovers (to his private delight) between "glossing" and "deception"; "the letter kills" (2 Cor 3:6 and Gregory the Great) is for this Friar a license to travesty the literal sense by way of glosses.[48] As if countering the Summoner's Friar, Chaucer's Parson reassures the pilgrims, in the prologue to his tale, that he will treat his moral subject matter in the manner of a simple preacher rather than that of a sophisticated cleric: "I am not textueel [a textual scholar]; / I take but the sentence [the plain meaning], trusteth weel" (*Canterbury Tales*, X: 57–58). The apparently throw-away half line "I wol nat glose" ("And therfore, if yow list—I wol nat glose— / I wol yow telle a myrie tale in prose," X: 45–46) contains, I think, a commitment to avoid traducing the literal sense of his sources, so he makes the decision not to gloss at all, in other words to introduce no element of interpretation. Chaucer's position on glossing, one supposes, lies somewhere between the two extremes represented by the Parson and the Summoner's Friar.

For all the Wycliffite distrust of glossing (particularly that arising from the "fantasie" [iii. 226/15] of non-Lollards), Wyclif himself was perfectly capable of glossing for his own ends, as David Aers has recently reminded us. In *De Officio Pastorali*, *De Officio Regis*, and *Trialogus*, Wyclif glosses, that is, interprets, New Testament texts in ways which, in Aers's view, offend against commonsense literal reading (this seems to me a highly tendentious claim), but which enable him to draw a sharp distinction between the discipleship of *clerici* and laity.[49] Doubtless Wyclif was confident that his glossing was consonant with "the honour of God and the advancement of the Church," which, in the course of discussing the prophets in his *Postilla super totam Bibliam*, he deems the *causa finalis* of Scripture.[50]

The decision of the Wycliffite translators, reported in the final chapter of the prologue to the Wycliffite Bible, to rework the highly literal Earlier Version into a version that sacrificed word-by-word literalism for the sake of accessible "sentence" [meaning] (i. 57/18) strongly suggests that the translators recognized the inevitability of supplementarity, and therefore of interpretation in translation. The writer's certainty that other translators, if not these present ones, will with the grace of God "make þe bible as trewe and as opin, ȝea and opinliere, in English þan it is in Latyn" (58/15–16), confirms his confidence that any element of interpretation they introduced would be faithful to the divine intention.

As a form of supplementation, and where they provide a variant reading, glosses must perforce be written outside the text. This, surely, is why Purvey recommends setting glosses in the margin where the Hebrew text differs from the Latin; he is assuring the reader that these glosses are necessary for understanding the literal sense of Jewish Scripture, not simply supplying spiritual interpretations or making polemical points.[51] A sample of this type of necessary marginal gloss in the Later Version comments on Jacob's question to Laban, "whi hast þou disseyued me?" (Gen. 29:25; *Wycliffite Bible*, i. 138). The gloss reads: "þis is þe verie lettre, as Lire seiþ here, but comyn Latyn bokis han þus 'whi hast þou priuyly put Lya to me?', but þis is fals lettre as Lire seiþ here."[52]

Not infrequently, a marginal gloss supplies a reading not incorporated in the translation: both Earlier and Later Versions say that the Israelites "brent wiþ desire of fleischis" (Num. 11:4; i. 395), but the gloss notes that "of fleischis" is itself an interpolated gloss: "þis word 'of fleischis' is not in Ebru neþer in bokis amendid [corrected texts], for þei desiriden fleischis and fischis and oþere þingis."[53] There are several glosses in which the Hebrew reading, following Lyra, is explicitly preferred to the Latin: the Latin translated as "o womman . . . hurtlide to þe heed of Abymelech and brak his brayn" (Judg. 9:53; i. 643) is glossed "in Ebreu it is his nol [head], for if sche hadde broke þe brayn he hadde be deed anoon."[54] Sometimes a Hebrew reading is preferred because it makes more sense in context: "ʒyue þou not . . . þi richessis to do awei kyngis [*ad delendos reges*, Vulgate]" (Prov. 31:3; iii. 50) is glossed "Ebreys seyen to make fatte kingis, and þis acordiþ betere to þe lettre suynge [A! Lamuel, nyle þou ʒyue wyn to kingis, Prov. 31:4]."[55] Glosses like these remind the Middle English reader that the Latin Old Testament is a translated text, and, cumulatively, persuade him or her that the Jewish Scriptures make good literal sense, and that Jewish scholars have been good literal readers.

Other marginal glosses found in many or several manuscripts are more broadly interpretive. Purvey intended, I believe, to reserve marginal glosses for commentary on the Hebrew text, while any interpretive glossing necessary to make the text of the Latin Bible "open" in English would be included in the text. This was partly because of a distrust of marginal glossing, but more importantly because Purvey wished the text to be "hool," to make good literal sense in itself, in Lyra's understanding of "literal," that is to say, including all the figurative senses intended by the writer and all the christological significations the Holy Spirit had inscribed within the text. The marginal glosses in the Pentateuch are largely reserved for commentary on the Hebrew text, but as soon as marginal glossing was introduced at all, glossing tended to move outwards from the text into the margin, in line with accepted editorial practice.[56] There are many cases where some manuscripts have a gloss within the text and others have the same gloss in the margin.

The Later Version is made more "open" to the reader than the Earlier Version, as Henry Hargreaves shows, by the addition of words, like parts of the verb "to be," by the repetition or recapitulation of words or phrases, and by the provision of glosses on difficult words.[57] The translators' source for this supplementary material was usually Lyra, and, given their dependence on him, it is not surprising that his "true literal" glosses sometimes become incorporated into the more "open" translated text. So, the Earlier Version's word-by-word "Fair in form befor þe sonus of men" (*speciosus forma prae filiis hominum*, Psa. 44:3; ii. 781), becomes in the Later Version, "Crist, þou art fairer in schap þan þe sones of men," incorporating within the text Lyra's literal-christological gloss on this verse. In a similar vein, the gloss on the title of Psalm 44, included in most manuscripts, states: "Þis salm is seid of Crist and of hooli chirche, modir and virgyn, for Poul in [Hebr. 1:8–9] aleggiþ þis salm seid of Crist to þe lettre."[58]

A reader illiterate in Latin, or without access to the Latin text, or anyone hearing this text read, would suppose that Christ was originally and quite literally written into this psalm, and would suppose the Jews to be remarkably bad readers if they failed to notice this. But then, Lyra and the translators did suppose the Jews to be bad literal readers of the Psalms, in the sense that they were blind to their alleged christological content. Hargreaves voices modern scholarly opinion in terming this type of supplementation "contamination,"[59] but since the Wycliffite translators evidently did not so regard it, we may infer that their educated contemporaries who approved of the Bible being translated into English also thought this kind of supplementation appropriate.[60]

What might have concerned a Latin-literate layman like Chaucer was the thought of simple men and women reading the Hebrew Bible in English without the help of interpretive glosses at all, especially books that were notoriously difficult such as the Song of Songs. In the second introduction to the Books of Solomon in the prologue to the Wycliffite Bible, the writer warns that the Song of Songs "seemiþ to fleschly men to sounne [signify] vnclene loue of leccherie" (i. 41/18), and "þerfore men moten be ful wel war to conseyue wel þe wordis of þe holy goost in þis book, and knowe whanne Crist spekiþ to þe chirche eiþir to þe synagoge, and whanne þe synagoge spekiþ to god, and whanne þe chirche spekiþ to Crist [etc]" (41/19–22). In the Earlier Version, as often in Latin bibles, glosses (or rubrics) written within the text indicate throughout the Song of Songs who is speaking to whom, but these glosses are omitted in the Later Version.[61] This seems very surprising, in view of the importance attached to identification of the speakers in the prologue, but the reason is that Lyra's postill on the Song of Songs, summarized in the prologue (41/12–15), is at odds with the earlier commentary tradition from which the speaker-rubrics derive.[62]

In Chaucer's *Merchant's Tale*, old January borrows words from the Song of Songs to exhort his young wife to go with him into their garden "to pleye":

Rys up, my wyf, my loue, my lady free!
The turtles voys is herd, my dowve sweete;
The wynter is goon with alle his reynes weete.
Com forth now, with thyne eyen columbyn!
How fairer been thy brestes than is wyn!
The gardyn is enclosed al aboute
(*Canterbury Tales*, IV: 2138–43; Song of Songs 2:10–13; 4:1, 10, 12)

Far from being aware who is speaking to whom at each point in the Song of Songs, January gives no indication of knowing that his words are those of Christ (or Yahweh) speaking to the church (or to the Jewish people). The scornful Merchant-narrator glosses January's words with precisely the carnal meaning that the Wycliffite writer of the prologue warns against: "Swiche olde lewed wordes used he" (2149; "lewed" is the opposite of both clerical and literate).[63] This is a moment of high comedy, but the Merchant's words are also shocking in their blindness to Jewish and Christian interpretive tradition, for both Christians and Jews had traditionally read the Song of Songs as being about love between the human and the divine. Would that understanding survive, Chaucer perhaps wondered, if simple readers read an unglossed English translation of the Song of Songs?

Jews and Christians share some interpretive traditions, yet dispute the meaning of their shared Scriptures; Jews are sometimes good literal readers and sometimes bad literal readers; the Jewish Scriptures should be open to "simple men's wit," but also are susceptible of dangerous misprision. These contradictory propositions can all be supported from the Wycliffite translation of Jewish Scripture, and from the glosses and prologues that supplemented it. The process of persuading the Jews of the truth of Christianity is there perceived to be a long and complex one, as long as the process of recovering the literal sense of Jewish Scripture and of teaching it to simple Christian readers. In sum, the translators view Jewish interpretive tradition with intense intellectual curiosity and, not infrequently, admiration. The literal-minded Jew is often a friend, while powerful Christians are all too often enemies. Chaucer was certainly not in the business of making enemies, but it is tempting to speculate that he read the translation of Jewish Scripture produced in his lifetime and shared the translators' estimate of the reading practices of the Jews.

Notes

I am grateful to Vybarr Creagan-Reid for his helpful comments on a draft of this paper.

1. Conrad Lindberg argues that work on the translation began with an interlinear version c. 1370, *The Middle English Bible: The Book of Judges*, vol. 3 (Oslo:

Norwegian University, 1989), 74. Most recently, Lindberg dates the conclusion of the work 1390, *King Henry's Bible, MS Bodl 277: the Revised Version of the Wyclif Bible*, vol. 1, Genesis to Ruth, *Stockholm Studies in English* 89 (1999), 47. Lindberg has always insisted that Wyclif played an active role in the project; Anne Hudson aptly says that "if not the immediate cause, Wyclif was the ultimate effective cause of the versions that have come to be known as the Wycliffite Bible": "Wyclif and the English Language," in *Wyclif In His Times* ed. Anthony Kenny, (Oxford: Oxford University, 1986), 85.

2. Steven F. Kruger makes this point, and discusses the consequences for medieval Christian attitudes to Jews in "The Spectral Jew," in *New Medieval Literatures* eds., Wendy Scase, Rita Copeland, and David Lawton (Oxford: Clarendon, 1997): 9–35. Kruger's provocative essay is much influenced by Jaques Derrida's *Spectres de Marx* (Paris: Editions Galileé, 1993), and in my view underestimates the extent to which Jews and Judaism were living realities for the medieval Christian.

3. I am inclined to believe that the customary identification is correct, although Anne Hudson has consistently reminded us of the lack of firm evidence for this; see in particular *Selections from English Wycliffite Writings* (Cambridge: Cambridge University, 1978), 173–74; and "John Purvey: A Reconsideration of the Evidence for his Life and Writings," in *Lollards and their Books* (London: Hambledon, 1985), 85–110.

4. Usually termed "the General Prologue," by analogy with the General Prologue to *The Canterbury Tales*. To avoid any confusion, I here refer to it as the prologue to the Wycliffite Bible. The Earlier and Later Versions (hereafter EV and LV in notes) were first identified, and edited as such, by Forshall and Madden, and their distinctiveness remains unchallenged, although "mixed," "intermediate," and post-LV versions have since been identified. See Josiah Forshall and Frederic Madden, eds., *The Old and New Testaments, with the Apocryphal Books, in the Earliest English Versions Made from the Latin Vulgate by John Wycliffe and His Followers* (Oxford: Oxford University Press 1850), iii. 842; hereafter cited in text as *Wycliffite Bible* and in notes as *WB*.

5. See Hudson's notes on these four stages, *Selections from English Wycliffite Writings*, 162–63, and her text, 67/26–68/35. The quotation is at 152.

6. *The Premature Reformation: Wycliffite Texts and Lollard History* (Oxford: Clarendon, 1988), 243.

7. Larry D. Benson, ed., *The Riverside Chaucer* (Oxford: Oxford University, 1988), 662, lines 39–40; hereafter cited in text as *Riverside Chaucer*.

8. For Trevisa's preface see R. Waldron, "Trevisa's Original Prefaces on Translation: A Critical Edition," in *Medieval English Studies Presented to George Kane*, eds., E. D. Kennedy, R. Waldron, and J. S. Wittig (Woodbridge, Suffolk: D. S. Brewer, 1988), 285–99 (text 289–95). For the arguments justifying translation in the prologue, *WB*, i. 58/22–59/36; two dates have been proposed for the prologue, 1388 and 1395, based on internal evidence from the passage in c. 13 bewailing the sorry state of Oxford. The earlier date sorts well with Lindberg's most recent dating of LV to 1390. Forshall and Madden argue for the earlier date, *WB*, i. xxiv, following Daniel Waterland, *The Works of Daniel Waterland*, vol. 10 (Oxford: Oxford University Press 1823), 385.

Hudson is not convinced by the evidence for 1395 in *Selections from English Wycliffite Writings*, 174, but accepts it in *The Premature Reformation*, 247.

9. See Hudson, "The Debate on Biblical Translation, Oxford 1401," in *Lollards and Their Books* (London: Hambledon, 1985), 67–84. Ullerston's *De Translacione* is unprinted; he became a defender of orthodoxy against Lollardy, and his support of Biblical translation in 1401 demonstrates that the Wycliffite Bible was not necessarily associated with the Lollard heresy.

10. "Geoffrey Chaucer," in *The Cambridge History of Medieval English Literature,* ed. David Wallace (Cambridge, England: Cambridge University, 1999), 582–83.

11. Usually followed by the canticles; they are nos. 16, 36, 37, 66, 72, 199, in Conrad Lindberg, "The Manuscripts and Versions of the Wycliffite Bible: a preliminary survey," *Studia Neophilologica* 42 (1970), 333–47; and Trinity College Dublin MS 72.

12. Lindberg lists 230 MSS, but, including fragments, the number is around 250; see Simon Hunt, "An Edition of Tracts in Favour of Scriptural Translation and of Some Texts connected with Lollard Vernacular Biblical Scholarship" (D. Phil. diss., University of Oxford, 1994), ii. 557–63. Five OTs are in EV and eighteen in LV; no. 103 lacks the Psalms.

13. *Enarrationes in Psalmos*, 54: 16; ed. E. Dekkers and J. Fraipont, *CCSL* XXXIX, ii (Turnhout: Brepols, 1956), 668–69.

14. In "Prologus Galeatus in Libros Regum," F. Stegmüller and N. Reinhardt, *Repertorium Biblicum Medii Aevi* (Madrid: n.p. 1950–80), no. 323; *WB*, EV, ii. 1–5; the apocryphal books of the Old Testament are named at ii. 4/17–25. This prologue is also included in 3 LV MSS: Cambridge University Library Addit. 6680, Hereford Cathedral Library O. VII. 1, and New College Oxford, 66.

15. The prologue to the Wycliffite Bible also reproduces Jerome's condemnation of 3 and 4 Ezra, i. 2/18–19, in his first prologue to Ezra, Stegmüller, *Repertorium Biblicum*, no. 330; *WB* ii. 477–88. In spite of Jerome's condemnation, all OTs in EV contain 3 Ezra, and MS Bodl. 277 contains 3 Ezra in LV.

16. *The Premature Reformation*, 230. *Doctrinale Antiquitatum Fideo Catholicae Ecclesiae*, Lib. II, cap. 20; ed. B. Blanciotti (Venice, 1757), i. 344–46.

17. MSS CEIMNPU (Forshall and Madden's sigla).

18. My references to Lyra are to the *editio princeps*, *Postilla litteralis et moralis in Vetus et Novum Testamentum*, ed. Sweynheym and Pannartz, 5 vols (Rome, 1471–72) [no quire or folio nos]. Quotations are from this edition: there is no modern edition. Four MSS add "kyng of Juda" after "Ezechie"; the gloss is found in MSS ACEGHKLPQb (Forshall and Madden's sigla), and Princeton, W. H. Scheide 12; *WB*, ii. 577 (MSS not recorded). MS N has a similar rubric.

19. Lincoln College Oxford Latin MS 119 omits this, beginning "þe book of Tobie is ful deuout." This MS, which prefixes the prologue's introduction to individual books to the books themselves, also omits the references to the non-canonicity of Judith and Ecclus.

20. See also Margaret Deanesly, *The Lollard Bible and Other Medieval Biblical Versions* (Cambridge: Cambridge University, 1920), 256.

21. Bodl. MS Douce 36; the initial is gold on a mauve and violet background, a fine example of a style commonly found in MSS of the Wycliffite Bible (e.g., GXDFKMOPQY; Forshall and Madden's sigla). Forshall and Madden's date "about 1440" (i. l) seems too late; perhaps 1410–1425.

22. "Proces" is the word almost invariably used in the prologue for Old Testament narratives, presumably to avoid any connotation of the fictional. Ruth, however, is a "storie" within Judges (9/23, 26).

23. Cambridge University Library MS Ii. 6. 26, treatise 1; see Hunt, "An Edition of Tracts in Favour of Scriptural Translation," ii. 265/249, 261–62. See also Deanesly, *The Lollard Bible*, 270–74; Deanesly attributes the treatise to Purvey and dates it 1382–1395, 70; Hunt perhaps post-1407, ii. 472.

24. From the rubric to Psalms in MSS ACLOP (Forshall and Madden's sigla).

25. The prologue's introduction to the Psalms, *WB*, i. 37/35–40/2, is contained in MSS Trinity College Dublin 72, BL Addit. 31,044, and Worcester Cathedral F. 172, as well as in complete copies of the prologue.

26. MS Bodl. 482, fol. 1v; quoted from Beryl Smalley, *The Study of the Bible in the Middle Ages*, 3rd ed (Oxford: Blackwell, 1983), 170–71.

27. "The Literal Sense of the Books of Samuel and Kings: from Andrew of St Victor to Nicholas of Lyra," in *Nicholas of Lyra: the Senses of Scripture*, eds. Philip D. W. Krey and Lesley Smith (Leiden: Brill, 2000), 81.

28. "Always to Keep the Literal Sense in Holy Scripture Means to Kill One's Soul': the State of Biblical Hermeneutics at the Beginning of the Fifteenth Century," in *Literary Uses of Typology from the Late Middle Ages to the Present*, ed. Karl Miner (Princeton, NJ: Princeton University, 1977), 47.

29. Rita Copeland, "Childhood, Pedagogy, and the Literal Sense," in *New Medieval Literatures* II, Scase, Copeland, and Lawton, 138.

30. "Childhood, Pedagogy, and the Literal Sense," 131–38. Copeland argues that in the late-antique period, literal reading and hermeneutics became separated.

31. "Childhood, Pedagogy, and the Literal Sense," 144–47; quotation, 147. On the date of the *Constitutiones*, see Hudson, *The Premature Reformation*, 15.

32. "Childhood, Pedagogy, and the Literal Sense," 142–43; Latin text quoted from Deanesly, *The Lollard Bible*, 424.

33. "Authority and Interpretation in Wycliffite, Anti-Wycliffite and Related Texts: c. 1375–c. 1430" (Ph. D. diss., University of Cambridge, 1995), 107. A version of this dissertation has been published as *The Wycliffite Heresy* (Cambridge, England: Cambridge University Press, 2001).

34. MSS ACEFGHIKMNPQRSUVXY (Forshall and Madden's sigla) and Cambridge University Library Addit. 6680, Princeton, W. H. Scheide 12, and John Rylands Library English 91. The Wycliffite prologue replaces Jerome's prologue (Stegmüller, *Repertorium Biblicum*, no. 482) even in those MSS which otherwise contain EV or revised versions of Jerome's prologues.

35. "in scripturis sanctis sine praevio et monstrante semitam non posse ingredi"; Lindberg, *The Middle English Bible: Prefatory Epistles of St. Jerome*, vol. 1 (Oslo: Norwegian University, 1978), 95/4–6 (LV text from New College Oxford MS 66).

36. See Gustav Benrath, *Wyclifs Bibelkommentar* (Berlin: Walter de Gruyter, 1966), 64–66, and Ghosh, " 'Authority' and Interpretation," 57–58.

37. Jerome's claim is also made in the *Epistola ad Paulinum*; Lindberg, *The Middle English Bible: Prefatory Epistles*, 129/158–59.

38. "Rhetoric and the Politics of the Literal Sense in Medieval Literary Theory: Aquinas, Wyclif, and the Lollards," in *Interpretation: Medieval and Modern*, eds., Piero Boitani and Anna Torti (Cambridge, Cambridge University, 1993), 20.

39. "What's A Good Soldier To Do? Scholarship and Revelation in the Postills on the Psalms," in *Nicholas of Lyra: the Senses of Scripture*, Krey and Smith, 127; see also Daniel J. Lasker, *Jewish Philosophical Polemics Against Christianity in the Middle Ages* (New York: Ktav, 1977), 4–6.

40. On the importance of FitzRalph to the Lollards, see A. J. Minnis, " 'Authorial Intention' and 'Literal Sense' in the Exegetical Theories of Richard FitzRalph and John Wyclif: An Essay in the Medieval History of Biblical Hermeneutics," *Proceedings of the Royal Irish Academy*, 75, Section C, no. 1 (Dublin, 1975), 1–31.

41. " 'Authority' and Interpretation," 155; see also his account of Nicholas Love's "resonable ymaginacioun," 188–190.

42. The prologue ends with some guidance for understanding "figuratif speche," moral figures intended by their authors, and therefore part of the literal sense, but liable to misreading; compare the much fuller discussion in the prologue to *WB*, c. 12; i. 43/43–46/15, and in the "Intermediate" Matthew prologue, ed. Hunt, "An Edition of Tracts in Favour of Scriptural Translation," ii. 370–82; the relationship between this prologue and the prologue to *WB* is discussed at i. 192–96.

43. As Hudson points out, the wording makes it clear that the writer's own knowledge of Hebrew is derivative, *Selections from English Wycliffite Writings*, 175–76.

44. *The Premature Reformation*, 235–36. *WB* does not provide a full record of which marginal glosses are in which manuscript, and fails to note where a "marginal" gloss is written within the text. Lindberg omits marginal glosses in all his editions, as he says in *The Middle English Bible: The Book of Judges*, 77.

45. On the Wycliffites and glosses see (*inter multa alia*) Ralph Hanna III, "The Difficulty of Ricardian Prose Translation: the Case of the Lollards," *Modern Language Quarterly* 51 (1990), 319–40 (esp. 337); and Ghosh, " 'Authority' and Interpretation," 88. On "naked text," particularly with reference to Chaucer, see Sheila Delany, *The Naked Text: Chaucer's Legend of Good Women* (Berkeley and Los Angeles: University of California Press, 1994), 41–42, 45–46, 83–85, and chapter 3.

46. On friars as "glosers" in *Piers Plowman*, and the apocalyptic dimensions of anti-mendicant satire, see Wendy Scase, Piers Plowman *and the New Anti-clericalism* (Cambridge: Cambridge University, 1989), 112–19.

47. A number of scholars helped to produce the *Glossa,* including Anselm of Laon, working in various northern French schools and religious houses between c. 1090 and c. 1140; see Beryl Smalley, *"Glossa ordinaria," Theologische Realencycop die*, vol. 13 (1984), 452–57; and Margaret T. Gibson, "The Glossed Bible," in *Biblia Latina cum Glossa Ordinaria*, facsimile reprint, vol. 1 (Turnhout: Brepols, 1992), VII–XI.

48. On glossing in the *Summoner's Tale*, see also David Aers, "Reflections on the 'Allegory of the Theologians,' Ideology and *Piers Plowman*," in *Medieval Literature: Criticism, Ideology and History* (Brighton: Harvester, 1986), 60–62. Aers claims that Chaucer is "intrigued by the way seemingly 'impersonal' discourses of the highest authority relate to specific interests of identifiable social groups," 62.

49. "John Wyclif's Understanding of Christian Discipleship," in *Faith, Ethics, and Church Writing in England, 1360–1409* (Cambridge: D. S. Brewer, 2000): 119–48. Aers concludes that "the way in which [Wyclif] dichotomized Christian discipleship, in the contexts of his ecclesiology and politics, outlines a *de-Christianization of the laity*," 147–48 (italics in original).

50. In the context of his discussion of Jer. 23:9; Benrath, *Wyclifs Bibelkommentar*, 79, text at n. 182.

51. Hargreaves says there is no controversial matter in the marginal glosses, "The vernacular Scriptures," 413, but see Exd. 6:11 (Corpus Christi College Cambridge MSS 147), *WB*, i. lvi, and Esther 3:2 (MSS BL Cotton Claudius E. II and Royal 1. C. IX, citing authorities on when it is lawful to kneel), ii. 643.

52. MSS CGQX (Forshall and Madden's sigla). This also corrects the Earlier Version's "whi vndurputtist þow Lya to me?"

53. MSS CGKQXd (Forshall and Madden's sigla; they omit K and d here).

54. BL MS Cotton Claudius E. II only. Other examples (all from this MS only) are at 1 Kings 14: 47 (*WB*, ii. 41), 2 Kings 1:18 (ii. 91), Prov. 31:19 (iii. 51) and Prov. 31:24 (ibid).

55. BL MS Cotton Claudius E. II only.

56. Cf. the scribal note in Lambeth Palace MS 1033 at the beginning of Isaiah, quoted by Hargreaves, "The vernacular Scriptures," 413. In Trinity College Dublin MS 67 the glosses at Isa. 17:6, 28:15 and 29:1 are written within the text, but the words of the text being glossed are omitted and later supplied in the margin.

57. "The Latin Text of Purvey's Psalter," *Medium Aevum* 24 (1955), 84. Added material is usually underlined, but not always, and not always accurately. Glosses on difficult words are also found regularly in EV from Ecclus onwards, except in in MSS Bodl. 959, Bodl. Douce 369 and Christ Church College Oxford 145. Forshall and Madden's choice of BL MS Royal 1. C. VIII as base text for LV, an MS which frequently "resolves" these glosses to one term, means that the LV text is often relegated to the textual variants.

58. MSS ACEGLPQSUXbi (Forshall and Madden's sigla), Bodl. 554 and Trinity College Dublin 72; *WB* records simply "A *et alii*". See Gross-Diaz's discussion of Lyra's christological reading of the Psalms by way of the New Testament, in *Nicholas of Lyra: the Senses of Scripture*, Krey and Smith, 126–28.

59. "The vernacular Scriptures," 413. Hargreaves cites several examples from Psalms.

60. Since LV did not supersede EV, according to Lindberg (*The Middle English Bible: The Book of Judges*, 71), some readers perhaps preferred a word-for-word translation. Hudson, however, supposes that LV did supersede EV: *The Premature Reformation*, 239.

61. They are included in one LV MS, Hereford Cathedral Library O. VII. 1.

62. The speaker-rubrics derive from Bede's commentary on the Song of Songs by way of Haimo of Auxerre's recension; see Mary Dove, *Glossa Ordinaria in Canticum Canticorum*, Corpus Christianorum Continuatio Medievalis 170, pars 22 (Turnhout: Brepols, 1987). On Lyra's postill on the Song of Songs, see Mary Dove, "Literal Senses in the Song of Songs," in *Nicholas of Lyra: the Senses of Scripture*, Krey and Smith, 129–46.

63. See further Dove, "Swiche olde Lewed Wordes: Books about Medieval Love, Medieval Books about Love, and the Medieval Book of Love," in *Venus and Mars: Engendering Love and War in Medieval and Early Modern Europe,* eds. Andrew Lynch and P. Maddern, (Perth: University of Western Australia, 1995), 11–22.

7

Reading Biblical Outlaws

The "Rise of David" Story in the Fourteenth Century

TIMOTHY S. JONES

From Edward I's expulsion of the Jews in 1290 until the late sixteenth century, Jews in England were few and far between.[1] But if flesh and blood Jews were absent, imagined Jews were not. They appear as the antagonists of Christ—in illustrations of the Crucifixion, the drama cycles, and narratives such as the *Siege of Jerusalem*—and as the antagonists of Christians in saints' lives, miracle tales, the Croxton *Play of the Sacrament*, stories of the finding of the True Cross, and Chaucer's *Prioress's Tale*. Despite the centuries between them, these two groups are often imaginatively collapsed into a single type, the stereotyped and demonized Jew who undermines the identity of Christian society through his unbelief and is stigmatized with a distinct iconography of otherness.[2] But there is another Jew in fourteenth-century England: the Jew of Hebrew Scripture. These men and women of the writings which Christians came to call the Old Testament presented a more complex challenge for medieval Christianity.

As Christianity spread from its Jewish origins to the gentile world of the Roman Empire it faced questions regarding the continuing value of traditional Jewish holy texts. Reconciling the beliefs of a new religion with the texts of an older one often required reading with a pre-established agenda, an interpretive practice which often did great violence to the stories by divorcing them from their historical and cultural context, silencing their polyphony in the interests of promoting a single meaning. Both the mechanics and effects of this practice are particularly evident in the interpretations and retellings of the story of David and Saul.

The story of David and Saul found in I Samuel is a complex composition. It is the story of a successful young man who is first embraced, then feared, then hunted by an aging and ineffectual king. This kind of story has been told throughout time and around the globe, usually during periods of political, social, or cultural turmoil. It is told in a variety of medieval English

texts: Hereward the Wake battles William the Conqueror at Ely; Fouke le
fitz Waryn confronts King John on the Welsh march; Robin Hood fights
the sheriff of Nottingham in Sherwood.[3] But while these stories exist on,
find their audience in, and take their meaning from the geographical and
cultural margins, the story of David and Saul resides at the center, preserved and reproduced in religiously and culturally authoritative texts. The
interests and values of the center, however, are potentially at odds with the
tales told at the margin. The outlaw story, for instance, is characterized by
elements which transgress established values and challenge those structures of authority which define the center: like his cousin the trickster, the
outlaw frequently inverts situations, plays semiotic games, turns hierarchies upside down, breaks taboos, endorses a pragmatic ethics, and
employs disguise.[4] But unlike the more mythic and anarchic trickster, the
outlaw is rooted in a particular time and place, and his transgressions
reflect the values and desires of a specific community. Thus the outlaw's
story appeals to an audience sympathetic to his goals: dispossessed Anglo-
Saxons in Cambridgeshire, barons of the Welsh March, or the rural gentry
of northern England. The story of David and Saul, however, was radically
removed from its point of origin, and medieval people encountered it not
as they did the "rymes of Robyn Hood," but as a religiously privileged
text.[5] Met in this context, the story of the outlaw presented an exegetical
challenge to readers and writers looking for a moral lesson or a secret spiritual meaning.

Medieval readers of Hebrew Scripture found two characters who could
easily be represented as outlaws and vilified: Satan and Cain. Satan was
imagined as an embodiment of evil who, in the apocryphal story of the Fall
of the Angels, fought a literal war with God.[6] Guilty of pride, treachery, and
mounting a primordial rebellion, he fails to inspire any sympathy. Medieval
literature knows nothing of the sort of characterization and motivation which
in Milton's *Paradise Lost* might inspire forbearance for Satan. Cain, however, as a human being is potentially sympathetic: his offering is rejected for
no preestablished reason, and he acts violently out of anger and frustration.
But although God is moved to be merciful with him, medieval Christian
exegetes were not, and Cain became a despondent wanderer and the progen-
itor of monsters.[7] David, however, presents a different problem. He is much
more like Robin Hood, a character whose guiding principle is to be admired,
even if certain of his actions are morally questionable. Medieval texts offer
two solutions to his problem, both with incarnations in fourteenth-century
England: typological exegesis, which appears in commentaries and devotional texts; and literal paraphrase, which has its origin in the *Historia
Scholastica* of Peter Comestor, and which is frequently employed in historical works. Each of these, in turn, has its own particular implications for the
representation of Jews and the uses of Jewish history.

The earliest Christians, of course, were Jews, and they continued to treat the Hebrew Scriptures as sacred texts. There is evidence already, however, in the Christian Bible that questions regarding the value of the Hebrew texts arose during the apostolic period as the new religion spread to the gentile population of the Mediterranean. The Acts of Apostles 16 and 21, Romans 3 and 14, and Galatians 3, 4, and 5 all describe conflicts regarding the value of circumcision and keeping the Jewish festivals and dietary laws; and II Timothy 3:16 iterates the continuing value of Hebrew Scripture: "All scripture is inspired by God and useful for teaching, rebuke, correction, and training in righteousness."[8] However, these writings were questioned in the second century. Some gentile Christians adopted a supersessionist position, arguing that the teachings of Jesus defined Christianity and made Hebrew Scripture and its law unnecessary. Marcion, denounced as a heretic, considered Hebrew Scripture obsolete and irreconcilable with the new gospel of Jesus Christ, but orthodoxy too struggled with the significance of the texts.[9] Two hundred years later, Augustine still felt the need to respond to these objections, though he imagined the question coming from Jewish critics of Christians: "For they say to us: 'Why do you read the law and the prophets when you do not want to follow the rules in them?' "[10]

Augustine's answer follows an exegetical practice patterned on the letters of Saint Paul, who had read events from Genesis, Exodus, and Numbers as typological anticipations of the Christ.[11] This led to the compilation of long catalogs of christological typology in Hebrew Scripture, and eventually to the elaborate allegorical readings of Clement, Origen, and the Alexandrian school. It also led to readings which interpreted the prophetic promises of the Scriptures as applicable to the Church, while prophetic criticism was applied to the Jews.[12] Although some of the more extravagant results of allegorical method were curtailed by the more sober historical and philological scholarship of the Antiochene school and its follower Jerome, and extremes of both schools were condemned by the Fifth Council of Constantinople in 553, this interpretive tool continued to be wielded throughout the Middle Ages. Nevertheless, the practice had the effect of divorcing biblical Jews from history and figuratively converting them to Christianity. As Stephen Wilson notes regarding Marcion's split with orthodoxy over Hebrew Scripture, "The one involved a radical break which left Judaism for the Jews; the other took what it wanted and, in effect, left nothing for the Jews. Or, to exaggerate a little, the one attacked the symbols but left the people alone; the other took the symbols and attacked the people" (Wilson, 58).

Yet Christianity couldn't leave Hebrew Scripture alone because these texts gave Christianity a claim to historical authority. During the first centuries of the Common Era, the Greco-Roman culture of the Mediterranean valued antiquity as an indication of authority and legitimacy. Such pressure impelled Flavius Josephus to write his *Jewish Antiquities* as a defense of

Jewish religion to skeptical Greeks. Similar criticisms were directed against Christianity, which had no such historical authority, and Christians responded by adopting Jewish antiquity as their own.[13] Typological hermeneutics itself exposes this desire, for the practice of reading Hebrew Scripture in order to find an already recognized meaning attributes no significant value to the narrative.[14] In a sense it does not matter what the Old Testament says, only that it is old. Because it is old, it provides Christianity with a usable past; because it can be interpreted to prophetically anticipate Christ, it simultaneously authorizes the Church and negates the Synagogue.

In introducing the story of David and its reception in European culture, Raymond-Jean Frontain and Jan Wojcik note that

> David's life . . . is crowded with more experiences than all the patriarchs' together, and in that mass of experience are so many contradictions that no easy statement can be made about him. Readers the first 2,000 years were so confused and even frightened by the mutivariousness of this hero, and by the implications of his experience, that they consistently tried to reduce him to a single meaning;[15]

The multivariousness of David is due in part to the composition of I Samuel 16 to 31, where David's rise to kingship is described. Biblical scholars describe at least three levels of composition for this text. The first was identified by Leonhard Rost as "The Rise of David Narrative," one of the earliest elements of the Davidic materials preserved in the Hebrew Bible, perhaps dating from the reign of David himself.[16] This material was combined at a later date with materials relating to the reign of Saul into a continuous narrative with a distinctly anti-monarchist orientation. Finally, this history of the kings of Israel was employed in turn by the so-called Deuteronomist, who assembled the current Scriptural text from Joshua through II Kings.[17]

Originating as it does in a period of political transition, the composition of the "Rise of David Narrative" is subject to disparate and conflicting values. A product of David's reign, it is sympathetic to him and opposed to the deposed dynasty of Saul. And like many medieval outlaw stories, it criticizes Saul as king but is supportive of monarchy as a divinely authorized institution.[18] However, the latter two layers of editing have worked the material into a larger story which criticizes the Israelite experiment with monarchy from a theocratic perspective. Needless to say, this complexity presented problems for anyone seeking a unified meaning of plot or character in the narrative.

In contrast, the Middle Ages preferred to recognize David as an exemplary poet, warrior, and king. The fourteenth-century *Alliterative Morte Arthure* gives a synopsis of these attributes in its description of David as a member of the Nine Worthies:

> The sexte was Dauid þe dere, demyd with kynges
> One of þe doughtyeste þat dubbede was euer;
> For he slewe with a slynge, be sleyghte of his handis,
> Golyas the grette gome, grymmeste in erthe,
> Syne endittede in his dayes all the dere psalmes,
> Þat in þe sawtire ere sette with selcouthe wordes.[19]

Thanks to their frequent role in the Christian liturgy, the Psalms were more often encountered than other texts of Hebrew Scripture, and it is as psalmist that David survives in most medieval literature. Of the eighteen references to him in Chaucer's poetry, fourteen introduce quotes from the Psalms, and Langland's proportion in *Piers Plowman* is eighteen of twenty-three. Nevertheless, incidents from the "Rise of David Narrative" and the rest of the Davidic material were also popular in the Middle Ages. Several events were, in fact, connected with specific psalms, and were frequently used to illuminate initials in Psalters: the fight with Goliath, as suggested by the quote from the *Alliterative Morte Arthure*, enjoyed special popularity and was frequently connected with Psalm 144 (Vulgate 143); Psalm 34 (33) was identified with David's visit to the city of Achish; Psalm 52 (51) with the slaughter of Achimelech and the priests of Nob; Psalm 54 (53) with David's flight into the Wilderness of Ziph; Psalm 59 (58) with his escape from his house; and Psalms 57 (56) and 142 (141) with the cave of Odallum.[20] In fourteenth-century England, Chaucer refers to the fight with Goliath in the *Man of Law's Tale* as an example of God's strength granted to the weak, and he includes Abigail, who turns David's wrath away from her husband, in lists of wise wives in both the *Merchant's Tale* and the *Tale of Melibee*.[21]

In his account of medieval illustrations of the Hebrew Bible, M. R. James noted that the David cycle was second only to Genesis in popularity.[22] The earliest of these cycles to survive, though only in fragments, is in the fourth-century Quedlinburg Itala manuscript (Berlin, Staatsbibliothek, Cod. Theol. Lat. fol. 485), while others appear on the doors of the basilica of St. Ambrose in Milan, a set of Cyprian plates, and a series of frescoes at Bawît.[23] Later extensive cycles juxtaposing the lives of David and Joseph are found on a casket at Sens Cathedral (tenth or eleventh century) and a marble screen in Naples Cathedral (eleventh century). Another casket at the Palazzo Venezia in Rome has scenes of David's life alone. Illustrated cycles also appear in English psalters, first in the Tiberius Psalter, and later in the Queen Mary Psalter; extensively in the Tickhill Psalter; and, in northern France, elaborately in the so-called Morgan Miniatures.[24] In the thirteenth and fourteenth centuries, cycles of illustrations appear in the *Bible Moralisée* and, with less scope, in the *Biblia Pauperum* and the *Speculum Humanae Salvationis*.[25]

The "Rise of David Narrative" is also retold in medieval written narrative, including commentaries, sermons, universal histories, and biblical paraphrases. The literature is substantial and includes several major pieces of Middle English religious literature, among them the *Cursor Mundi*, William Caxton's translation of the *Legenda Aurea*, and the *Mirror of Man's Salvation*.[26] However, the most interesting text for our purposes is a fourteenth-century poem with the ungainly title of the *Middle English Metrical Paraphrase of the Old Testament*. One of the more ambitious pieces of medieval English writing, the *Metrical Paraphrase* consists of 1,531 twelve-line stanzas, covering Genesis, Exodus, Numbers, Joshua, Judges, Ruth, I and II Samuel, I and II Kings, Jonah, Job, Tobit, Ester, Judith, and selections from II Chronicles and II Maccabbees.[27]

These two sets of texts respond both typologically and historically to what can be called the outlaw elements in the David story: inversions of situations and hierarchies, incidents of disguise, broken taboos, and ethics of self-interest. Typology, the practice to which Frontain and Wojcik refer when they note attempts to "reduce [David] to a single meaning," when applied to David and Saul led to a transformation of the outlaw narrative in which the historical and political rebellion of I Samuel was rewritten as a spiritual revolution: the outlawed David who overthrows the dynasty of Saul becomes the outlawed Christ, champion of grace, who overthrows the dispensation of the Jews and the tyranny of Mosaic law. That is, the rebellion of the outlaw against a literal and historical king is transferred symbolically to a socially and religiously acceptable target, the Jewish religion perceived as a form of tyranny. This is the strategy which dominates texts concerned with elaborating the spiritual meaning of Scripture: the visual depictions of the David cycle found in Psalters, the devotionally oriented *Mirour* and *Bible Moralisée*, and many medieval commentaries on I Samuel and the Psalms. It is also included in the *Cursor Mundi*, but in the apocryphal additions rather than the paraphrase of the canonical text itself.[28]

In contrast, the *Metrical Paraphrase* follows the second method, one established by Peter Comestor in his *Historia Scholastica*, which emphasizes the literal and moral levels of the story. Rather than transferring the outlaw elements to a more acceptable level of meaning, this narrative approach allows the most innocuous to stand, while ignoring, hiding, or recontextualizing the more disturbing. But although this literal or historical method might appear to offer a more generous treatment of the Jews in its choices about how to represent the text for a fourteenth-century audience, the *Metrical Paraphrase* ends up erasing much that is distinctly Jewish.

The introductory stanzas of the *Metrical Paraphrase* give an introduction to the poet's project which shows that he is well aware of traditional Christian concerns about the value and meaning of Hebrew Scripture. He begins by invoking the Father, Son, Holy Ghost, and Virgin Mary to aid his composition, "Begynnyng, myddes, and end, / that yt be to goddes pay" (ll.11–12), and proceeds to describe his purpose:

> This buke is of grett degre,
>> Os all wettys that ben wyse,
> ffor of the bybyll sall yt be
>> The poyntes that ar mad most in price,
> Als maysters of dyuinite
>> And on, the maystur of storyse,
> ffor sympyll men soyn forto se,
>> Settes yt þus in this schort assyse;
> And in moyr schort maner
>> Is my mynd forto make yt,
> That men may lyghtly leyre
>> to tell and vnder take yt. (ll. 13–24)

The "maystur of storyse" is, of course, Peter Comestor, the thirteenth-century professor at the University of Paris who compiled his *Historia Scholastica* from the Hebrew Scripture, Josephus, classical history, and other sources.[29] But the poet's purpose is really not the same as Peter's, for the *Historia Scholastica* does not just retell the "poyntes that ar mad most in price," but rather supplements the biblical narrative with apocryphal material, etymological analysis, and explanatory comment. In contrast, the *Metrical Paraphrase* prefers story to commentary, and sticks more closely to the biblical text, elaborating in order to add drama and detail.

In the third stanza of his introduction, however, the poet feels the need to defend the value of these stories:

> This boke that is the bybyll cald,
>> And all that owtt of yt is drawn,
> ffor holy wrytt we sall yt hald
>> And honour yt euer os our awn;
> All patriarkes and prophettes yt told,
>> So euer þer saynges sekerly ar knawn,
> And all wer fygurs fayr to fald
>> How coymmyng of crist my3t be kawn.
> God graunt vs crist to knaw
>> All our form faders crauyd
> And so to lere is law
>> That our sawlis may be sauyd. (ll. 25–36)

By "the bybyll" the author here means Hebrew Scripture, for he contrasts it with the gospels in line four, "our awn" holy writ, but concludes that both are to be "honoured." This is an argument drawn directly from the II Timothy text cited above, and it expresses the same concern regarding the value of the Hebrew Scripture for Christians. Like the early Christians, the poet finds an answer in typology, a practice to which he alludes when he claims that these characters "all wer fygurs fayr to fald / How coymmyng of crist myg3t be kawn." But despite locating this value in the Hebrew Bible, the poet concludes the stanza with a prayer that clarifies the incompleteness of this metaphorical revelation: May God allow us to know Christ, all that our former fathers desired, and to learn his law so that our souls might be saved. That is, reading the Jewish text may enable Christians to know Christ better because they have already encountered him through the gospels, yet these same texts were insufficient for the Hebrews, "our form faders," who could only desire the Christ. Here succinctly stated is the complex attitude toward Hebrew scripture and the Jews which Jeremy Cohen finds in in Raymond Martini's *Pugio fidei* and determines to be characteristic of later medieval Christian thought: the patriarchs of Hebrew tradition are the spiritual ancestors of Christians, but their story and faith are insufficient.[30] Salvation is attained through learning Christ's law, which commonly stands in contrast to the law of Moses known to the patriarchs, and to which Jews still cling.

One might well ask whether there are any Jews in the *Metrical Paraphrase*. The term itself shows up infrequently; the poet prefers "Ebrews" for the people ruled by Saul and David, but employs "jews" on occasion where it fits the alliteration: "A jew, jesse, of jacob kyn" (l. 5874), "Jesse, þat gentyll jew, he fand" (5883), and "þat day was joy to many jew" (6127). The poet uses the terms interchangeably where the Vulgate uses "Israhelitae" or "viri Israhel," but it is notable that these ethnic identifications show up almost exclusively in descriptions of battle where they are opposed to the "Phylysteyns." This is the difference which is of most interest to the poet, for there are two general categories of people: those who follow God's law and those who do not. Many of the "Ebrews" do; the "Phylysteyns" do not. After Saul is defeated at the battle of Mt. Gilboa, the Philistines celebrate by worshipping their "mawmentes," and by offering Saul's armor to their god, "Astrott."

A distinct Hebrew or Jewish identity, however, suffers from the same sort of anachronistic medievalizing that characterizes Chaucer's *Troilus and Criseyde* and *Knight's Tale*. Rather than typologizing, the poet of the *Metrical Paraphrase* converts the Jews by augmenting the biblical text with elements of romance. The Hebrew warriors address each other as "ser," and medieval titles are attached to ancient Israelite characters: "bishop" Abimelech and "Duke" Abner. Saul's army is identified as "chevalry"; David and his men are "knyghts"; and stock romance phrases like "in ylke feld he bare þe flour" (l. 6184) describe biblical events. Occasionally a whole descriptive passage is inserted. The account of the siege of Keilah, for instance, is enhanced with a stanza which might be applied to any medieval military campaign:

> Now in þis meyn tyme herd þei tell
> > with folke þat ferd þore to and fray
> how the phylysteyns, fers and fell,
> > in seged a cyte þat heght Ceilay,
> And how þei made maystrays o mell
> > and sayd þat þei suld bryn and slay
> Ebrews þat in þat Cete dwell
> > and all þer thresour to þem ta.
> Þei brynt and wold not blyn
> > a bowt both lenh and brede.
> Þen þei þat ware with in
> > lyfed in grett dole and drede. (6505–16)

These additions may have the effect of making the actions of the plot more comprehensible to fourteenth-century English Christians, but they also erase the historical identity of the characters. Unlike the characters of Chaucer's *Knight's Tale*, who are similarly medievalized, but get to retain their religious practices of praying to Mars, Venus, and Athena, the Hebrews of the *Metrical Paraphrase* lose the few distinctly Jewish religious practices cited in I Samuel in favor of a generalized devotion to the law of God. The books of the law, Leviticus and Deuteronomy, are excised in the interest of story, but so are many smaller details. In I Samuel 23:6–12, for instance, David calls Abiathar the priest to bring the *ephod*, an instrument of divination, in order to seek Yahweh's advice, but in the *Metrical Paraphrase* this becomes a simple prayer uttered directly by David (6517–20). The consecrated bread which Abimelech offers to David in I Samuel 21:4 loses much of its significance, as the proscription against sexual impurity which accompanies it is ignored in the paraphrase. Even David's grotesque circumcision of one hundred Philistines killed in battle in I Samuel 18:27 is replaced by the presentation of one hundred heads as a dowry for Saul's daughter Michal. Here the poet follows Josephus and the tradition of biblical illustration rather than the *Historia Scholastica* or the Vulgate, which specifies *praeputia* rather than *capita*.[31] While the poet may be consciously using "heads" euphemistically, his choice of words, and the choice of most other texts to ignore the episode, exhibits the same revulsion found in the *Dialogus de Altercatione Ecclesiae et Synagogae*: "Her sign of election, circumcision, is itself disgraceful, for it signs an organ which must be covered and is used only for shameful deeds, while the Christian is chastely signed on the forehead."[32] Though the *Metrical Paraphrase* does not go so far as to make the Philistines into Saracens as the *Cursor Mundi* does,[33] there is little to distinguish the men of I Samuel from Christian knights.

These romance conventions complicate the presence of many of the outlaw elements in the story of David and Saul, for the codes of behavior of the knight and the outlaw are often at odds. The story of David opens with an inversion of expectations, and elevation of the weak in the choice of the new king. The biblical text makes a point of contrasting Yahweh's judgment with Samuel's as all the sons of Jesse are brought forward and all are rejected. Though the prophet is impressed by stature and appearance, Jesse is forced to call in the youngest son who had been left to guard the flocks before the prophet finds his man. The *Cursor Mundi* neglects the dramatic potential in this scene and the thematic emphasis which comes with it by having the Lord tell Samuel,

> "Þe yongest is he þat I neven
> Boþe wis hende [and] of good fame
> David he hette bi his name." (Trinity, ll. 7368–70)

When he goes to the home of Jesse, the prophet then walks right by the six older sons and asks for David. The *Metrical Paraphrase*, on the other hand, not only follows the biblical account closely with regard to the selection process, but adds a dinner scene in which David is seated on one side of Samuel, and Jesse and his other sons are seated on the other "ylkon in þer degree" (5915). Thus the poem reiterates the disruption that David causes to the order of things.

The triumph of the weak is most notable and probably most acceptable in the story of David's fight with Goliath. Chaucer, for instance, uses the event for just such a purpose in the *Man of Law's Tale* when he compares the plight of Custance to that of David (ll. 932–38). The narrative emphasizes both David's youth and inexperience and the Philistine's size and equipment. He defeats Goliath with a creative strategy when he rejects Saul's offer of weapons and armor and chooses the sling and stones. The enemy is monstrous and already demonized, so it is no surprise that Goliath is read as a type of the devil, and the whole story connected with the temptation of Christ in the wilderness. Thus the *Mirour* summarizes: "And that Crist temptid of pride the feend ouercomen was, / Prefigured Dauid sometyme when he slew Golias" (1577–78).[34]

But there is even more to the story than this. David also employs the challenging and potentially insulting questions that are common to the outlaw in order to expose the weaknesses in the status quo. Arriving in the Israelite camp with supplies for his brothers, David probes the fearful soldiers: "What will be given to the man who kills this Philistine, and takes away the disgrace from Israel? For who is this uncircumcised Philistine who challenges the armies of the living God?" (17: 26).[35] The question is, of course, a reproach to the Israelite soldiers as well as to Goliath. If one is fighting for the living God, why should one fear the enemy? And furthermore, why should one need the additional impetus of a monetary reward?

David's brother recognizes this challenge from his younger sibling and becomes angry with him. David responds that it was "only a question," but it is question which calls into question the behavior of the powerful.

This may not appear to be a particularly disturbing challenge to authority, but the *Cursor Mundi* ignores the conversation completely, allowing David to hear Saul's lament and promise of a reward directly, and to immediately offer his service to the king. Perhaps this can be attributed to a desire to streamline the narrative and get on with the action of killing the giant. On the other hand, the *Metrical Paraphrase* includes a brief interaction between David and his brothers, but without any hint of reproach or antagonism.[36] But if the paraphrases choose to ignore the scene, the exegetes foreground it. Caesarius of Arles, for instance, asserts the common paradigm for typologically reproducing the story of David for a medieval Christian audience. "That older brother," he writes, "who rebuked David, the type of Christ, in a display of malice, signifies the people of Judea, who out of envy slandered the Lord Christ, who came for the salvation of humankind, and they frequently caused many injuries."[37] This reading not only deletes the irritating questions and provocation of the story, preferring to acknowledge only David's victory over the giant, but also transfers the outlaw narrative to a more acceptable theater of conflict.

I Samuel 19 describes a rather more disturbing transgression, one with clear associations with the carnivalesque images and practices identified by Mikhail Bahktin.[38] Fleeing from Saul, David goes to Samuel in the town of Ramah, a community of prophets. When Saul hears of this, he sends three rounds of soldiers to capture David. However, each group in turn is overcome by the spirit of God and falls into a prophetic frenzy. Finally, Saul himself goes to Ramah, where he too falls into a frenzy, strips off his clothes, and lies "naked all that day and all that night" (19:24). Here is a striking inversion: the king writhing naked on the ground in ecstasy. While such behavior might be comprehensible in a culture which combines religious and secular authority, here it aims at showing Saul's subjection to a power of a different order. In fact, Julius Wellhausen argues that this episode was not in the earliest versions of the "Rise of David Narrative," but was added later by the theocratically inclined Deuteronomist editor who was distrustful of the institution of monarchy.[39] Because he does not respect the interests of Yahweh as conveyed by the priests, Saul is stripped of his power to command, to act, and perhaps even to reason.

Such a critique of monarchy disturbed the medieval imagination, or at least the imaginations of those at the centers of political and cultural power, and the image of the naked and ecstatic Saul is not to be found in the *Historia Scholastica*, *Cursor Mundi*, or *Metrical Paraphrase*, although all three describe the soldiers sent by Saul being overcome. Only Caxton's *Golden Legend* includes the king: "And he prophesied when he came also, and took off his clothes and was naked all that day and night before Samuel" (2.18). Visual artists, on the other hand, appear to be less squeamish. The Morgan Miniatures show a group of knights throwing down their weapons and waving their arms in ecstasy as the spirit of God descends between them and the priests, and in the next panel Saul drops his crown and begins to pull off his clothes (f. 31r and 31v). The Tickhill Psalter pushes this a step farther, depicting Saul naked, crownless, and seated among fully clothed prophets, a scene which appears to amplify rather than occlude the carnivalesque inversion (f. 25v and 26r).

As Wellhausen shows, the subjection of the king to the power of Yahweh and his intermediary, the prophet Samuel, would have a clear appeal to the Deuteronomist and his theocratic politics, but it is more difficult to understand its appeal to the creators of medieval biblical illustrations. Perhaps it is merely the visual drama of the scene which is attractive, but two other possibilities occur to me. First, the image of Saul dropping his crown and removing his clothing contains hints of the iconography of Synagoga in medieval illustrations of the crucifixion. Often in these scenes, the deposed Synagoga is shown with a broken staff, a fallen crown, and her robe in disarray, while Ecclesia assumes the throne and attributes of royal power.[40] This corresponds with the typological reading of the transfer of kingship from Saul's to David's family as the transference of God's favor from Jews to Christians. Bede, for example, writes his controlling idea in the introductory comments to the third book of his commentary on I Samuel: "David anointed king instead of Saul signifies the reign of the Jews that was changed by law to the reign of Christ and the Church."[41] It is also possible to find a rationale in the nature of the audience for deluxe illustrated psalters as opposed to narrative poems. The former were often produced for royalty, and showing a naked king to a reigning king might have served as a moral warning, like the falling figure designated "regnavi" ("I have reigned") in pictures of the Wheel of Fortune. On the other hand, describing a king naked and out of his mind to the lower clergy, students, or gentry who made up the audience for the *Historia Scholastica*, the *Metrical Paraphrase* or *Cursor Mundi* might incite disrespect or insurrection.

Outlaws are commonly masters of disguise and deception, employing them for self-preservation, to discomfit the powerful, and to expose the hypocritical. David uses these tools almost exclusively for the first of these causes. In I Samuel 19:11–18, Saul sends his soldiers to David's house to kill him, but Michal, Saul's daughter and David's wife, warns him and helps him to escape out of a window.[42] She then places an idol in his bed, puts some goat's hair on its head, and covers it with a blanket. The ruse delays the soldiers long enough for David to escape. Now if you were like me, you asked your Sunday School teacher what David was doing with an idol in his house when this was strictly forbidden in the Ten Commandments. "It must have belonged to Michal," was my teacher's response. This answer deflects the transgression from our hero, but no more so than the footnotes in many modern Bibles which inform us that the nature of the *teraphim* is obscure or the medieval retellings which sanitized the episode.[43]

The *Cursor Mundi* turns this whole incident into a simple escape: "But his wif bi nygt him oute lette / Out at a prive posterne" (Trinity, 7674–75). In contrast, the *Metrical Paraphrase*, which plays up the romance between Michal and David, takes advantage of the potential here. When Michal is first introduced, her love for David is elaborated beyond the biblical precedent and along the lines of medieval lovesickness:

> And mycoll, þe kynges doyghtur dere,
> David hyr hert all holy hade.
> When he was moved to make yll chere,
> no myrth on mold mygt make hyr glad.
> And when þe pepyll hym plessed,
> and scho hys conforth kend,
> yf oþer had hyr dys[pl]essyd,
> þat medcyn moght amend. (6197–204)

And when the troubled Saul hurls his spear at David, it is Michal's cry of warning which prevents him from being harmed. When she learns that Saul's men are lying at wait at the door, she urges David to flee "For bettur is þou lyfe and lende / þen [þat] we both to dede be dygt" (6307–308). There is no threat to her person in I Samuel; rather it is a detail added to emphasize the romantic passion, and perhaps to provide an excuse for David to flee rather than stand up to his enemy in this case. She persists cleverly with the deception of the soldiers, though here the *teraphim* (*statuam* in the Vulgate) becomes "a dry stoke" and later "a mekyll tree," and thus less problematic.

In I Samuel 21:11–16, David puts on his own disguise in order to effect an escape. In Gath in the court of King Achish, David begins to fear for his life and pretends to be mad: "He changed his appearance in their presence and feigned madness while in their hands. He beat upon the doors of the gate and let the spittle run down his beard."[44] Like the ecstatic prophecy of Saul, this scene is ignored by all three of the narrative texts, though it seems to have been popular with visual artists. The *Cursor* and *Golden Legend* say nothing of it, and the *Metrical Paraphrase* passes over this incident (and nothing else) with the lines

> yt ware long tyme to tell
> how [he] lys cowrse kest
> And what ferlys be fell
> or he was broygt to rest (6489–492)

In contrast, this incident provided no trouble for the allegorical exegetes: David's mad behavior was read as a precursor of the Christ's incarnation, for just as David hid his identity from Achish, so Jesus hid his divinity from the Devil and the Jews.[45] This behavior, however, may have struck the romance reader as unchivalrous and even cowardly, and certainly at odds with the bold and powerful David that the *Cursor* and *Metrical Paraphrase* take pains to emphasize.[46]

While these transgressions are largely symbolic, the narrative moves on to more morally disturbing actions by David. Perhaps the chief of these is David's treatment of Ahimelech and the priests at Nob. Running from Saul in I Samuel 21, David comes to Nob looking for help, but he lies to Ahimelech about being on a mission from the king and convinces the priest to hand over the consecrated bread and the sword of Goliath. Putting the sacred bread to a common and pragmatic use is a behavior typical of the outlaw, but more damaging here is the deception of Ahimelech, which leads to the slaughter of the whole city when Saul hears that they have aided David.[47]

The *Cursor Mundi* has nothing to say of this, moving directly on to the two episodes where David spared Saul's life, and then Saul's death. The *Metrical Paraphrase* includes the scene and David's lie, but the business of the sacred bread is played down. Later, when David learns of the slaughter he laments, "alas / þat folke for me ar dede!" While there is clearly regret here, it is ambiguous as a recognition of guilt. Does he mean "these folk have died for my sake" or "these folk are dead on account of my actions"? The Vulgate is much less ambiguous, though perhaps no more encouraging: "I knew on that day that when Doeg the Idumaean was there that he would declare it to Saul. I stand accused of the souls of all your fathers."[48] Here David admits guilt, but also a prior knowledge that might have saved the priests.

Christian exegetes enjoyed a gospel precedent for excusing David's profane consumption of sacred bread: in Mark 2:23–28, Jesus is admonished by the Pharisees when his men pluck and eat grain on the Sabbath, but he responds by citing the example of David. They are more cagey, however, about the deception of the priest. Rather, they are quick to point fingers at Doeg and Saul as the guilty parties and to overlook David's self-interested behavior. "Necessitas non habet legem [necessity has no law]," notes Peter Comestor with respect to David's consumption of the consecrated bread, but the phrase might just as well apply to David's lie as well.[49]

A second episode, in I Samuel 25, involves David in behavior more typical of a fourteenth-century outlaw. While living near Carmel, David sends some young men to demand that a wealthy local man, Nabal, give them some of his livestock. Nabal refuses and David angrily determines to ride into his camp and slaughter everyone. His plan is prevented, however, when Nabal's wife, Abigail, intercepts him on the road and offers him gifts. When he hears what his wife has done, Nabal suffers a stroke and dies, enabling David to marry Abigail and claim all the property.

Nabal's name means "fool" in Hebrew, and this fact combined with David's marriage to Abigail encouraged typologically oriented exegetes to read the story as an account of the transmission of God's favor from the Jews to the Christians. Rhabanus Maurus, who commonly summarizes popular commentaries, writes: "For Nabal, about whom it is said that he was an obstinate, most noxious, and malicious man, is a type of the people of the Jews. . . . In fact, Abigail, about whom scripture reports that she was a most prudent and beautiful woman, is a type of those folk who endeavored to please God by conversion from the Jews to the faith."[50] In this rewriting of the story, the Jews are foolish because they do not recognize Jesus as the Messiah and so they forfeit their property to the Church.

The *Metrical Paraphrase* attempts to deflect any criticism of David from the beginning by defining the religious status of Nabal and describing the rationale for David's action. The Vulgate characterizes Nabal as "pessimus et malitiosus" and Abigail as "prudentissima et speciosa," but the English poet asserts that Nabal "lyfed not by þe law / of moyses and Iosue" (6803–804), a detail at odds with the Bible's identification of the man as a Calebite of the tribe of Judah, and that Abigail "wrschept god in all hyr lyfe / and at hyr mygt mayntened his lay" (6811–12). Having thus established a conflict along the lines of his usual dichotomy, the poet proceeds to establish David's cause for intervention:

> David oft with hyrdes mett
> > And mayntend þem als his menege.
> Wyld wulfes and lyons oft he lett
> > to do dysese to Naball fee.
> All yf his fod was ferre to fett,
> > No thyng unto rewll take wold hee. (6819–24)

This information is taken from I Samuel, but there it does not come until David's irate response to Nabal's refusal: "Truly, all this is pointless which I have done to preserve this man's property in the desert so that nothing whatsoever was lost, for he returned me evil for good."[51] But by moving this material forward in the story, the poet not only builds early sympathy for David, but also preempts Nabal's counterargument. When David's men present their request, Nabal

> sayd þei suld be schamed and schent
> > As felons þat ar fayn to flee.
> "He is þe kynges enmy
> > And hath full wekydly wroygt." (6847–50)

This is a legitimate and law-abiding response. The maintenance of felons was a major legal issue in fourteenth-century England and the practice had been specifically proscribed in law codes since the eleventh century.[52] What is more, the poem has shown the potential result of offering aid to David two hundred lines earlier, where Saul slays Ahimelech and the priests of Nob. Nabal seems hardly the fool that his name suggests. However, by insisting that David has first "mayntend" Nabal's shepherds, the poet reverses the relative positions of the parties, making David's action risky and generous while emphasizing Nabal's parsimony and ingratitude. As a result, when David benefits from Nabal's death by taking his property, he appears to be claiming his right as lord rather than taking advantage of opportunity as an outlaw.

While the Middle English poems show a regular pattern of hiding or dismissing many of the outlaw elements in the "Rise of David Narrative," they, like the pictorial sequences, embrace the two episodes where David has the opportunity to kill Saul but refuses to press his advantage. In the first of these, narrated in I Samuel 24, Saul enters a cave at Odallum to relieve himself. David has taken refuge in the same cave, and his men urge him to seize the opportunity to kill Saul and claim the throne. David refuses but cuts the hem from Saul's robe and then confronts him with the evidence after he has left the cave. In I Samuel 26, in a similar incident David slips into Saul's camp past sleeping guards, but again rebukes the companion who offers to kill Saul, and takes away a spear and drinking cup instead. Once again Saul is abashed by David's mercy when he is shown the evidence.

The *Metrical Paraphrase* narrates the events at Odallum tersely, but with a few significant changes in detail. When David's men urge him to seize the opportunity and kill Saul, David responds, "god forbede! / he is A kyng enoynt" (6741–42). This is a more general ethical pronouncement than what is found in the Vulgate: "I will not set my hand against him because he is the anointed one of God" (I Samuel 24: 7). Because the medieval reader may have considered all kings to be anointed by God and thus to be respected, the writer makes it explicit that David will not raise his hand against any king, not only Yahweh's anointed king.

The poet also alters the ending of the episode, apparently in an attempt to turn the episode into a full military confrontation:

> [Saul] saw David was well Arayd
> > With feyghyng folke full fayre in fere
> And toygt, yf he to batell brayde,
> > Who so suld wyn wrschepe wore in were.
> Þerfor all sothly þus he sayd,
> > "David, þis ded þou hath done here

>   And þi grett meknese made me payde;
>   I grawntt þe peyse be my powere. (6769–76)

The details here concerning the strength of David's army are not only not found in the Vulgate, but they stand in contrast to the earlier explanation for David's presence in the cave:

>   And David durst not well abyd;
>   So ware þe kynges folke ferly fele.
>   Under A hyll he con hym hyde
>   In a depe hole to hald his hele `
>   So þat þe kyng suld passe be syd,
>   And noþer suld with oþer dele. (6723–28)

The added material suggests that David has the opportunity for an upfront military victory, not just a covert assassination. This has the dual purpose of doubling David's generosity and portraying him as a noble warrior and vassal, not merely an outlaw in the bushes.[53]

In analyzing the nature of the trickster figure, Karl Kerényi made some observations about how these characters change over time. His model can be usefully applied to the outlaw as well and the story of David in particular. Arguing that the "true" trickster can only function in an archaic social order, Kerényi writes that one of three transformations occurs when the figure is translated into a more mature culture: (1) the trickster is assimilated into the form of a cultural hero; (2) the trickster is transformed into a devil; (3) the ridiculous aspects of the trickster are emphasized, reducing the myth to entertainment.[54] The first two options result from a human penchant for binary simplicity—a reader/writer annihilates the characteristic ambiguity of the trickster by selecting to preserve only the creative (heroic) or destructive (demonic) aspects of the trickster. The third option preserves the ambiguity of the trickster but robs it of its seriousness by moving it into a context of pure play. In the case of David, the third option is ruled out because of the authoritative position occupied by the Bible in medieval Christian culture, so biblical outlaws must become either heroic or demonic. The behavior of Satan and Cain is destructive and any ambiguities are easily erased, but David is a more complex case. Although some of his behavior is destructive and disruptive, he is more easily reconciled with standard models of heroism. This is the work of the *Metrical Paraphrase*, which casts the Israelites of Hebrew Scripture as characters recognizable to fourteenth-century readers of romance. Thus David becomes a knight and lover, but ironically also less of a Jew.

It is notable that the typological texts often embrace what the historical try to hide. From the patristic age until the fourteenth century the outlaw ele-

ments which are aimed at structures of authority are retained but then translated through the interpretive process so that they apply to different characters and conflicts. This is the essence of the outlaw, a character whose story
grows up along a border of values. He or she champions an "us" against an
often more powerful "them." But if the "us" and "them" of the original historical context disappear, the outlaw can survive by being relocated to a new
border. So where the anti-monarchical agenda of the Deuteronomist found no
sympathetic audience in medieval Christendom, a new plot was found in the
desire of Christianity to define itself in opposition to its parent religion.
David's tricks and inversions and lies do not disturb the medieval status quo
when they are directed toward the Jews, just as William Wallace's do not
when they are aimed at the despised English, and Robin Hood's do not when
they are directed at a corrupt clergy and sheriff.

Both of these methods of rereading the story of David and Saul reveal
simultaneous desires: to embrace Hebrew Scripture as containing an historical narrative which is authentic and authoritative, and to rewrite that narrative
to make it more useful to the medieval Christian audience. At this point the
literary history of David and Saul and of the tales of Robin Hood and other
outlaws converge, for like David, Robin Hood has become an historically
authoritative figure whose story is invoked again and again for new uses.[55]
Like medieval readers who saw Christ in David, we may see a neo-pagan
environmentalist in Robin Hood, or a Reform Party populist in William Wallace. Despite our new values, we continue to tell old stories.

Notes

A different version of this essay was presented at the International Medieval
Congress, Kalamazoo, May 2001. My thanks to Norbert Wetherington for
assembling the panel, Sheila Delany for taking an interest in the essay, and
Murray Haar and Michelle Bartel for their advice.

1. On the events leading up to the expulsion of the Jews and its immediate effi-
    cacy, see Robin R. Mundill, *England's Jewish Solution: Experiment and
    Expulsion, 1262–1290* (Cambridge: Cambridge University Press, 1998).
2. See Joshua Trachtenberg, *The Devil and the Jews: The Medieval Conception
    of the Jew and Its Relation to Modern Anti-Semitism* (New Haven: Yale Uni-
    versity Press, 1943); and Ruth Mellinkoff, *Outcasts: Signs of Otherness in
    Northern European Art of the Late Middle Ages*, 2 vols. (Berkeley and Los
    Angeles: University of California Press, 1993), 1.41–43, 61–94, 127–29 and
    the corresponding illustrations in volume 2.
3. See Maurice Keen, *The Outlaws of Medieval Legend*, rev. ed. (London: Rout-
    ledge and Kegan Paul, 1987); Thomas Ohlgren, ed., *Medieval Outlaws: Ten
    Tales in Modern English* (Phoenix Mill: Sutton, 1998).
4. The trickster appears in folklore and mythology around the world. William
    Hynes has identified six features common to this figure: an ambiguous and
    anomalous personality, deceptive behavior, shape shifting, inversion of situa-

tions, imitation of the gods, and a mixture of sacred and lewd. See William J. Hynes and William G. Doty, eds., *Mythical Trickster Figures* (Athens: University of Georgia Press, 1993), 33–45.

5. The contrasting values of the outlaw story and biblical narrative are famously juxtaposed by William Langland in the confession of Sloth in *Piers Plowman*:

> I kan noght parfitly my Paternoster as the preest it syngeth,
> But I kan rymes of Robyn Hood and Randolf Erl of Chestre,
> Ac neither of Oure Lord ne of Oure Lady the leeste that ever was maked.
> (V.395–97)

(The Vision of Piers Plowman: A Critical Edition of the B-Text Based on Trinity College Cambridge Ms. B.15.17, ed. A. V. C. Schmidt, [2nd ed. London: Dent, 1995], 82).

6. The story of the Fall of Angels was pieced together by early Christian writers from a brief reference in Revelation 12:7–9 and figurative prophecies in Isaiah 14:12–15 and Ezekiel 28:2–19. The Book of Enoch offers a more developed narrative (*The Book of Enoch,* trans. Robert Henry Charles [1917; London: Society for the Preservation of Christian Knowledge, 1972]), while Augustine wrote a more theologically rigorous account in books 11 and 12 of *The City of God* (ed. and trans. John William Charles Wand [London: Oxford University Press, 1963]). For a description of related Middle English texts and their sources, see Rosemary Woolf, *The English Mystery Plays* (Berkeley and Los Angeles: University of California Press, 1972), 105–113.

7. Grendel is the most recognized product of this tradition, but the "kin of Cain" appear throughout medieval culture. See John Block Friedman, *The Monstrous Races in Medieval Art and Thought* (Cambridge, MA: Harvard University Press, 1981), 87–107; Ruth Mellinkoff, *The Mark of Cain* (Berkeley: University of California Press, 1981); Gilbert Dahan, "L'exégèse de l'histoire de Cain et Abel du XIIe au XIVe siècle en Occident. Notes et texte (à suivre)," *Recherches de Théologie ancienne et médiévale* 49 (1982), 21–89.

8. "omnis scriptura divinitus inspirata et utilis ad docendum ad arguendum ad corrigendum ad erudiendum in iustitia." All translations are my own unless otherwise indicated.

9. See Stephen G. Wilson, "Marcion and the Jews," *Anti-Judaism in Early Christianity: Vol. 2, Separation and Polemic,* Stephen G. Wilson, ed. (Waterloo: Canadian Corporation for Studies in Religion/Wilfrid Laurier University Press, 1986), 45–58. On Apostolic exegesis in general see Karlfried Froehlich, ed. and trans., *Biblical Interpretation in the Early Church* (Philadelphia: Fortress, 1984); and Richard N. Longenecker, *Biblical Exegesis in the Apostolic Period,* 2nd ed. (Vancouver: Regent College; Grand Rapids, MI: Wm. B. Eerdmans, 1999).

10. "Dicunt enim nobis, Quid apud vos facit lectio Legis et Prophetarum, cuius praecepta servare non vultis" (*Tractatus adversus Judaeos, Patrologia Cursus Completus, Series Latina [Patrologia Latina],* ed. J-P. Migne, 221 vols. [Paris, 1844–55], 42:52).

11. See, for example, Romans 5:14 and I Corinthians 10:1–22; on the development of patristic and medieval hermeneutics regarding the Old Testament, see

Henri de Lubac, *Medieval Exegesis: Volume 1, The Four Senses of Scripture*, trans. Mark Sebanc (Grand Rapids, MI: Wm. B. Eerdmans; Edinburgh: T & T Clark, 1998), 225–67.

12. See Rosemary Reuther, *Faith and Fratricide: The Theological Roots of Anti-Semitism* (New York: Seabury Press, 1974), 131–37. Reuther concludes that "possibly anti-Judaism is too deeply embedded in the foundations of Christianity to be rooted out entirely without destroying the whole structure" (228). The essays in Alan T. Davies, ed., *Antisemitism and the Foundations of Christianity* (New York: Paulist Press, 1979), provide a variety of responses to Reuther's argument. See especially John C. Meagher, "As the Twig Was Bent: Antisemitism in Greco-Roman and Earliest Christian Times," who critiques Reuther's overly unified picture of early Christianity; and Douglas R. A. Hare, "The Rejection of the Jews in the Synoptic Gospels and Acts," who locates several varieties of anti-Judaism in the triumphalist theology of the earliest Christian texts. This latter argument is made in greater detail by John Dominic Crossan, *Who Killed Jesus? Exposing the Roots of Anti-Semitism in the Gospel Story of the Death of Jesus* (San Francisco: HarperSanFrancisco, 1995).

13. James Parkes, *The Conflict of Church and Synagogue: A Study of the Origins of Antisemitism* (New York: Hermon, 1934), 97. Parkes cites as examples Tatian's address to the Greeks and Theophilus' letter to Autolycus.

14. David Lawton notes that this practice devalued the importance of a complete text: "The allegorical exegesis of the early fathers puts no premium on completeness. If the parts are in harmony, any can stand in the place of, or as well as, another" ("Englishing the Bible, 1066–1479" in *The Cambridge History of Medieval English Literature*, ed. David Wallace [Cambridge: Cambridge University Press, 1999], 456). See also A. J. Minnis et al., *Medieval Literary Theory and Criticism, c.1100–c.1375: The Commentary Tradition* (Oxford: Clarendon, 1988), 4.

15. Raymond-Jean Frontain and Jan Wojcik, eds., *The David Myth in Western Literature* (West Lafayette, IN: Purdue University Press, 1980), ix.

16. Leonhard Rost, *Die Überlieferung von der Thronnachfolge Davids*, Beiträge zur Wissenschaft vom alten und neuen Testament III.6 (Stuttgart: W. Kohlhammer, 1926).

17. See the summary of scholarship by P. Kyle McCarter, Jr. in the Introduction to *I Samuel: A New Translation with Introduction and Commentary*, Anchor Bible 8 (New York: Doubleday, 1980), 12–30.

18. Consider, for instance, the scene in the *Lytel Geste of Robyn Hood*, where Robin recognizes the disguised King Edward and agrees to enter his service, and together they march off to fight the corrupt sheriff (ed. R. B. Dobson and J. Taylor, *Rymes of Robyn Hood: An Introduction to the English Outlaw*, rev. ed. [Stroud: Sutton, 1997], 108–109).

19. *The Alliterative Morte Arthure: A Critical Edition*, ed. Valerie Krishna (New York: Burt Franklin & Co., 1976), ll. 3416–21.

20. Most commentaries on the Psalms made these connections. See, for instance, Augustine's *Enarrationes in Psalmos*, ed. A. Wilmart, *Corpus Christianorum, Series Latina (CCSL)*, 38–40 (Turnholt: Brepols, 1954). On the varieties of Psalter illustration, see John Jacob Tikkanen, *Die Psalterillustration in*

Mittelalter (1895–1900); Victor Leroquais, *Les Psautiers manuscrits latins les bibliotheques publiques de France*, 3 vols. (Macon: Protet frères, 1940–41); and Andrew Hughes, *Medieval Manuscripts for Mass and Office: A Guide to their Organization and Terminology* (Toronto: University of Toronto Press, 1982). On the insular Psalter tradition, see Kathleen M. Openshaw, "The Symbolic Illustration of the Psalter: An Insular Tradition," *Arte Medievale*, 2nd series, 6 (1992): 41–60.

21. *Man of Law's Tale*, ll. 932–38; *Merchant's Tale*, ll. 1369–71; *Tale of Melibee*, ll. 1094–1101.

22. M. R. James, "Illustrations of the Old Testament" in *A Book of Old Testament Illustration of the Middle of the Thirteenth Century*, ed. W. O. Cockerell (Cambridge: Roxburghe Club, 1927), 46. Reprinted as *Old Testament Miniatures: A Medieval Picture Book with 283 Paintings from the Creation to the Story of David* (New York: George Braziller, [1969]). On Old Testament illustrations, see also Nigel Morgan, "Old Testament Illustration in Thirteenth-Century England" in *The Bible in the Middle Ages: Its Influence on Literature and Art*, ed. Bernard S. Levy (Binghamton: MRTS, 1992), 149–98; Patrick J. Collins, "Narrative Bible Cycles in Medieval Art and Drama" in *The Drama of the Middle Ages: Comparative and Critical Essays*, ed. Clifford Davidson, C. J. Gianakaris, and John H. Stroupe (New York: AMS, 1982), 118–39.

23. For illustrations of the doors of the church of St. Ambrose, an account of their relation to other early pictorial cycles, and further bibliography, see Teresa Mroczko, "The Original Programme of the David Cycle on the Doors of San Ambrogio in Milan," *Artibus e Historiae* 6 (1982), 75–87.

24. London, BL Cotton Tiberius C.vi; London, BL Royal 2.B.vii, "The Queen Mary Psalter"; New York, Public Library, Spencer 26. "Tickhill Psalter"; New York, Morgan Library 638. James notes similarities between the Morgan Miniatures and several elaborate psalters and writes, "It is just possible that they were intended to preface a Psalter, of so magnificent a kind as to have been almost certainly for royal use. But it is far more likely that they formed something resembling the 'Bible historiée et toute figurée à ymages' which belonged to Queen Jeanne of Evreux" (58).

25. The *Bibles Moralisées* contain the most complete set of illustrations. The Vienna manuscript edited in facsimile by Gerald B. Court, *Bible Moralisée: Codex Vindobonensis 2554 Vienna . . . sterreichische Nationalbibliothek* (London: Harvey Miller, 1995) includes forty-two illustrations stretching from the anointing of David to the death of Saul (fols. 37v–43r). The *Bibliae Pauperum* contains five scenes: David killing Goliath, the women praising David, David fleeing his house, the slaughter of the priests of Nob, and David crowned king. See, for example, the Vatican manuscript edited in facsimile by Christoph Wetzel and Heike Drechsler, *Biblia Pauperum: Die Bilderhandschrift des Codex latinus 871 im Besitz Bibliothek Apostolica Vaticana* (Stuttgart and Zurich: Belser, 1995). The *Speculum Humanae Salvationis*, composed about 1324 by a Dominican monk at Strasbourg, included seven scenes from the "Rise of David Narrative" among its forty-five chapters, including David killing a lion and bear, fighting with Goliath and being praised by the women, Saul throwing his spear at David, Michal mourning

her wedding to another man and later helping David escape his house, and Abigail appeasing David. See Edgar Breitenbach, *Speculum Humanae Salvationis: Eine Typengeschichtliche Untersuchung* (Strassbourg: Heitz, 1930).

26. *Cursor Mundi: A Northumbrian Poem of the XIVth Century in Four Versions*, ed. Richard Morris, EETS os 57, 59, 62, 66, 68, 99, 101 (London, 1874–93); William Caxton, *The Golden Legend*, 7 vols. (London: Dent, 1900); *The Mirour of Mans Salvacioune: A Middle English Translation of Speculum Humanae Salvationis*, ed. Avril Henry (Philadelphia: University of Pennsylvania Press, 1987).

27. The first five hundred lines of the poem were edited by Herbert Kalén in *A Middle English Metrical Paraphrase of the Old Testament*, Göteborgs Högskolas Årsskrift 28, vol. 5 (Gothenburg: Elanders, 1923). The project was completed by Urban Ohlander in *Gothenburg Studies in English*, vols. 5, 11, 16, 24 (Stockholm: Almqvist and Wiksell, 1955, 1960, 1963, 1972). See also Laurence Muir, "Translations and Paraphrases of the Bible, and Commentaries" in *A Manual of the Writings in Middle English 1050–1500*, ed. J. Burke Severs, vol. 2 (Hamden: Connecticut Academy of Arts and Sciences, 1970), 382, 535–36; and James Morey in *Book and Verse: A Guide to Middle English Biblical Literature* (Urbana: University of Illinois Press, 2000).

28. This was cogently argued by Guy Trudel in his paper "History and Typology: Structural Devices and Didacticism in the *Cursor Mundi*" at the International Medieval Congress, Kalamazoo, May 2001.

29. See James Morey, "Peter Comestor, Biblical Paraphrase, and the Medieval Popular Bible," *Speculum* 68 (1993): 6–35.

30. Jeremy Cohen, *The Friars and the Jews: The Evolution of Medieval Anti-Judaism* (Ithaca: Cornell University Press, 1982), 129.

31. The Morgan Miniatures depict David and his men offering piles of enemy heads to Saul (30v); the Tickhill Psalter shows both the slaughter of the Philistines and the presentation of heads, some impaled on swords and spears (20r). For a facsimile of the Morgan Miniatures see Cockerell, *A Book of Old Testament Illustration*. For the Tickhill Psalter see Donald Drew Egbert, *The Tickhill Psalter and Related Maniscripts: A School of Manuscript Illumination in England during the Early Fourteenth Century* (New York and Princeton: New York Public Library and the Department of Art and Archaeology of Princeton University, 1940).

32. "Vides ergo te non accepisse in signum salutis circumcisionem, sed in signum potius pudoris rt turpitudinis. Nam putas signum esse quod vestitu tegitur, quod prae verecundia non profertur, quod uxori tantummodo debitum ess cognoscitur. . . . Populus autem meus signum salutis in fronte gestando, totum hominem, viros ac mulieres" (*Patrologia Latina*, 42:1154–55); trans. in Ruether, who repeats an erroneous attribution to Augustine (*Faith and Fratricide*, 136). Among the more comprehensive retellings of the David story, Caxton's *Golden Legend* and the *Bible Moralisée* ignore the scene, and the *Cursor Mundi* uses "hedes" (l. 7638).

33. The Philistines are called "sarazins" in lines 7589, 7751, 7766, 7779, 7806.

34. The *Cursor Mundi* expands Goliath's monstrosity and connection to the devil: "grete he was and unsemele / him semed satanas on to se" (Fairfax, 7445–46).

35. "quid dabitur viro qui percusserit Philistheum hunc et tulerit obprobrium de Israhel quis est enim hic Philistheus incicumcisus qui exprobravit acies Dei viventis." Biblical scholars identify evidence for two distinct giant-fight stories in I Samuel 17 and 18. The material which is of interest here is almost entirely from the second story, which appears in the Masoretic texts but not the Septuagint. See McCarter, 295–98, 306–309.

36. Josephus tells the story in a similar fashion, saying that David volunteered to fight the giant but was rebuked for youthful exuberance (*Jewish Antiquities*, 6.9.2).

37. "Frater isto senior, inquit, qui David typum domini gerentem per malitiam increpavit, significavit populum Iudaeorum, qui per invidiam Christo Domino, qui pro salute humani generis venerat, dextraxerunt, et multis frequenter iniuriis adfecerunt" (Sermo 121, *S. Caesarii Arelatensis Sermones*, ed. D. Germani Morin, *CCSL* 103 [Turnholt: Brepols, 1953], 505).

38. Mikhail Bahktin, *Rabelais and His World*, trans. Hélène Iswolsky (Bloomington: Indiana University Press, 1984).

39. Julius Wellhausen, *Prolegomena to the History of Ancient Israel*, trans. Munzies and Black (Cleveland: World, 1961), 267–68. Cited by McCarter, 330.

40. See Wolfgang S. Seiferth, *Synagogue and Church in the Middle Ages: Two Symbols in Art and Literature*, trans. Lee Chadeayne and Paul Gottwald (New York: Frederick Ungar, 1970); Gertrud Schiller, *Iconography of Christian Art*, trans. Janet Seligman, 2 vols. (London: Lund Humphries, 1972), 2.110–12; and Mellinkoff, *Outcasts*, 1.48–50, 64–65, 217–20.

41. "pro Saule Dauid unctus in regem significat regnum Iudaeorum quod per legem erat Christi et ecclesiae regno mutandum," Bede, *In Primam Partem Samuhelis Libri IIII*, ed. D. Hurst, *CCSL*, 119 II.2 (Turnholt: Brepols, 1962).

42. The soldiers of Saul are depicted in the Tickhill Psalter's illustrations (fol. 22v and 23v) with the clothing and grotesque facial features which characterize the medieval iconography of Jews.

43. On the other hand, my colleague Murray Haar has pointed out that Michal's willingness to put the idol to this use indicates that she venerates it no more than a bedspread or a bolster.

44. "et inmutavit os suum coram eis et conlabebatur inter manus eorum et inpingebat in ostia portae defluebantque salivae eius in barbam."

45. Augustine, commenting on Psalm 33, writes "He changed then His Countenance in the Priesthood, and sent away the kingdom of the Jews, and came to the Gentiles [Mutavit ergo uultam suum in sacerdotio, et dimisit gentem Iudaeorum, et uenit ad gentes]" (*Enarrationes in Psalmos, CCSL*, 38).

46. Although romance heroes like Lancelot, Yvain, and Tristan endure periods of madness, these come as the result of psychological distress rather than as disguises assumed to effect an escape. See David A. Sprunger, "Depicting the Insane: A Thirteenth-Century Case Study" in *Marvels, Monsters, and Miracles: Studies in the Medieval and Early Modern Imagination*, ed. Timothy S. Jones and David Sprunger (Kalamazoo, MI: Medieval Institute Publications, 2001).

47. In his commentary on Psalm 52, Augustine reads David's consumption of the sacred bread as an indication of his own "priesthood" (*Enarrationes in Psalmos, CCSL, 38*).

48. "sciebam in die illa quod cum ibi esset Doec Idumeus procul dubio adnuntiaret Saul. ego sum reus omnium animarum patris tui."

49. Peter Comestor, *Historia Scholastica*, *Patrologia Latina*, 198:1315.

50. "Nabal enim de quo dictum est quod vir durus et pessimus et malitiosus esset, typum tenet populi Judaeorum. Quorum aliqui uva fellis, et botro amaritudinis inebriati, dura cervice, et incircumcisis cordibus semper Spiritui sancto resistebant, atque carnalem sensum in lege sequentes, stulti facti sunt. . . . Abigail vero, de qua refert Scriptura quod mulier prudentissima et speciosa fuerit, typum tenet plebis illius, qui ex Judaeis ad fidem conversi Domino placere meruerunt," (*Commentarius in Libros IV Regum*, 1.25; *Patrologia Latina*, 109:64).

51. "vere frustra servavi omnia quae huius erant in deserto et non periit quicquam de cunctis quae ad eum pertinebant et reddidit mihi malum pro bono," I Samuel 25:21.

52. See J. G. Bellamy, *Crime and Public Order in England in the Later Middle Ages* (London: Routledge and Kegan Paul; Toronto: University of Toronto Press, 1973).

53. For an example of this incident employed to interpret events in medieval history, see my "The Outlawry of Earl Godwin from the *Vita Ædwardi Regis*" in Ohlgren, 1–4.

54. Karl Kerényi, "The Trickster in Relation to Greek Mythology" in *The Trickster*, ed. Paul Radin (London: Routledge and Kegan Paul, 1955), 186.

55. See Stephen Knight, *Robin Hood: A Complete Study of the English Outlaw* (Oxford: Blackwell, 1994); and Thomas Hahn, ed., *Robin Hood in Popular Culture: Violence, Transgression, and Justice* (Cambridge, England: D. S. Brewer, 2000).

8

Robert Holcot on the Jews

NANCY L. TURNER

The influential Dominican theologian Robert Holcot[1] (d.1349) lived and died in an England entirely bereft of Jews. It is of course possible that Holcot encountered an occasional Jewish merchant on one of the major English trade routes, but it appears highly unlikely that Holcot would ever have encountered a family, much less a substantial community, of Jews at any point in his lifetime. Yet, just as is the case for Geoffrey Chaucer, despite the absence of Jews from England during Holcot's lifetime, issues concerning Jews and Judaism are by no means absent from Holcot's works.

We know that Holcot's scholastic reputation and influence were considerable since his works were cited by many thinkers during his own century and continuing into the sixteenth century.[2] Holcot was the author of numerous well-known theological treatises, but his greatest fame among medieval and early modern colleagues came from his commentary on the apocryphal Wisdom of Solomon (known today as the Book of Wisdom).[3] In fact, although Holcot is not mentioned by name, scholars have determined that Geoffrey Chaucer drew upon Holcot's Wisdom commentary for much of the knowledge about dream theory he displays in the amusing debate between Chauntecleer and Pertelote in *The Nun's Priest's Tale*.[4]

Yet dreams would not be the only subject on which Holcot could instruct the poet. While Holcot's influence on Chaucer's dream theory has long been recognized, his teachings on Jews have not yet been explored in this connection. Holcot discusses issues concerning Jews and Judaism frequently in several works. He discusses the Jews' knowledge of Christ's divinity and their culpability for His death at some length in his Wisdom commentary, and devotes an entire treatise to a discussion of Mosaic law.[5] Furthermore, in his commentary on the *Sentences* of Peter Lombard, Holcot discusses the soteriological benefits conferred by the Jewish rite of circumcision. His writings also include a short discussion on the baptism of Jewish children. Determining the

influence of Holcot's writings upon Chaucer's attitude toward Jews is a difficult and speculative task, due largely to the fact that Chaucer's attitude toward
Jews cannot be determined with certainty, so skillful are his ironies and narrative ploys; but we can at least examine the sources from which Chaucer would
have learned about Jews, with a view to evaluating the cultural context of his
works.

Holcot's most detailed treatment of Jews and Judaism occurs in the same
book Chaucer knew: his commentary on the apocryphal Book of Wisdom, a
text often analyzed by Bible commentators throughout the high and late Middle Ages. Holcot's most extended treatment of Jews occurs in his comments
on the following passage:

> "Let us lie in wait for the righteous man, because he is inconvenient to us
> and opposes our actions; he reproaches us for sins against the law, and
> accuses us of sins against our training. He professes to have knowledge of
> God, and calls himself a child of the Lord. He became to us a reproof of our
> thoughts; the very sight of him is a burden to us, because his manner of life
> is unlike that of others, and his ways are strange. We are considered by him
> as something base, and he avoids our ways as unclean; he calls the last end
> of the righteous happy, and boasts that God is his father. Let us see if his
> words are true, and let us test what will happen at the end of his life; for if
> the righteous man is God's, he will help him, and will deliver him from the
> hand of his adversaries. Let us test him with insult and torture, so that we
> may find out how gentle he is, and make trial of his forbearance. Let us con-
> demn him to a shameful death, for, according to what he says, he will be
> protected."
>
> Thus they reasoned, but they were led astray, for their wickedness
> blinded them, and they did not know the secret purposes of God, nor hoped
> for the wages of holiness, nor discerned the prize for blameless souls; for
> God created us for incorruption, and made us in the image of his own eter-
> nity, but through the devil's envy death entered the world, and those who
> belong to his company experience it. (Wisdom of Solomon 2:12–24,
> *[Oxford] Revised Standard Version with Apocrypha*)

The customary medieval Christian reading of this passage interpreted
"we" and "they" as Jews, the "righteous man," persecuted and tortured by the
unrighteous, as Christ. Holcot expands enormously upon previous discussions
of this text, devoting six lectures—roughly thirteen folio pages—to it,
expounding upon its supposed insight into the character and motivation of the
Jews in their attack against Christ. Where Bonaventure and Nicholas of Lyra
simply draw a few, almost cursory, connections to the Jews, Holcot proclaims
that this passage describes the conspiracy of the Jews to ensnare and kill Christ,
and explains what motivated them to do so. He enumerates twelve accusations
made against Christ, devoting three lectures (23–25) to deriving these accusations from the passage and explaining them, often with great ingenuity.[6]

In his exposition, Holcot calls upon Thomas Aquinas' depiction of Jewish behavior and character.[7] Holcot, too, depicts the Jews as inspired by malice and jealousy in their decision to crucify Christ. He states in his Wisdom commentary that upon seeing Christ preaching, the Jews "were very jealous" and "betrayed [Christ to Pilate] out of envy." He attributes their ignorance to "an unnatural malice" which rendered them "indisposed to knowing." In this context, Holcot quotes the first line of Aristotle's *Metaphysics*: "All men by nature desire to know."[8] By describing Jews as creatures with "unnatural" emotions and who are disinclined to "know," Holcot classifies the Jews as beings who are somehow unhuman, or, at the least, cognitively abnormal. According to Holcot, these unnatural qualities left the Jews spiritually and developmentally diminished, for, as he states, "wisdom will not enter a spiteful soul."

On the issue of the Jews' motivations in killing Christ, Holcot adopts Aquinas' teachings on Jewish ignorance and envy almost verbatim, demonstrating that the negative depictions of Jews that appear in Aquinas' teachings were clearly retained and passed on within the teachings of the Dominican Order. Holcot, using nearly the same wording as Aquinas,[9] asks "whether the persecutors of Christ knew him to be God." In replying, he, like Aquinas, distinguishes between the knowledge of Jewish leaders and that of the general Jewish populace. Holcot concludes, as does Aquinas, that the leaders "recognized him to be promised in the law by the deed and sign which he made." Holcot explains that the Jews' desire to remain ignorant of Christ's character was brought on by their desire to live a bad life and by their love of sensual pleasure, injustice, and [of taking] "liberties" (*libertates*). Holcot declares that the Jews turned against Christ because their evil character and customs made them feel antagonism to the goodness in Christ. He expands upon this by arguing that the Jews perceived Christ as being different from them in that "they were evil" while he was conceived, born, and behaved without sin.

Though he clearly draws upon Aquinas' teachings, Holcot develops his own allegations concerning the Jews' motivations for attacking Christ: they kill Christ as an experiment to test whether Christ was the son of God as He claimed, as suggested in Wisdom 2:17, "Let us see if his words are true; and let us test what will happen to him in the end." Holcot continues, "It is to be noted that they knew how to see nothing of the good that could come about to them from the death of Christ except a certainty of experience as to whether he was the true son of God or not." With such statements, Holcot embodies the medieval tendency to see Jewish thought and behavior as strongly influenced by materialism, rationalism, and empiricism. By the thirteenth and fourteenth centuries, empiricism and an interest in physical experimentation had gained positive interest among many Christian thinkers, particularly those trained at Oxford.[10] But the empiricism with which Holcot associates the Jews is not one which late-medieval thinkers considered admirable;

instead, Holcot declares that the Jews were motivated solely by "a cruel curiosity" to witness the outcome of Christ's death, not by a desire to use experimentation for the purpose of increasing philosophers' understanding of the physical world.

Holcot presents a particularly antagonistic, almost inflammatory image of the Jews immediately following this in his discussion of Wisdom 2:19–20. The narrators' scheme: "Let us test him with insult and torture . . . and make trial of his forbearance. Let us condemn him to a shameful death." Holcot begins his analysis of this passage with the declaration: "It was arranged by a conspiracy of the Jews that Christ was to be killed." He then argues that the Jews contrived a death for Christ that would be painful, dishonorable, and foul:

> And therefore, since they wished to test the humility of Christ, they wished to insult him. And as they wished to test his patience, they wished to cause him the distress of tortures. They say therefore thus: "With insults and torment let us interrogate him so that we may know his reverence," that is, his humility; "and let us test his patience," namely, through torments.
>
> Consequently, where [the text reads] "through the most disgraceful death," they ordained that his death would be dishonorable, and this through the disgracefulness of worthlessness. Whence they say, "Let us condemn him through the most disgraceful death," that is, through death of the cross with the most disgraceful circumstances. (*Sapientiae*, lect. 27, fol. 26rb)

Thus Holcot strongly highlights what he sees as the cunning, premeditated character of the tortures and humiliations the Jews inflict upon Christ. To emphasize further the despicableness of the Jews' actions, later in this lecture Holcot describes how the "beautiful face of the son of Man" was befouled by the Jews' spit (*"sputis iudeorum deturpatur"*).

Yet despite Holcot's clearly negative depiction of Jews, there is a markedly detached and abstract quality to his overall treatment. He often presents Jewish behavior and belief solely for the purpose of illustrating larger points concerning philosophy or proper Christian belief. For instance, Holcot devotes nearly two folio pages to Wisdom 2:21, "Thus they reasoned but they were led astray, for their malice blinded them." He makes it clear at the outset that it is the actions of the Jews against Christ to which the passage refers; yet his actual, explicit discussion of the Jews in this context amounts to only three lines. Holcot focuses instead on the reference in this passage to thoughts and emotions that befuddle one's reason, choosing to use this focus as a vehicle to expound in some depth on general types of error and their causes. Jews do make an appearance in the discussion, but only as examples used to illustrate his broader point about the distinction between conquerable (*vincibile*) and invincible error. He explains that errors which are invincible can be excused; not, however, errors which an individual could have avoided, but did not.[11] Here, Holcot uses the Jews' antagonism toward Christ as an example of easily conquerable error. Only at this point does Holcot refer to the Jews, and in a way that indicates that he is alluding to them in order to clarify which type of error and sin he means: "Such malice was the cause of the ignorance of the Jews, that is, a scorn for knowing together with a will to live a bad life."

Holcot immediately follows this pronouncement by stating that the Jews sinned in this way because they erred in their reasoning on three points: "they did not know the sacraments of God" which are necessary for salvation, they did not reason correctly about the punishment for their actions, and they did not know about the rewards of the afterlife. Holcot does not mention the Jews' sins for the rest of the lecture.[12] Thus, Holcot uses the sins of the Jews against Christ as a vehicle for introducing several fundamental issues of Christian theology, but Jewish belief and behavior are not in any significant way the focus of the discussion which they ostensibly inspire.

A similar strategy informs Holcot's analysis of Wisdom 2:19, "Let us test him with insult and torture." Holcot begins this lecture by interpreting the text as a reference to a conspiracy of the Jews first to disgrace and dishonor Christ with insults (*contumelia*), and then to torture Him before they kill Him. This assertion prompts Holcot to present a lengthy sermon on the "seven sins of speaking, by which a person injures his neighbor," and "the four good qualities in a person which another person may injuriously strive to diminish or take away." He mentions the Jews' sins on these counts again only briefly and only as a transition to his next topic, which is a discussion of the commonly debated question of whether Christ was violently killed or voluntarily died.

Here, too, even in an explicit discussion of Christ's passion and death, the actions of the Jews serve mainly as a starting point for a lengthy discussion of Christ's character and the presentation of basic Christian doctrines about Christ's death. Holcot pronounces that the Jews' determination to test Christ's temperament and divinity can be used to explain the time, place, and method of Christ's death, the decision to execute Him alongside thieves (as his fellows, or *socii*), and the "painful," "ignominious," and "unjust" elements of His execution. Holcot then ignores the Jews for pages, and instead goes into great detail about the nobility of Christ's sacrifice and about the particulars of the Crucifixion. Thus, although the Jews are mentioned at the beginning of the lecture, and the discussion ostensibly is a commentary on their actions and behavior, the Jews are not its central focus.[13]

Later, Holcot mentions the Jews' act of turning Christ over to Pilate as an example to introduce his analysis of false friends and false judges who consciously deny the truth. Holcot uses the Jews in this incident to represent all false judges, "who knowingly subvert the truth and who form an opinion which they know is false for a reward, or out of fear and threats withdraw from the truth." Although his treatment here is harsh, Holcot's primary motivation for including the Jews in the discussion at this point is to use their actions to condemn and admonish Christians, who, he says, are often as bad as the Jews: "There are many today who curse the act of a Jew while they do the same act. For when they give false testimony for a reward, they sell God, who is truth."[14] The focus of Holcot's condemnation from this point on is Pilate, whom he condemns for listening to the Jews' accusations against Christ and for acceding to their requests. Thus the Jews represent individuals who, for ulterior motives, can lead one away from the truth.

The call for crusade by John XXII in 1331[15] inspired Holcot to another discussion on Jews (along with Muslims). In lecture 65 of his Wisdom commentary he comments on the theory and practice of attacks on infidels and non-Christians, addressing the question "whether it is licit and meritorious for a Christian to kill an infidel by force, such as an invading pagan." Holcot first presents many of the standard arguments against violent attacks on non-Christians, stating that "God does not want the death of a sinner, but rather that a sinner be converted and live." The task of the Church, he writes, is to pray for those who have not yet converted, not to kill them; there are many non-Christians who would want to believe "if they had instruction in the faith," but who are not allowed to receive such instruction "because of the power of their princes." As a result, he argues, their error is invincible hence exculpating; it is not their fault they are not Christians, and they should not be killed.

Having dutifully presented these arguments against killing non-Christians, Holcot proceeds to arguments justifying an attack on the Muslims occupying the Holy Land:

> Those pagans are unjustly occupying through force and arms the land which was promised to Abraham and his seed by God; . . . therefore, it is licit . . . to resist those who are unjustly struggling against us, because it is licit to fight for one's fatherland . . . or to expel an unjust occupier, or if such a one does not want to believe, to kill the invader.

Holcot takes great pains, however, to make it clear that he is not advocating violence against all non-Christians. He cautions against indiscriminate attacks on non-Christians because "there are . . . distinctions among infidels." Those who accept ecclesiastical authority are to be distinguished from those who are "rebels against the church, persecutors of Christians, and insulters of Christian doctrine." Holcot lists "various sects of infidels," among which Jews make their appearance: "Some are gentiles or pagans who have nothing but the laws of nature. Some are Jews. Some are Saracens. Some are idolators. Some are heretics." In keeping with his desire to support a crusade, Holcot asserts that the Muslims are the most odious in their offenses against Christianity, hence most deserving of having action taken against them; they "do not admit preachers of God," and order that anyone who preaches against the law of "Machomet" is to be killed. Holcot argues that this fact justifies aggressive action against Saracens because "there is no hope of converting them;" a Christian may "invade with force and arms, plunder and kill them, and acquire their goods for the faithful." At this point, Holcot, aware of massacres of the Jews at the hands of zealous crusaders in previous centuries,[16] takes some pains to state explicitly that his words should not be taken to endorse violence against Jews, for "the church permits them, explicitly, to live." His Scriptural prooftexts are Romans 9:27 and Isaiah 10:22 which, according to Catholic interpretation, pronounce that a remnant of Israel must be present in the final days. Thus, he concludes, "different indeed is the cause of the Jews from [that of] the Saracens."

Perhaps the best evidence that for Holcot, issues concerning the treatment of Jews were not an active daily concern, is the fact that Holcot's writings lack any real discussion of the practical and directly applicable issue of the forcible baptism of Jewish adults or children—a topic analyzed in great depth by many of Holcot's continental contemporaries. John Duns Scotus (d. 1308), for instance, devotes page after page of his *Sentences* commentary to the question of whether Jewish adults should be forcibly baptized. He concludes in the affirmative, and then declares that the potential for apostasy among these forcibly converted Jews should be of little concern; he states that even if such adult Jews do not remain faithful to Christianity, less evil results from preventing Jews from observing their law than from allowing them to practice their religion with impunity. Scotus also insists that even if these adult Jews are not faithful to the Christian religion, nevertheless their children, if educated in the faith, would be faithful by the third or fourth generation.

On the question of baptizing Jewish children without their parents' consent, Scotus sees such an action as fully defensible if carried out by a prince or other "public person." He states that a prince has the right, even the duty, to override parental rights and to fulfill God's desire to have all people baptized into the Christian faith. In order to adhere to the requirements presented in Romans 9:27 and Isaiah 10:22, Scotus argues that a handful of Jews should simply be preserved "on an island somewhere."[17]

The French theologian Peter Aureol (d. 1322) also devotes many folio pages to an examination of the issue of the forcible baptism of Jews. After a thorough discussion of whether recipients of baptism must consent in order for the sacrament to be valid, Aureol concludes: "I think it should be said . . . that if an individual exhibited at least interpreted consent, that is, that he consented outwardly . . . however much he might dissent inwardly, he would receive the perfect character [of baptism]." Aureol further argues that should such an individual return to his previous faith after having received baptism, he should be treated as a heretic.

Aureol takes a somewhat less direct stand on the licitness of the baptism of Jewish children. He presents Scotus' argument in favor of allowing "public persons" to remove children from their parents and baptize them against the wishes of the parents, juxtaposing this position with that of Aquinas, who argues that children are legally the property of their parents and should not be removed from their parents' possession (*Summa Theologiae* 2a2ae.10.12). Aureol does acknowledge the legal status of children as the property of their parents; however, he ultimately declares that it would be wrong to condemn a "public person" who baptizes a child against the will of the parents if the public person were "inspired by the piety of faith" (Turner, 134–39).

In contrast to these two thinkers, Holcot is not much interested in the topic of the forcible baptism of Jews. To find his discussion of the issue, we must turn to his *Sentences* commentary, where he does briefly discuss the baptism of a Jewish child against its parents' will. But he brings up this complex question only as a hypothetical instance of what to do about a non-Christian child who is about to die while separated from its parents. This is Holcot's only pronouncement on the issue of the forced baptism of Jewish adults or children. Living in a region that was devoid of Jews throughout his lifetime (which was not the case for either Scotus or Aureol), Holcot probably devotes little energy to this issue because it had no direct empirical relevance for him.

Yet the theology of forced baptism is not the only Jewish-related issue on which Holcot shows considerably less interest than Scotus and Aureol. Also missing from Holcot's *Sentences* commentary, but found in great detail in the works of several of his immediate predecessors, is extensive discussion of the meaning and legitimacy of circumcision and whether, when, and why it was superseded by baptism. Holcot does not completely ignore all discussion of circumcision; perhaps simply following tradition, he alludes to circumcision in Book 4, question 1 of his *Sentences* commentary and makes a perfunctory attempt to discuss it. But Holcot does not seem quite to have understood the question. In contrast to Aquinas, Scotus, and Aureol, who spend many folios investigating when and why circumcision was instituted, whether it conferred grace, and when it lost its validity, Holcot writes, rather obtusely, "I take a circumcized child and a baptized child. . . . Each one is saved; but I ask whether they have equal reward or not." By way of answer, he explains that although circumcision did have the power to remove original sin, nonetheless, as Peter Lombard had already argued,[18] it does not act as an aid to performing good works or in "restraining one from concupiscence." Holcot also offers the argument, which he attributes to Aquinas, that baptism is superior to circumcision because it can confer grace upon women as well as men. For these reasons, Holcot concludes that baptism is the more perfect sacrament, and that the Jewish and Christian child do not receive the same reward. Unlike many previous thinkers, then, Holcot simply repeats previous arguments briefly and offers no new opinions or insight.

Holcot's interest in the standard comparison of Old Law and New Law is similarly truncated and uninspired. Missing from Holcot's commentary on Book 3 of the *Sentences* is the discussion found in works of his continental contemporaries concerning the difficulty of following the laws of the Old versus those of the New Testament. Holcot does not, however, entirely ignore a discussion of Old Law. He devotes a *Quodlibetal* question to the discussion of "whether the observation of the Mosaic Law by the Jews merited them eternal life," a text stemming from an actual university debate.[19] Holcot begins by making it clear that he is aware of the basic arguments and issues involved in comparing Old Law and New, demonstrating his familiarity with the standard arguments found in Aquinas and others.

Holcot responds in the affirmative to the basic question posed in the *Quodlibet* and goes on to present the Old Law in a traditionally positive light. He states that "every just man is worthy of eternal life, and every observer of the Mosaic Law is just before God,"[20] an argument which he supports with several passages from the New Testament and the *Glossa Ordinaria* on the Bible. He lists seven individuals from the Hebrew Bible who, according to Christian teaching, merited eternal life: Moses, Joshua, Samuel, David, Ezekiel, Josiah, and Judas Maccabee. When Holcot briefly considers the role of grace in Old and New Laws, once again his real interest is not Jewish doctrine, but rather his aim is to refute a fellow student (*socius*) who had denied that grace is required in order to merit eternal life. Old Law and Jews appear for the remainder of the question and when they do, Holcot uses them merely to support his larger point or to demonstrate that his opponent has misunderstood scriptural and patristic writings on baptism, circumcision, or grace.

Given that there is barely a generation between the lives of Aquinas, Scotus, Aureol, and Holcot, the latter's lack of attention to practical issues is striking. Perhaps without an active Jewish presence to remind this fourteenth-century English theologian that there was a living challenge to Christianity within Europe itself, he felt little interest in analyzing practical issues such as baptism and conversion. Yet on the question of Jewish character and behavior, Holcot makes many determinedly negative pronouncements, generally presenting Jews as stylized stereotypes exemplifying negative qualities such spite, cunning, and sensuality. A lay reader like Geoffrey Chaucer would have drawn from Holcot's works the image of Jews as cruel, rationalistic, vaguely unhuman, and filled with malicious envy toward Christ. We cannot be certain how Chaucer evaluated this or any other depiction of Jews, or what his own sentiments were; what he made of such images we can only infer from his multivalent work.

Notes

1. Scholars do not know Robert Holcot's birthdate or birthplace with certainty, but it is quite likely that he trained and professed at the Dominican Priory in Northampton near Holcot, a village in Northamptonshire. We know that Holcot delivered the required lectures on his *Sentences* commentary in Oxford from 1331 to 1333. It is claimed by tradition that Holcot died of the plague in 1349 while ministering to the sick. We have no evidence that Holcot ever left

the island of England. See Beryl Smalley, "Robert Holcot O.P.," *Archivum Fratrum Praedicatorum* 26 (1956), 7–8; Katherine H. Tachau, "Introduction," in *Seeing the Future Clearly: Questions on Future Contingents* by Robert Holcot, eds. Paul A. Streveler and Katherine H. Tachau (Toronto: Pontifical Institute of Mediaeval Studies, 1995), in *Studies and Texts 119*, 27; Katherine H. Tachau, *Vision and Certitude in the Age of Ockham: Optics, Epistemology and the Foundations of Semantics 1250–1345*, (Leiden: Brill, 1988), 243–245.

2. Tachau, *Seeing the Future Clearly*, 3; Smalley, "Robert Holcot," 10. See also Beryl Smalley, *English Friars and Antiquity in the Early Fourteenth Century*, (Oxford: Blackwell, 1960), 133–202. Holcot's views on God's conferral of grace were known and condemned by Martin Luther; see Heiko A. Oberman, "Facientibus quod in se est deus non denegat gratiam": "Robert Holcot, O.P. and the Beginnings of Luther's Theology," *Harvard Theological Review* 55 (1962), 336.

3. At least 175 fourteenth- and fifteenth-century copies of Holcot's Wisdom commentary survive. It was unusually long and thorough, and perhaps owing to this fact, as Beryl Smalley reports, "every well-stocked library came to possess [it]." Smalley, "Robert Holcot," 10, and Smalley, *English Friars and Antiquity*, 133–202.

4. See Robert A. Pratt, "Some Latin Sources of the Nonnes Preest on Dreams," *Speculum* 52 (1977), 538–49.

5. "Utrum observantia legis mosaycae fuit Judaeis meritoria vitae aeternae," in Paolo Molteni, ed., *Roberto Holcot O.P.: Dottrina della Grazia e della Giustificazione con due question quodlibetali inedite* (Pinerolo: Alzani, 1967).

6. Bonaventure, *Opera Omnia*, II vol. (Quarracchi: Collegii S. Bonaventurae, 1903), 6:122–24; Nicolaus de Lyra, *Postilla super totam bibliam* III, (Strassburg, 1492) [Minerva Gmbh, Frankfurt/Main, 1971]. Much of the information for this article was drawn from my dissertation. For the full Latin passages of the English translations, see Nancy L. Turner, 'An Attack on the Acknowledged Truth': French, English and German Theologians on the Jews in the Fourteenth Century" (Ph.D. diss., University of Iowa, 1996); hereafter cited in text. All English translations of Latin passages throughout the article are mine.

7. John Y. B. Hood, *Aquinas and the Jews*, (Philadelphia: University of Philadelphia Press, 1995); Alexander Broadie, "Medieval Jewry Through the Eyes of Aquinas," in *Aquinas and Problems of His Time*, eds. G. Verbeke and D. Verhelst (Louvain: Leuven University Press, 1976), 57–68; Hans Liebeschuetz, "Judaism and Jewry in the Social Doctrine of Thomas Aquinas," *Journal of Jewish Studies* 13 (1962), 57–81; J. Guttmann, *Das Verhaeltnis des Thomas von Aquino zum Judenthum und zur juedischen Litteratur* (Goettingen: 1891).

8. *Super Libros Sapientiae* (Hagenau, 1494), lect. 28, fol. 27ra: "et hec est innaturalis malitia, quia omnis homo natura scire desiderat; et talis malitia facit hominem se indisponere ad sciendum"; hereafter cited in text.

9. Thomas Aquinas, *Summa Theologica* 3.47.5 (New York: McGraw Hill, 1962–76), 54–67.

10. John E. Murdoch, "The Development of a Critical Temper: New Approaches and Modes of Analysis in Fourteenth-Century Philosophy, Science and Theology," *Medieval and Renaissance Studies* 7 (1978), 51–79.

11. *Sapientiae,* lect. 28, fol. 27ra. On the issue of the compatibility of error and meritorious action, Holcot sustained a running debate with his fellow Oxford theology student, William Chitterne, OFM; see Katherine Tachau, "Robert Holcot on Contingency and Divine Deception," in *Filosofia e teologia nel trecento: Studi in ricordo di Eugenio Randi,* ed. Luca Bianchi (Louvain-la-Neuve: Féderation internationale des institutes détudes médiévales, 1994), 182–89, 192.

12. Instead, Holcot uses this reference to the issues of reason and the path to salvation as an opportunity to present, develop, and defend his famous argument that "if an individual does what is in him, he will be well enough informed about those things which are necessary for salvation"; for a detailed analysis of this argument, see Oberman, "Facientibus quod in se est," 322–30.

13. In a similar vein, in *De imputabilitate peccati* (Lugduni, 1518), sect. zv, col. a, Holcot again refers to the Jews' ignorance of Christ's nature, but in this case, he does so solely in order to provide his reader with an example of "careless" ignorance. He devotes many columns to a very wide-ranging discussion of whether individuals who are ignorant in some way about a sin they are committing are fully culpable for that sin. Among the many issues concerning ignorance which he addresses in this lengthy discussion is that of the distinction between ignorance which is sincere and not willed, and ignorance which stems from laziness; that is, when a fact or event is willfully ignored. To illustrate what he means when using the term "lazy," Holcot uses the actions of the Jews as an example. He states, "the ignorance of the Jews is of this type, by which up to now they have ignored the coming of Christ in the flesh." For more examples of Holcot's use of Jewish beliefs and actions to illustrate complex philosophical points concerning ignorance, semantics, epistemology, and faulty logic, see Turner, " 'An Attack on the Acknowledged Truth,' " 163–69.

14. For an analysis of the common medieval practice of condemning the behavior of Christians by comparing it to the practices or behaviors of Jews or other little-respected members of European society, see Marc Saperstein, "Christians and Jews—Some Positive Images," *Harvard Theological Review* 79 (1986), 236–46; and Robert Levine, "Why Praise Jews: Satire and History in the Middle Ages," *Journal of Medieval History* 12 (1986), 291–96.

15. Jonathan Riley-Smith, *The Crusades: A Short History* (New Haven, CT: Yale University Press, 1987), 226.

16. Robert Chazan, *European Jewry and the First Crusade*, (Berkeley: University of California Press, 1987); Shlomo Eidelberg, ed. and trans., *The Jews and the Crusaders: The Hebrew Chronicles of the First and Second Crusades* (Madison: University of Wisconsin Press, 1977); Hans Liebeschuetz, "The Crusading Movement in its Bearing on the Christian Attitude towards Jewry," *Journal of Jewish Studies* 10 (1959), 97–111.

17. In *Sententias* Book 4, distincton 4, questions 4 & 9, in *Joannis Duns Scotus opera omnia*, ed. Luke Wadding, (1639; repr. by Vives: Paris, 1891–95),

Vives XVI; see also Turner, " 'An Attack on the Acknowledged Truth,' " 85–90.

18. Peter Lombard, *Sententiae in IV Libris Distinctae* (Rome: 1971), 237–38.

19. In a theology student's final year as a bachelor of theology and in his first years as a master, he was required to take part in theological disputations known as *quodlibetal* debates. During these debates, questions on "any topic whatsoever" (hence the label *quodlibetal*, derived from the Latin for "whatsoever") were posed. A student was at first allowed only to oppose or respond to arguments in these disputations; as he became more advanced, he was allowed to "determine," or sum up, a debate. Modern scholars are still uncertain how, or by whom, the topics of debate were chosen; nevertheless, all evidence suggests that each *quodlibetal* dispute took place as a real debate in which the participating individuals were expected to demonstrate thorough knowledge of the issue under debate and to argue their positions clearly and persuasively. For more on the format of *quodlibetal* debates, see William J. Courtenay, *Schools and Scholars in Fourteenth-Century England,* (Princeton, NJ: Princeton University Press, 1987), 45.

20. Gilbert Dahan, in his brief analysis of Holcot's treatment of the Mosaic law, makes a not uncommon mistake, taking Holcot's presentation of another thinker's views in his *Quodlibetal* question for Holcot's own views. Based upon his reading of a sentence which Holcot starts with the word *dicitur* (it is said), Dahan incorrectly concludes, "la response de Robert Holcot est pourtant négative: puisqu'il était impossible d'observer intégralement la Loi, la grace était nécessaire pour faire mériter la vie éternelle," *Les intellectuels Chrétiens et les Juifs au Moyen Age* (Paris: Editions du Cerf, 1990), 560. What Holcot actually believes is: "Quantum ad primum dico quod sic et ratio est quia illa observantia esse non potuit sine gratia et iustitia. Tunc arguo sic: Omnis homo iustus apud Deum dignus est vita aeterna, omnis observator legis mosaycae iustus est apud Deum, igitur etc."

9

The Protean Jew in the Vernon Manuscript

DENISE L. DESPRES

Oxford Bodleian Library Ms. English Poetry a. 1., best known as the Vernon manuscript, is a remarkable compilation of Middle English vernacular literature, providing students of medieval devotional culture with evidence of the rich generic breadth and stylistic compass of English texts available to fourteenth-century lay readers.[1] The manuscript is unusual in size (403 items), generic inclusiveness, and high degree of English content.[2] It displays little evidence of contemporary theological debates about Lollards, interest in theological scholasticism, or even the continental ecstatic or mystical texts such as we see in Margery Kempe's *Book* and other spiritual literature.[3] Although much exciting work is being done in medieval devotional culture on marginal and heretical groups in late-medieval England, the Vernon manuscript offers little to that conversation.[4] Rather, the manuscript exemplifies a rich vernacular theology through popularized doctrinal discourse and a repertoire of symbols familiar from homilies and exempla, miracles, homiletic romances, lyrics, and disputation literature, much of it of thirteenth-century origin. The Vernon manuscript's doctrinal and spiritual program is in keeping with the lay educational directives of the Fourth Lateran Council's *Omnius utriusque sexus* in its focus on prayer, the commandments, sacraments, and works of mercy, disseminated in England as early as 1219 through Richard Poore's Statutes of Salisbury.[5]

Its religious conservatism and generic variety make the Vernon manuscript fertile ground for exploring the ambivalent representation of Jews in Middle English devotional culture. Recent literary scholars have reduced the Jew in late-fourteenth-century English literature to a "pedagogical category" in view of the 1290 expulsion, dangerously refashioning anti-Judaism a "deviant tropological bigotry which is relocated onto other groups"—such as the currently ubiquitous Lollards.[6] In her exploration of anti-Judaism in the fourteenth-century *The Seige of Jerusalem*, Elisa Narin van Court convincingly argues against a "monolithic and static bigotry which can accommodate any group," establishing a historical and ideological context for the Yorkshire poem consonant with the wide literary interest in Jews reflected in late-medieval English homiletic, devotional, and dramatic literature.[7] *The Siege of Jerusalem* shares with the Vernon *Disputation* an instability in its representation of the Jew and demonstrates a similar need to press the various and sometimes conflicting characteristics attributed to Jews in Middle English writings. In displacing the Jew for the Lollard, or other heretical groups, scholars distort the essential relationship of Jew to Christian in the construction of Christian identity; a bond that exists even in the absence of Jewish communities. The displacement of Jews by Lollards thus leads to historical revisionism, deceptive in its implication that Jews were thus relieved of their responsibility for the Crucifixion— the foundational Christian sacrifice—hence the distinctive place they held in medieval Christian culture, where they were never displaced by heretical or deviant groups (such as witches) in medieval and early modern history.[8]

The devotional and catechetical texts that emerged in the thirteenth century, a period of confusion and religious classification, reflect the myriad ways in which a discourse of Jewish identity developed and was made comprehensible to lay audiences. The use of specific genres and rhetorical conventions in anti-Judaic narrative reflects the diversity of audiences as well as emphasis on different facets of the project of differentiation between Jews and Christians. Although the Jew is consistently the "other" in works as varied as Marian miracles and Jewish-Christian debate, the representation of what constitutes "otherness" depends upon the rhetorical aim of the genre and thus its specific argument about Christian identity. A close reading of a variety of anti-Judaic narratives in Middle English manuscripts produces not a static demonized Jew, but a Jew whose danger is located in his protean nature, in his very ability to play the wide variety of roles assigned to him in an evolving and wide-ranging literature about Jews in relation to Christian identity.[9] Typically, Christian sacramentalism and cultic purity are foregrounded in Marian and eucharistic miracles, whereas Jewish rationalism figures largely in debate literature. The genres themselves, we must remember, have their origins in historical moments when the Christian endeavor to define "the Jew" required actual debate and legislation, because the separation of peoples within close-knit medieval communities was a daunting task. Like all literatures of racial or religious exclusion, medieval anti-Judaic narratives reveal inconsistencies, anxieties, and ambivalences that are elucidated by the historical documentation of actual attempts to impose separation.

In this essay, I will point out the markedly different ways that narratives in the Vernon manuscript investigate the Jew through competing and distinctive literary genres. This critical enterprise is particularly intriguing in the historical absence of Jews from England, challenging us to account for the impetus to perpetuate a particular social myth or negative representation, such as the Jew as usurer. The Vernon manuscript, in its diverse representation of Jews for a post-expulsion audience, replicates the conflicts and inconsistencies that even the Fourth Lateran anti-Judaic Canons could not mask or elide.

The literature that was produced to implement the 1215 Canons of the Fourth Lateran Council reflect the Council's essential task in defining orthodox Roman Catholicism against the Albigensian revival of Manicheism, particularly the refutation of its position on the essential evil of matter.[10] The central theme of somatic and spiritual unity underscores the Council's treatment of trinitarian and especially incarnational doctrine, eucharistic and marital sacramentalism, sexual and commensal purity, and cultic identity. Contrary to R. I. Moore's assertion that the Council's influence was "slow, piecemeal and haphazard"[11] in its gradual reshaping of Catholic society, the Council's catechetical program accounts for an impressive body of penitential lyrics, gospel harmonies, and sermon literature, largely produced by the Franciscans and Dominicans, whose urgent task it was to preach to the laity in the vernacular to combat heresy. Canons 67, 68, and 69—legislation dealing exclusively with the Jews—were formulated in the context of the Council's concern with Christian identity and purity, in an effort to unify the material and spiritual realms of Christian experience.[12] The appearance of Jews in tandem with issues of bodily, eucharistic, or communal purity in late-medieval vernacular devotional compendia emerges from the Council's own logic of exclusivity.

The Council of Oxford, presided over by Archbishop Stephen Langton in 1222, took place the second Sunday after Easter; its central purpose was to promulgate the Fourth Lateran legislation in England, and the Oxford canons became the basis of local English Church law in the later Middle Ages. The council is also notable for its conviction of a deacon of apostasy to Judaism, for which he was burnt in the "first clear case of the death penalty for heresy being exacted in England."[13] The case, which also records the deacon's purported sexual relations with a Jewess, underscores the principle of separation outlined by the Lateran anti-Jewish Canons. In social reality, however, Jews and Christians lived in close proximity in thirteenth-century England. The attention devoted in Council and Synod documents to the Jewish badge suggests greater anxiety about than confidence in the project of differentiation. In fact, the repetition of injunctions about the size and nature of the Jewish badge might well be interpreted as evidence of the legislation's impotence. The Council of Oxford, for example, "decreed that the sign should be of a different color than the garment to make it visually distinct and its size was increased," as it was again in 1275 by Edward I, who specified a length of six fingers.[14] Henry III renewed the Oxford "badge" clause in 1253, "ordering the tabula to be borne in a prominent position," an injunction refined by Edward I in the matter of color and physical placement: the cloth was to be of yellow taffeta—the color yellow signifying carnality, and associated in a medieval visual semiotics with "bile, urine, and feces."[15] The badge was to be worn by every Jew over the age of seven, dramatically covering the heart. This requirement was extended to women in 1279 and the cumulative legislation repeated by ecclesiastical injunction at the Synod of Exeter in 1289. The English Christian audience for such signs required ongoing clarification until the matter was solved in a series of local expulsions followed by national expulsion in 1290.

Devotional manuscripts like the Vernon, rather than supplying evidence for uniformly demonized representation of Jews, demand ongoing reflection about the essential nature of the Jews and its centrality to the definition of Christian identity. Scholars need to consider the context of reading and reception in a manuscript culture to imagine just "how" a medieval Christian reader of Marian miracles and disputation literature understood the Jew. The Vernon manuscript is particularly impressive for its inclusiveness of older, authoritative texts like St. Edmund's *Speculum Ecclesiae, Ancrene Riwle,* and Grosseteste's *The Castle of Love,* along with contemporary works by Walter Hilton and *Piers Plowman* (Henry, 89). The variety of texts suggests that Vernon readers possessed a broad and sophisticated facility in literary interpretation. The exemplary romances, Marian miracles, mystical and catechetical works in the Vernon manuscript invite the audience to synthesize or meditatively process doctrinal and devotional models in the readerly act of *collatio.* This process of reflecting, internalizing, and thus remembering, demanded a kind of generic cross-pollination in the medieval reading process whether in vernacular or Latinate textual communities.[16] A manuscript like the Vernon produced the kind of colloquy central to all devotional reading and listening: the reader or listener is invited to synthesize and assimilate texts that ultimately have moral or spiritual application. The visual apparatus in the Vernon substantiates and facilitates this medieval reading process; the extant illustrations and diagrams aid meditative reading in stimulating "memorial *compositio:*" the recollective process by means of which a particular reader engages a particular text (with all that includes) on a particular occasion (Carruthers, 256).

One sees the same kind of invitation to weigh, compare, and track themes and images in an experimental work like Chaucer's *Canterbury Tales,* where, fragmented or not, the inclusivity of the collection deliberately poses interpretive challenges to the reader. Chaucer's dramatic interludes and introductions to the tales and critical responses by characters to previously told tales, reinterpreting—even misinterpreting as the Miller does—the moral thrust of a specific tale and its genre, are evidence of the lively nature of medieval readerly reconstruction. Clearly the Vernon manuscript, whose principle of inclusion is governed by another aesthetic and purpose than Chaucer's, is less experimental in its juxtaposition of texts. Still, Chaucer's *Prioress's Tale,* whose analogue appears in the Vernon's (now incomplete but once extensive) *mariale*, seems less anomalous when we consider its prominence as an illustrated tale in a prestigious volume like the Vernon. Whereas Chaucer's compilation offers us nothing else to construct the contemporary idea of the "Jew," the Vernon's generically rich collection of texts featuring Jews considerably complicates any attempt to define the idea of the Jew in fourteenth-century England.[17]

In the Vernon manuscript, the Jewish-Christian disputation is collated with the Marian miracle, but each genre conforms to narrative conventions and expectations expressive of its historical origins and function. Of course, the disputation genre is no more realistic in its representation of Jews than is the Marian miracle. Amos Funkenstein notes that anti-Jewish polemic by Christians took the same "dangerous" turn for Jews in the twelfth century as did miracle tales, both informed by the religious impulses concretized in the Fourth Lateran legislation against Jews, heretics, lepers, and women.[18] Whereas polemical literature in antiquity and the early Middle Ages served the dual purpose of converting Jews to Christianity while simultaneously teaching Christians, late-medieval disputation literature portrayed Jews to serve internal theological needs, as did the miracle tale (Funkenstein, 2). The Vernon manuscript enables us to address the difficult issue of representation and reception of the historically absent Jew midway between the expulsion and the readmittance of Jews to England.[19]

Undoubtedly, such a task is distasteful, for anti-Judaism is powerfully present in the Vernon manuscript. In the Vernon "Miracles of the Virgin" (fols. 124r–126v), once the most complete *mariale* in Middle English, virulent anti-Judaism is heightened by the inclusion of an analogue of Chaucer's *Prioress's Tale* and the "Jew of Bourges," both provided with detailed and evocative illustrations.[20] Since forty-one leaves are missing from the Vernon miracles, it is difficult to know how representative the focus on Jewish venality and rage was in the overall program, but four of the nine surviving narratives do substantiate the myths of Jewish usury and of conspiracy in host desecration and ritual murder. The additional expense of illustrating these particular stories is significant even in such a luxurious manuscript. The rich color scheme of green and rust signifies Jewish perfidy and corporeality in the tradition of anti-Judaic imagery in Northern European manuscript illustration.[21] Such meditative imagery helps to interpret the text, rather than merely illustrate it, in a larger nexus of symbols linking Jewish perfidy in Gospel narrative to medieval Jewish blasphemy and the sabotage of Christian culture.[22]

The analogue to *The Prioress's Tale* entitled "Hou þe Jewes, in despit of ure lady, þrewe a chyld in a gonge" and "The Jew of Bourges," "hou a Jew putte his sone in a brennyngge ouene, for he was communed wit oþur cristene children on þe pask-day," rank among the most widespread and long-lived Marian miracles, their popularity evidenced in stained glass, manuscript illumination, and homiletics throughout Europe from the thirteenth century. Miri Rubin's sensitive reconstruction of such "gentile tales" and their resilience in medieval Christian and early modern print culture sets forth the chronology of their dissemination, and accounts for their pervasive influence. Rubin's account acknowledges historical place and moment, and thus adds the difficult issue of reception to our reconstruction of their meaning, for the same story could be introduced "into a multiplicity of contexts—literary, devotional, visual—and could acquire a variety of tones eliciting different moods" (Rubin, *Gentile Tales*, 22). Marian contexts for tales about Jews tend to foreground the linked theme of bodily and sacramental purity. Chaucer's *Prioress's Tale* and "The Jew of Bourges" share a liturgical imagery, for in both "eucharistic associations are implicit . . . The oven-hearth is related to the punishment of the Jew but also gestures towards Christ's own death and rebirth as bread" (Rubin, *Gentile Tales*, 27).

By the fourteenth century, variants of such tales illustrating the power of the eucharist, bodily incorruptibility, resurrection, and Marian intercession had mutated into self-replicating tales of Jewish host desecration and the ritual murder. In England, where such dark fantasies had already contributed to the general expulsion of the Jews, these tales proliferated in a different environment from that of communities where Jews physically constituted the other. The familiar narrative elements that resonated with credibility continued to do so in England—even in the absence of Jews—for the emotional impact of these stories depended upon the "mundane setting" of medieval town life with its veneer of security and control (Rubin, *Gentile Tales*, 70). One might think, for example, of contemporary horror film classics like *Hallowe'en*, in which obscene violence is predicated upon the existence of familiar domestic spaces wherein we locate our greatest security and comfort. Such tales are broadly applicable, traveling over time, and a fear of the predatory "other" was especially powerful in an insular England where the Jews had been expelled and foreigners tended to concentrate only in major urban areas (at their own peril, as London's Flemish clothworkers learned during the 1381 revolt). The tale's portability was rooted in the timeless nature of eucharistic ritual, wherein sacred space and community were tangibly and continually reclaimed as ever-present realities. This heightened sense of reality transformed the familiar geographies of the fragmented, fallen, and polluted world into a sacralized world; it extended to the corporate body the purity accessible to the individual Christian through the sacraments of the mass, wherein was dramatized again and again Christ's sacrificial crucifixion. The Jews at the heart of such pervasive narratives, however, did not become blurred, or indistinct, nor did they lose the symbolic characteristics that distinguished them as Jews in a Northern European taxonomy of otherness. Cultic anti-Judaism stems from a belief that sacramental realities enable the first persecutors, Jews, to repeat their tormenting of Christ's sacred body. Lollards, however they objected to transubstantiation, never assumed the full semiotic identity of the "other" that led to, for example, the symbolic representation of the hanging of Jews upside down with dogs and apes in works like *The Siege of Jerusalem* (Narin van Court, 231). They did not bear the historical burden of the Crucifixion; consequently, their rejection of the real presence in the eucharist lacked the element of ritual revenge accorded to Jewish host profanation.

The Vernon miracle illustrations participate in this semiotic, visually rendering the basic elements of the mythology in detail familiar from altarpieces, stained glass, books of hours, and sermons. These elements in medieval culture, individually or in combination, are the drama of Jewish depravity and carnality. In the Vernon manuscript, the images are performative, almost displacing the text below; the blasphemous events occur sequentially in compact space, as in a cartoon, observed by medieval Christians who share the role of witness with the manuscript reader.[23] Characters gesture with pointed fingers, signals of declamation; their hands are outstretched in lamentation or clasped in prayer. Speech scrolls in this illustration provide the directive to listen, enabling the medieval reader/viewer to hear the "Alma Redemptoris" sung by the child in the privy—the dark, round hole that symbolizes Jewish physicality, corruptibility, and filth—both revealing the crime and denying its efficacy. This is surely among the most violent extant illustrations of ritual murder.

The miniaturist of the Vernon Marian miracles conforms to a demonized medieval stereotype in representing Jews with hooked noses and unkempt reddish-tinged beards (Mellinkoff, 128, 147–50). Jews are also disproportionately enlarged for emphasis so that the eye naturally fixes upon them. On f. 125r, in the illustration of "The Jew of Bourges," the enraged Jewish father, bearing a broom, dwarfs his small son who stands on the threshold of the Church; the father's face is parallel to the rose window. Both his angry expression and his enlarged hands reflect his capacity for hasty violence, which is rendered efficiently in the sweep of his garments as he thrusts his small son into the oven because he has innocently partaken of the eucharist. In the right hand corner, the child basks serenely in a glowing oven, his hands clasped in prayer, and the flames form a burning halo around his head. In contrast, the boy's mother kneels beside the oven, her features and clothing indistinguishable from a Christian woman's, as she reports the events to mayor and bailiffs.[24] Any reader of the Vernon manuscript would know this tale, and thus of the subsequent conversion of the mother after the Virgin appears and saves the little boy. Carol Meale has reflected upon the illustrator's interesting choice of not representing the Virgin (Meale, 129). The Virgin Mary's absence from the illustration creates anticipation and suspends the longed-for movement from sacrifice to sacramental wholeness symbolized by the boy's emergence from the virginal womb, the oven.[25] The illustrator has presented the story with impressive economy and feeling, but with simplicity in contrast to the operatic orchestration of movement on f. 124v illustrating "*the child in Paris killed by the Jews.*" The frame of this illustration cannot contain the complex sequence of action; the right and left margins of the illustration are balanced with church and secular authorities breaking out of the frame to create a sense of spatial depth similar to that of a stage.

The visual action moves from the lower right foreground, where the weeping mother begs secular officials for help in finding her boy, to the slightly receding threshold of the house where the Jew beckons to the child. The narrative moves leftward on the upper plane to the central image of the Jew slitting the kneeling child's throat, despite his prayerful gestures. The Vernon illustration is among the most brutal renditions of this story, for the artist avails himself of the full horror of the story with fierce energy. The cramped, dark, and slightly receding space of the Jew's house underscores the link between this polluted place and the gaping black privy into which the Jew disposes of the body. They are ideologically one and the same. The frame of the house separating the Jewish from the Christian world (we see through the walls to the pathetic scene) hides evil (the murder), yet fails to protect Christians by confining Jews or permanently separating them; thus the Jew is made predatory. The square bier in the left foreground is paired with the square privy seat, yet the child's now cleansed and linen-clothed body, miraculously upright with hands joined in prayer, presents a study in symbolic contrasts: resurrection in contrast to bodily putrefaction; innocence in contrast to depravity; white in contrast to black. The child chorister's shrouded body enters into public space like a relic for witnessing, the bier's long handles stretched to the left out of the picture margins where a bishop blesses the child and holds the lily he has removed from his throat. To the right, the boy's mother kneels, her pathos reminiscent of the Virgin Mary's at the foot of the cross. In a sense, the picture makes a narrative circle, which is appropriate given its eternal message and the ominous lack of closure central to this tale that promises the repetition of such evil wherever there are Jews, innocent children, and a lack of Christian vigilance.

Yet Jews figure differently in other didactic narratives in the Vernon manuscript, particularly the generically hybrid *Disputation between a Christian and a Jew* (f. 301v). In contrast to the nine extant (of an original forty-one) Marian miracles, which focus typically and thematically on bodily purity and wholeness, matter historically central to the unique and highly specific vernacular theology of Marian miracles, the *Disputation* explores the relationship between reason and revelation, constructing a Christian paradigm of wholeness by mapping the relationship of soul to senses. While the Jews in both genres share some characteristics, their different roles in the production of Christian identity defy reductive categorization

Disputation literature tends to acknowledge rather than to dismiss or mystify the role of material experience in human comprehension of the world and self. Hence, rather than being entirely "other" or monstrous in the *Disputation*, the Jew shares the Christian's "epistemological limitation and potentiality," indicative of the self-defining purpose of anti-Jewish polemical writings.[26] This is the shared ground upon which Jew and Christian can converse; thus, Steven Kruger perceptively links disputations to medieval dream visions, which also present us with a refracted self in the interior dream mirror that is "affiliated with the lower realm of the sense."[27] Christians in dream visions are reduced to a literal, rather than spiritual, comprehension of reality because of their sin, but their pilgrimage inward restores to them spiritual vision. To say then that the Jew in the Vernon *Disputation* is merely a "projection" of Christian anxiety is not quite accurate, for this formulation both avoids the question of *which* anxiety is engaged and dismisses the theme of legitimate sensual experience in the ascent to God. The Jew surely functions to acknowledge and explore shared epistemological territory in the demarcation of Christian and Jewish identity; however, these boundaries are explored and identified through religious symbols of late-medieval Christianity that function in a broad range of rituals and discourses in late-medieval culture and are themselves polyvalent. One might say the same for the figure of the Jew in various literary genres. Margery Kempe, for example, chastises the Jews in her vivid Crucifixion meditations; but she acknowledges the Jew as one category of otherness in a complicated taxonomy of identity when she is identified by layfolk and clergy in York as a Lollard, a virgin wearing white, a potential martyr, and a Jewess.[28] Similarly, the identity of the Jew in the Vernon manuscript reflects the evolving role of the Jew in Christian thought: Scriptural Jew, rational Jew, conspiratorial Jew.

The medieval Jewish-Christian disputation is a significant literary genre in medieval polemical writing, whether in Latin or vernacular, because it has plagued historians with its indeterminate function.[29] Historians acknowledge that the eleventh- and twelfth-century intellectual dialogues about faith, individual and social identity, epistemology, and Biblical authority might derive from genuine conversations between Christians and Jews, although some are simply academic treatises.[30] Modern readers appear to expect both toleration and narrative realism from medieval intellectuals who may have actually known Jews. Odo of Tournai's *Disputatio contra Judaeum Leonem nomine de adventu Christi filii Dei* (ca. 1105), which claims to record an actual conversation with a learned Jew of Senlis, is indeed less virulently anti-Judaic than the polemics of Peter the Venerable, whose purely exegetical treatises on the Jews bear no evidence of genuine exchange or interest in Jewish law and custom.[31] In Odo's treatise, Leo the Jew presents his opponent with authentic, well-reasoned logic in response to Christian doctrine deemed blasphemous or ridiculous by Jews, such as the Incarnation, a Trinitarian God, and virginal conception. Odo's conclusion to the treatise acknowledges the very real appeal of Judaism to Catholics, most particularly its compatibility with

Aristotelian observation of experience: "I presented these reasoned arguments to the Jew regarding the advent of Christ, because some people urged me to argue more subtly for certain Catholics who had sided with the views of the Jew" (Resnick, 97). Odo's thoughtful representation of the Jew, in contrast to Peter the Venerable's more typical employment of the Jewish straw man who exemplifies a narrowly literalist understanding of Scripture, may be grounded in his familiarity with the wealthy and cultivated Jewish community of Senlis. In any case, his conclusion establishes the dual purpose of refuting legitimate Jewish arguments against Christian doctrine to convert Jews and wooing rationalist Christians away from Judaism.

Although some disputations prior to the expulsions of the Jews from France and England may reflect a genuine interest in converting Jews, the majority of extant dialogues between Christians and Jews appear to be little more than theological exercises providing the occasion for Christian anti-Jewish polemic. Disputation literature, however, still underwent significant alterations according to intellectual developments from the early *Tractatus contra Judaeos* to the rationalistic polemics of prescholastic thinkers like Peter the Venerable and Gilbert Crispin.[32] When Christian scholars, through their newly acquired knowledge of anti-Christian Hebrew texts and the Talmud, reconceived the threat Judaism posed to Christianity, they altered the identity of the blind Scriptural Jew to the conspiratorial Jew (Cohen, *The Friars and the Jews*, 242–64). The evolving and sometimes contradictory representation of the Jew in monastic and scholastic disputation literature can help us gage the nature of and rationale for medieval Christian anti-Judaism, for literary conventions themselves are perceptual indicators of genuine realities—audiences understood specific narrative patterns, images, and symbols because they received them in particular cultural contexts where they both interpreted and constructed reality. And this is especially true of any religious literature purporting to construct Christian identity in a highly ritualized, sacramentalized culture of reception. Christian identity in disputation literature reflects the dynamism of late-medieval religious culture, especially in the thirteenth and fourteenth centuries, when we have a myriad of new devotional forms and images.[33]

Jewish identity cannot be static in a literature of Christian identity that evolves over the centuries in appeal to evolving lay and clerical audiences. We readily recognize that the romance genre, as transmitted to England, underwent significant shifts in form and function reflective of its varied audience and their political and cultural expectations.[34] The same is surely true of Jewish-Christian debate literature; certainly the Vernon *Disputation* offers us a hybrid narrative: polemical dialogue, landscape and plot of romance, eucharistic symbolism, each component offering a competing notion of identity and discourse of the "self." The disputation conflates eucharistic and romance imagery in a vision that is subsumed into the consecrated host and concludes with the conversion of its Jewish character after much debate with the Christian, Sir Walter. The text resembles twelfth-century disputes in focusing on scriptural hermeneutics and in the absence of thirteenth-century elements such as a conspiratorial Jew masking violent intentions against the host. The evidence of host desecration narrative and imagery elsewhere in the Vernon manuscript underscores the generic complexity of the Vernon *Disputation* as it transforms the romance journey and polemical debate into a eucharistic miracle; after all, the textual community of the Vernon manuscript was familiar with the late-medieval narrative demonization of Jews, and could not have discounted the images presented so vividly in the Marian miracle illustrations in visualizing the Jew.

In marked contrast to the vicious Jew of many exempla and tales, the Jew who accompanies "Sir Walter" in the Vernon *Disputation* is "wys" (479: 7); "A Mon muchel of his miht" (479: 26); and a University of Paris clerk of divinity like the Christian who is his intellectual friend and debating partner.[35] Despite the improbability of a Jew permitted to become a "Maister" of divinity with an English clerk, the narrative conjures a debate reminiscent of Odo of Tournai's with the Jew Leo, who is rational, eloquent, and worthy as a sparring partner. Leo's specific identity—for Jews are often unnamed in anti-Jewish Christian polemic—and his resistance to conversion at the dialogue's conclusion provide Odo's disputation with a touch of realism lacking in the Vernon narrative. In the Vernon *Disputation*, the Jew listens patiently to Sir Walter's claim of Christ's dual nature as the Son of God, his messiahship, as well as to a description of Mary's virginal conception of Christ (485–86: 33–48). These are among the tenets of Christianity that real as opposed to fictional Jews found blasphemous, ridiculous, or offensive.

Although the Christian's response to Jewish disbelief is predictably vehement—he threatens the Jew with beating, prison, and damnation—the Jew's position is firmly based in his monotheism, his belief in God as the sole creator of "þe sonne and þe Moone" (480: 54), and his rejection of the theory of atonement and God's incarnation (55–56). When the Christian sets a wager, promising to show the Jew Christ at His death, the Jew's response is calm and lacking in ridicule:

> So const þou not do
> ffor al þi clergye; þerto,
> As haue I reste oþer Ro,
> þi Reson is nouȝt. (*A Disputation*, 481: 93–96)

To the Jew, there is no such thing as original sin, and thus no necessity for atonement for it; his comprehension of Genesis 1–3 has nothing to do with an Augustinian "fall," but is clearly informed by a Jew's sense that Adam and Eve are our first natural parents: "Boþe of Adam and of Eue / Of hem we weore alle I-wrouhte" (481: 83–84). Undoubtedly this Jew shares the pervasive characteristic of the "blind" Jews, who cannot read the Book of the World in reference to God's Word, and thus the Word made flesh, in late-medieval literature; his desire to witness Jesus's crucifixion is in keeping with the role of Jew as materialist rationalist in anti-Jewish Christian polemics. Yet in his literal seeing, his progress toward a mystery, and his need to apply his own senses to the full experience, he is as much "like" as unlike the Christian. Their quest for the ultimate reality of the transubstantiated host in the Man of Sorrows occurs in the landscape of romance, with its implicit invitation to self-discovery, misreading, and the experience of ambiguity and misdirection. And like the romance landscape, the Vernon disputation's geography dissolves into a dreamlike, spiritual and psychological realm, a hall of mirrors that presses the participants to define "reality" in the face of illusion and disorientation. The hall wherein Sir Walter and his companion witness a eucharistic miracle is a splendid metaphor for the process of spiritual conversion and the kind of interior "sight" that such transformation entails.

The narrative incorporates elements of both the dream vision and romance as it charts the liminal journey to miracle, an episodic journey that explores "the relationship between nature and revelation" and thus material and spiritual seeing.[36] As in roughly contemporary dream visions such as *Pearl*, the disputation between the literal-minded protagonist and the enlightened guide is meant to mediate between the spiritual and corporeal realms. This hard-won knowledge in late-medieval dream visions depends upon an Aristotelian acceptance of the senses and the imagination, though they have a lower place than spiritual sight. In assigning the primary role of Reason to the Jew, but not rejecting the legitimacy of reason in the spiritual ascent, the Vernon *Disputation* conforms to more illustrious late-medieval models of spiritual illumination, such as Dante's *Commedia* or Bonaventure's *Itinerarium*. However, the Christian in the Vernon disputation is not the equal of a Beatrice, Lady Philosophy, or the *Pearl* maiden; spiritual physicians whose allegorical authority depends upon noncorporeal vision. Rather, the Christian, while more receptive to the mystery he will witness by virtue of faith, inhabits with the Jew the sacramental world where faith is nourished by the sensual celebration of the mass. This sacramental emphasis, much as at the end of *Pearl*, where the dreamer embraces his partial revelation in reception of the eucharist, is manifested by the unconsecrated host the Christian carries as a talisman so that that the fiend will not trouble them. The distribution of paxbread at the end of the mass, a substitution for the eucharist, and the tradition of the kissing of the pax or osculatorium—an object made of wood or precious metal bearing an image of the lamb or a crucifixion scene—was common in England from the thirteenth century. Just as Sir Walter will gain his identity (a central theme of romance), and the Jew will convert to a neoplatonic or sacramental view of reality, so must the pax transform from sacred bread into the literal body and blood of Christ, as it does when Sir Walter elevates it at the bewitching feast in the hall of mirrors. In fact, this sacramental realization of the commensal symbol alone can effect Christian identity and conversion.

The landscape the Christian and Jew traverse is typical of romance geography and dream vision, exteriorized states of liminality inviting self-discovery. Both genres feature a protagonist's struggle to comprehend his "corporeal and spiritual" nature, a knowledge that in late-medieval dream visions depends upon an Aristotelian acceptance of the legitimacy of sensual experience (Lynch, 46–76). The Jew and Christian follow strange paths until they reach a city that appears to be an earthly paradise. Here, amidst birdsong and the smell of herbs and spices, they enter a hall that turns out to be King Arthur's, and they witness the joyful gathering of the Round Table knights. They pause here briefly before traveling on to a "Nonnerie" where "þer was mony a derworþe dame / in Dyapre dere" (490: 199–200). Amidst much courtly splendor, Sir Walter is personally welcomed and invited to a sumptuous banquet with "schire cloþes and schene," "Riche metes" and bountiful wines "In Coupes ful gret" (490: 209–24). The eucharistic altar was a place for the distinction of "apparitions and illusions: the former were divine, the latter satanic. But it was not always easy to distinguish which was which."[37] Walter's suspicions about the "nonnerie," with its potential distractions of "murþe and munstralysy" are confirmed when he becomes aware of a crucifix at the far end of the room. The image of Christ on the cross, attended by Mary and John, is familiar from penitential lyrics, but this bleeding Man of Sorrows conforms to the more specific, eucharistic iconography of the "Mass of St. Gregory." In this seventh-century miracle tale, popularized in the vernacular from the thirteenth century, St. Gregory proves Christ's presence in the eucharist by requesting that a doubting woman be granted a vision of the host transformed into bleeding flesh.[38] Images of the Man of Sorrows, Christ bleeding into the chalice on the altar, were commonly depicted in English books of hours, often in conjunction with prayers for the elevation of the host and the feast of Corpus Christi. When framed within the story of the Mass of St. Gregory, the Man of Sorrows image invites meditation on spiritual and corporeal sight, a theme of some significance in eucharistic miracle stories which frequently featured Jews, rather then women, as unbelieving. Jews appeared widely in tales involving punishment for host desecration or illustrating their conversion after they witness an anthropomorphic vision of the Real Presence (Despres, "Cultic Anti-Judaism," 416–21). Indeed, the Vernon manuscript includes a variant of this story in its compilation of Corpus Christi sermon exempla (f. 196r) (Despres, "Cultic Anti-Judaism," 420–21).

The Vernon Corpus Christi exemplum, however, incorporates a critical element of anti-Judaic iconography that subtly links its eucharistic imagery to that of the Marian miracles and the *Disputation*: the bleeding child as host motif. The exemplum begins much like the *Disputation*, with a Jew and a Christian traveling together.[39] When the Christian hears the mass bell ring, he enters the church, leaving his companion outside impatiently awaiting his return. When the Jew enters to retrieve the Christian, he witnesses the elevation of the host, which appears to him as a bleeding child that multiplies upon its distribution to those kneeling to receive the eucharist. By the fourteenth century, this tale, which has numerous analogues, connected the sacrament of the eucharist to tales of host desecration and ritual murder, wherein the child becomes Christ's surrogate in a literal reenactment of the Crucifixion performed by vengeful Jews. The inclusion of "The Jew of Bourges" and the analogue to *The Prioress's Tale* in the Vernon *mariale* is evidence of the conflation of eucharistic iconography and Jewish perfidy in the late-medieval religious imagination. The Jew's very presence before the crucifix in the Vernon *Disputation* suggests the potential for sacrilege and violence, or half-hearted and thus counterfeit conversion, as does that of the Jew in Vernon Corpus Christi exemplum who merely wishes to repress the grisly sight of the host as bleeding child.

The Vernon *Disputation*, however, avoids these predictable conclusions in its investigation of spiritual and literal ways of seeing. Sir Walter abstains from the carnal feast and his eucharistic fast has been rewarded by this vision of Christ's bleeding body on the cross. The discourse is no longer the "rational" argumentation of the disputation, nor the specular language of distorted images and doubtful sight in the romance or vision; now the language is that of the eucharistic miracle, in which a reality based upon the Word made flesh the Real Presence prevails. No conversion based upon earthly sight or potential illusion will suffice for conversion in the poem's eucharistic idiom.

Sir Walter takes the paxbread from his pocket and elevates it before the crucifix, a para-liturgical gesture that transforms the table into an altar for a sacramental rather than an earthly feast:

> Þe Cristen Mon hedde a derworþ þinge,
> On his Bodi, he gon hit brynge:
> Þat a prest schulde wiþ synge
> Whon Masse schulde be don.
> "ȝif þou be god so fre
> Þat for me diȝed on pe tre,
> Here þi sone mai þou se,"
> And heold him a-bouen. (491: 245–52)

The moment of elevation, or sacring, in the liturgy was perhaps the most private and individual in the entire mass. When the sacring bell rang and the host was elevated, the devout would kneel and offer up prayer that, in effect, summed up individual and collective Christian identity: confession, prayer for the dead, personal petitions and intercessions, and prayer for the Christian community. Given the culmination of the mass in the elevation, "the overwhelming majority of prayers provided for the laity at Mass were, therefore, elevation prayers" (Duffy, 119). Increasingly, English books of hours and prayer books provided "private" moments of devotion to the eucharist by illustrating the elevation. Through such meditations, the devout could imaginatively re-experience this sacred moment, recovering imaginatively the sensual effects of the bells and incense. Yet this highly sensual experience, rather than belonging to the realm of the ordinary senses, occurred in the miraculous space between natural law and unseen realities. In Pietro Camporesi's graphic words,

> The awesomeness of the sacrifice caused the dislocation of natural laws. It violated them through a series of impossible alchemic reactions that upset the relationship between substances and accidents. Color, odor, flavor survived the annihilation of the substances that expressed them. By turning into flesh and blood, the primary substances—bread and wine—changed radically in essence, but their physical attributes survived their metamorphosis. . . . God has introduced himself into a balsamic "mysterious food" in order to modify and remold those who ate and digested it, without being modified Himself. (Camporesi, 226)

The visual experience of transubstantiation prior to actual reception and ingestion of the host necessarily increased the participant's awareness of the sacrament's transformational effect on all matter, all reality, and particularly on the bodily corruptibility of the recipient. Through the eucharist, God provides believers with an earthly experience of the ultimate reality—wholeness, individuality, and incorruptibility—at the final resurrection. Unlike Adam and Eve, whose eating resulted in mortality, medieval Christians eat to return to the incorruptibility denied them by original sin.

Perhaps this is why when Sir Walter elevates the host, the illusory building, with its bright candles and mirth, "barst." The "sonne" and "mone," that the Jew appropriated in his early argument as evidence of God's creative act, are darkened, as at the Crucifixion; and with the recension of this light, "Al þe gere þat was gay / Was þenne I-wasted a-way" (491: 252–58). In the darkness, the Jew and the Christian must determine reality without relying on human sight or other earthbound experience. Only upon his emergence from darkness does the Jew acknowledge that the Arthurian hall, the nunnery, and the earthly feast—corporeal delights to be enjoyed in the here and now—were fiendish illusions. Rather than offering the reader or listener a fearful or punitive sense of Jewish conversion, the conclusion of the Vernon *Disputation* is joyful, and these new "brothers" walk back to the city together, where they share a meal in what is clearly a reference to unitive Christian eating at mass.

The prospect of reconciling this converted Jew to the enraged father in "The Jewish Boy" (ff. 124–25), or the murderous Jews in "The Child Slain by the Jews" (f. 124) is difficult, yet the practice of reading as collation demands a synthesis. Social iconologies reflect and create social memory, and narratives thereby influence present reality as much as they reconstruct the past. The attention to Jews and "Jewishness" in the Vernon manuscript, especially in the absence of a Jewish community, witnesses to the continued importance of Jews in the construction of Christian identity. But it also provides us with important evidence of conflicting attitudes towards the Jew, who emerges from these narratives simultaneously as intellectual, criminal, convertable, and equally resistant to genuine conversion.

Chaucer's inclusion of *The Prioress's Tale* in *The Canterbury Tales,* followed by an admonitory reference to Hugh of Lincoln's "historical" ritual murder, dramatizes the way in which medieval stories were recollected, linked to social memories, and pressed for their spiritual relevance by individuals through meditation. Modern readers might have rather different conversations about Chaucer's own anti-Judaism had he incorporated *another* tale featuring Jews—like the Vernon *Disputation*—into his compendium of significant stories and genres. In its very breadth and conflicting representation of the Jews, the Vernon manuscript offers us the protean Jew who anticipates Shakespeare's Shylock in his refusal to be either the Scriptural Jew or the demonic usurer. Far from being anomalous, Shylock typifies the ambiguous Christian representation of the Jew as romantic comedy hovers on the edge of tragedy.

Notes

1.   I would like to thank the University of Puget Sound Enrichment Committee for the purchase of a microfilm of the Vernon manuscript. The manuscript is also available in facsimile; see *The Vernon manuscript: a facsimile of Bodleian Library, Oxford, Ms. Engl. Poet.a.1 with an Introduction by A. I. Doyle* (Cambridge, England: D. S. Brewer, 1987).

2.   Kathleen Scott has described this hefty volume, originally boasting 420 to 422 leaves, as "a virtual library with approximately 403 separate items,": *A Survey of Manuscripts Illuminated in the British Isles, Later Gothic Manuscripts 1390–1490,* Vol. II (London: Harvey Miller, 1996), 19, no. 1. A. I. Doyle concurs that the Vernon manuscript, compiled not in London but by a provincial team over several years' time, to the costly tune of 50 to 100 pounds, contains "a considerable proportion of what we know to have been written in the relevant genres up to that period;" see Doyle, "The Shaping of the Vernon and the Simeon Manuscripts," in *Studies in the Vernon Manuscript,* ed. Derek Pearsall (Cambridge, England: D. S. Brewer, 1990), 6. Scholars have also noted its English contents, citing provision for English translations from the Latin and French throughout and the emphasis on native saints and writers such as Walter Hilton, William Langland, and Richard Rolle.

3.   See Avril Henry, " 'The Pater Noster in a table ypented,' and Some Other Presentations of Doctrine in the Vernon Manuscript," in *Studies in the Vernon Manuscript,* 89: hereafter cited in text. For a comprehensive treatment of Continental mysticism's influence on the book culture of late-medieval En-

gland and English devotionalism, see *Prophets Abroad: The Reception of Continental Holy Women in Late Medieval England*, ed. Rosalynn Voaden (Cambridge, England: D. S. Brewer, 1996); *De Cella in Seculum, Religious and Secular Life and Devotion in Late Medieval England*, ed. Michael G. Sargent (Cambridge: D. S. Brewer, 1989).

4. The single allusion to Lollards in the Vernon manuscript occurs in reference to a Lollard proposal for Church disendowment and appears in conjunction with the redaction of Aelred's *Inclusarum*: Arne Zetterson and Bernard Diensberg, *The English Text of the Ancrene Riwle, The "Vernon" Text* (Oxford: Oxford University Press, 2000), xii.

5. *Councils & Synods with Other Documents Relating to the English Church, Vol. 2, A.D. 1205–1313, Part I*, eds. F. M. Powicke and C. R. Cheney (Oxford: Clarendon Press, 1964), 57–96. Avril Henry outlines the various texts in the Vernon manuscript fulfilling the directives of *Omnius utriusque sexus*, 106–11; see also Vincent Gillespie, "Vernacular Books of Religion," in *Book Production and Publishing in Britain 1375–1475*, eds. Jeremy Griffiths and Derek Pearsall (Cambridge, England: Cambridge University Press, 1989), 317–44.

6. Elisa Narin van Court, "The Siege of Jerusalem and Augustinian Historians: Writing About Jews in Fourteenth-Century England," *The Chaucer Review* 29 (1995), 227–29, and reprinted in this volume.

7. Van Court, 232. Van Court rebuts the tendency to displace Jews as "figurative references to other groups" in Mary Hamel, "The Seige of Jerusalem as a Crusading Poem," *Journeys Toward God: Pilgrimage and Crusade*, ed. Barbara N. Sargent-Baur (Kalamazoo, MI.: Medieval Institute Publications, Western Michigan University, 1992); also Gail McMurray Gibson, *The Theater of Devotion* (Chicago:, 1989), 35–38. See also Cecilia Cutts's classic essay, "The Croxton Play: An Anti-Lollard Piece," *Modern Language Quarterly* 5 (1944), 45–60; and Victor I. Scherb, "Violence and the Social Body in the Croxton Play of the Sacrament," in *Violence in Drama: Themes in Drama* 13, ed. James Redmond (Cambridge, England: Cambridge University Press, 1991), 69–78.

8. Anna Foa's essay "The Witch and the Jew: Two Alikes that Were Not the Same" provides a methodology in its exploration of why the Inquisition did not launch an anti-Jewish campaign in tandem with the witchcraft hunts; given the medieval association between Jews and demon worship, this is surely what we might expect to have happened. See A. Foa in *From Witness to Witchcraft, Jews and Judaism in Medieval Christian Thought*, ed. Jeremy Cohen (Wiesbaden, Germany: Harassowitz Verlag,1996), 361–74.

9. The Jewish protagonist in disputation literature, in sermon exempla, and in Marian miracles is always male; I know of no disputation narrative featuring a woman, and although women do appear in sermon exempla and miracles, they often convert to Christianity, whereas the male Jew usually perpetrates the crime and is unrepentant. On gender and Jewishness, see Ivan G. Marcus "Jews and Christians Imagining the Other in Medieval Europe," *Prooftexts* 15 (1995), especially 218–20.

10. A translation of the Fourth Lateran Canons appears in *Readings in Medieval History*, ed. Patrick J. Geary (Lewiston, NY: Broadview Press, 1989), 460–85.

11. R. I. Moore, *The Formation of a Persecuting Society* (Oxford: Blackwell, 1987), 7.

12. The literature on the Fourth Lateran Council and medieval anti-Judaism is vast. The primary documents are printed in Shlomo Simonsohn, *The Apostolic See and the Jews: Documents: 492–1404* (Toronto: Pontifical Institute of Medieval Studies, 1988); for an excellent summary of the Church's historical position on Judaism see Kenneth R. Stow, "Hatred of the Jews or Love of the Church: The Policy of the Medieval Papacy Toward the Jews," in *Anti-Semitism through the Ages*, ed. Shmuel Almog (New York: Pergamon Press, 1988), 71–89. An essential work on the Franciscan role in the cultivation of a virulent anti-Judaism is Jeremy Cohen's *The Friars and the Jews: The Evolution of Medieval Anti-Judaism* (Ithaca, NY: Cornell University Press, 1982); hereafter cited in text.

13. *Councils & Synods, with other Documents Relating to the English Church,* Vol. 2, 100.

14. Michael Camille, *The Gothic Idol, Ideology and Image-Making in Medieval Art* (Cambridge, England: Cambridge University Press, 1989), 182.

15. See Cecil Roth, *A History of the Jews in England* (Oxford: Oxford University Press, 1964), 95–96; Ruth Mellinkoff, *Outcasts: Signs of Otherness in Northern European Art of the Late Middle Ages* (Berkeley: University of California Press, 1993), 35–37; hereafter cited in text; on badges see 43–47.

16. Mary J. Carruthers, *The Book of Memory, A Study of Memory in Medieval Culture* (Cambridge: Cambridge University Press, 1990), 217; hereafter cited in text.

17. Jeremy Cohen, *Living Letters of the Law, Ideas of the Jew in Medieval Christianity* (Berkeley: University of California Press, 1999), 2: "In order to meet their particular needs, Christian theology and exegesis created a Jew of their own . . . a hermeneutically and doctrinally crafted Jew." Also see Denise L. Despres, "Cultic Anti-Judaism and Chaucer's Litel Clergeon," *Modern Philology* 94 (1994), 413–27; hereafter cited in text.

18. Amos Funkenstein, "Basic Types of Christian Anti-Jewish Polemics in the Later Middle Ages," *Viator* 2 (1971), 1–2; hereafter cited in text.

19. I acknowledge the argument of James Shapiro that the 1290 expulsion has been sanitized by historians to deflect attention from the brutal impoverishment and evisceration of Jewish communities in England prior to 1290 in a period of nascent nationalism, producing a satisfying narrative of their national past,: *Shakespeare and the Jews* (New York: Columbia University Press, 1996), 42–55. The scholarship on the Jews in England is considerable; I refer readers to Gavin Langmuir's magisterial works; Robert C. Stacey's important essay, "The Conversion of the Jews to Christianity in Thirteenth-Century England," *Speculum* 67 (1992), 263–83; and my bibliography in "Cultic Anti-Judaism and Chaucer's Litel Clergeon." Miri Rubin's recent study *Gentile Tales: The Narrative Assault on Late Medieval Jews* (New Haven, CT: Yale University Press, 1999; hereafter cited in text) moves literary discussions of English texts and images into the broader realm of cultural studies, and reflects upon the dissemination of anti-Judaic tales throughout Europe, taking into account the cultural context of recep-

tion. See also D. L. Despres, "Mary of the Eucharist: Cultic Anti-Judaism in Some Fourteenth-Century English Devotional Manuscripts," in *From Witness to Witchcraft: Jews and Judaism in Medieval Christian Thought*, ed. Jeremy Cohen (Wiesbaden, Germany: Harrassowitz Verlag, 1996), 375–401; D. L. Despres, "Immaculate Flesh and the Social Body: Mary and the Jews" *Jewish History* 12.1 (1998), 47–69; and Robert C. Stacey, "From Ritual Crucifixion to Host Desecration: Jews and the Body of Christ," *Jewish History* 12.1. (1998), 11–28.

20. Carole M. Meale, "The Miracles of Our Lady: Context and Interpretation," in *Studies in the Vernon Manuscript*, 115–36; hereafter cited in text.

21. For a survey of Jewish demonization in late-medieval art, see Moshe Lazar, "The Lamb and the Scapegoat, The Dehumanization of the Jews in Medieval Propaganda Imagery," in *Anti-Semitism in Times of Crises*, ed. Sander L. Gilman and Steven T. Katz (New York: New York University Press, 1991), 38–80; and Debra Hassig, "The Iconography of Rejection: Jews and Other Monstrous Races," in *Image and Belief, Studies in Celebration of the Eightieth Anniversary of The Index of Christian Art*, ed. Colum Hourihane (Princeton, NJ: Princeton University Press, 1999), 25–37.

22. See Suzanne Lewis, *Reading Images, Narrative Discourse and Reception in the Thirteenth-Century Illuminated Apocalypse* (Cambridge, England: Cambridge University Press, 1995), 215–21.

23. The Vernon illustrations to "the child in Paris killed by Jews" and "the Jewish child thrown in an oven" are reproduced in Doyle's *Facsimile*, f. 124v and f. 125r.

24. Both Meale and Rubin have noted the importance of mothers as witnesses in anti-Judaic narrative; Rubin discusses the paradoxical dangers of feminine fluidity and their greater ability to convert to Christianity.

25. See Despres, "Mary of the Eucharist," 391–93; Carra Ferguson O'Meara, " 'In the Earth of the Virginal Womb': The Iconography of the Holocaust in Medieval Art," *Art Bulletin* 63 (1981), 75–88.

26. Steven F. Kruger, *Dreaming in the Middle Ages* (Cambridge, England: Cambridge University Press, 1992), 144.

27. Kruger, 139. Kruger notes that "in the dialectic between Christian and Jewish ways of reading, dreams play a crucial role," as in the conversion narrative of the Jewish Hermann of Cologne (*Opusculum de conversione sua*), 158. Jeremy Cohen provides a fascinating analysis of this text in *Living Letters of the Law*, 291–305.

28. *The Book of Margery Kempe,* ed. Sanford Brown Meech and Hope Emily Allen. Early English Text Society, o.s., 212 (Oxford: Oxford University Press, 1940), 124, 30–32. On Kempe's references to Jews see Judith Rosenthal, "Margery Kempe and Medieval Anti-Judaism," *Medieval Encounters* 5 1999).

29. David Rokeah, "The Church Fathers and the Jews in Writings Designed for Internal and External Use," in *Anti-Semitism Through the Ages*, 39–69. Historians speculate that eleventh-century disputations may be a response to Christian awareness of a tradition of Jewish anti-Christian polemical literature dating from the ninth or tenth century in Jewish communities within Islam.

See also David Berger, "The Jewish-Christian Debate in the High Middle Ages," in *Essential Papers on Judaism and Christianity in Conflict from Late Antiquity to the Reformation*, ed. Jeremy Cohen (New York: New York University Press, 1991), 484–513. For an overview of the subject, see Gilbert Dahan, *The Christian Polemic against the Jews in the Middle Ages*, trans. Jody Gladding (Notre Dame, IN: University of Notre Dame Press, 1998).

30. Anna Sapira Abulafia, "Jewish Christian Disputations and the Twelfth-Century Renaissance," *Journal of Medieval History* 15.2. (1989), 105.

31. Odo purports to have "had an encounter and discussion with a Jew when he had attended a council at Poitiers (the council was held on 18 November 1100) and had been called upon to dispatch some business involving this Jew and the community of Senlis." See Irven M. Resnick, *On Original Sin and A Disputation with the Jew, Leo, Concerning the Advent of Christ, The Son of God* (Philadelphia: University of Pennsylvania Press, 1994), 29; hereafter cited in text.

32. See Funkenstein, 373; and Abulafia, on the transformation from the "rational" Jew to the "neutral debating partner," 107–108.

33. Thomas Bestul has recently argued against the tendency to universalize even crucifixion narratives; for example, the emphasis on filth and excrement in Latin passion narratives reflects historically evolving strategies of Jewish degradation. See chapter 3, "The Representation of the Jews in Medieval Passion Narratives," in *Texts of the Passion, Latin Devotional Literature, and Medieval Society* (Philadelphia: University of Pennsylvania Press, 1996), 69–110.

34. See, for example, Susan Crane's discussion in *Insular Romance, Politics, Faith, and Culture in Anglo-Norman and Middle English Literature* (Berkeley: University of California Press, 1986), 10–11: "Genre was not an important concept for medieval theorists . . . thus, insofar as observations about the generic nature of medieval romance can be made, they must be fluid and contingent, seeking to clarify the nature of single works rather than to classify them."

35. "A Disputation between a Christian and a Jew," in *The Minor Poems of the Vernon Manuscript, Part II*, ed. F. J. Furnivall (London: Kegan Paul, 1901), 484–93; hereafter cited in text by page and line number.

36. Kathryn L. Lynch, *The High Medieval Dream Vision, Poetry, Philosophy, and Literary Form* (Stanford, CA: Stanford University Press, 1998), 50; hereafter cited in text.

37. Piero Camporesi, "The Consecrated Host: A Wondrous Excess," in *Fragments for the History of the Human Body*, ed. Michel Feher (New York: Zone, 1989), 225–27; hereafter cited in text.

38. See Rubin, *Corpus Christi, The Eucharist in Late Medieval Culture* (Cambridge, England: Cambridge University Press, 1991), 308–310; Eamon Duffy, *The Stripping of the Altars: Traditional Religion in England, 1400–1580* (New Haven, CT: Yale University Press, 1992), 238–40; hereafter cited in text.

39. *The Minor Poems of the Vernon Manuscript, Part I*, ed. Carl Horstmann (London: Kegan Paul, 1892), 174–77.

10

The Siege of Jerusalem and Augustinian Historians

Writing about Jews in Fourteenth-Century England

ELISA NARIN VAN COURT

After years of critical neglect, *The Siege of Jerusalem*[1] recently has been the focus of two fine studies—studies that invoke earlier assessments of the poem and then propose new contexts for understanding either the composition or the reception of this work. Notorious for its violence and virulent anti-Judaism, this late-fourteenth-century alliterative narrative was dismissed years ago by Derek Pearsall as a "model of decadent poetic."[2] Ten years later, A. C. Spearing recoiled from its "horrible delight in the suffering of the Jews," and concluded that the poem "leaves no unresolved ambiguities in the reader's mind."[3] Unlike Chaucer's *Prioress's Tale*, which has been for years the subject of a lively debate about the nature and significance of its anti-Judaism, the graphically violent and seemingly unambiguous bigotry of *The Siege of Jerusalem* convinced critics that the work was a repellently conventional, if somewhat overwrought, model of late-medieval sentiment about the Jews. Invoking and then echoing these earlier assessments, Ralph Hanna decries the poem's "gratuitous" and "cheerfully sanctioned violence."[4] He goes on to suggest the suitability of its composition in Yorkshire, where two hundred years earlier the Jews of York had been massacred in one of the most infamous episodes in the history of medieval English Jewry.[5] Nonetheless, Hanna then proposes a fifteenth-century reception and Lancastrian reading of the poem in which flayed Jewish flesh is transformed into flayed Lollard flesh. In a methodologically similar reading, Mary Hamel argues that the poem was composed in response to the briefly resurgent crusade fervor of the late fourteenth century. In her cogent discussion, the object of the poem's "repugnant brand of anti-Semitism" is not the Jews, but the Saracens.[6]

Both Hanna and Hamel join the small but unanimous group of critics of this otherwise little remarked-upon poem who are repulsed by the anti-Judaism evident in both subject matter and language; yet they go further than earlier assessments when they propose that either in its composition or in its reception, the poem's anti-Judaism is a deviant tropological bigotry which is relocated onto other groups. In essence, they both decry the poem's anti-Judaism and then suggest that the poem is not about Jews.

These readings of displacement, wherein Jews are read as figurative references to other groups, are understandable: the Jews were not materially present in England after the expulsion of 1290, and it is possible that in their absence their presence in narratives becomes a kind of pedagogical category into which other sources of anxiety are displaced. Much has been written, for example, about the Jew as Lollard in the Croxton *Play of the Sacrament*.[7] Therefore, I do not want to suggest that the Jews are *never* used as a trope for other heterodox, heretical, or marginal groups. Nonetheless, I fear that this kind of interpretive supersession elides the very real issue of Jewish presence in Christendom that continues to concern the Christian community even in the absence of Jews. We need to remember, for example, that the Talmud was burned in France *after* the Jews were expelled from that country in the early decades of the fourteenth century.[8] We need also to recognize that the proliferation of late-fourteenth-century Middle English narratives which directly address the issues of Jew *qua* Jew in relationship to the Christian community indicates a significant and ongoing interest in Jews and Judaism.

Equally at issue here is the modern critic's impulse to dislocate the Jews from this text. This procedure assumes a monolithic and static medieval bigotry against *any* group perceived to threaten a coherent Christian community. Such an assumption, I think, denies both the specificity and the complexities available in the *Siege*. While the modern reader may be tempted to group Jews, Saracens, and heretics into one vast homogenized group in antagonistic relation to Christianity, medieval writings, even when grouping these varieties of unbelievers, maintained distinctions among them.[9] In *The Siege of Jerusalem* particularly, the peculiar form of bigotry which often seems on the verge of deconstructing itself, testifies to the equally peculiar and *very specific* relationship between Judaism and Christianity. I will offer in this essay a reading of *The Siege of Jerusalem* in which I reinscribe the Jews as the subject of the poem; reevaluate the ways in which the Jews are represented in the poem; and discuss the possibilities of this poem's place in a particular tradition of historical writing in England. I will argue that not only is the poem really about Jews, but that in addition to the graphically violent anti-Judaism of the poem, there is a competing sympathetic narrative strand that complicates what has been considered a straightforward and brutal poetic.

Hanna tells us that *The Siege of Jerusalem* was probably composed in the last decades of the fourteenth century in far west Yorkshire (Hanna, "Contextualizing," 114–15). Its learned source texts suggest that it was composed in a monastic setting, and the eight surviving manuscripts testify to a wide popularity. Drawing on chronicles and legendary materials, including Josephus's first-century account of the *Jewish War*, Higden's *Polychronicon*, the *Bible en françois* of Roger d'Argenteuil, and the *Legenda Aurea*,[10] the *Siege* poet constructed a detailed alliterative narrative that relates the story of the destruction of Jerusalem in 70 C.E. and the dispersion of the Jews. This is a text which announces itself as an exemplar of Christian thinking about the Jews: the destruction and dispersion are a favorite theme of patristic literature offered as testimony to Jewish apostasy, the supersession of Judaism, and the triumph of Christianity.[11] Yet patristic writers did not have to turn to learned source texts for their material, for Jesus's prophecy (*ex eventu*) of the destruction of Jerusalem in Luke 19 is repeatedly invoked as proof that the destruction of the Temple is the Lord's vengeance against the unbelieving Jews: "For the days shall come upon you, when your enemies will cast up a bank about you and surround you, and hem you in on every side, and dash you to the ground, you and your children within you, and they will not leave one stone upon another in you; because you did not know the time of your visitation" (Luke 19:43–44). Significantly, this Lucan version of the destruction of Jerusalem was not only the subject of patristic writings; it was an integral part of the common heritage of medieval Christendom. By the fourth century, this passage was included in the lectionary as the Gospel text for the tenth Sunday after Pentecost.[12] Enshrined in the homiletic tradition of the medieval Church, the story of the destruction of Jerusalem acquired an allegorical interpretation when Gregory the Great urged Christians to identify with the Jews of Jerusalem: the state of the Christian soul was, in Gregory's sermon, "identical to that of a city under siege" (Wright, 24). This allegorical reading of the Luke passage dominated the sermon tradition for centuries until Nicholas of Lyra, in writings calculated to contribute to increased hostility against the Jews, popularized the restoration of the *sensus literalis* in the fourteenth century.[13] What had been read allegorically with moral implications for the Christian soul is once again read in the fourteenth century as historical testimony to Jewish apostasy and supersession. And in yet another revival of interest in reconstructing this narrative of destruction and dispersion, and again as part of the increased polemic against the Jews, the first dramatizations of the destruction of Jerusalem also appear in the mid-fourteenth century (Wright, 33).

The *Siege* poet's choice of this narrative, then, which is not only retold annually as part of the liturgy, but is *specifically* in the fourteenth century reliteralized in sermons and represented in dramatic performances, signals his participation in the discourse of displacement and supersession currently in vogue, and directed quite specifically against the Jews. Moreover, the poet not only draws on the Lucan image of no stone upon another, he insists upon it. Where his sources invoke this passage once to correct Josephus's secular rationale for the destruction, the *Siege* poet invokes it four times in the course of his narrative. Vespasian, envisioning himself as the agent of the fulfillment of the prophecy, vows that "Schal no ston vpon ston . stonde by y passé"

(352), a vow which is repeated twice more before he returns to Rome and the imperial crown. The Lucan lines are invoked a final time at the end of the poem when, after Titus and his men destroy the temple and the city walls, indeed, "nas no ston in þe stede . stondande alofte" (1285).

Yet, in an even more emphatic gesture of specificity, the *Siege* poet recreates a dramatic and exegetically perfect scene of supersession. The Roman and Jewish troops are arrayed outside the walls of Jerusalem; before the battle, Caiaphas, the High Priest of the Jews, comes out with his scribes to inspire the Jewish troops with readings from the Hebrew Scriptures:

> Lered men of þe lawe, . þat loude couþe synge,
> With sawters seten hym by . & þe psalmys tolde
> Of douȝty David þe kyng, . & oþer der storijs
> Of Joseph, þe noble Jewe, . & Judas þe knyȝt.
> Cayphas of þe kyst . kyppid a rolle
> & radde, how þe folke ran . proȝ þe re[d]e wa[ters],
> Whan Pharao & his ferde . wer in þe floode drouned;
> & myche of Moyses lawe . he mynned þat tyme.
> Whan þis faiþles folke . to þe feld comen,
> & batayled after þe bent . with many burne kene. (473–82)

Directly after this scene, Vespasian comes out to encourage *his* troops with a retelling of Christ's passion:

> Byholdeþ þe heþyng . & þe harde woundes,
> Þe betyng & þe byndyng, . þat þe body hadde:
> Lat neuer þis lawles ledis . lauȝ at his harmys,
> Þat bouȝt vs fram bale . with blod of his herte.
> . . . .
> Þat preueþ his passioun, . who so þe paas redeþ. (493–96)

This is a striking textual moment of oppositions: the Jews and their texts are superseded in the chronology of the poem by the Christians and *their* texts; but, of course, the supersession is not limited to the temporality of the narrative. We should note in passing the distinctions made between Scriptural and historical Jews: on the one hand, "douȝty David" and "Joseph, þe noble Jewe," on the other, "þis faiþles folke" who come out onto the field to fight. But more to the point are the two competing narratives offered here: the Jews tell the story of the Exodus, and Vespasian tells the story of Christ's passion. These are, of course, the foundational tropes of these two religions. The Exodus signifies both freedom from bondage and the giving of the covenant of the Law; the Passion signifies freedom from original sin through Christ's death and the giving of the "new" covenant of grace. In Christian typological exegesis, the Exodus is a prefigurative type of the Passion, just as Moses is a prefigurative type of Christ.[14] In this scene then, the Jewish narrative is fulfilled and superseded by the Christian, just as the Mosaic Law is evacuated when Vespasian calls the Jews "lawles" (495), even as Caiaphas relates "myche of Moyses lawe" (480). In this moment of exegetical supersession, the *Siege* poet introduces the main action of the poem—that action of destruction and dispersion—with a model of exegetical reading; a model for reading the main action of the poem as the culminating proof of the exegetical reading it contains.

These kinds of specific articulations of Jewish-Christian relations found in the poet's invocations of the Lucan passage and the competing biblical narratives can be found in smaller ways throughout the poem. When Hanna invokes flayed Jewish flesh as being read as that bared and flayed Lollard body under Lancastrian rule, he is referring to the execution of Caiaphas. But flaying is only a part of the death scene. The Jewish priest is flayed, drawn, and hung upside down with cats, dogs, and apes attached to him. And while flaying may resonate in the fifteenth century in particular ways, there is an even more striking historical resemblance: by the end of the fourteenth century: "In cases of capital punishment, it was an established custom . . . to hang a Jew by the feet and sometimes to hang beside him a fierce wolfdog as well."[15]

While it may be tempting to read Jew as "Jew" (or symbol for the unbelieving Lollard), as Gail McMurray Gibson does in her analysis of the Croxton *Play of the Sacrament*, even a superficial glance at fourteenth-century writing testifies to a continuing and, at times, radically ambivalent, interest in the Jews. Langland, Chaucer, Gower, the *Corpus Christi* plays, and the siege narratives come under this rubric; but additionally, many post-expulsion sermons preach Jewish conversion, *Mirk's Festial*, a homily collection, contains many stories of the miraculous conversion of the Jews, and the one surviving copy of Peter of Cornwall's *Disputation with Symon the Jew* survives in a fourteenth-century manuscript.[16] These are only a few examples of a substantial body of work that addresses the problems of Jewish presence in Christendom. And what is particularly intriguing about these fourteenth-century productions is that in the absence of the Jews, a number of these narratives demonstrate an ambivalent instability in their response to or representation of the Jews.

In her discussion of *The Siege of Jerusalem* as a crusade narrative, Hamel notes that its language is "oddly, less violent than some of the language used of the Saracens in the crusade texts," and that in its pity for the Jews, the poem is, in some respects, a "work of moderation"[17] compared to the crusade literature. I think that these observations are very apt; the most compelling argument I can make that this poem is about Jews is to demonstrate the nuance and ambivalence with which the *Siege* poet represents the

Jews, for it is in the simultaneous brutality and sympathy offered in this work that we find the dualistic Christian ideology about the Jews most fully and emphatically expressed. The representation of the Jews in most medieval narratives is, predictably, anti-Judaic. But the representation can also be complex and finely nuanced, a reflection (at least in part) of the centuries-old dualistic Christological perspective inherited in Church doctrine. This dualism, which originates in the Pauline injunctions: "As regards the gospel, they are enemies of God, for your sake; but as regards election they are beloved for the sake of their forefathers" (Rom. 11:28–29), was developed by Augustine and others into what is called the doctrine of relative toleration. With a patristic reading of Psalm 59:12 ("Slay them not, lest my people forget") as its central text, the doctrine of toleration enunciated a theological formula in which the Jews are accorded a role in Christendom: alive, but in servitude; alive, but socially and economically degraded; alive, but as symbols of Christ's passion. In an attempt to protect the Jews from massacre during preparations for the Second Crusade in the twelfth century, Bernard of Clairvaux, in both letters and sermons, drew on this doctrine of toleration, and, invoking Psalm 59:12, formulated explicit distinctions among Jews, Saracens, and heretics. The Jews, protected by biblical injunction, were "not to be persecuted, killed, or even put to flight."[18] Unfortunately, Saracens and heretics were *not* accorded this special dispensation. About the Saracens Bernard writes: "As they have now begun to attack us, it is necessary for those of us who do not carry a sword in vain to repel them with force" and in regard to heretics: "it is better to coerce heretics at sword point than to permit them to 'draw away many other persons into their error' " (in Berger, 91, 92). The sword is not to be raised against the Jews, yet they are not to be granted the same rights and privileges given to Christians. The complexities and ambivalent gestures of the Augustinian position, in which toleration is yoked inextricably with persecution, dominated most medieval Christian writing about the Jews, at least until the thirteenth and fourteenth centuries.[19] At this time, the policy of toleration began to come under increased scrutiny and in concert with increasing social, economic, and legal pressures a "new, more hostile ideology" began to inform ecclesiastical, secular, and popular writing about the Jews.[20] The narratives which draw on this Christian ideology are, like the ideology itself, complex and sometimes ambivalent. There is a fair amount of slippage as texts negotiate both the pressures exerted by long-standing and doctrinally sanctioned formulas (which are in the process of being revised) and their own historical and authorial contexts.

What is noteworthy about *The Siege of Jerusalem* is that even within the context of the doctrine of toleration, the poem exhibits a tenuous but fully articulated sympathy toward the Jews, and does so at a time when the doctrine of toleration had almost entirely yielded to a more hostile ideological and practical treatment of the Jews. This narrative is, on the one hand, outrageously violent and outrageously bigoted: fields run with blood and gore, and metal runs through "vn-mylt hertes" (556); the Jews are "þe heþen here" (307) "þe fals men" (551), "þis folke faiþles" (481), who "on no grace tristen" (515). When Titus and Vespasian set out for Judea, the narrative warns:

> Cytees vnder S[yon], . now is ʒour sorow uppe:
> Þe deþ of þe dereworþ Crist . der schal be ʒolden.
> Now is, Bethleem, þy bost . y-broʒt to an ende;
> Jerusalem & Iericho, . for-juggyd wrecchys,
> Schal neuer kyng of ʒour kynde . with croune be ynoyntid,
> Ne Jewe for Jesu sake . [i]ouke in ʒou more. (295–300)

Passages such as this, in which brutality against the Jews is justified as fitting revenge for Christ's death, join with the inescapable and excessive detail of violence and bloodshed in the poem to produce an *almost* convincing demonstration of a straightforward and brutal anti-Judaic poetic. I emphasize *almost* because I do not wish to fault earlier critics who focused upon what they saw as *the* anti-Judaism in the poem. There is much that *is* anti-Judaic in the *Siege* poet's narrative. There is, however, another inflection, another narrative strand, which continually intrudes upon and undermines the seemingly unambiguous anti-Judaism. For instance, in the simile that describes their flight into Jerusalem from the Romans they "flowen, as þe foule doþ, . þat faucoun wolde strike" (310), fall on the battlefield as "hail froward heuen" (598), and "wy[nn]en with mycel wo . þe walles with-ynne" (612). When the poet explains why there are so many Jews in Jerusalem (it is the Passover holiday), he departs from his sources and enlists the rhetoric of individuation as he refers to

> Princes & prelates . & poreil of þe londe,
> Clerkes & comens . of contrees aboute. (313–14)

This rhetorical catalogue effectively differentiates among Jews; they are not simply "þe faiþles," but varied social types. And in a related gesture the *Siege* poet undermines the stereotypes of his sources. In Josephus's *Jewish War* and Higden's *Polychronicon*, the Jews are persistently characterized as acting in "impetuosity and unbridled rage"[21] or "furor cum temeritate"[22]—what Trevisa translates as "woodnesse and folye" (429). In *The Siege of Jerusalem* the Jews speak "mekly" (338), and in their fighting are "ferce men & noble" (867), while the unbridled rage is transferred onto Vespasian, who is variously described as "wroþe" (371), "wode wedande wroþ" (381), and "wroþ as a wode bore" (781).

   There are many such small, unexpected moments in this poem, moments which startle the reader out of his or her complacent assessment of a conventional and anticipated representation of the Jews. (In one strikingly appropriate departure from his sources, the *Siege* poet has the Romans not only blockade the water sources for the city, but attempt to contaminate them with carcasses and filth. This is, of course, one of the more insidious accusations against the Jews during the plague years: that they intentionally contaminate wells to poison all of Christendom.) But, however fascinating these small, and frequent, disjunctions that undermine a stereotyped representation of the Jews, I would like to turn to an extended passage which, more than any other, exemplifies the nuanced account of the Jews which the *Siege* poet offers. This passage is a "set-piece" in the various siege narratives, significant both for its local effect and for its subtext. In this scene, a woman suffering from the siege-inflicted famine kills and eats her child. This act of cannibalistic infanticide in the sources is used as dramatic testimony to Jewish barbarity and becomes the final rationale for their destruction. The *Siege* poet reworks the rhetoric of his sources and produces a sympathetic account that invites not disgust but sorrow from the reader.

In the sources, the scene is prefaced by a pointed rendition of "you are what you eat" calculated to degrade and dehumanize the Jews. In Josephus, the starving Jews eat sewage, cow dung (V. 571), and "objects which even the filthiest of brute beasts would reject" (VI. 197). The *Polychronicon*, in even more explicit fashion, lists shield leather, filth which clung to stinking walls, vomit, cow dung, snake skins, and horse carcasses among the foodstuffs (4:438). Only the *Legenda Aurea* shows restraint as it reports that the Jews ate shoes, but it shares with the other narratives a second set of prefatory remarks in which children snatch food from parents, parents from children, husbands from wives, and wives from husbands.[23] All this is by way of introducing the infanticide and cannibalism. Josephus begins the scene with the claim that "I am here about to describe an act unparalleled in the history whether of Greeks or barbarians, and as horrible to relate as it is incredible to hear" (VI. 199). In his version, the mother is a woman of fortune who has lost her wealth in the siege. As a result, "the fire of rage was more consuming even than the famine," and she kills and eats her child "impelled by the promptings *alike* of fury and necessity" (VI. 204; *italics mine*). Her act is called the "abomination," and when the news spreads to the Romans, "the effect on the majority was to intensify their hatred of the nation" (VI. 214), and to justify Titus's resolve to destroy the city. The *Legenda Aurea*, with its usual economy, merely reports that the townspeople ran trembling and terrified away. In the *Polychronicon*, however, this "infamous" and "horrible" act impels Titus to exclaim as Trevisa translates, "We come to a bataille of men, but now I see þat we fiȝteþ aȝenst bestes; ȝit bestes rampaunt spareþ her owne kynde, be þey nevere so nedy, and helpeþ her owne children; but þese men devoureþ here owne children: þanne destroye we hem, for alle hir dedes stinkeþ"(447).

In *The Siege of Jerusalem*, the poet introduces the scene by noting the "hard hunger" (1063–65) that has befallen the town. The elaborate detail of disgusting foodstuffs is deleted and replaced with a detailed account of what they *do not* have: neither fish, nor flesh; bread, nor broth; water, nor wine "bot wope of himself" (1068–70): they drink their own tears.[24] Even when the narrative notes that they ate old shields and shoes, it is not, as in Josephus, "the shameless resort to inanimate articles of food" (VI. 199), but another reason to pity them, for the shields are difficult to chew ("þat liflode for ladies . was luþer to chewe" [1072]). The poet also deletes the prefatory remarks in which children and parents and husbands and wives snatch food from one another, and although he replaces this with the observation that they acted like wolves—the strong made war on the weak—even this is qualified by the first half-line: "wo wakned þycke" (1075).

In the *Siege* poet's account the mother is a "myld wyf" (1077) who addresses her child with "rewful wordes" (1079); she is "þat worþi wif" who tells the townspeople that "in a wode hunger" she roasted her own child (1089). And it is in the townspeople's response especially that the poet radically revises his sources. The response, whether here or in the sources, is essential to the episode; it is what sets the interpretive spin, as it were, the "right reading" with which the audience is expected to concur. In the *Siege* poet's "right reading" the townspeople hear what the mother has done and

> A-way þey went for wo . wepyng echone,
> & sayn: "Alas, in þis lif . how longe schule we dwelle?
> Ʒit beter wer at o brayde . in batail to deye,
> Þan þus in langur to lyue, . & lengþen our [p]yne." (1093–96)

They make a decision "pat deil was to hure" (1097): to kill everyone who is dying from hunger. There is no source for this self-massacre—in the *Vindicta Salvatoris* eleven thousand kill each other to prevent the enemy from claiming the glory of their deaths, but here in the *Siege* the slaying is prompted by moral imperative. Significantly, Jewish self-massacre had assumed, by the thirteenth and fourteenth centuries, the dimensions of spiritualized martyrology as a *kiddush ha-shem*, or sanctification of God's name, through which each victim "commits" an "act of ultimate piety." Although the appearance of the ideal of martyrdom in the Jewish communities is not easily explained, Kenneth Stow suggests that when eleventh-century Jewish messianic expectations were "replaced by wholesale massacre, the Jews sought a redemption of their own making: they took their lives 'sacrificially' as martyrs for the 'Sanctification of the Holy Name' . . . Israel had truly become the holy people, a nation of priests, itself the *agnus dei*, as if in open competition with the Christian claim that Christ alone was the perfect sacrifice."[25]

In a narrative whose purported object is vengeance for Christ's perfect sacrifice, the *kiddush ha-shem* of the Jews is a persuasive counterpoint to the source narratives' (and contemporary) accounts of the bestial Jews. Clearly, the local effect of this episode in *The Siege of Jerusalem* is radically different from its sources, where the act of cannibalism heightens the hatred and disgust directed at the Jews; here, disgust is transformed into sorrow and pity. Yet there is a subtext here that resonates beyond the local moment. When Josephus introduced this scene in his *Jewish War* with the claim that he would describe an act unparalleled in history, he was being more than a little disingenuous. This cannibalistic act, particularly when enacted by parent upon child, is part of the literature of prophetic warnings found throughout the Hebrew Scriptures. Leviticus, Deuteronomy, Kings, Jeremiah, Baruch, and Lamentations all have versions of cannibalism either prophesied or enacted in consequence of disobedience to God.[26] When these source narratives showcase this episode by making it both central and emphatic, they are demonstrating that Scriptural prophecy has been fulfilled. In his recasting of this episode then, the *Siege* poet not only transforms a local moment; he also comments, if only indirectly, on the fulfillment of Scripture which his entire narrative signifies.

If this were the only transformation the *Siege* poet made from his sources, it would be enough, I think, to encourage us to question the conventional wisdom of literary criticism concerning his representation of the Jews. As we have seen, however, in smaller and more subtle ways the poet complicates his narrative's anti-Judaism. And, there are other, less subtle passages in which the poet articulates his sympathy for the Jews. After the Romans execute Caiaphas and the scribes,

> Þe Jewes walten ouer þe walles . for wo at þat tyme,
> Seuen hundred slow hem-self . for sorow of her clerkes,
> Somme bent her heer . & fram þe hed pulled,
> & somme [down] for deil . dasch[e]de to grounde. (709–12)

The *Siege* poet's representation of Jewish woe and sorrow is uncompromised by the slightest suggestion that their hardship is either deserved or justified; there is no subtextual sneer to mar this straightforward and emotional account of the Jews' reaction to the death of their priests. When the Romans burn the bodies of Caiaphas and the scribes they

> Suþ went to þe walle . on þe wynde syde,
> & alle a-brod on þe burwe . blewen þe powder:
> "Þer is doust [to] ȝour drynke!" . a du[ke] to hem crieþ,
> & bade hem bible of þat broþ . for þe bischopes soule. (717–20)

This passage of vindictive brutality is then followed by the justification that "coursed Cayphas . & his clerkes alle" (721) were killed "in tokne of tresoun" (723) against Christ. The *Siege* poet demonstrates, within the space of sixteen lines, three disparate interpretations or responses to the death of Caiaphas: Jewish sorrow accompanied by the *kiddush ha-shem*, and devoid of the language of automatic anti-Judaism; Roman brutality as they blow the ashes of the dead priests over the walls and mock the Jews; and the traditional, increasingly threadbare Christian justification for the murder of the Jews.

In later passages, the three-fold nature or exegesis of these scenes of brutality is refashioned into a singular perspective as the poet lingers over piteous and graphic descriptions of the starving and defeated Jews, and there is nothing triumphant in these scenes as he mourns the people that were a "pite to beholde":

> Wymmen falwed faste & her face chaungen,
> Ffeynte & fallen doun, þat so fair wer;
> S[ome] swallen as swyn, som swart wexen,
> Som lene on to loke, . as la[n]terne-hornes.
> Þe morayne was so myche, . þat no man couþe telle
> Wher to burie in þe burwe . þe bodies þat wer ded,
> Bot wenten with hem to þe walle . & walten [hem o]uere;
> n-to þe depe of þe diche . þe ded doun fallen. (1143–50)

And when the Jews finally yield to the Romans:

> Bot vp ȝeden her ȝates . [þeyl ȝelden hem alle,
> Without brunee & briȝt wede, . in her bar chertes;
> Ffram none tille þe merke ny3t . neuer ne cesed,
> Bot man after man . mercy bysouȝt.
> Tytus into þe toun . takeþ his wey:
> Myȝt no man st[e]ken [i]n þe stret . for stynke of ded corses;
> Þe peple in þe pauyment . was pite to byholde,
> Þat wer enfamy[n]ed for defaute . whan hem fode wanted.
> Was noȝt on ladies lafte . bot þe lene bones,
> Þat wer fleschy byfor . & fayr on to loke;
> Burges with balies . as barels or þat tyme,
> No gretter þan a grehounde . to grype on þe medil.
> Tytus tarieþ noȝt for þat, . bot to þe temple wendiþ. (1237–49)

Particularly striking about these passages describing the emaciated and suffering Jews is the absence of the vocabulary of automatic anti-Judaism: the Jews here are, simply, "Jewes," "wymmen," "ladies," "man," "burges,"

and "peple." As the level of suffering in the narrative increases, there is a concomitant decrease in accusatory and hostile language to describe the Jews.
Moreover, the poet emphasizes that Titus does not delay because of the starving Jews, but goes directly to what has been, all along, the main agenda: the
destruction of the Temple. Yet even the destruction of the Temple in the *Siege*
poet's version is oddly subdued with its stately and funereal cadence:

> Nas no ston in þe stede . stondande alofte,
> Morter ne m[o]de walle . bot alle to mulle fallen—
> Noþer tymbr ne tre, . temple ne oþer,
> Bot doun betyn & brent . into blake erþe. (1285–88)

The Siege of Jerusalem is a violent and militant narrative, but it is neither
cheerful nor unambiguous. Indeed, the poem is fully aware of the terrible
practical consequences of its own Christian militancy and is relentless in
detailing, with uncommon sympathy, the suffering of the Jews. The poem is
compounded of unequal measures of assertive bigotry and melancholy
apologetic, and this ambiguity of representation belies long-held critical
assumptions both about this specific poem, and about a conventional monolithic anti-Judaism in late-fourteenth-century Middle English texts.

If anti-Judaism is *not* inevitable in these narratives, then an investigation
of its historical mutability could help determine the contexts for the variety
of representation in literary texts. I would like, in conclusion, to contextualize *The Siege of Jerusalem* and its representation of the Jews, by placing the
anonymous *Siege* poet and his narrative in a particular tradition of English
historical writing.

To do this we need to turn to Yorkshire, where the poem was composed,
and where, two hundred years earlier in 1190, there had been a brutal massacre of the Jews of York. Now, while Yorkshire has a tradition of violently
enacted anti-Judaism, it also has another, less dramatically expressed, tradition of Augustinian historicism and toleration. The chronicle of William of
Newburgh,[27] Augustinian canon in Newburgh, Yorkshire, contains some of
the most complete and graphic accounts of the anti-Jewish riots in England in
1189 through 1190. Although set within the context of his own Christian
anti-Judaism, which sees the Jews as that "perfidious" race who should
remain in servitude as remembrance of Christ's passion (Newburgh, 316–17;
Stevenson, 568). Newburgh's records are relentless both in their detailed
descriptions of Jewish suffering and in their condemnation of the barbarous
cruelty and greed of the Christian townspeople. Newburgh's account of the
massacre at York is of particular interest. The chronicler begins by decrying
the privileges accorded the Jews under Henry II: it is only fitting that this
blasphemous people should be the victims of Christian zeal at the beginning
of the reign of Richard I. Yet the chronicler also invokes Psalm 59:12—"Slay

them not, lest my people forget"—the standard proof-text of the doctrine of toleration. As Newburgh reports, at the end of the York pogrom the Jews are besieged in Clifford Tower, where they enact the Masada scene from Josephus's *Jewish War*: they kill themselves to avoid capture and probable death at the hands of the Christian townspeople. The similarities between the real York events and the historicized account in Josephus do not escape Newburgh. As his entry unfolds, Newburgh becomes increasingly involved in the plight of the Jews, and begins to draw on Josephus's narrative to dramatize his own. Newburgh gives to the leader of the Jews of York a poignant speech derived from that of the leader of the Jews in Josephus's work, embellishes details about the "machines" used to besiege Clifford Tower, and then cites Josephus in his explanation for the self-immolation of the Jews.[28] The more Newburgh is drawn into sympathetic alliance with the Jews, the more nuanced his account, until his dramatic condemnation of Christian barbarity against the York Jews emphatically competes with his earlier anti-Judaic pronouncements: "With regard to these persons, who were thus butchered with savage ferocity, I will affirm, without hesitation, that if, in their entreaty for holy Baptism, there was no fiction, they were baptized by their own blood, and were by no means defrauded of its efficacy; but whether they sought the holy font feignedly or unfeignedly, the inexcusable cruelty of those murderers is to be execrated."[29] Newburgh's chronicle demonstrates, both in its detail and in its emotional reaction, the chronicler's fidelity to his conception of what it is to record contemporary events, even when these events resist a pious and Christian interpretation. In Book Four of his chronicle, he has recorded with great "clarity of vision" the violence against the Jews in London, Stanford, Lincoln, and York, and as Nancy Partner notes: "no rule of history or theology impelled him to report the shabby and revolting story as honestly as he did" (*Serious Entertainments*, 227). If anything, the contrary was true; and Newburgh does attempt to offer a coherent Christian historical view in his assertions that the pious interpretation of these events is that of a happy "presage of the advancement of Christianity."[30] Yet, divided between the "sad welter of a conscientious religious purpose and the ugly facts . . . of Christian greed, violence, duplicity, and bloodiness" (Partner, 226), Newburgh chooses to record for posterity the events in all their brutal detail accompanied by elaborate and outraged personal commentary. In the face of real violence against the Jews, the chronicler's almost automatic anti-Judaism (like that of the *Siege* poet) collapses as he recognizes the practical consequences of an inhumane ideology.

We have, then, a late-twelfth-century chronicle history and a late-fourteenth-century poetic history, composed in the same general locale (Yorkshire), drawing on the same historical source (Josephus), and promoting similar sympathetic and protective gestures toward the Jews. *The Siege of Jerusalem* and Newburgh's chronicle both propose a pious and Christian interpretation of events, for the *Siege* is framed by the explicit desire to avenge the death of Christ, while Newburgh attempts to contextualize his graphic accounts as a happy presage for Christianity. Yet both poet and chronicler demonstrate a curious symmetry of unresolved *ambigua* as they recognize that no pious interpretation suffices to explain the brutality against the Jews, which they both record in unflinching detail.

An argument could be made that the *Siege* poet knew William of Newburgh's chronicle and was influenced by it in his choice of material and manner of representation. There is, however, no material proof that the poet had access to the chronicle. On the other hand, there is a late-thirteenth-century copy of Newburgh's chronicle at Osney, in Oxfordshire, where another Augustinian canon, Thomas Wykes, writing a chronicle in the late thirteenth century, is similarly nuanced in his accounts of the Jews: Wykes condemns the violence perpetrated against the Jewish community in London in 1263 as " 'forgetful of humanity and piety' "; writes with unhidden disgust about the Londoners' cruelty in "murdering all those Jews who did not pay large sums or allow themselves to be baptized"; and, like Newburgh, invokes a biblical injunction (Isaiah 10:22) as testimony to the Jews' eschatological significance in his outraged report of their murders.[31] He also deplores, at some length, the expulsion of the Jews from England in 1290. Wykes cites Newburgh in the introduction to his own chronicle, and draws on Newburgh's accounts for historical material from the twelfth century.[32]

Noting the old adage that twice makes custom, we may hypothesize the existence of an Augustinian tradition. Both Newburgh and Wykes belong to the Augustinian canons, an order known for its scholarship and its writers, and, even more importantly, for the humane moderation of its rule and its ideology. Indeed, the order does not have a rule, in the monastic sense of the word, but draws its inspiration first from a letter of spiritual advice by Augustine, and then from the corpus of Augustinian writings. As R. W. Southern notes: "as a 'rule' its great beauty was that it left so much to the imagination, and it could be developed in various ways by the communities which adopted it."[33] The Augustinian canons' adherence to the writings of Augustine would include, of course, a recognition of the doctrine of relative toleration. Introduced into England in the late eleventh to early twelfth centuries, the Augustinian order quickly expanded to numerous small houses throughout England. Gerald of Wales, writing of the Augustinians in the twelfth century, claims that they are "more content than others with a middling and modest position; . . . though placed in the world, they live uncontaminated by it, not known as litigious or quarrelsome, they fear public scandal too much to be tempted by luxury or lust" (Partner, 53). More importantly, the "judicious, finely balanced ideal which Augustine had lived and preached," lived again in the Augustinian order. The extreme asceticism of the twelfth century was unlikely to disturb the moderate tenor of Augustinian life, and "discerning minds . . . realized that the regular canonical ideal, far from being a spiritual second best, as the monks were apt to regard it, was an ideal worthy of the highest admiration, and in its distrust of the rather fussy puritanism of the time it certainly strikes a curiously modern note."[34]

For the most part, the Augustinians were moderate and humane both in their conventual life and in their writings. Unlike the Cistercians, for example, the Augustinian canons did not become deeply involved economically with the Jews, and the writings, at least of Wykes and Newburgh, do not contain the unrelieved polemic found in Cistercian writings. This is not to suggest that every Augustinian demonstrated the extraordinary humanity toward the Jews that we find in Newburg and Wykes; there is, however, another Augustinian chronicler, Walter of Guisborough, writing either at the end of the thirteenth or the beginning of the fourteenth century, whose histrionic account of the brutality against the Jews upon their expulsion from England testifies to a later, if overly dramatic, sympathy for Jewish suffering.[35] Furthermore, there is an intriguing footnote to the Oxford Council of 1222. One of the decrees promulgated at this council forbade the Jews from owning Christian slaves and from constructing synagogues; it further enjoined them to be bound to the churches in their parishes in respect to tithes. Another decree demanded that they wear a distinguishing linen patch. After issuing these decrees, Stephen Langton, the Bishop of Lincoln, and Hugo de Welles, the Bishop of Norwich, published an injunction to the effect that "no Christian shall have any communication with the Jews, or sell them provisions, under pain of excommunication."[36] Although the King later overturned these injunctions, some of the clergy had already disregarded the orders of both Council and bishops: " 'At this time the prior of Dunstable granted several of them [the Jews] free liberty to reside within the Lordship and to enjoy the privileges of it, in consideration of the annual payment of two silver spoons.' "[37] Not surprisingly, the priory at Dunstable at the time was Augustinian, founded c. 1132.[38]

The Augustinian connection is, I think, an important one, for if the intensified anti-Judaism of the thirteenth and fourteenth centuries was due, at least in part, to an attenuation of the doctrine of toleration, then it could be argued that those who continued to adhere to the old Augustinian position ("Slay them not, lest my people forget") would respond to violence against the Jews with sympathy and outrage. We have seen that Newburgh and Wykes do this in their chronicles, and I suggest that the policy of toleration, which "did not always yield immediately to the new, more hostile ideology" (Cohen, *Friars and Jews*, 226) was transmitted to the *Siege* poet, who, within the context of his originary narrative of destruction and dispersion, echoes these earlier accounts of Jewish victimization under a relentless militant Christianity.

In a paper presented at the International Congress of Medieval Studies at Kalamazoo in 1991, Hanna proposed three possible locations for the *Siege* poet: Sawley, Whalley, and Bolton. Bolton had an active Augustinian priory in the late fourteenth century,[39] and taking into consideration the transmission of sympathetic representation of the Jews from Newburgh to Wykes to Guisborough, and the similarities between the chronicled representation and the poetic, I proposed, in a paper at the New Chaucer Society Congress in 1992, that the anonymous *Siege* poet was an Augustinian canon writing at Bolton Priory. At this time I was unaware of Hanna's then-forthcoming article in which he fine-tunes his earlier proposal, and also locates the poet at Bolton Priory on the basis of manuscript evidence: a copy of the *Bible en françois*, another source text, has been found there, as has a scribal copy of *The Siege of Jerusalem* (Hanna, "Contextualizing," 115–16). Hanna notes that Sawley and Whalley were the sites of Cistercian houses, while Bolton's religious house was Augustinian; yet the issue of the poet's religious affiliation is not an issue for Hanna, who approaches the problem of location through manuscript and patronage evidence. Working independently of one another, and coming at the text from different directions, we have arrived at similar inferences about the location of the poet and his poem. Hanna's conclusions provide me with the external evidence necessary to make my claim more than speculative, yet surely of equal importance are the representational strategies of the *Siege* poet that connect him with the earlier Augustinian historians. Continuing a particular tradition of Augustinian historical writing, the *Siege* poet recalls, not the massacre at York or the London riots, but the originary event of destruction and dispersion that serves as template for all subsequent narrations of violence against the Jews. The poet takes from the chronicles, particularly from Newburgh's detailed and sympathetic accounts, a measure of toleration that he expresses in striking revisions of his sources and in his sympathetic descriptions of the piteous, defeated Jews. By means of historical recollection, the *Siege* poet brings the Jews into fourteenth-century England, where there are no Jews. His narration can be read as a poetic commentary reaching back to the events in twelfth-century Yorkshire, and it can be read as another historical account in the humane traditions of his order written to condemn fourteenth-century violence against the Jews enacted throughout Europe with little regard for the doctrine of toleration. Whatever we choose to believe, it is clear that even if *The Siege of Jerusalem* does not explicitly invoke Psalm 59:12, it does demonstrate, in its persistent and sympathetic detailing of Jewish suffering, the practical consequences of abandoning this Augustinian formula for toleration.

Ralph Hanna begins his article with the compelling claim that "*The Siege of Jerusalem* has a perfectly deserved reputation as the chocolate-covered tarantula of the alliterative movement. Indeed, the poem is so offensive as to exist on the suppressed margins of critical attention, unaccompanied by commentary" ("Contextualizing," 109). To extend this marvelous metaphor, I think that there is more chocolate here than tarantula albeit bittersweet, but very rich indeed. *The Siege of Jerusalem* invites and deserves a fully nuanced reading which recognizes that what animates this narrative is not a univocal and monolithic anti-Judaism, but ambivalence and, at times, a profound confusion about Jews, Christians, and violence.

Notes

A version of this paper was first presented at the New Chaucer Society International Congress in Seattle in 1992. I wish especially to thank Professor Carolyn Dinshaw for the opportunity to present my views of *The Siege* in a context where I was assured of a very effective response.

1. E. Kölbing and Mabel Day, eds., *The Siege of Jerusalem,* EETS, OS 188 (Oxford: University Press, 1932). All quotations are from this edition, cited by line number.

2. Derek Pearsall, *Old English and Middle English Poetry* (London, Henley, and Boston: Routledge and Kegan Paul, 1977), 169. Although Pearsall acknowledges the "brilliance" of the poem's "technique," he concludes that "the poet's failure is that he embellishes without establishing any imaginative control of his own, and that an accomplished brutality of the visualizing imagination is in the end put at the service of a crude and narrow vindictiveness. The *Siege* is a model of decadent poetic."

3. A. C. Spearing, *Readings in Medieval Poetry* (Cambridge, England: Cambridge University Press, 1987), 167, 172. Like Pearsall, Spearing recognizes the "brilliance" of the poem: "*The Siege of Jerusalem* is a brilliant and repellant work of art" (172); yet he simplifies his otherwise astute analysis of the poem with the claim that it is "permeated by *the* antisemitism that was so common in the Middle Ages" (167, italics mine). This kind of assessment of anti-Judaism in medieval literature, an assessment that assumes a "common" convention, a monolithic and static representation, undercuts a real understanding of the complexities in the representations of the Jews in the Middle Ages, and especially in *The Siege of Jerusalem.*

4. Ralph Hanna, "Contextualizing *The Siege of Jerusalem,*" *Yearbook of Langland Studies* 6 (1992), 111, 110; hereafter cited in text. Hanna and David Lawton are at work on a new edition of the *Siege* (forthcoming, Colleagues Press).

5. Hanna notes "although it is difficult to claim any one area of Europe as more given to anti-Semitism than any other, Yorkshire is one particularly noxious locale" (114). See R. B. Dobson, *The Jews of Medieval York and the Massacre of March 1190,* Borthwick Papers 45 (York, England: St. Anthony's Press, 1974).

6. Mary Hamel, "*The Siege of Jerusalem* as a Crusading Poem," *Journeys Toward God: Pilgrimage and Crusade,* ed. Barbara N. Sargent-Baur (Kalamazoo, MI: Medieval Institute Publications, 1992), 177–94 (178).

7. Cecilia Cutts, "The Croxton Play: An Anti-Lollard Piece," *Modern Language Quarterly* 5 (1944), 55. See also Gail McMurray Gibson, *The Theater of Devotion* (Chicago: University of Chicago Press, 1989), 35–38.

8. Jeremy Cohen, *The Friars and the Jews* (Ithaca, NY: Cornell University Press, 1982), 193; hereafter cited in text.

9. As I will note later, Bernard of Clairvaux makes explicit distinctions between Jews and Saracens in which the sword is not to be raised against the Jews (protected as they are by biblical injunction), but should be raised against the Saracens. Peter the Venerable, on the other hand, believes in a reconstructed Islam and evangelism of the Saracens. See Avery Dulles, *A History of Apologetics* (New York: Corpus; Philadelphia: Westminster; London: Hutchinson, 1971), 82. See especially A. Lukyn Williams, *Adversos Judaeos: A Bird's-Eye View of Christian Apologiae Until the Renaissance* (Cambridge, England: Cambridge University Press, 1935).

10. Contrary to the conclusions of Kölbing and Day, Hanna and Lawton believe that the *Siege* poet did have access to Josephus's *Jewish War* in Latin: "About fifteen English manuscripts of the work survive, nearly all of the late twelfth or early thirteenth centuries and most with secure monastic provenances (none from the north)" (Hanna, 113 n. 9). Hanna notes that he overlooked a northern copy of Josephus at Durham. See also Phyllis Moe, "The French Source of the Alliterative *Siege of Jerusalem*," *Medium Aevum* 39 (1970), 147–54.

11. For a fine and comprehensive summary of this theme in patristic literature, see Rosemary Radford Ruether, "The Negation of the Jews in the Church Fathers," in *Faith and Fratricide: The Theological Roots of Anti-Semitism* (New York: Seabury Press, 1974), 117–82. See also Marcel Simon, *Verus Israel*, trans. H. McKeating (Oxford: for the Littman Library by Oxford University Press, 1986), 65–68.

12. Stephen K. Wright, *The Vengeance of Our Lord: Medieval Dramatizations of the Destruction of Jerusalem* (Toronto: Pontifical Institute of Mediaeval Studies, 1989), 23; hereafter cited in text..

13. Wright, 26 n. 64. See Nicholas of Lyra, *Postilla super Totam Bibliam* (Strassburg, 1492; rpt. Frankfurt: Minerva, 1971), 4, fol. 112. See also Cohen, *Friars*, 170–95.

14. This is, of course, a commonplace of typological exegesis found in most patristic literature. However, a good starting point for understanding the development of this thematic is the Gospel of John with its repeated comparisons between Moses and Christ, between wilderness manna and the bread of life given by Christ.

15. Leon Poliakov, *The History of Anti-Semitism: From the Time of Christ to the Court Jews*, trans. Richard Howard (New York: Schocken, 1974), 121.

16. See Bernard Glassman, *Anti-Semitic Stereotypes without Jews* (Detroit, MI: Wayne State University Press, 1975), 28–36; Thomas Wimbledon, Wimbledon's *Sermon Redde Rationem Villicationis Tue: A Middle English Sermon of the Fourteenth Century*, ed. Ione Kemp Knight (Pittsburgh, PA: Duquesne University Press, 1967); John Mirk, *Mirk's Festial: A Collection of Homilies*, ed. Theodore Erbe (London: Kegan Paul, Trench, Trübner & Co., 1905). For a comprehensive discussion of the sermon manuscripts from 1350 to 1450, see G. R. Owst, *Preaching in Medieval England* (Cambridge, England: Cambridge University Press, 1926); note especially Owst's discussions of John Bromyard throughout. R. W. Hunt, "The Disputation of Peter of Cornwall Against Symon the Jew," *Studies in Medieval History*, ed. R. W. Hunt, W. A. Pantin, R. W. Southern (Oxford: Oxford University Press, 1948; rpt. 1969), 145. Hunt writes

that the fourteenth-century manuscript was "written in England, and it is note-worthy as showing that the problem presented by the refusal of the Jews to accept Christ as the true Messiah continued after the Jews had been expelled from England" (145).

17. Hamel, 184, 185. This is precisely the point that most critics, with the exception of Professor Hamel and myself, have failed to notice. And while my conclusions concerning this offered "pity" differ from Hamel's, I am grateful for her confirmation of my reading of the representation of the Jews in this poem.

18. David Berger, "The Attitude of St. Bernard of Clairvaux Toward the Jews," *Proceedings of the American Academy for Jewish Research* 40 (1972), 90; hereafter cited in text.

19. N.B.: "*most* medieval Christian writing": for the exigencies of this short essay, I have simplified what is a fairly complex and varied response to the Jews. There are those, like Bernard of Clairvaux, who follow Augustinian doctrine concerning the Jews; there are others, such as Peter the Venerable, who conclude that " 'if any man is naturally endowed with the mental faculties to recognize the truth of Christianity and the Jews have not acknowledged that truth, then the Jews must not be human,' " Cohen, 24.

20. Cohen, *Friars*. See also Jeremy Cohen, "The Jews as the Killers of Christ in the Latin Tradition: From Augustine to the Friars," *Traditio* 39 (1983), 1–27.

21. Flavius Josephus, *The Jewish War*, Books IV–VII, trans. H. St. J. Thackeray, Loeb Classical Library (Cambridge, MA: Harvard University Press, 1928; rpt. 1990), bk. VI, 159.

22. Ranulph Higden, *Polychronicon, Together with the English Translation of John Of Trevisa and an Unknown Writer of the Fifteenth Century*, ed. Churchill Babington and Joseph R. Lumby, 9 vols. (London: 1865–86), 4: 428.

23. Jacobus de Voragine, *Legenda Aurea*, ed. Th. Graesse (Leipzig, 1850). In translation, *The Golden Legend*, trans. William Granger Ryan, 2 vols. (Princeton: Princeton University Press, 1993), 1: 275. Also *The Legends of the Saints in the Scottish Dialect of the Fourteenth Century*, ed. W. M. Metcalfe (London: 1896). In *Legenda Aurea*: "*tanta fames omnes tenuit quod parentes filiis et filii parentibus, viri uxoribus et uxores viris cibos non tanturn e manibus, sed etiam ex ipsis dentibus rapiebant. . . . Tanta enim ibi fames erat, quod calceamenta sua et corrigias comedebant*" (Metcalfe, 125).

24. Tears as a sign of sanctity and piety are a common motif in both orthodox Christian writings and in Christian mysticism. There is copious weeping in *The Siege of Jerusalem* by the Jews, and this drinking of their own tears suggests a sanctified self-consumption to counterbalance the later cannibalism. At the very least, it would be worthwhile to compare this scene with tears of sanctity in mystical and hagiographical writings. See, for example, Pierre Adnès, "Larmes," *Dictionnaire de Spiritualité* (Paris: 1976), 19: 287–303.

25. Kenneth R. Stow, *Alienated Minority* (Cambridge, MA: Harvard University Press, 1992), 116–18. Kölbing and Day find no source for this self-massacre (102 n. 1097–1100).

26. Leviticus 26:27–29; Deuteronomy 28:52–57; II Kings 6:24–30; Jeremiah 19:9; Baruch 2:2–3; Lamentations 4:10. We should note that at least one patristic writer, John Chrysostom, draws on these biblical passages when he

accuses the Jews of cannibalism in his *Fifth Oration Against the Jews*: "The like of what does he mean? The eating of little children by their mothers! Moses foretold it, and Jeremiah reported its fulfillment." See John Chrysostom, *Eight Homilies Against the Jews, Patrologia Graeca* 48: 843–942; Chrysostom's *Homilies Against the Jews*, ed. and intro. C. Marvyn Maxwell, (Ph.D. diss., University of Chicago, 1966), 133.

27. William of Newburgh, *Historia Rerum Anglicarum*, in *Chronicles of the Reigns of Stephen, Henry II, and Richard I*, ed. Richard Howlett (London, 1884–89); hereafter cited in text. In translation, *The Church Historians of England*, vol. IV, part 11, trans. Joseph Stevenson (London: 1856); hereafter cited in text.

28. The citation of Psalm 58:12 is found in Newburgh, 316: "*Ne occidas eos, nequando obliviscantur populi mei.*" The speech drawn from Josephus is found in Newburgh, 318–19; the direct citation of Josephus at 320.

29. Newburgh, 321–22, trans. Stevenson, 571; I have restored the "inexcusability" that Stevenson omits. For a fine discussion of the significance of Newburgh's detailed accounts and outrage over Christian brutality, see Nancy Partner, *Serious Entertainments: The Writing of History in Twelfth-Century England* (Chicago and London: University of Chicago Press, 1977); hereafter cited in text. See also Antonia Gransden, *Historical Writing in England c.550 to c. 1307* (Ithaca, NY: Cornell University Press, 1974), 265.

30. Newburgh, 297–98, trans. Stevenson, 557. Partner's discussion of this passage is an astute analysis of Newburgh's attempted resort to a *regulum* to frame the *ambigua* of events, 226–27.

31. Thomas Wykes, *Chronicon vulgo dictum Chronicon Thomæ Wykes, Annales Monastici*, ed. Henry Luard (London: 1869), 4: 141–42, 326–27. Quoted from Gransden, 466. Unlike Newburgh, Wykes is also concerned with the financial aspects of Jewish-Christian relations: "One reason why Wykes deplored this destruction of the London Jewry was financial. He says the damage done to the royal treasury was inestimable" (Gransden, 466). The financial issue also partially motivates his disgust with the expulsion of the Jews.

32. N. Denholm-Young, "Thomas de Wykes and his Chronicle," *English Historical Review* 61 (1946), 172.

33. R. W. Southern, *Western Society and the Church in the Middle Ages* (Middlesex, England: Penguin, 1970; rpt. 1985), 241–42.

34. Rev. J. C. Dickinson, *The Origins of the Austin Canons and Their Introduction into England* (London: SPCK, 1950), 177, 179.

35. *The Chronicle of Walter of Guisborough*, ed. Harry Rothwell, Camden Series (London: 1957), 226–27.

36. Solomon Grayzel, *The Church and the Jews in the XIIIth Century* (New York: Hermon, 1966), 314–15. In this section about the Oxford Council of 1222, Grayzel gives the texts of decrees 39 and 40.

37. Grayzel, 315. This footnote to the Oxford Council is literally a footnote in Grayzel's text where he quotes from Tovey, *Anglia Judaica* (Oxford, 1783), 83.

38. David Knowles, *The Religious Houses of Medieval England* (London: Sheed and Ward, 1940), 83.

39. David Knowles and R. Neville Hadcock, *Medieval Religious Houses, England and Wales* (New York: St. Martin's Press, 1971), 148.

11

"House Devil, Town Saint"

Anti-Semitism and Hagiography in Medieval Suffolk

ANTHONY P. BALE

"... the English are known to be of a polite persuasion and their
anti-Semitism is of the most courteous kind." Bernice Rubens, *I, Dreyfus*

Who produced images of Jews in medieval England? Who was involved in
the transmission of such images? And who consumed them? This essay aims
to address these questions, using the meagre yet fecund remnants of the cult
of the alleged ritual murder victim Robert of Bury St. Edmunds. By reconstructing and interpreting the context in which images of the murderous Jew
were conjured, we shall see what purposes this imaginary Jew served for a
group of writers, readers, and worshippers in medieval Suffolk.

Recent scholarship has devoted much useful study to the early development of the ritual murder allegation in medieval England.[1] Such work has
been focused on the twelfth and thirteenth centuries, that period in which
anti-Jewish writing and iconography became innovative and shockingly fan-
tastical and which, before the expulsion of the Jews from England in 1290,
was transmitted in the context of everyday contacts with England's Jewish
community. Emerging from pan-European discourses surrounding the sacrificial, sacramental Christ child and the dangerous Jew, the myth of ritual
murder was first given the form of a church-sponsored cult in the 1150s,
around the figure of William of Norwich.[2] William's shrine was popular and
lucrative; Thomas of Monmouth's written *vita* of the boy was instrumental in
the early promotion of the cult.[3]

The present study is concerned not only with the origins of Robert of
Bury's cult, but also with its later manifestations, revivals, and ultimate
silencing. What circumstances made the image of the Jew slaying a Christian
child enduringly popular, fresh, and meaningful?

I. *Inventio:* The Origins and Early Development of the Cult of Robert

In the last twenty years of the twelfth century a new saint's cult developed at the Benedictine abbey at Bury St. Edmunds (Suffolk). A local child, Robert, was said to have been killed in 1181 by the city's Jews, as noted by the celebrated historian of Bury St. Edmunds, the monk Jocelin of Brakelond (d. 1202?):

> It was at this time also [1181] that the saintly boy Robert was martyred and was buried in our church: many signs and wonders were performed among the people.[4]

Comments made about Robert of Bury by the coeval historian Gervase of Canterbury (d. *c.* 1205) fill in some of the details, adding that Robert was martyred by Jews, and miracles were worked at his tomb.[5]

Even Jocelin's elliptic remark gives us useful information. The burial of Robert in the church suggests a shrine or even a chapel. The "signs and wonders" attributed to the boy formed some kind of written record—perhaps a list of *miracula*, a proto-hagiographic document or, less likely, a *vita*. Jocelin was writing within the abbey precincts and had spent his life in Bury, first as a citizen of town and then, from 1173, as a monk at the ancient and venerable Abbey of St. Edmund. Why would the Benedictines of Bury St. Edmunds have wished to develop a boy-martyr cult, particularly when Bury was already the center for the veneration of the East Anglian king St. Edmund (841–869)? I will briefly sketch the possible stimuli for the initial development of Robert's cult.

First, we must consider Bury's position with regard to nearby Norwich, and in particular the repeated claims made by the abbey at Norwich of episcopal supremacy over Bury. In the 1160s the early boy-martyr story of William of Norwich had been developed by Bishop Turbe (bishop from 1146 to 1174); the development and transmission of Thomas of Monmouth's *vita* of the boy have been well-documented elsewhere.[6] It suffices here to state that the abbey at Norwich, and Bishop Turbe in particular, clearly marketed the veneration of their own boy-saint in order to boost local prestige and to garner the financial benefits of having a popular shrine in the abbey. In the Norfolk area William's cult was widespread and remained under the sponsorship of the abbey and, later, of parish churches, and even a guild.[7]

Circumstantial evidence suggests that in the 1150s and '60s Bishop Turbe of Norwich may have made renewed claims of episcopal authority over Bury St. Edmunds.[8] Bury was granted fully independent status by Pope Alexander III in 1175, making the abbey exempt from the control of the diocese of Norwich. It is no coincidence that the abbey at Bury, under the vigorous Abbot Samson (abbot from 1182), decided to develop its very own boy-saint cult in the 1180s, to amplify its independent identity and create a rival center for this particular brand of boy-martyr veneration. The sources do not exist to show that the development of Robert's cult was explicitly an answer, or rebuke, to Norwich; but there is a telling symmetry in Bury's development of its own boy-saint with its corresponding independence from Norwich.

Joe Hillaby has shown that the growth of Robert's cult must be considered against the backdrop of ecclesiastical rivalries at Bury in the 1180s, which culminated in the expulsion of Bury's Jews in 1190 (Hillaby, 87–89). Abbot Samson developed Robert's cult not only as a way of bringing in revenue but also as a snub to his rival at Bury, William the Sacrist, who had close financial links with the town's Jews. The Jews were manipulated, slandered, and finally expelled, caught in the micro-politics of the abbey. In 1189 a wave of anti-Jewish feeling swept eastern England, starting at the coronation of Richard I (1157–1199) in September, continuing in incidents at Stamford, Lincoln, Huntingdon, and Lynn, and climaxing in the notorious slaughter of York's Jewish community on March 15, *shabbat ha-gadol* (the great sabbath), 1190.[9] The precise circumstances of the expulsion from Bury are vague, but we might usefully turn again to Jocelin of Brakelond, who records that

> [In 1190] the abbot asked the king [Richard I] for written permission to expel the Jews from St Edmund's town, on the grounds that everything in the town and within the *banleuca* [the greater jurisdiction of the abbey] belonged by right to St Edmund: therefore, either the Jews should be St Edmund's men or they should be banished from the town. Accordingly, he was given permission to turn them out, but they were to retain their movable possessions and also the value of their houses and lands. When they had been escorted out and taken to various other towns by an armed troop, the abbot directed that in future all those who received back Jews or gave them lodging in St Edmund's town, were to be excommunicated in every church and at every altar.[10]

Which came first—the veneration of the boy or the expulsion of the Jews? Did the development of the cult in the 1180s pave the way for the expulsion of 1190, demonizing the Jews for the practical purpose of their expulsion? Or did the cult develop later as a form of justification and maintenance of the Jewish absence? Jocelin's chronicle was compiled from the mid-1190s and it is tempting to assume that he wrote the *vita* of Robert at the same time, to both explain and maintain the absence of Jews from the town.

It is clear that the veneration of Robert was established, at least within the abbey precincts, by 1202, the probable date of Jocelin's death, and scattered references in financial and other records attest to the continued existence of the cult through the subsequent centuries. Later fragments of the cult include a prayer to St. Robert written by John Lydgate (?1371–1449), monk of Bury, which uniquely appears in a late-fifteenth-century manuscript, Oxford, Bodleian Library MS Laud misc. 683 (hereafter Laud 683) and a late-fifteenth-century miniature from an illuminated bible from Bury which features Robert's passion. We shall return to both Lydgate's prayer and the miniature in greater detail below.

A 1520 feretrar's account roll from Bury, compiled by John ffynyngham, Robert Lanaym and Simon Berdwell, records payments to *cantores* (singers or minstrels) in St. Robert's chapel on his saints day.[11] The nature of these entertainments is not clear; whilst Gail McMurray Gibson hints that they might have been miracle plays based on Robert's *vita*, they could also have been liturgical—though, in the latter case, it is unclear as to why singers might have been employed from outside the abbey.[12] Lawrence Clopper has demonstrated that a whole range of performances—from sports to liturgy— was associated with saints' days; saints' celebrations certainly did not always take the form of a dramatized *vita*. Most likely, these *cantores* were hired to sing carols—those vernacular, liminal devotional pieces which were so much a part of fifteenth-century devotion. Whatever the nature of these entertainments, we can be sure that Robert's day was celebrated at the abbey into the sixteenth century.[13]

II. "Blyssid Robert, Innocent and Virgyne": Lydgate's "Praier to St. Robert"

The one literary remnant of Robert's cult is John Lydgate's "Praier to St. Robert" (see appendix on p. 209), the unique copy of which appears in a late-fifteenth-century manuscript collection of Lydgate's poetry, Laud 683. The "Praier" is in a series of verse saints' lives by Lydgate, which reached its zenith in the *Lives of SS. Edmund and Fremund* (written for the young Henry VI), the *Life of St. Alban*, and the ambitious and ubiquitous *Lyf of Ovr Lady*.[14] Lydgate's vernacular verse hagiography was later developed by other East Anglian clerics, among them Osbern Bokenham and John Capgrave.[15]

Lydgate's "Praier" addresses "blyssid Robert, Innocent and Virgyne, / Glorious marter, gracious & riht good" (lines 1–2), against whom "the Iewys were so wood" (5). Lydgate's poem takes for granted the fact that Robert's story is well-known; he gives few details, instead referring the reader to Robert's *vita* ("Lyk as thy story makyth mencyoun") (6). In this way the "Praier" appeals to common memory, placing the book in a subsidiary role to communal *memoria*.[16] Lydgate may be referring to a written *vita* here (with which he is likely to have been familiar *via* the abbey's library, if such a text ever existed). Robert's "story" was more likely that which formed the content of the performances at Robert's shrine, together with details of his *vita* which may have been known through ecclesiastical art, books of hours, rumor, and anecdote. Lydgate's "Praier" does not give the precise details of Robert's life, for its function is the creation of a shared, memorial community. The "Praier" is inherently exclusive, open only to those who had participated in Robert's cult in another medium, such as images, songs, or liturgy. Alternatively, Lydgate may not have been aware himself of any further details of the cult: for Lydgate's poem, the basic Jewish murder is all that is needed in order to enter the idiom of boy-martyr veneration.

The "Praier" draws conventional parallels between Robert's passion and that of Christ ("Only for Crist, crucyfied for our goode, / In whos despit al sangweyn was thy weede": lines 19–20), and it seems that the story of Robert was similar to coeval ritual murder narratives. As with William of Norwich, Harold of Gloucester, Hugh of Lincoln, and the "Miracle of the Boy Singer" which Chaucer wrote as *The Prioress's Tale*, the Jews are said to torture and murder a passive, innocent child. Indeed, Lydgate's poem emphasizes the boy's mute, robotic inertia ("thou myghtyst crie, thou spak no woord parde, / with-oute language makyng a pitous soun") (13–14), a body in pain whose subjectivity has been erased as the body becomes social, communal.[17] Robert is described as having "purpil blood allayed with mylk whiht" (26), not only recalling the royal and religious significations of this color, but also linking with Lydgate's poem to St. Edmund ("Benygne and blissed, o gemme purpurat!") in Laud 683 (ff. 19r–21r).[18] The boy's body evokes the sacrificial Christ child which, in turn, appeals to a particularly maternal sense of pity:[19] Robert is described as "a sowkyng childe, tendre of innocence" (11) and, later, as "Fostrid with mylk and tendre pap" (17).[20] The final stanza of the "Praier" recalls the town of Bury, "that hast among hem a chapel & a shryne" (34) to Robert. St. Edmund is also invoked, "Kyng of Estynglond, martir and virgyne" (36), suggesting a particularly local brand of veneration, and, likewise, the two saints are described as "strecchyng [their] stremys thoruh al þis regioun" (38).

Lydgate's poem is not an anti-Jewish invective; it is, rather, unquestioning in its acceptance of anti-Semitic epistemologies of ritual child murder. I would argue, however, that the poem can be termed "anti-Semitic," for it says things about Jews which are neither true nor positive, and which serve to slander the Jewish religion and those identified as Jews. That Jews might murder a Christian child is taken for granted; indeed, this murder defines these characters as Jews. The poem demonstrates the various ways in which this murder can be interpreted and replayed in religious practice. The murderous Jew—in the background of (and yet integral to) the "Praier to St. Robert"—functions as the agent which enables the coalescence of various forms of worship: parental, particularly maternal, piety; local panegyric; devotion to the suffering body of Christ.

III. St. Robert's Manuscript Context

The "Praier to St. Robert" must be located within the frame of the unique manuscript, Laud 683, in which it is found and a review of this manuscript's contents is instructive. Laud 683 comprises regional eulogy of Suffolk and East Anglia, texts concerned with the household or domestic service, parental (mostly maternal) material and standard devotional fillers.

Together with Robert's "Praier", the prayer to St. Edmund (ff. 19r–21r) and the "Miracles of St. Edmund with a prayer" (ff. 42r–53r) are the most obvious instances of localized eulogy.[21] The "Legend of St. Gyle" (ff. 33v–42r), written in 1431 for abbot William Curteys, was "emphatic verse propaganda about the jealously-guarded "franchise" of the Liberty of St. Edmund";[22] once again, the independence of Bury is figured through tailor-made local devotion.[23] The prayers to Thomas of Canterbury (f. 23v) ("vertu-ous primat off Ingelond") and St. George (f. 24v) ("of Ynglond callyd protectour & patroun"), together with *Guy of Warwick* (ff. 65r–78r), display a more general patriotism.

Similarly, the "Prayers to Ten Saints," a series of short, 9-line prayers, praise ten favourite figures of English domestic piety (Saints Denis, George, Christopher, Blaise, Giles, Katherine, Margaret, Martha, Christina and Barbara), emphasizing servitude, charity, motherhood, virginity and repetitive rituals of devotion.[24] The structure of these prayers—five male saints followed by five female—sets up a balanced economy of veneration in which female devotion answers and balances models of male capacity. In general, these hagiographic prayers inscribe models of service and, in particular, they constantly, insistently, impress the importance of virginity in the lives of both male and female saints.

These saints' lives—accessible verses concerned with local identity, Englishness, doctrine and deportment—complement the more explicitly didactic courtesy texts in the collection. The latter poems are more secular, but are explicitly instructional. "A dyte of womenhis hornys" (ff. 53r–54v; known as "Horns away") is Lydgate's notorious sumptuary satire against women's modish, immoderate headgear. The "Doctryne of ffesyk" (f. 60r) and "Doctryne of pestilence" (f. 62r) are didactic poems on the correct ways to live healthily, exhorting the reader to avoid fruit, to eat chicken and to sleep late. *Stans Puer ad Mensam* (ff. 62fv–65r) is addressed to a male child and instructs him, among other things, not to pick his nose at table. The other texts of Laud 683, such as the "Tretys of Crystys Passyoun" (ff. 15v–17r), "Five Joies of Oure Lady" (ff. 18v–19r), "Praier to the Holy Sacrament" (ff. 30v–31r) and the *Pater Noster* (f. 81r) are all vernacular, straightforward devotional pieces. Some of these have a particularly parental resonance, such as the charming Christmas carol, "A babe is born to blis vs bringe" (f. 105v).

Uniting these concerns is "The Order of Foolis" (f. 56r–60r), which inveighs against a range of sins. The "cheef of alle folys" is said to be

> he that nouther loveth God nor dredith,
> Nor to hi chirche hath noon advertence,
> Nor to his seyntys doth no reuerence,
> And hath dysdeyn of ffollk in poverte (f. 56r)

Obligations to saints and an inclusive vision of a Christian community are paramount in the models of conduct thus set out in Laud 683.[25] Likewise, the "Praier to St. Robert" promotes a combination of local devotion, familial bonds and accessible piety, figured through the sacramental body of the little virgin boy.

In this way the "Praier to St. Robert" should not be seen as a sophisticated or theologically substantive *contra Judaeos* text; it is, rather, firmly within the framework of standard hymns, easy doctrine and everyday devotion of this manuscript. Laud 683 contains simple prayers and verse, which fuse undemanding morality with elementary storytelling. The "Praier to St. Robert" is not only formulaic in its general sentiments and images, but seems to engage explicitly with a notion of repetitive piety: the recurring last line of each stanza, "That do reuerence on-to thy passioun" and the objectified, automatic boy-hero suggest a faith in the worth of communal rituals of restatement and easy duplication. Like the other poems of Laud 683, the "Praier to St. Robert" appeals to the fundamental spheres of body, family, home and church, creating a Jewish assault on each of these spheres in order to reassert their strength and preeminence.

IV. "Mastres cole," Social Memory, and the Domestic Jew

Laud 683 is a small book (140mm x 200mm) with little decoration or ornament, dating from towards the end of the fifteenth century. Verse is written out as prose throughout the manuscript. The contents described above, with their Bury and East Anglian sympathies, suggest a Bury provenance. An inscription, at f. 105r, states that "thys boke is mastres [i.e. mistress] coles boke" in a hand from the end of the fifteenth century.

This inscription proves that the manuscript was owned or handled by a woman, and the choice of material suggests that it was put together for or by a female reader or writer.[26] The preponderance of Marian material and female saints' lives, together with the overall emphasis on virginity and maternity, points to a female audience (though this is not to suggest that only women read such texts).[27] Moreover, recent research has shown that several very similar small books were owned by women, possibly as girdle-books or as portable pious reading for domestic consumption.[28]

It is now well-known that women read, and formed reading communities, in medieval England. The fact that women could read should no longer be seen as a conclusion in itself; we might now take the issue of ownership one step further to place the book in a more dynamic position within the household. I suggest that Laud 683 was used in a domestic setting (which included women but may have also included men) for group instruction and devotion.[29] The intended audience may have included children (particularly boys) and domestic servants.

Most of the poetry in the section of Laud 683 which includes the "Praier to St. Robert" is arranged in poetic lines and stanzas but occupies the whole page, largely unrubricated. The pages of the manuscript look like prose, as is the case with several coeval and similar manuscripts.[30] Laud 683 presents a mass of text which only becomes organized as poetry at the moment at which it is read aloud. Such presentation hinders rather than aids memory, but it does save space on the page and relegate the visual appearance of the word to a status below that of the word's actual iteration. That is to say, this format makes the *content* of reading (the message of the text) and the audience more important than the self-reflexive act of reading or the physical presentation, the status symbol, of the book. The visual format of Laud 683 then suggests that this book was used for reading aloud to a group of listeners, possibly to an audience which included the illiterate or barely literate. In particular, the presence of the "Praier to St. Robert" and *Stans Puer ad Mensam* suggests that a son or young boy may have been in the audience, as we know is the case with another Lydgate manuscript, Cambridge, Sidney Sussex College, MS 37.

Sidney 37 is a mid-fifteenth-century *deluxe* book of hours with a selection of Lydgate poems similar to those found in Laud 683; the donor of the book was a woman, possibly Richard III's sister Anne Plantagenet (1439–1475/6), who appears kneeling, in a red cloak, before a desk on which is a book (f. 116v).[31] On a blank folio at the end of the book is the early-sixteenth-century inscription "Edmovnd churche ys a good son for he ys wyllyng to lern" (f. 154v), and later "Thys my boke edmovnd churche" (f. 156r), and other notes by and about Edmund Church. The book was commissioned by a woman but was later used, or shared with, by a mother and son. Rather than being designed for use by either men or women, such manuscripts were designed to appeal to a group, to be read by or to men, women, *and* children.[32] Like Sidney 37, Laud 683 seems to have been read out to a varied audience, and it is not surprising that at each turn its texts seek to evoke a sense of *communitas* and corporate identity—of familial, local, and national bonds, as well as bonds of obligation, service, and devotion; concerns which coalesce in the "Praier to St. Robert."

Unfortunately, we have scant information about the identity of the one-time owner of Laud 683, "mastres cole." Her hand is of the late fifteenth century and the contents of Laud 683 possibly reflect her reading tastes. The book may come from any number of families in Suffolk, Norfolk, or Essex, or even from an East Anglian family living in London.[33] Mistress Cole does not appear in Samuel Moore's broad survey of patrons of letters in fifteenth-century Suffolk; indeed, her inscription appears to have gone largely unnoticed by codicologists.[34]

Although the identity of Mistress Cole remains unknown, the internal evidence of Laud 683 suggests that she was a well-to-do gentlewoman, standard in her reading tastes, her piety, and her cultural frame of reference. Her anonymity is not surprising, for she was probably an unexceptional East Anglian woman who happened to own a fairly standard, formulaic, and fashionable book. The "Praier to St. Robert" is, likewise, thoroughly standard. Laud 683 leads us to a reading community accepting of the image of a domestic, murderous Jew, replaying this twelfth-century homicide allegation in the fifteenth-century household.

V. Hiding the Light of God: The Bury Bible Miniatures

The sole known visual representation of Robert's cult is found in the Bury bible miniatures (*olim* Dyson Perrins MS 1).[35] The manuscript, now in a private collection, comprises a set of twelfth-century biblical illustrations that probably once accompanied or preceded a psalter. In the fifteenth century a further set of fifty-eight (relatively crude) illustrations was added, together with prayers. Neither the patron nor the fifteenth-century owner of the manuscript is known, but in the sixteenth century it belonged to "susana flint and joanes pinchbeck," as marked on the flyleaf.[36] Later in the sixteenth century the book was in Norfolk.[37]

The fifteenth-century additions attach (and sometimes duplicate) an extra set of subjects for the Aves of the Rosary, including a four-part miniature of the passion of St. Robert, and an *oratio sancti Roberti*, a conventional prayer to the boy. As a whole, the fifteenth-century illustrations are eschatological, running from the Deity (f. 6r) and the Creation (f. 7r) to the apocalypse (ff. 98r–105v). The miniature of Robert (see fig. 5) appears (at f. 44r) between the Adoration of the Shepherds (f. 30v) and the Transfiguration of Christ (f. 55v). In the miniature of the Transfiguration, Christ stands between Elias and Moses (who holds the tablets of the Law). Below are Peter with a key, James with a scallop-shell and John with a palm branch.[38]

The image of Robert of Bury appears here at a clear junction, a temporal intersection: Robert's life is removed from Bury in the 1180s and is placed at the moment of the generation of Christianity, the moment at which Judaism becomes the Old Law (represented by Moses' tablets in the Transfiguration miniature) and faith is transformed. The illuminator, or patron, of the manuscript conceived the typological value of Robert's story as follows: Jews, whether pre- or post-Christ are antique and must be seen in their gospel and

Figure 5. *Martyrdom of Robert of Bury,* twelfth century. Courtesy of the Conway Library, Courtauld Institute of Art.

medieval role.[39] The Jewish murder at this point is what allows Christianity to depart from its antecedent.

The miniature shows a woman holding the boy's corpse at a well; the corpse is then seen in a ditch (in which stands the tree alluded to in Lydgate's "Praier") whilst an archer shoots heavenwards (recalling St. Edmund's death—he was tied to a tree and martyred with arrows). At the top of the frame Robert's soul ascends to heaven, which is connected *via* a prayer to a tonsured figure, in reddish garb, at prayer.[40] This man prays to an icon of Robert—a red-breasted robin with a large charter and seal (which possibly signifies the Liberty of St. Edmund).[41] In as much as the miniature offers an opportunity to reconstruct Robert's *vita*, the story of the boy's passion seems very standard: the boy was killed, his body was thrown in a well, it was discovered, and subsequently venerated.

Under the prayer, on the facing page, (see fig. 6) is the ensemble of stag (*cervus*), chained bear (*ursus*), panther (*pantera*), and a cow-like animal. Given that these illustrations were added to the book in the fifteenth century as an illustrative scheme, and that the animal group fits into the layout of the page, it would seem likely that the beasts are contingent on the prayer and miniature for their meaning. The stag (the "good friend" and a Christ-figure) and the panther (an image of Christ, with sweetly fragrant breath, who is loved and followed by other creatures) are often found together (in London, British Library Royal MS 12.F.XIII [f. 9r], the *Rochester Bestiary*, for example).[42] Bears were known for nursing their cubs, for having the power to heal their own wounds, and for their mimetic human qualities (although the chain around the bear's neck in this illustration suggests a shackled, or tamed, beast).[43] The bovine figure may be a bonnacon, the "ox-like beast with the flexible horns" of the bestiary, known for expelling noxious, burning substances from its anus to harm its enemies (Hassig, 165). The bonnacon offers an anti-Semitic image, in common with the owl, hoopoe, and hyena in the bestiary, linking Jews with excrement in a eucharistic slander (the Jews' incorrect incorporation is reflected in excretion, whilst eucharism suggests correct appetite).[44] The sweet breath of the true panther contrasts with the corrupt body of the bonnacon.[45] The beasts may then depict Christ or Robert (the panther), his followers (the stag), the good, or corrected, parent (the bear), and the Jews (the bonnacon). Alternatively, and perhaps more likely, the last beast may be a cow (*vacca*), which stands for the sacrifice of Jesus: "His human form was made red by the blood of the passion. His humanity is without blemish."[46] Whereas the bonnacon is usually depicted with curly horns, images of the cow are very similar to that found in this illustration, and the allegorical understanding of the beast has obvious relevance within the vocabulary of Robert's cult.

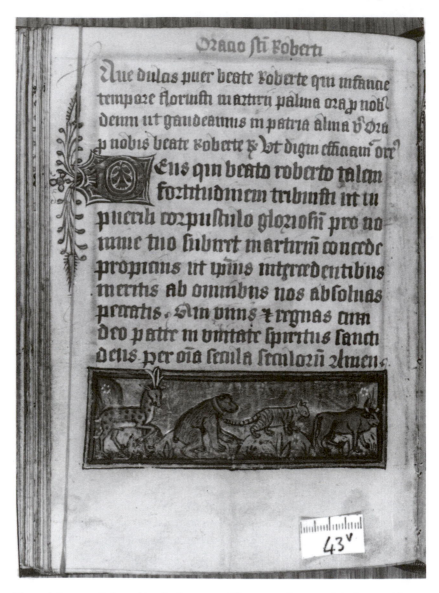

Figure 6. Prayer to Robert with animal group, twelfth century. Courtesy of the Conway Library, Courtauld Institute of Art.

Above the female figure is the legend, *"Voluit sed non potuit anus abscondere lucia dei"* ("the old woman wished but was not able to hide the light of God"). This woman is Robert's murderess or the character employed to dispose of the body.[47] The monkish figure, meanwhile, utters a prayer to Robert, *"Meritis sancti Roberti hic et in euum misereatur mei"* ("may he have mercy on me by the merits of St. Robert now and forever"). He appears to be the book's donor, which has led Nicholas Rogers to suggest that the illustration is a product of the book workshop at Bury in the mid-fifteenth century.[48]

The inclusion of the miniature again shows that the cult was still alive in the fifteenth century, and was possibly enjoying a revival. Moreover, Robert's story had its own iconographic register (the robin, charter, and seal). The cult was also apparently gendered in some way. The woman perverts the originary rite of baptism by placing Robert's body in a well. Meanwhile the pious man in the miniature has access to Robert. He prays to an image of Robert (the robin), and his prayer connects with Robert's ascendant soul (visually further separating the woman from Robert's body). The male (cleric) has intercessory access to Robert whilst the woman's behavior is warped.

The choice of a female protagonist works as a clear negative *exemplum* to women and children in particular. The monk shows the ladies of Bury how to practice the cult; the murderess offers an obscene, horrifying transgression—her presence in the manuscript is at once shocking, admonitory, and redemptive, for it leaves the pious women of Bury with a model of what they are not. The figure is not a distant caricature, but a rather elegant image of a being at once close to and distant from the very worshippers at whom it was aimed—a fifteenth-century gentlewoman (nominally a murderess and possibly a Jew) as the paradigm of alterity.

VI. An Audience with Anti-Semitism

The evidence of Laud 683 and *olim* Dyson Perrins 1 suggests that whilst the cultic memory of Robert was sustained by recital and ritual at the boy's shrine, it was in the household that the veneration took root. It was in this milieu that the cult was revived, through Lydgate's poem, in the fifteenth century. If we are to consider the narrative functions and workings of anti-Semitism, we must ask who was exposed to this narrative, and in what narrative context this exposure took place. As Denise Despres has written about anti-Semitic miracles of the Virgin, such texts

> occur at specific historical moments and are recalled deliberately to underscore the doctrinal and theological imperatives at the heart of their iconography—images that reinforce a late medieval notion of community, sacramental efficacy, and ritual responsibility.[49]

Laud 683 was clearly organized around accessibility to a group of readers and listeners of mixed gender and a variety of ages. Not only do we find here the subculture of "women talking about the things of God," as identified by Felicity Riddy, but also a mixed-sex reading/listening community in the medieval urban household.[50]

Gory stories about Jews here accompany miracles of the Virgin as texts used by women (as well as men). It is noteworthy that in Gloucester Cathedral the shrine to the similar boy-martyr Harold of Gloucester was in the Lady Chapel (Hillaby, 83). As Chaucer's assignment of a boy-martyr story to the Prioress suggests, such tales were particularly associated with women's piety. Indeed, Mistress Cole, the one-time owner of Laud 683, might have been rather similar to the Prioress: a well-presented gentlewoman with all the trappings of bourgeois success, confident in her faith in Church Triumphant's defeat of Synagoga.

The manuscript context of Lydgate's "Praier to St. Robert" thus leads us to a sobering and somewhat shocking image: that of Mistress Cole, in her comfortable urban household in fifteenth-century Bury, gathering round her family, her charges and her servants to partake in a quotidian corporate devotion central to which is the image of a Jew murdering a Christian child in old Bury. Here, anti-Semitism literally begins at home. The "Praier to St. Robert" strikes a chord with all present: the mother responds to the potent image of the suckling child; the son responds to pious little Robert; those close to the abbey respond to the evocation of Robert's shrine, the locus of the repeated regeneration of his passion; those from the Bury area are touched by the prayer's appeal to their provincial identity; all those present respond to the link made between saints Robert and Edmund, which forges a genealogy for each citizen of Bury from the cradle to the Crown. To become pious, to become a devout mother, to become a boy, to become a citizen, to become a Christian: in fifteenth-century Bury these processes started with the recurrent work of resurrecting the long-vanished Jewish community and staging or reiterating its repeated vilification and, less explicitly, its expulsion. It is through this revived Jew that the later-medieval people of Bury conjured a corporate identity and a polity accessible to all. Thus my title, "house devil, town saint": an Ulster saying about children who are naughty at home but who behave in public. Robert is enabled socially to be a saint by the diabolical Jew-figure of domestic readings; and children who are taught the "Praier" or similar materials are domestic misbehavers made to learn public piety and propriety.

Yet St. Robert was no St. Edmund.[51] Edmund, the royal martyr and nostalgic symbol of East Anglia, was the public, grand Bury saint; indeed, Lydgate famously wrote the *Legend of St. Edmund* for Henry VI.[52] St. Robert's cult was useful to the abbey, and complemented the cult of Edmund, precisely because it was private, diminutive, open, almost unofficial. Robert's story was known, and Robert was venerated, but through centripetal social memory, "common knowledge," and domestic piety rather than orthodox, centrifugal display. The paucity of material remains of Robert's cult—images, prayers, and the like—may be a consequence not only of the Reformation, but also of a cult sustained by rumor, oral traditions, drama, and local lore rather than grand iconography.[53] We might here usefully make a distinction between the Lydgate currently in critical vogue—royal, propagandist, "laureate" Lydgate—and the Lydgate of Laud 683—Suffolk, bourgeois, and, perhaps, monkish Lydgate. Lydgate's Lancastrian maneuvers, exemplified by the *Legend of St. Edmund*, have eclipsed his role as versifier of the gentry, of the upper middle class, of private devotion, of literate women, and of fifteenth-century fads. Yet it would be incorrect to set up a firm boundary between gentry fashion and royal iconography: the two frequently exist in symbiosis. The evidence leads us directly from Robert of Bury's household image to Henry VI (1421–1471): boy-king, Lancastrian catastrophe, and, eventually, pseudo-saint.

The sources available to us suggest that Robert's cult was dormant in the fourteenth century and enjoyed a revival in the fifteenth. Lydgate's use of the cult of St. Edmund in his commissions for Henry VI is well-known, and both Lydgate and his abbot, William Curteys, were instrumental in shaping Henry's self-image and his posthumous iconography. Henry VI stayed at St. Edmund's abbey, first as a twelve-year-old in 1433; in 1434 he was formally received, with the Earl and Countess of Warwick and Humphrey Duke of Gloucester, into the Fraternity of the Convent of Bury. Henry VI visited Bury throughout the 1440s and must have been familiar with Robert's shrine.

The resurgence in the popularity of boy-martyr iconography may well have been a part of the symbolic register of Henry VI's reign and his posthumous sanctification.[54] It is significant that two East Anglian representations of Robert's avatar, William of Norwich—at Eye (Suffolk) and Litcham (Norfolk)—place the boy-martyr adjacent to Henry VI on rood screens (dated to c. 1470 and 1536, respectively). This strand of Henry VI's iconography may have been adopted and embraced by both clerical and lay people in the period during and following Henry's reign, and both Henry VII (1485–1509) and Henry VIII (1509–1547) energetically developed the cult of Henry VI during the period in which Laud 683 and *olim* Dyson Perrins 1 were circulating.[55] That Henry VI should be depicted with the victims of Jewish ritual murder offers us a remarkable instance of the integral role of Judaism (and its vilification) in the formation of the royal identity, the paradigm of Englishness. Such iconography does not present the king as defender of the faith, but as victim of Jewish perfidy.

VII. Conclusion: The End of Robert's Cult

The Macro *Castell of Perseverance* play, which also has a Bury provenance, seems to quietly acknowledge this symbolically central and constant performative resurrection of the murderous Jew, expressing exasperation that "þe Jves wolde not ses" (1. 3555) their tormenting of Christ.[56] The Jewish *topos* could not cease in fifteenth-century Bury, for its regeneration served crucial communal functions. Jews—whether used for the discussion of identity, monarchy, or sacramentality—could act as a transcultural cynosure to create an adversary for the entire community beyond distinctions of gender, class, religion, and literary. Indeed, the slandered image of the Jew was almost omnipresent in late-medieval Bury—not only in the cult of St. Robert, but also in the drama (the Croxton *Play of the Sacrament*, the Digby plays, the Macro plays, and the N-Town plays have all been given a Bury connection or provenance, and all discuss the Jewish image) whilst the wall paintings at the abbey included a narrative of the "Jewish boy of Bourges," said to have been killed by his father in an oven.[57]

In the 1537 and 1538 accounts of Edward Rowgham it is only the Chapel of St. Laurence for which any revenue is received, and the oblations at crosses and altars including that of St. Robert have entirely disappeared.[58] If Bale was correct in placing a written *vita* of Robert with the Protestant iconoclast in the mid-sixteenth century, it is hardly surprising that such a text was disposed of at some point in this tumultuous period.[59] The boy's cult was a perfect example of all that was seen to be encoded—diminutive piety, faith in saints and their images, ritual rather than substance—in the old religion.

Yet the rumor of Robert's passion lived on after his shrine had been dismantled and his altar neglected. As late as 1593 the name St. Robert's Hall was used in property deeds to describe a house in Hatter Street, Bury.[60] Hatter Street was also known throughout the medieval period as "Heathenmen's Street," and this street contained a large number of stone houses, which were, until recently, associated with Jewish occupation.[61] In particular, Moyses Hall, a stone building likely to have been erected in the 1180s by the abbey, continues to be said to have been a Jew's house. We see a need, on the part of the Christian citizens of Bury, to create a domestic Jewish presence in the town, an apparition of its twelfth-century Jewish community. As in the repeated performances of the Croxton *Play of the Sacrament* there is some communal work—reflected in the variety of people exposed to these artifacts—of expelling the Jews, a task which it was felt had to be repeatedly performed.

We must take care, however, not to mistake this polite, pervasive, and stealthy ubiquity of Robert's cult—and those of similar boy-martyrs—for innocence and naïveté. Some reports state that fifty-seven Jews were put to death in Bury on Palm Sunday, 1190, and the allegation of ritual murder may well have been a key component in fuelling the violence.[62] In Lincoln, in 1255, the ritual murder charge led to the execution of nineteen Jews.[63] The allegation has had ferocious consequences throughout history, and remains a staple subject of anti-Semitic "revisionist" historiography.

Conversely, we ought also not to place Robert's cult in a transhistorical narrative which pays little attention to distinctive local and temporal stimuli. Robert's cult may well have been the product of discourses which have become inherent in the stereotyping of Jews by their neighbors, but the cult also responded to elements of devotional practice specific to medieval Bury. In revealing how Robert's cult, with its image of the murderous Jew, was sustained for some four centuries in a provincial town, we witness the multimedia dynamism of medieval English anti-Semitism: its omnipresence as an imagistic system, its openness to recontextualizations of medium and audience, its varied uses, purposes, and ideological destinations. Discourses such as that of the ritual murder allegation can only take root once they have penetrated, infiltrated, indeed saturated, a more general consciousness—in this case the quotidian devotion and the literary and artistic artifacts through which this devotion was taught and replayed.

The cult of St. Robert reinvented Bury's past for everyday rehearsal and consumption. As Miri Rubin asks, "Does the making of memory not involve the act of self-exculpation, the action of justification, and in so doing is it not also an admission of guilt?"[64] The concern we have seen with the revived Jew makes sense of the Bury community's expulsion and the sense of temporal rupture, discontinuity, and violence surrounding the events of 1190. The cult of Robert, its narratives and images, reconfigured historical time, making Christian sense of Jewish history, incorporating Jewish time at the most basic level of Christian praxis. It was through the Jew, and through the communal work of restaging the vilification of the Jew, that obedience and faith were taught and polity achieved. It was through the absent presence of the Jew that history and identity in Bury could be given the impression of concordance, stability, and wholeness.

Notes

I would like to thank the many people who have shared information about aspects of Robert's cult and offered their helpful comments: Rosemary Appleton, Sheila Delany, Brian Faulkner, Gail McMurray Gibson, Alexandra Gillespie, Antonia Gransden, Jane Griffiths, Lara McClure, Diarmaid Mac-Culloch, Linne Mooney, Tim Phillips, Emily Rose, Helen Spencer, Margaret Statham, and Paul Strohm. All interpretations and conclusions, and any errors, are my own. I am grateful to the Vidal Sassoon Center for the Study of Antisemitism at the Hebrew University of Jerusalem for its generous financial support in the form of a Felix Posen Fellowship and to the British Academy/Arts and Humanities Research Board for a Postgraduate Research Studentship.

1. On twelfth-century cases at Norwich, Gloucester, and Bristol respectively, see John McCulloh, "Jewish ritual murder: William of Norwich, Thomas of Monmouth, and the early dissemination of the myth," *Speculum* 72 (1997), 698–740; Joe Hillaby, "The ritual-child-murder accusation: its dissemination and Harold of Gloucester," *Transactions of the Jewish Historical Society of England* 34 (1994–96), 69–109; hereafter cited in text; Robert Stacey, "From ritual crucifixion to host desecration: Jews and the body of Christ," *Jewish History* 12 (1998), 11–28.

2. McCulloh, *passim*. Israel Yuval, "Vengeance and Damnation, Blood and Defamation: from Jewish martyrdom to blood libel accusations," *Zion* 58.1 (1993), 33–90, argues that the allegation emerged from the Continent. On the figure of the little boy in medieval devotional culture, see Miri Rubin, *Gentile Tales. The Narrative Assault on Late Medieval Jews* (New Haven, CT: Yale University Press, 1999), 7–39.

3. Thomas of Monmouth, *Life and Miracles of St. William of Norwich*, ed. Augustus Jessop and M. R. James (Cambridge, England: Cambridge University Press, 1895), for the *vita* and *miracula*.

4. Jocelin of Brakelond, *Chronicle of the Abbey of Bury St. Edmunds*, trans. and eds. Diana Greenaway and Jane Sayers (Oxford: Oxford University Press, 1989), 15. For original, see *The Memorials of Saint Edmund's Abbey*, ed. T. Arnold, vol. 1 (London: Eyre and Spottiswode, 1890), 223.

5. Gervase of Canterbury, *Opera Historica*, ed. William Stubbs (London: Longman, 1879), 1.296.

6. Thomas of Monmouth, *Life and Miracles*; McCulloh, "Jewish ritual murder."

7. The guild of St. William was founded in Norwich in 1376. M. Carey Evans, *The Legend of St. William Boy-Martyr of Norwich* (Norwich, England: Norwich Cathedral, n.d.), 6.

8. *The Customary of the Benedictine Abbey of Bury St. Edmunds in Suffolk*, ed. Antonia Gransden (Chichester: Henry Bradshaw Society, 1973), xv–xvi.

9. Barrie Dobson, *The Jews of Medieval York and the Massacre of March 1190* (York, England: St. Anthony's Press, 1974), 17–27.

10. Jocelin, *Chronicle*, 42. For original, see *Memorials* 1.249–50.

11. London, Public Record Office SC 6/HENVIII/3397.

12. Using dramatic and sermon evidence, Lawrence Clopper suggests that patron saints appeared in community drama, "that the parishioners [were] engaged in an attempt to coerce protection for another year" ("English drama: from ungodly *ludi* to sacred play," in *The Cambridge History of Medieval English Literature,* ed. David Wallace [Cambridge, England: Cambridge University Press, 1999], 739–66, 744). See also Siegfried Wenzel, "*Somer Game* and Sermon References to a Corpus Christi Play," *Modern Philology* 86 (1989), 274–81. The early-fifteenth-century *Tretise of Miraclis Pleyinge*, ed. Clifford Davidson (Kalamazoo, MI: Medieval Institute Publication, 1993) states that "no man shulde usen in bourde and pleye the miraclis and werkis that Crist so ernystfully wroughte to oure helthe" (93, ll. 23–25). The *Tretise* makes it

clear that saints' lives were frequently performed, although whether these performances appeared to the general community as devotion or as unholy burlesque is not clear (for the author of the *Treatise* it was clearly the latter). Clopper writes, "The bishops disliked . . . *ludi* [*inhonesti*] because they were inappropriate—in taking place within sacred space—and sacrilegious—in deriding, making fun of Christ and the saints," "English drama" (744). However, the evidence of PRO SC 6/HENVIII/3397 (the feretrar's accounts) suggests that the performances in St. Robert's chapel were within the financial ambit of the abbey, and were therefore at least allowed to continue (if not encouraged).

13. See Malcolm Godden, "Fleshly Monks and Dancing Girls: Immorality in the Morality Drama," in *The Long Fifteenth Century. Essays for Douglas Gray,* eds. Helen Cooper and Sally Mapstone (Oxford: Clarendon, 1997), 205–28, on dramatic performances in fifteenth-century Bury.

14. For a summary of Lydgate's life and literary career, see Derek Pearsall, *John Lydgate (1371–1449), a bio-bibliography* (Victoria, Canada: University of Victoria, 1997).

15. On Bokenham and the culture of fifteenth-century hagiography in Suffolk, see Sheila Delany, *Impolitic Bodies: poetry, saints and society in fifteenth-century England: the work of Osbern Bokenham* (Oxford: Oxford University Press, 1998). For a survey which contextualizes and connects Lydgate, Bokenham, Capgrave, Thomas Chaucer, and others, see Samuel Moore, "Patrons of Letters in Norfolk and Suffolk, *c.* 1450," in two parts, *Publications of the Modern Language Association* 27 (1912), 188–208, and *Publications of the Modern Language Association* 28 (1913), 79–105.

16. "*Memoria* . . . was a part of *litteratura*: indeed it was what literature, in a fundamental sense, was for." Mary Carruthers, *The Book of Memory: A Study of Memory in Medieval Culture* (Cambridge: Cambridge University Press, 1990), 9. Carruthers goes on to suggest that "it was in trained memory that one built character, judgment, citizenship, and piety" (9).

17. I am here reminded of Elaine Scarry's proposal in her *The Body in Pain: the Making and Unmaking of the World* (New York: Oxford University Press, 1985). Scarry writes "what assists the conversion of absolute pain into the fiction of absolute power is an obsessive, self-conscious display of agency" (27). In the case of ritual murder, the situation is reversed—the Jews' agency is foregrounded in order to invest the Jews with threatening physical potency. Michael Jones has recently offered a reading of anti-Semitic narratives which highlights their performativity, in " 'The Place of the Jews': Anti-Judaism and Theatricality in Medieval Culture,' *Exemplaria* 12 (2000), 327–59.

18. Moreover, in the twelfth-century ritual murder story of Adam of Bristol, the boy-martyr is seen by the Jewish villains in the arms of Mary, garbed in purple. The story of Adam, which possibly developed as parish drama at Bristol, is found in only one manuscript (London, British Library Harley MS 957) which belonged to William Spynk, prior at Norwich Cathedral, in the fifteenth century. Christoph Cluse, " 'Fabula inepitissima': Die Ritualmordlegende um Adam von Bristol nach der Handschrift London, British Library,

Harley 957," *Aschkenas* 5 (1995), 293–330, 294; Stacey, *passim*, on the story's possible dramatic provenance.

19. Leah Sinanoglou, "The Christ Child as Sacrifice: A Medieval Tradition and the Corpus christi Play," *Speculum* 43 (1973), 491–509. Sinanoglou discusses *exempla* in which the Christ child is dismembered and devoured in order to convert Jews (43). In this way, the Christ child, in this case Robert, is consumed as a sacrament at his altar.

20. The allusions to milk and suckling in Lydgate's poem have a purchase on conventional imagery of the Christ child and Mary's milk. On such imagery, see Caroline Walker Bynum, *Holy Feast and Holy Fast. The religious significance of food to medieval women* (Berkeley and Los Angeles: University of California Press, 1987), figs. 17–27.

21. The prayer to St. Leonard (patron of pregnant women and captives; ff. 21r–23r) mentions the saint's "servantis resortyng to þis place," which Mac-Cracken suggests is Norwich, where there was a hospital of St. Leonard. There was, however, also a hospital of St. Leonard at Ipswich, which was certainly within the ambit of Robert's cult. The standard printed edition of these, and other, Lydgate poems is *The Minor Poems of John Lydgate*, ed. H. N. MacCracken, 2 vols. (London: Oxford University Press, 1911).

22. Gail McMurray Gibson, *Theater of Devotion: East Anglian Drama and Society in the Late Middle Ages* (Chicago: University of Chicago Press, 1989), 33.

23. St. Christina (f. 26v), who features in the "Prayers to Ten Saints," was martyred with arrows, like St. Edmund, a further link with Bury.

24. Likewise, St. Christopher (f. 25r), the "Geant of Stature / that bar Iesu over the sterne fflood," offers an image of quasi-parental responsibility. Gabriel (ff. 24r–v; also unique to Laud 683) has an obvious relevance to mothers, and Gabriel's parental role is drawn out: "Blissed Gabriel, wich broughtest first tydying / On-to Marye, knelyng on thy kne . . ."

25. "The Order of Foolis" is often accompanied in manuscripts by marginal illustrations of owls, the filthy "Jewish" animal of the bestiary. The owl was thought to shun the light of God, to nest in its own excrement, and to be mobbed by the good, but smaller, Christian day birds. This particular scheme of illustration would seem to then place "Jews" as a shorthand for folly. Kathleen Scott observes that the owl is often seen "on the arm of a jester or in the company of a fool,": "A Mid-Fifteenth-Century English Illuminating Shop and its Customers," *Journal of the Warburg and Courtauld Institutes* 31 (1968), 170–96, 172. I am grateful to Alexandra Gillespie for this observation.

26. There are a number of similar manuscripts, containing Lydgate's texts, which were also known to have female owners. These include Oxford, Bodleian Library MS Hatton 73 (Lydgate's *Life of Our Lady*), which belonged to "Dame Elizabethe Wyndesore"; Oxford, Bodleian Library MS Ashmole 39 (*Life of Our Lady*), inscribed with the name "Anne Andrew," wife of Sir Thomas Bourchier; Durham, University Library Cosin MS V. II (*Life of Our Lady*, which belonged to "Jane Fitzlewis"; Cambridge, Trinity College MS O.52 (*Troy Book* and *Siege of Thebes*), owned by Anne Knevet of Buckenham, Norfolk, in the 1480s; Oxford, Bodleian Library MS Laud 416 (a miscellany, including Lydgate's *Siege of Thebes*) owned by a Syon nun, "syster

Anne Colvylle"; Oxford, Bodleian Library Rawlinson poet. 144 (*Troy Book*), owned by "elysabeth peche." On these manuscripts, see Carol M. Meale, " '. . . alle the bokes that I haue of latyn, englisch, and frensch': laywomen and their books in later medieval England," in ed. Carol M. Meale, *Women and Literature in Britain 1150–1500* (Cambridge: Cambridge University Press, 1993), 128–59. Moreover, a variety of Lydgate's poems were commissioned by women, notably the "Invocation to St. Anne" (Anne, countess of Stafford, daughter of Eleanor Bohun), the "Legend of St. Margaret" (Anne Mortimer), the "Fifteen Joys of Our Lady" (Isabella Despenser), and *Guy of Warwick* (Margaret Beauchamp, later Talbot, wife of John Talbot, earl of Shrewsbury). Meale, 137. *Guy of Warwick*, the poems to St. Anne and St. Margaret and the "Fifteen Joys" all appear in Laud 683.

27. Jocelyn Wogan-Browne, "Saints' Lives and the Female Reader," *Forum for Modern Language Studies* 27 (1991) 314–32, shows that female saints were perceived as "particularly relevant models for female audiences."

28. A. S. G. Edwards, "Gender and design in Cambridge University Library MS Add. 4122 and some related fifteenth-century hagiographical collections," *Yearbook of English Studies* 33 (forthcoming, 2003).

29. It should be added that even books commissioned by women were not necessarily always owned by women. For example, Margaret Beaufort left a copy of Lydgate's *Troy Book* to her son, Henry VII, in 1509 (Meale, 141).

30. For example, Cambridge University Library MS Add. 4122; Oxford, Bodleian Library MS Douce 1.

31. On this manuscript, see Anne F. Sutton and Livia Visser-Fuchs, *The Hours of Richard III* (Stroud: Alan Sutton, 1990), 109 n. 267.

32. For fascinating evidence from similar books, see Cullum and Goldberg, *passim*.

33. Two wills, one from 1449 and the other from 1464, record two Suffolk women named Margaret Cole—the former living at Stoke juxta Clare, the latter at Stoke by Nayland. There were also wealthy testators by the name of Cole at Bury (Thomas, d. 1478), Mildenhall (Richard, d. 1480), Wattlesfield (Thomas, d. 1481), Risby (John, d. 1514), and Thelnetham (John, d. 1527). This is just a sample, from the "Calendar of Pre-Reformation Wills, Testaments, Probates, Administrations, Registered at the Probate Office, Bury St. Edmunds," ed. Vincent B. Redstone, *Proceedings of the Suffolk Institute of Archaeology and Natural History* 12 (1906). A detailed examination of testamentary evidence may well produce further documentation of Robert's cult.

34. For example the Laud collection catalogue explicitly occludes the female inscription: "Codex membranaceus, in 4to minori. ff. 151, secc. xv. et. vii; quondam _____ Cole". H. O. Coxe and R. W. Hunt, *Laudian Manuscripts* reprinted with corrections and additions (Oxford: The Bodleian Library, 1973), 26. Laud 683 has been considered by Julia Boffey and John Thompson as a miscellany rather than as a woman's manuscript, in "Anthologies and Miscellanies: production and choice of texts," *Book Production and Publishing in Britain 1375–1475*, eds. Jeremy Griffiths and Derek Pearsall (Cambridge: Cambridge University Press, 1989), 279–315.

35. A full description of the manuscript can be found in George F. Warner, *Descriptive Catalogue of illuminated manuscripts in the library of C. W. Dyson Perrins* (Oxford: Oxford University Press, 1920), 1, 5, on St. Robert. Shorter notices appear in Sotheby & Co., London, *Sotheby's 216th Season* [October 1959–July 1960], (London: Sotheby & Co., 1960), 94; and in Lawrence Witten, *Important Books, Manuscripts, Documents and Autographs 10th to 19th Centuries* [catalogue #5] (New Haven, CT: Lawrence Witten, 1962), 12. The notice and description of the manuscript given in H. Copinger Hill, "S. Robert of Bury St. Edmunds," *Proceedings of the Suffolk Institute of Archaeology* 21 (1931–33), 98–109, should be used with caution.

36. Pinchbeck is a village near Spalding (Lincolnshire), also in the east of England.

37. An inscription at f. 41r shows that by the 1590s the manuscript was at Foulsham (Norfolk), and belonged to Robert Themilthorpe, Rector of Foulsham. Warner, 8.

38. The above is based on Warner's manuscript description; should the manuscript be made available for inspection, new material may come to light.

39. Likewise, the early-fifteenth-century panel of William of Norwich at Loddon (Norfolk) places this boy's martyrdom next to the Annunication—the point at which Jesus is brought into being is again accompanied by the genesis of medieval anti-Semitism.

40. As Bury was a Benedictine foundation one would expect the monk's habit to be black.

41. The link with the robin may not only be because of the name "Robert," but also because of lore surrounding the figure of the robin which connects it with Christ's blood. "The tradition is that when Our Lord was on His way to Calvary, a robin picked a thorn out of his crown, and the blood which issued from the wound falling on the bird dyed its breast red," recorded in *Brewer's Dictionary of Phrase and Fable*, ed. Ivor H. Evans (London: Guild, 1985), 955.

42. Debra Hassig has chapters on both the stag and the panther in *Medieval Bestiaries: Text, Image, Ideology* (Cambridge, England: Cambridge University Press, 1995); hereafter cited in text. The *Northumberland Bestiary* (*olim* Alnwick Castle MS 447, f. 16v), and the *St. John's Bestiary* (Oxford, St. John's College MS 178, f. 158v) have similar combinations of the panther with an adoring stag. The panther was not thought of as a black animal. It was glossed as the beast which comes back to life after the scourging of the Jews, citing Psalms 45:2.

43. On the bear, see Ann Payne, *Medieval Beasts* (London: British Library, 1990), 42.

44. In Paris, Bibliothèque Nationale MS fr. 14969, a late-thirteenth-century bestiary from Oxford or London, an owl (the most common "Jewish" bestiary animal) sits in the panther's entourage with his head turned away, as the Jews were believed to turn away from Christ (Hassig, 162).

45. Hassig offers an intelligent discussion of the anti-Semitism implicit in the images of the panther and its followers, and describes the bonnacon as the panther's "antithetical counterpart" (Hassig, 156–66).

46. Richard Barber, *Bestiary* (Woodbridge, England: Boydell, 1993), 92. The cow was also resonant with images of sacrifice and was glossed with Leviticus 9:3–8; Numbers 18:17; 1 Samuel 28:24.

47. It is not clear if this figure is supposed to be Jewish. In the fifteenth-century wall painting of the Jewish woman cured by the Virgin, at Eton College chapel (Berkshire), the Jewess looks no different from the other women in the picture.

48. Nicholas Rogers, "Fitzwilliam Museum MS 3–1979: A Bury St. Edmunds Book of Hours and the Origins of the Bury Style," in *England in the Fifteenth Century: Proceedings of the 1986 Harlaxton Symposium,* ed. Daniel Williams (Woodbridge: Boydell and Brewer, 1987), 229–43.

49. Denise Despres, "Immaculate Flesh and the Social Body: Mary and the Jews," *Jewish History* 12 (1998), 47–71, 60.

50. Felicity Riddy, " 'Women talking about the things of God': a late medieval sub-culture," in Meale, *Women and Literature,* 104–28.

51. The monastic sign list from Bury, which was used by monks to communicate whilst maintaining their vow of silence, includes signs for Saints Mary, Benedict, and Edmund, but not for Robert. David Sherlock and William G. Zajac, "A fourteenth-century monastic sign list from Bury St. Edmunds Abbey," *Proceedings of the Suffolk Institute of Archaeology and History* 36:4 (1988), 250–73, 257. Moreover, Robert does not appear in Oxford, Bodleian Library MS Bodley 240, an anthology of materials including John of Tynemouth's saints' lives composed by the monks of Bury St. Edmunds. The omission is startling, as Bodley 240 is essentially a propagandist compendium of all that made Bury St. Edmunds and its abbey spiritually distinctive. John of Tynemouth's saints' lives are insistently East Anglian and his enormous account of the life and miracles of St. Edmund is also found in the manuscript. It is unusual then that Robert was omitted—rather like Worcestre's incomplete record of Robert's saint's day, the negative evidence of Bodley 240 suggests that the cult of Robert was dormant or muted at the abbey and was revived or practiced outside its precincts. Tynemouth's saint's lives are printed in *Nova Legenda Anglie,* ed. Carl Horstmann (Oxford: Clarendon Press, 1901), 2.538–688.

52. On "laureate Lydgate" (Pearsall's phrase) see Derek Pearsall, *John Lydgate* (London: Routledge and Kegan Paul, 1970), 160–91; also Walter F. Schirmer, *John Lydgate: a study in the culture of the XVth Century,* translated by Ann E. Keep (London: Methuen, 1961), 100–108, 130–43. Also on Lydgate's laureate texts, see Paul Strohm, "Hoccleve, Lydgate, and the Lancastrian Court," in *The Cambridge History of Medieval English Literature,* ed. David Wallace (Cambridge: Cambridge University Press, 1999), 640–61; and, focusing on Lydgate's relation to Henry V, Lee Patterson, "Making Identities in Fifteenth-Century England: Henry V and John Lydgate," in *New Historical Literary Study: Essays on Reproducing Texts, Representing History,* eds. Jeffrey N. Cox and Larry J. Reynolds (Princeton: Princeton University Press, 1993), 69–108. On Lydgate's royal patrons, see Lois Ebin, *John Lydgate* (Boston: Twayne, 1985), 80–86.

53. The remarkable study of rumor and anti-Semitism by Edgar Morin *et al., Rumour in Orléans,* trans. Peter Green (London: Blond, 1971) amply shows how rumor-based cults can spread and develop, and be inculcated across the community, without the need for material objects.

54. Both the cults of Edmund and Henry VI put a special emphasis on miracles concerning children. See Eleanora C. Gordon, "Accidents among medieval children as seen from the miracles of six English saints and martyrs," *Medical History* 35 (1991), 145–64. On Henry's cult, Fr. Ronald Knox and Shane Leslie, *The Miracles of King Henry VI* (Cambridge, England: Cambridge University Press, 1923).

55. This cult includes a book of *miracula* (English version *c.* 1486; Latin *c.* 1501). These are respectively London, British Library Royal MS 13.C.VIII and London, British Library Harley MS 423. E. Ettlinger, "Notes on a wood-cut depicting King Henry VI being invoked as a saint," *Folklore* 84 (1973), 115–19. In 1479 Lawrence Booth, archbishop of York, forbade the veneration of Henry; in 1504 Pope Julius II endorsed the cult and permitted the translation of Henry's body to Westminster (Knox and Leslie, 3, 5); Henry VIII made a pilgrimage to the tomb of Henry VI in 1529.

56. *The Macro Plays,* ed. F. J. Furnivall and Alfred W. Pollard (London: Kegan Paul, Trench, Trübner and Co., 1904), 183. Gail McMurray Gibson gives the manuscript of the Macro plays (Washington, Folger Library MS V.a.354) a Bury provenance, "Bury St. Edmunds, Lydgate, and the *N-Town Cycle*," *Speculum* 56 (1981), 56–90, 57.

57. On the Bury provenance of the drama, see Gibson, "Bury St. Edmunds," *passim*. On the ecclesiastical art at Bury, see M. R. James, *On the Abbey of S. Edmund at Bury* (Cambridge, England: Cambridge Antiquarian Society, 1895), 143.

58. London, Public Record Office SC 6/HENVIII/3398. It should be noted, however, that the payments for boy-bishop festivities continue.

59. On iconoclasm at Hadleigh, see Diarmid MacCulloch, *Suffolk and the Tudors. Politics and Religion in an English County, 1500–1600* (Oxford: Clarendon, 1986), 171.

60. Margaret Statham, personal communication, June 20, 2000.

61. Robert Halliday, "Moyses Hall, Bury St. Edmunds," *Suffolk Review: Bulletin of Suffolk Local History* n.s. 25 (1995), 27–44; Edgar Samuel, "Was Moyses Hall, Bury St. Edmunds, a Jew's House?", *Transactions of the Jewish Historical Society of England* 25 (1977), 43–47. There was also a St. Robert's Hall in Bury; see *Wills and Inventories from the registers of the commissary of Bury St. Edmunds,* ed. Samuel Tymms (London: Camden Society, 1850), 8–9.

62. Joseph Jacobs, *The Jews of Angevin England* (London and New York: Putnam, 1893), 75.

63. Gavin Langmuir, *Toward a Definition of Anti-Semitism* (Berkeley and Los Angeles: University of California Press, 1990), 258.

64. Rubin, 134. Such an "admission of guilt" has been made explicit at Lincoln and Norwich cathedrals, where plaques have been erected which rescind the ritual murder allegation. Likewise, regarding Robert of Bury, the "Catholic Online Saints" site states that his story "is entirely fictitious and owes its propagation to the rampant anti-Semitism of the period." See http://saints.catholic.org/saints/robertofburystedmunds.html.

Appendix
John Lydgate, "Praier to St. Robert"

Edited from Oxford, Bodleian Library MS Laud misc. 683, ff. 22v–23r. Minimal punctuation added.

Here begynneth a praier to seynt Robert
O blyssed Robert, Innocent and virgyne,
glorious marter, gracious & riht good,
to our prayer thyn eris doun enclyne,
wich on to crist offredyst thy chast blood,
ageyns the the Iewys were so wood,   5
lyk as thy story makyth mencyoun,
pray for all tho, to crist that starff on rood,
that do reuerence on to thy passioun.
Slayn in childhood by mortal violence,
allas it was a pitous thyng to see   10
a sowkyng child, tendre of innocence,
so to be scourged, and naylled to a tre;
thou myghtyst crie, thou spak no woord parde,
with-oute language makyng a pitous soun,
pray for alle tho, knelyng on thy kne,   15
that do reuerence on-to thy passioun.
Fostrid with mylk and tendre pap þi foode
was it nat routhe to se þi veynes bleede
only for crist, crucyfied for our goode,
in whos despit al sangweyn was thy weede,   20
slayn in erthe, in hevene is now thy meede,
among marteris, vp on thy hed a crown,
O gracious Robert to pray for hem tak heede
that do reuerence on to thy passioun.
Suffredist deth or thou koudist pleyne,   25
thy purpil blood allayed with mylk whiht,
oppresid with turment koudest no woord seyne,
ffer ffro thy norice, founde no respight;
be grace enspired, Ihesu was thy delight,
thy sowle vpborn to the hevenly mansioun,   30
pray for alle folk that haue an apetyght
to do reuerence on-to thy passioun.
Haue vpon Bury þi gracious remembraunce
that hast among hem a chapel & a shryne,

with helpe of Edmund, preserve hem fro grevaunce,   35
kyng of Estynglond, martir and virgyne,
with whos briht sonne lat thy sterre shyne,
strecchyng your stremys thoruh al þis regioun,
pray for alle tho, and kepe hem fro ruyne,
that do reuerence to both your passioun.   40
Explicit.

PART III

Chaucer, Jews, and Us

12

Englishness and Medieval Anglo-Jewry

COLIN RICHMOND

I frequently ask myself: What would a Jewish history of Europe be like? Sitting in the Botanical Gardens at Oxford one summer's day recently, I pondered what such a history of England would consist of. What would it say about this beautiful place, for example: its honey-colored stone walls, the goldfish among the water lilies, the immaculate lawns? Beyond the green water of the Isis, on which a punt was being indolently poled along, a cricket match was in progress: middle-aged men in garishly-colored caps trundled after the ball on Magdalen School field. A slow bowler (rarest of sights) was hit for six, and the silence was scarcely broken by that particularly English sound of summer: random applause from pavilion and deck chairs. This side of the river a family of foreign tourists (Spanish? Italian? Greek?) watched uncomprehendingly. Over the trees Magdalen College tower rose (as one might say) timelessly, while Merton College clock struck the quarter-hour: it was 4:15 and I was due to take tea in Magdalen cloister. Here, as any Englishman was bound to think, was Grantchester. I *was* thinking that. I was also thinking that here until 1290 had been the cemetery of the Jewish community of Oxford, and moreover that the cemetery had occupied the other side of the road as well as this until 1231, when the pious Henry III granted it as a building site to the hospital of St. John the Baptist, which itself gave way to Magdalen College in the fifteenth century.[1]

I had not learned these facts from *Medieval Oxford* by the Reverend H. E. Salter, Fellow of Magdalen College and doyen of the historians of medieval Oxford. Jews feature neither in the index of that book, published in 1936 by the Oxford Historical Society, nor (so far as I can detect) in its 150 pages of text. The information came from Cecil Roth's *The Jews of Medieval Oxford,* published by the same society in 1951. The moral is obvious. It would require no elaboration were it not for its utter neglect by English historians and because of my failure to comprehend it in the question I pondered in the Botanical Gardens: What would a Jewish history of England consist of? The moral is this: Why does it have to be a history of the Jews in medieval Oxford which discusses the Jews of Oxford in the Middle Ages? They were not unimportant (whatever that means); quite the contrary—on any measurement of "importance," whether social, economic, political, cultural, or intellectual, for two hundred years the Jewish community of Oxford was important. Were this simply a matter of "out of sight utterly out of mind," this article might be unnecessary. History, however, is more than heritage; indeed, this case demonstrates that it has to be unswervingly anti-heritage, for it is precisely those aspects of the English past which are out of sight that have to be kept in mind. "Have to be" if history is not to succumb to myth, as well as to that invidious convention, more racialist than nationalist, that Jewish history is only for Jews. Do not Frenchmen write about the history of England, Englishmen about Polish history? Jewish history permeates European history; its absence from the history of Oxford and England tells us at once a great deal about Englishness.

Have things changed since 1936? It may be thought that they have. Professor Barrie Dobson is an Englishman who not only has written about medieval English Jewry, but also has become president of the Jewish Historical Society of England. He has said that "At the end of the twentieth century it often seems that the treatment of their Jewish minorities by Edward I, Philip the Fair, and *los reyes catolicos,* much as those monarchs would have been disconcerted by the thought, is more 'relevant' to our own problems than any other feature of their respective reigns."[2] Gavin Langmuir, a non-Jewish American, is more specific: "To explain what Hitler had done, scholars found they had to rewrite sections of earlier history."[3] In other words it has become essential to recycle the past if the *Shoah* is not to slip entirely into that historical limbo which is half-heritage (it is happening, it is happening) and half-entertainment (it has happened, it has happened). One cause of the *Shoah* was that non-Jewish historians ignored the Jews, as—to take what seems so trivial an instance but is not—H. E. Salter ignored them in writing the history of medieval Oxford. A masterly non-Jewish historian in the course of mourning a majestic Jewish one has put that ignorance into crystalline perspective: "This refusal to see permanent value in the particularity of the Jews had left Christian countries morally impotent, when the Nazis proposed annihilation as the alternative to absorption."[4]

Oh, but that did not happen here—might be an Englishman's answer. Oh, but it would have—has to be the response of historians of twentieth-century England. There is, therefore, no excuse for those English historians who have not changed their ways, who write as if the *Shoah* had not happened. Take Edward I, the English king whom Barrie Dobson singled out and who was a pioneering anti-Semite when he expelled the Jews from the kingdom of England in 1290: he was the first European ruler to make his state permanently *Judenrein.* He, or one of his civil servants, was a pioneer in small things as in great. "The fatal step," as Cecil Roth describes it, "was taken on 18 July 1290 by an act of the king in his Council. It happened to be (as was long after remembered with awe) the fast of the ninth of Ab, anniversary of manifold disasters for the Jewish people, from the destruction of Jerusalem onwards."[5] That neutral phrase, "it happened to be," may have been carefully chosen, for Professor Roth, even though writing without our knowledge of the Nazi habit of deliberately selecting the Holy Days of Judaism on which to initiate atrocities against Jews, must have suspected that Edward I knew (or was reminded) what day it was on July 18, 1290. English historians ought to remember (with a good deal more awe than they have done hitherto) not only the vindictiveness Edward displayed, but also the political connection he was making, when he chose the fast of the ninth of Ab.

Edward knew what he was doing on July 18, 1290. This is evident from his close association with the construction of the shrine to little St. Hugh in Lincoln Cathedral in the first half of the 1290s. As David Stocker has shown, the shrine was of a design similar to that of the Eleanor Crosses, notably the cross at Waltham; they shared the same contractor, sculptor, and master mason. The shrine, he suggests,

> belongs to a group of Edward I's projects which bring with them an element of political propaganda . . . Edward clearly wanted the new shrine to be associated with the Crown; not only was he the sole monarch recorded as giving alms at the shrine, but it appears he may have provided expertise from the royal workshops to create this monument, which may even have been intended to remind pilgrims of the Eleanor Crosses. To reinforce the connection between the saint and the Crown, the royal arms were prominently displayed . . . Edward had a strong interest in emphasising both the alleged criminality of the English Jewry and the Crown's position as a principal defender of the English Christians. Edward's apparently enthusiastic support for the shrine of Little St. Hugh suited this royal purpose very well.[6]

Such demonstrable enthusiasm might lead one to believe that a Jewish policy was close to Edward's bigoted heart, that the king placed himself, in the words of Paul Hyams, "at the head of anti-Jewish forces, which were not necessarily any stronger in numbers than a century earlier."[7] Yet, even the expulsion itself is fleetingly dealt with in Michael Prestwich's biography of Edward I. In a text of 567 pages the Jews get less than three. It is also evident that, however pressing were the financial circumstances, it was Edward's religious bigotry that impelled him to expel the Jews in 1290. Despite this, Professor Prestwich's paper entitled "The Piety of Edward I" makes no mention of the expulsion. One's suspicions that these omissions are more than simple negligence are deepened by some of the little Prestwich has to say on Jewish topics in his book. He writes, for example, that "there were stories of ritual child-murder and torture, which, although they now *appear* groundless on the basis of the recorded evidence, were generally believed," and that "the expulsion itself went surprisingly smoothly, and was not the occasion for massacres, *as it might well have been*" (my italics).[8]

This reminds me of the evening I was at the heart of Englishness. In Shakespeare's schoolroom at Stratford-on-Avon I had given a lecture on the expulsion and was answering questions and listening to comments; one of the latter was to the effect that the expulsion had been conducted in a comparatively humane manner, and I was to realize (was the implication of the tone of the communication) that this was a reason for self-congratulation. There was no indication that the speaker was aware the expulsion could have been avoided. What confronted me in that most English of English locales was the terrible and terrifying habit of viewing the past as inevitable. Moreover, when historians write about Edward I in the way Professor Prestwich has, the *Shoah* will disappear into the predetermined as the expulsion has done, for as historians our approach to both is bound to be identical.

I am not (as we shall see) singling out Professor Prestwich. Edward I, on the other hand, deserves picking on. It must be a measure of Englishness that he is recognized as the Hammer of the Welsh and Scots, but has no such reputation where the Jews are concerned, despite perpetrating "the largest ever massacre of English Jews,"[9] in the notorious coin-clipping affair of 1278. On a charge of filing the edges of England's silver pennies, the head of every Jewish household was arrested and imprisoned in the Tower of London; after hanging 269 of them (along with twenty-nine Christians) Edward got over £16,000 from the sale of their forfeited property. This was the gamekeeper turned poacher with a vengeance. Philip the Fair was no innovator when he turned on the Jews and Templars in France a generation later. How remarkable that the English king who is remembered for his legislation had no greater regard for legality than Adolf Hitler did.

Or, possibly, than his father did. This, however, may be unfair to Henry III. It is true, as Gavin Langmuir has pointed out,[10] that when Henry III had nineteen Jews of Lincoln hanged in 1255 for the alleged murder of little St. Hugh he was the first major authority in Europe to order executions for so-called ritual murder: Henry too was a pioneer. Yet we must assume Henry was genuinely scandalized by the story extracted under torture from the Jew Copin; thereafter he duly applied the law to those guilty of this heinous crime. The case, which "entered into the folk-lore of the English people,"[11] was also cause and consequence of what Robert Stacey has called a "watershed in Anglo-Jewish relations,"[12] when in the middle years of the thirteenth-century victimization of the Jews by king, Church, and top people plumbed new depths. An historian, Matthew Paris, was on hand to chronicle and explain the "new themes" of anti-Semitism: "magic, murder, and excrement" (Stacey, 149–50). Yet, we are told by Professor Richard Vaughan that

"Matthew to his credit had no very deep-seated prejudices against the Jews, perhaps because of his sympathy for them as victims of royal extortion."[13] Here is the sympathetic Matthew:

> Though miserable, they [the Jews] deserved no commiseration, for they were proved to have been guilty of forgery, both of money and seals. And if we are silent about other crimes, we have decided to include one of them in this book, in order that their wickedness may be better known to more people. There was a certain quite rich Jew, Abraham by name but not in faith, who lived and had property at Berkhamstead and Wallingford . . . In order to dishonour Christ the more, this Jew bought a nicely carved and painted statue of the blessed Virgin, as usual nursing her son at her bosom. This image the Jew set up in his latrine and . . . he inflicted a most filthy and unmentionable thing on it, daily and nightly, and ordered his wife to do the same.[14]

It is necessary to grasp the fact that to a thirteenth-century mind a religious image was not the simple representation it would be to a twentieth-century one, in order to appreciate the disgust a fastidious monk would have felt when told this story. Can a historian afford such credulity? Moreover, does not credulity in a historian exactly coincide with his prejudices, shallow or deep? I do not think Professor Vaughan can get away with his Matthew Paris any more than Professor Prestwich can with his Edward I.

Nothing of this is to be found in the large volumes on the reign of Henry III by Sir Maurice Powicke. That gentlest of historians and most sensitive of men was writing during and just after World War II; his sympathetic understanding of the plight of the English Jewry in the thirteenth century, especially at the hands of royal tax collectors, is evident in a number of passages. He has not one word on little St. Hugh. It is almost as if a Christian English gentleman, of which Powicke was a near perfect example, did not speak of such things. On Powicke's part we may talk of innocence, not ignorance; on the part of so many others it was (and is) that ignorance which, because it is of the ostrich variety, will not save them from condemnation at the bar of History.

Powicke certainly made no bones about Simon de Montfort: Simon "hated Jews."[15] He does not deal with what have been called the "savage anti-Semitic riots" in London of April 1264, when over five hundred Jews were killed and robbed, beyond a neutral "the Jews were attacked"; but we should not expect him to: he was not writing about Simon.[16] But David Carpenter was, yet in his article[17] the Jews do not feature. There is every reason that they should, because Dr. Carpenter's theme is that Simon was an enthusiastic bigot who knew how to manipulate the instincts of the English political nation, not excluding the baser ones. Simon was zealous for political reform: so were many of "the knights, gentry and those below them in the counties of

England." He seemed to desire reform in the Church: "reform-minded eccle-siastics" rallied to him. "Equally significant was Simon's skill in exploiting the question of the aliens": here, at last, I anticipated a sentence on the way in which Simon's anti-Semitism endeared him to knights and gentlemen, those *buzones* or bigwigs of the English provinces, whose hatred of the Jews was even sharper than that of the civil servants at Westminster. There was no such sentence. An opportunity had been missed. We are bound to ask: Why such forgetfulness? Why is it that something which stares one historian in the face escapes the attention of another?

Simon de Montfort, apart from initiating pogroms in English cities, was among the first to expel Jews from an English town. Simon was granted the earldom of Leicester in August 1231; this included lordship of the town of Leicester; by the end of the year the Jews had gone. Simon's charter of 1253 making Leicester *Judenrein* for all time survives in the borough archives: "Know . . . that I, for the good of my soul, and the souls of my ancestors have granted . . . that no Jew or Jewess, in my time or in the time of any of my heirs to the end of the world, shall within the liberty of the town of Leicester, inhabit or remain or obtain a residence."[18] This is the authentic voice of the founder of Parliament, a man who "is much commemorated in Leicester—a square, a street, and a concert hall are named after him, his statue adorns the Clock Tower."[19] So writes Professor Jack Simmons; his only other comment is that "the town's deepest cause of gratitude to Simon de Montfort is nega-tive: that he did not involve it in the turmoils of the close of his life." Jews and their expulsion are not mentioned.

According to Matthew Paris, Simon's confessor was Robert Grosseteste. Sir Richard Southern confronted head-on Grosseteste's attitude towards the Jews; the passage in which he does so commands even greater admiration as one senses in reading it how hard Professor Southern found it to write: he has never been an historian to lack courage. In 1231 Grosseteste was archdeacon of Leicester; the Jews of that town after their expulsion in that year went to Winchester, where they were welcomed by the Countess of Winchester. But Grosseteste, not content with having got rid of the Jews from his own archdeaconry, sent the Countess a letter bitterly condemning her hospitality. After summarizing the letter, Professor Southern comments: "I have softened rather than exaggerated the violence of Grosseteste's words, which extend to four pages of print." He continues:

> Here we see Grosseteste in an unfavourable light. . . . It is unfavourable to him, because it shows that in an area of conduct where brutality was the rule, he was prepared to go to even greater lengths of brutality, because he took the principles on which it was based more seriously than most men. He thought with more energy, with more fierce commitment, and with a more urgent desire to give practical expression to his thoughts than most men in

high positions, who had worked their way to the top by many compromises. Grosseteste had risen almost by a single bound. He had had no lessons in keeping silent. He was a man of the people, and he spoke with a peasant's violence and passion to those above him as well as those beneath.[20]

Grosseteste was born about 1170, almost certainly in a village near Bury St. Edmunds. Until 1230 his life was difficult. His long and tough route to high office—he became bishop of Lincoln in 1235—followed (and this is Professor Southern's highly original conclusion) an entirely English education, for Grosseteste never attended the schools of France. It was just this "provincial career" which made Grosseteste original and complicated. He was impatient of academic constraints; intellectually he was both reckless and broad; in life he followed the Gospels; he had a prophetic clarity of vision which enabled him to tell the Pope to his face that what was wrong with Christendom was the Papacy; he was a cheerful man who loved music, and a moral fanatic who wanted compulsory Christianity; he was "one of the most independent and vigorous Englishmen of the Middle Ages—a medieval Dr. Johnson in his powers of mind and personality." Because they had rejected the Incarnation he hated the Jews. That such an Englishman, so principled an Englishman, so English an Englishman hated Jews explains a good deal—perhaps all we need to know—about the precocity of English anti-Semitism.

Yet not quite all for there may be a connection which Professor Southern does not make. It is the Bury St. Edmunds connection. Anti-Jewish feeling among the monks at Bury was a consequence of their ambition to build and to adorn their abbey in the grandest style; no doubt they believed themselves to be glorifying God and honoring St. Edmund by doing so. In order to do so they had to borrow from God's murderers, and the outcome of this paradox was an animosity fuelled by guilt and self-contempt. The notorious Bury St. Edmund's ivory cross is a product of that tension. Its inscriptions, as Elizabeth Claridge has written,

> don't mince words. "The synagogue falls after vain and stupid effort," reads one part of a Latin hexameter; and elsewhere, "The Jews laugh at the death agony of God." The words inscribed on the cross at Calvary are reputed to have read "Jesus of Nazareth, King of the Jews," but even this sarcastic reference was too much for the ivory cross artist. His inscription reads "Jesus of Nazareth, King of Confessors."[21]

In 1181 the monks were involved in a ritual murder accusation against the Jews of the town. In the following year Samson was elected abbot. This middle-aged ex-schoolmaster, like Grosseteste a country-boy in origin but from Norfolk, and unlike him in that he had studied in Paris, set about freeing the monastery from debt. On Palm Sunday 1190, fifty-seven Jews were killed in the town by crusaders. Shortly afterwards, Abbot Samson petitioned the Crown for permission to expel the surviving Jews. Permission was granted and the Jews of Bury were dispersed. Jocelin of Brakelond, the Bury chronicler, observed dryly: "The recovery of the manor of Mildenhall for eleven hundred paltry marks of silver, and the expulsion of the Jews from the town of St. Edmund, and the foundation of the new hospital of Babwell are all proofs of the Abbot's excellence."[22] Presumably Grosseteste heard of Abbot Samson's expulsion of the Jews from his old home town. Was he influenced by any of this? Southern believes that Grosseteste "may himself have been the instigator of their [the Jews] expulsion from Leicester by Earl Simon." Samson, ever since Thomas Carlyle made him famous in *Past and Present*, has been thought of as a type of Englishman: rightly so. Perhaps, therefore, one extraordinary Englishman made a formative impression upon another.

The massacre at Bury in March 1190 inevitably brings us to York and the eve of the "Great Sabbath" (*shabbat ha-gadol*) before Passover 4950. There is, however, no need to dwell on that particular massacre and mass suicide: Barrie Dobson has written an account which is a minor classic. "The Dead have no voice of their own," but in Dobson the York Jews of 1190, whose bones eight hundred years later lie beneath a supermarket car park, have a historian who has done them justice—all an historian is able to do.[23] Nonetheless, three observations are worth making. First, while we should not be surprised that Rabbi Yom-Tob has not entered any pantheon of English heroes, it is significant that Richard Malebisse's name did not become a household term for evil, like that of King John, the sheriff of Nottingham, or Guy Fawkes. Secondly, it should be noted that not only were no converts made (or rather, such was the mentality of the crusaders, no prisoners taken), but also that although some rebels were fined, the Archbishop of York did not condemn the atrocities. The failure of the English Church *ever* to condemn either the excesses of rioters or the exactions of the state against the Jews should be stressed, as this dereliction lays bare the moral ambivalence of the Roman Church's attitude towards the Jews. Thirdly, in the words of Professor Dobson, "the York massacre was not only a tragedy but an influential tragedy: it helped to promote the closest relationship between state and Jewry yet seen in western Europe and to bring about a decisive transformation in the constitutional position of the medieval English Jews" (*Jews of Medieval York*, 30). How typical it was that the consequence of a tragedy (on such a scale, in England's second city) was more and, therefore, worse government for the Jews.

It is one of the truisms of English history that England has been tightly and closely governed since the tenth century, first from Winchester and subsequently from Westminster. The Norman Conquest altered little in that regard. It is also generally held that this has been to the advantage of Englishmen and women. That is one of those pernicious myths that rulers put about in order that the ruled may be quietly governed. The history of the Jews in England enables us to see that it is myth: there England's rulers are revealed to be without clothes; naked and unashamed they go about to despoil their subjects in order to benefit themselves. Is this not why the Jewish history of England is not taught in schools—because it is a type of anti-history as perceived by those who finally determine national curricula? I write in anger as well as sorrow.

The result of the tragedy at York was "the compulsory registration of all Jewish bonds and chattels in a few fixed urban centres, the critical step in the complete reorganization of royal control over the English Jewry," that is the establishment of the Exchequer of the Jews (Dobson, 30). It is, therefore, yet another paradox of Jewish history that what began as "a financial conspiracy" of the Yorkshire gentry and ended for them as "a murderous [and entirely successful] business affair," should be for English Jews the beginning of the process that would destroy them,[24] for from the mid-1190s kings of England had the means to tax the Jews to extinction and did not hesitate to do so. Hubert Walter, Archbishop of Canterbury and Chancellor of England in the 1190s, was a bureaucratic genius: he made the essential first moves towards a final solution of the Jewish "problem" in England. Their destruction was not to come about by the forces of popular anti-Semitism, but by the agency of that authority which was their chief protector: the government. What a familiar ring that has to it for the post-Auschwitz generation!

Where the kings of England are concerned, rapacity is a word that comes almost naturally to mind. King John's Bristol tallage of 1210 is a remarkable example of the ruthlessness of that monarch, as well as of how government may be transformed into its opposite. Sir James Holt also showed us how rapacious were the English baronage of the late twelfth and early thirteenth centuries—for land, for wardships, for widows. It is, therefore, sad (not to say astounding) to discover the following sentence in *The Northerners:*

> Treacherous country full of ugly scenes and vistas, of pogroms, cheating, traffic in mortgages, and dispossession, a country in which baron and knight were involved in an obscure and unwholesome conflict with the rapacity of the Jew, the acquisitiveness of monastic houses, and the interest of the King as the residuary legatee to whom, in the end, the profits of usurious transactions descended.[25]

It is unnecessary to italicize the phrase "the rapacity of the Jew": no emphasis is required to identify the chaff among the grain. We are bound to inquire: what was Professor Holt thinking of? If he is to be caught nodding, all the worse; dropped casually, such a phrase is even more revealing of a frame of mind. Unconscious Anglo-Saxon attitudes make for bad history. That is the case here. In reality, it was a king consumed by the desire to recover Normandy, along with acquisitive lords and gentlemen, who were rapacious. Jewish financiers, who were no more than one Jew in a hundred,[26] provided the means by which the rapacity of others was accomplished. From 1980 to 1984 Professor Sir James Holt was president of the Royal Historical Society of England.

Anglo-Saxon attitudes are also to be detected in accounts of Magna Carta. The sins in this instance are ones of omission. I am not competent to challenge Professor Holt's dismissal of the anti-Jewish clauses 10 and 11 as "superficial,"[27] but I am sure it should not have been left to Cecil Roth to reveal that "when London was occupied on 17 May 1215, the Jewry was the first objective of the [baronial] insurgents. It was ruthlessly sacked, the houses being demolished and the stone used to repair the City walls." It is Cecil Roth also who points out a difference the loss of Normandy made which is unnoticed by English historians: "To the Jews the consequences were no less momentous than to the country at large. They, too, were henceforth cut off to a considerable extent from the great centres on the Continent" (Roth, *Jews of Medieval England*, 34, 36). If the loss of Normandy was the start of that long process by which "Little Englanders" came into being, it must also have quickened the demise of English Jewry. Increasingly isolated from intellectual and social contact in France and Germany, the community turned in upon itself; there is some evidence of contact with the German Hasidic movement of the early thirteenth century, but it amounts to very little.[28] In addition, financial business was circumscribed once it became more difficult to make and maintain continental connections. The loss of Normandy was truly England's loss.

One matter cannot be avoided. It is an English "first" which is the most shameful of them all. Between Norwich in 1144 and Kielce in 1946 there is an unbroken thread of ritual murder charges. The inventor of the first of these and of its sacrificial boy-victim, St. William of Norwich, was Thomas of Monmouth, a Benedictine monk; one presumes he was English and not Welsh. Gavin Langmuir writes:

> We may feel reasonably sure that the fantasy that Jews ritually murdered Christians by crucifixion was created and contributed to Western culture by Thomas of Monmouth about 1150 . . . He did not alter the course of battles, politics, or the economy. He solved no philosophical or theological problems. He was not even noteworthy for the holiness of his life or promotion to monastic office. Yet with substantial help from an otherwise unknown converted Jew [Theobald of Cambridge], he created a myth that . . . caused, directly and indirectly, far more deaths than William's murderer could ever have dreamt of committing . . . Those deadly consequences should not blind us, however, to the creative imagination with which Thomas manipulated religious symbols and his perception of events in his environment in order to . . . mould the religiosity of others to support his own. For Thomas was more concerned to strengthen his own Christian cosmos than to destroy Jews.[29]

The last sentence apart, the latter portion of this quotation reminds us of Adolf Hitler. Both these monsters must make the historian of today pause, for we are too ready to de-individualize history. Gibbon would have been better able to find a place for them. Nor are we yet prepared to give due weight to fantasy, the irrational, and myth as powers to move mankind. A single Englishman was the sole begettor of a lie that had more life in it than most truths have; that lie led to terrible and untold suffering. I do not think, however, that Englishness, the Englishness of Thomas himself, or of the people of Norwich and East Anglia, is relevant: this lie could have had its origin in almost any city or town of twelfth-century Europe: man and moment—with a great deal of heaving and shoving from the man—coincided at Norwich in the 1140s. Where responsibility is involved, what may be far more relevant was a visit to northern France in 1171 of William Turbe, an English monk who spent all his life at Norwich, who was an enthusiast for the cult of St. William, and who was bishop of Norwich from 1146 to 1174. Not coincidentally, the second ever ritual murder accusation occurred at Blois in spring 1171, and more than thirty Jews were burned by order of the Count of Blois on May 26, 1171.

William Turbe, as Dom David Knowles describes him, was "a man of learning in the monastic literary tradition."[30] Being learned in that tradition did not prevent a man being bigoted and credulous; quite the opposite. For instance, *The Dialogue of Miracles* by Caesarius of Heisterbach, written about 1230, opens the window wide on medieval monastic culture. A monk was prone to believe anything; he was particularly ready to believe the worst about Jews, women, and his fellow monks. The friars thought they knew more than monks, and they undoubtedly did; their greater knowledge made them even more zealous to make Christians of everyone: ordinary men and women, heretics, pagans, and Jews. They could be deliberately provocative, founding their houses bang in the middle of urban Jewish communities, as at Oxford and at Cambridge, where the Franciscans set themselves up in a former synagogue.[31] In the twelfth century, many monks were bishops; in the thirteenth, a number of friars were. The point I seek to make here is that the anti-Semitic notions of the English people had their origins in the religious culture of monks and friars. Moreover, they were violent men, at any rate in their language—and it was by their words that they communicated their ideas to ordinary folk. This is Richard of Devizes, a Benedictine monk, on the massacres of March 1190:

> On that same coronation day, at about the hour of that solemnity in which the Son was immolated to the Father, they [Londoners] began in the city of London to immolate the Jews to their father, the Devil. It took them so long to celebrate this mystery that the holocaust was barely completed on the second day. The other towns and cities of the country emulated the faith of the Londoners, and with equal devotion they dispatched their bloodsuckers bloodily to hell . . . Winchester alone spared its worms.[32]

Here is the familiar temptation intellectuals perennially fall for: the pornography of bad language. When ideologues speak like this synagogues burn.

In England they did not. Kings had to pull them down. After all, ordinary people are far less gullible than intellectuals; the anti-Semitic notions of monks and friars had far less impact than credulous historians tell us they had. At Winchester, Northampton, Hereford, Canterbury, and in other English towns in the thirteenth century, Christians and Jews rubbed along as neighbors;[33] no doubt they would have continued to do so were it not for the intervention of their spiritual, social, and political "betters." It is there that the blame has to be lodged, with those who maintained that to be a proper Christian you had to hate Jews. We should not mistake the message. The identity of Christendom and of Christians was the issue; the more Christian one was the more potent one's anti-Semitism. Once rulers got the message then there was no hope for the Jews: a Christian king had to rule a Christian kingdom. Edward I got the message.

There is, nonetheless, another issue. If by 1290 being Christian meant being anti-Jewish, did being anti-Jewish mean being English? The expulsion has been said to have been a "popular" measure. What may be meant by this is that it was done to please the parliamentary classes, who in the summer of 1290 granted the taxes Edward had asked them for.[34] The only people in England in 1290 who may have regarded themselves as English were those parliamentary classes: the king, his bishops, his clerical bureaucrats, the judges, the barons, the knights, urban businessmen. These, I venture to suggest, were anti-Semites. It is, in other words, and entirely as one would expect, the governing elite who first equate Englishness with non-Jewishness.

Jews disappeared from England in 1290; "the Jew" did not. In wall paintings, as at Chalgrove in Oxfordshire and in St. Stephen's Chapel, Westminster, or in wall tiles, like those at Tring, now in the British and Victoria and Albert Museums, he could have been seen. He was also visible onstage in the Croxton (or Babwell) *Play of the Sacrament,* as well as in Passion plays. One company of players called themselves "the Jeweis de Abyndon"; they performed interludes at Christmas 1427 for the five-year-old Henry VI.[35] There was also a handful of converted Jews, who lived in the *Domus Conversorum* in London. Michael Adler published a poignant paper about them in 1939.[36] Working in the Public Record Office, which is on the site of the *Domus Conversorum,* and looking through the Wardens' accounts, which run in an unbroken sequence to 1609, is to know firsthand what Englishness is. That continuity, on which the English pride themselves, is evident in these neatly written account rolls in their trim white-leather pouches, reminiscent of whited sepulchres because there is no life within them. The salaries of the warden, two chaplains, and a clerk after the mid-fourteenth century invariably come to three or four times what it costs to keep two or three converted foreign Jews. The institution that survives long past its active life, no longer serving its original purpose: that is very English—just think of parliament, the monarchy, the Church of England.

Yet very English, too, is the idiosyncracy of the *Domus Conversorum* in the first place, for, as Adler notes, England is the only country where a king founded a home for converts. Henry III established the house in 1232. His son, Edward I, did an equally English thing when in the 1280s, for the upkeep of the *Domus Conversorum,* he established a poll tax of 3d a head on the Jews of England who refused conversion. Collectors of the tax were the chaplains themselves, usually converts; the dispatch of William le Convers to gather the tax in his own former community at Oxford shows the nasty logic of which English government is capable: the predictable assault duly occurred. With this incident we get close to the moral ambivalence which is at the root of so much that is regarded as typically English. When the *Daily Telegraph* tells us that "Raffles must be accounted one of the most powerful myth figures of popular fiction," we have to sit up and listen. Yet Raffles, "a public-school man of the best sort," an elegant clubman, and "the finest slow bowler of his time," was a common thief. This is the gentleman who is the hero of the English reading classes.[37] In the story "A Costume Piece," the reader is left in no uncertainty as to Raffles' attitude towards Reuben Rosenthall of St. John's Wood. The genteel anti-Semitism of the uniquely English Raffles has a very long history.

I end with a thought from a Polish masterpiece, *The Beautiful Mrs Seidenman,* by Andrzej Szczypiorski. It concerns the Poles of Warsaw, who were "unaware that they were maimed, for without the Jews they are no longer the Poles they once were and should have remained for ever."[38] Might this be said of the English after 1290?

Notes

1. Cecil Roth, *The Jews of Medieval Oxford.* (Oxford Historical Society, 1951), 107–108.
2. In a note distributed to members of the Ecclesiastical History Society, of which President Professor Dobson was president in 1991; the note was an introduction to the Society's annual conference, whose theme was "Christianity and Judaism."
3. Gavin Langmuir, *History, Religion, and Antisemitism* (Berkeley: University of California Press, 1990), 351.
4. Professor Peter Brown's obituary of Professor Arnaldo Momigliano, *Proceedings of the British Academy* Vol. 74 (1988), 434.
5. Cecil Roth, *A History of the Jews in England* (Oxford: Clarendon Press, 3rd ed. 1964), 85.
6. David Stocker, "The Shrine of Little St. Hugh," *Transactions of the British Archaeological Association Conference* 8 (1986), 115.
7. Paul Hyams, "The Jewish Minority in Medieval England, 1066–1290," *Jour-*

nal of Jewish Studies 25 (1974), 293.

8. Michael Prestwich, *Edward I* (London: Methuen, 1988), 345 and 346; "The Piety of Edward I" in W. M. Ormrod ed., *England in the Thirteenth Century: Proceedings of the 1984 Harlaxton Symposium* (Woodbridge, Suffolk: Boydell Press, 1986).

9. Archie Baron, "Hidden Exodus," *The Listener* (1 November 1990).

10. Gavin Langmuir, "The Knight's Tale of Young Hugh of Lincoln," *Speculum* 47 (1972), 479.

11. Roth, *A History of the Jews in England,* 57.

12. Robert Stacey, "1240–60: A Watershed in Anglo-Jewish Relations?", *Historical Research* 61 (1988), 135–50.

13. Richard Vaughan, *Matthew Paris* (Cambridge, England: Cambridge University Press, 1958), 143.

14. Richard Vaughan, trans., *Chronicles of Matthew Paris: Monastic Life in the Thirteenth Century* (Gloucester, England: A. Sutton, 1984), 214–15.

15. F. M. Powicke, *King Henry the Third and the Lord Edward: The Community of the Realm in the Thirteenth Century* (Oxford: Clarendon Press, 1947), ii, 447.

16. Ibid., 461. The phrase "savage anti-Semitic riots" comes from Gwyn A. Williams, *Medieval London. From Commune to Capital* (London: Athlone Press, 1963), 217 and 224. Dr. Huw Ridgeway has kindly supplied me with a reference to another, hitherto unrecorded, anti-Jewish (as well as anti-government) incident: "On about 6 May 1260, during an abortive rising led by Simon de Montfort and the Lord Edward, the Wardrobe of the Jewry at the Exchequer, Westminster, was broken into and records stolen" [London, Public Record Office, E.159/33, m.10].

17. David Carpenter, "Simon de Montfort: The First Leader of a Political Movement in English History," *History* 76 (1991), 3–23.

18. S. Levy, "Notes on Leicester Jewry," *Transactions of the Jewish Historical Society of England* 5 (1902–5), 39.

19. Jack Simmons, *Leicester Past and Present,* 2 vol. (London: Eyre Methuen, 1974), i, 25.

20. R. W. Southern, *Robert Grosseteste: The Growth of an English Mind in Medieval Europe* (Oxford: Clarendon Press, 1986), 244–49.

21. Elizabeth Claridge, *Sunday Times Colour Supplement* (1974); for the cross, see Norman Scarfe, "The Bury St. Edmunds Cross," *Proceedings of the Suffolk Institute of Archaeology* 33 (1974), 75–85.

22. H. E. Butler, trans., *The Chronicle of Jocelin of Brakelond* (London: T. Nelson, 1949), 45; Roth, *The Jews of Medieval England,* 25.

23. Barrie Dobson, *The Jews of Medieval York and the Massacre of March 1190,* Borthwick Papers No. 45 (York, England: St. Anthony's Press 1974). The quotation is from Gordon J. Horwitz, *In the Shadow of Death. Living Outside the Gates of Mauthausen* (New York: Free Press, 1990), 180.

24. The phrases are from the "Timewatch" programme, "All the King's Jews," written and produced by Archie Baron, and shown on BBC 2 on Oct. 31, 1990.

25. James Holt, *The Northerners: A Study in the Reign of King John* (Oxford: Clarendon Press, 1961), 165.

26. V. D. Lipman, "The Anatomy of Medieval Anglo-Jewry," *Transactions of the Jewish Historical Society of England* 21 (1968), 64–77.

27. James Holt, *Magna Carta* (Cambridge, England: 1965), 233.

28. See V. D. Lipman, *The Jews of Medieval Norwich* (London: Jewish Historical Society, 1967), 148–49, for Joseph the Hasid of Bungay; Cecil Roth, "Elijah of London, the most illustrious English Jew of the Middle Ages," *Transactions of the Jewish Historical Society of England* 15 (1939–45), 52–53.

29. Gavin Langmuir, "Thomas of Monmouth: Detector of Ritual Murder," *Speculum* 59 (1984), 842 and 844–45.

30. David Knowles, *The Episcopal Colleagues of Archbishop Thomas Becket* (Cambridge, England: Cambridge University Press, 1951), 32.

31. John R. H. Moorman, *The Grey Friars in Cambridge, 1225–1538* (Cambridge: Cambridge University Press, 1952), 8.

32. J. T. Appleby, ed. and trans., *The Chronicle of Richard of Devizes* (London: T. Nelson, 1963), 3–4.

33. Michael Adler, "Benedict the Gildsman of Winchester," *Miscellanies in Honour of E. A. Adler* (London: Jewish Historical Society, 1942), 1–8; A. J. Collins, "The Northampton Jewry and its Cemetery in the Thirteenth Century," *Transactions of the Jewish Historical Society of England* 15 (1939–45), 151–64; Roth, *Jews of Medieval England* 77; Michael Adler, "The Jews of Medieval Canterbury," in his *Jews of Medieval England* (London: Jewish Historical Society, 1939), 49–103.

34. F. M. Powicke, *The Thirteenth Century, 1216–1307* (Oxford: Clarendon Press, 2nd ed., 1962), 513.

35. William Tydeman, *The Medieval Theatre* (London: 1978), 218–19. For the *Play of the Sacrament*, see Norman Davis, ed., *Non-Cycle Plays and Fragments*, Early English Text Society Supplementary Text No. 1 (London: Oxford University Press, 1970). If the play is to be associated with Babwell rather than Croxton (near Thetford), then we return to the Bury St. Edmunds connection: Babwell is only a mile from Bury.

36. Adler, "The History of the Domus Conversorum," in *Jews of Medieval England*, 277–379.

37. Raffles is the hero of a series of novels and stories by E. W. Hornung. He is described as "amateur cracksman" in the stories collected under that title (New York: Charles Scribner's Sons, 1907 [c. 1902]), which includes "A Costume Piece." A "cracksman" is a burglar. [S.D.]

38. Trans. Klara Glowczewska (New York: Grove Press, 1989).

13

Teaching Chaucer to the "Cursed Folk of Herod"

GILLIAN STEINBERG

While teaching a British Literature survey at Yeshiva University earlier this year, a student asked me whether we could read the works of any famous Jewish poets even though none were listed on the syllabus. Some others chimed in: "Yeah, where are all the Jewish poets?" I mentioned, off the top of my head, a strange mix of American and European, of contemporary and early writers: Allan Ginsberg, Yehuda Ha-Levi, Carolyn Kizer, David Ignatow, Yehuda Amichai, Marge Piercy, Hannah Senesh, Emma Lazarus. The students had heard of none of these, save the last, and were disappointed to find that none of the writers in our Norton Anthology were Jewish. For our next class, I brought in selected works of a few of these poets dealing with specifically Jewish subjects, and the students were surprisingly disappointed. They wanted a Jewish Spenser, a Semitic George Herbert; they weren't at all satisfied with overtly Jewish references written for a Jewish audience. Aside from their dissatisfaction with the quality of writing, they were concerned with the poets' Jewishness. "Were these writers observant?" they demanded. Sure, they were born Jewish, the students acknowledged, but how religious were they? This question loomed largest in their minds and most influenced their judgments. If these Jewish poets were merely secular, then they should write poetry of the caliber of Sidney and simply restrict themselves to Judaic references. If they were observant, however, they could be forgiven much more in their choice of language and subject. Jewishness and level of observance are the lenses, I have learned, through which all writing, all art, all science, is judged at Yeshiva University.

When I step into a classroom at Yeshiva—a room filled with twenty-year-old men in yarmulkes who have spent their lives in all-male learning spaces studying the minutiae of Talmud and Gemara (elaboration of Talmud), and who have just returned from at least one full year at an Israeli religious school—and offer them *The Waste Land* or *David Copperfield* or

Astrophil and Stella, I know that every question and every response will grow from Jewish thought. "I got an e-mail forward that said Eliot was an anti-Semite. Is that true?" "Weren't some of David's actions a *chilul Hashem?"* (profanation of God's name). "Sidney's writing reminds me of *Shir Hashirim"* (Song of Songs). The challenges provided by the most seemingly innocuous secular works in these circumstances might indicate that reading *The Merchant of Venice* or *The Prioress's Tale* would be nearly impossible. How can students with this background at this institution be expected to read such overtly anti-Semitic texts? Perhaps surprisingly, inclusion of such texts is both possible and productive at Yeshiva University, but the differences between reading these texts at Yeshiva and anywhere else are striking.

I should note here that Yeshiva University, while all male and all ortho-dox, is uniform in almost no other ways. Students come from a variety of backgrounds, with different levels of religious observance, Zionist feeling, and Judaic learning; some are converts to Judaism or newly observant, while others have grown up overseas in countries where religious (or at least Jew-ish) practice was not tolerated. A number attended public high schools. Many are deeply inquisitive young men who have chosen a religious path, yet desire a contemporary secular education. The students I discuss in the fol-lowing pages probably comprise the majority of those I encounter on a daily basis, but that is not to say that a significant number of Yeshiva students are not intimately familiar with secular and/or multicultural settings, or open to certain secular ideas. The students whose opinions appear in this paper are the more typical ones whose childhoods were spent in the yeshivas and orthodox Jewish communities of New York, Baltimore, Miami, Cleveland, Los Angeles, and Toronto, and whose parents likely also attended Yeshiva University or someplace similar.

Many of these students have not learned, as most religious, ethnic, or racial minorities in America have had to, how to look at the world both through the narrow lens of one's own culture and through the wider lens of mainstream society. Nothing in their lives has required such secularism, and anything that did would almost certainly be feared and avoided. For most largely secularized Jews, myself among them, mainstream America poses some problems of difference (choruses of "Merry Christmas" everywhere one goes, for instance, or childhood soccer practices scheduled for Saturday mornings), but otherwise the meshing of the Jewish-American life and the "Good Ol' American" life proceeds smoothly. For the orthodox students I teach, however, the sense of encroaching secularism often prompts a "build the walls higher" mentality; the lifestyle that has been practiced and rever-enced by thousands of generations of Jews is truly threatened in contempo-rary America, and these students feel a genuine personal responsibility to maintain the values, beliefs, and commitments that have allowed Judaism to survive for as long as it has. One way to prevent the gradual degeneration of the Jewish people, these students believe, is by remaining isolated socially; another is by putting their time and energy into studying the texts that are central to Jewish survival—namely, the Torah and the Talmud. Of course, these students are also torn between aspects of secular and religious life; for the most part, they aspire to secular jobs, and therefore find Yeshiva a "safe" place to prepare for a secular career; there are no distractions from women, schedules accommodate the Jewish calendar, and, most importantly, many hours are reserved each day for the Jewish learning that is absolutely central to their lives.

While I feel both admiration for and indebtedness to the attitude these students have towards their traditions and religion, as a secular instructor I feel compelled to challenge them to read and discuss that which is unfamiliar to them. Therefore I have them read both anti-Semitic and otherwise non-Jewish texts. The challenges posed by Chaucer for these orthodox men are multifold. First, many of them have absolutely no conception of Christianity except as a violent and proselytizing component of the *goyish* world—one of God's other nations for whom Jews serve as a model but with whom they do not interact. The students have, in large part, played ball in all-orthodox leagues and attended orthodox camps and schools and have had no exposure, short of popular music, film, and television (for those who choose to expose themselves to such things), to anything outside of a very insular Jewish world. So Chaucer requires that we start from the very basics, including nuns and priests, cathedrals, Christmas and Easter (which, of course, they have heard of but know little or nothing about), and the Christian Bible, which many of them have been forbidden to read by their rabbis. While one might argue that Chaucer cannot be read without some understanding of Catholic theology, one might also argue that knowing such details is unnecessary to understanding some of the stories and characters Chaucer creates or for appreciating his poetry. For many Yeshiva students, however, the lack of understanding they have about Christianity translates to a sense of foreignness that can make texts impenetrable. Merely knowing that the works we read grow out of Christian thought and practice proves an obstacle to reading and understanding texts.

To teach either secular or overtly Christian materials to these students, I find that I have several choices. The easiest choice is to teach them as I have taught at secular institutions, not altering my plans for a specifically Jewish audience and answering theological questions as though they were mere vocabulary. Initially, I did teach that way, especially since I did not want the students to think of me as a fellow Jew but as a secular (and secularly trained) English professor. I learned quickly, though, that the methods that had worked best when I was a teaching assistant in Delaware were the least successful at Yeshiva, not only because of the students' widely divergent levels of religious understanding at the two institutions, but also because the

Yeshiva students tended to be radically dismissive of that which was not specifically Jewish. They have been taught to favor Jewish texts above others and to find non-Jewish (and certainly overtly Christian) texts suspect in method and motivation.

The students react negatively to writing when they believe that the author himself is an anti-Semite; therefore one of the earliest steps in teaching Chaucer is to ensure that students understand that Chaucer creates characters and that *The Canterbury Tales* is not an autobiography. Of course, for any group of students such an understanding is necessary, but at Yeshiva, I believe, it is even more so. When I taught at the University of Delaware, students might misinterpret the divide between speaker and poet ("So Robert Browning really ordered that Elizabeth Barrett Browning be killed?"), but they would seldom give up reading because of it. At Yeshiva, however, students sometimes feel compelled by their religious interests to ignore the words of proclaimed anti-Semites. And while one of Yeshiva's prominent rabbis, Shalom Carmy, includes *Mein Kampf* in a course on "Nationalism and Patriotism," and has cited numerous rabbis who believe in the importance of understanding the enemy's words in order to counter them, students still feel understandable hesitation and may balk at the thought of reading and studying the writings of anti-Semites. Therefore, I begin with Chaucer by explaining the difference between the author's beliefs and those of the characters he has created. A few students are appeased by the thought that Chaucer himself only creates his characters and does not necessarily agree with them. The analogy of a play helps them. We have discussed the university's production of *Primal Fear*[1] in this context: the lead actor, a student, isn't a murderer, but he played the part of a murderer in that show. Students generally accept this analogy, but, problematically, I have no clear proof that Chaucer was *not* an anti-Semite, and many of the other authors we read during the semester certainly were. Consequently, I hope to instill in the students not only an understanding of the divide between speaker and writer, but also a sense that an author might be worth reading even if his personal motivations and beliefs are antithetical to theirs. In any case, most students argue that "Chaucer still spreads anti-Semitic ideas through his writing, even if those beliefs aren't really his own." In other words, although Chaucer may not be an anti-Semite, he still inhibits the progress of the Jews and, perhaps, encourages his readers to be anti-Semitic.

Interestingly, for many of the students, the main problem with *The Prioress's Tale* is that it is being read at secular colleges by non-Jews, who may uncritically absorb its characterization of Jews as "cursed folk of Herodes al newe" (VII, 574). While many of my students are offended by the tale on a personal level, they are far more concerned that students at "some hick Southern college" might use this tale as a basis for their misunderstanding of Jewish behavior and belief. In fact, although several students said that reading the tale was important for Yeshiva students because "we need to know what people think of us," nevertheless they hesitate to allow others to see those same stereotypes for fear, understandably, that they will be believed or, as one student put it, that "students at a Christian college might take these stories as truth." Part of this fear, I think, comes from the students' own misperceptions of minorities other than Jews. I am constantly shocked to hear the racist comments my students make about the African-Americans they encounter on subways or, more often, the Dominicans who live in the neighborhood surrounding our college. Because many of our orthodox students do not accept or appreciate diversity, they naturally assume that no other group could have non-prejudiced feelings towards them. This sentiment, combined with the many horrors of Jewish history and the twenty-four-hour surveillance of our campus for terroristic or anti-Semitic attacks, prompts students to fear the outsider and his perception of Jews. As a Jewish student in North Carolina and Delaware, I often felt myself compelled to be a defender of the Jews in all of my classes, from history to English to foreign languages. At Yeshiva, I find myself more often defending non-Jews against the misunderstandings and counter-anti-Semitism that the students have learned in their often isolated Jewish communities.

To deal with the problem of Chaucer's propagation of anti-Semitism, we look to the personalities exhibited throughout *The Canterbury Tales*. The tales of the Wife of Bath and the Pardoner reveal far more about the Wife and Pardoner than about their stories' characters. These two tales, the students recognize, are meant to show the hypocrisy and posturing of their tellers. Students immediately understand the mocking of the Pardoner, although they have never heard of indulgences nor do they know much of the Catholic conceptions of heaven, hell, and purgatory. They notice the Wife of Bath's lecherous nature quickly and, for both these works, see what Chaucer means to do by having his narrators tell self-revealing tales. To explain further the way that speakers might reveal information about themselves through their stories, certain Jewish analogies work well for the students. For instance, the *Haggadah* recited at the Passover seder retells the stories of four sons, each of whom asks a question about the exodus from Egypt and each of whose personalities is revealed by the manner in which he phrases his question. The emphasis of this fable, as traditionally explained by rabbis, is less on the content of the questions than on the varying degrees of righteousness of the questioners.

In some ways, I wish not always to turn to Jewish analogies because I want the students to move away from the areas in which they are most comfortable. I would like them to be able to see the common humanity between these pilgrims and their own communities without putting everything so bluntly into Jewish terms. Even when I avoid making direct references to Jewish subjects, however, the students do so. One student recently told me that the blood libel we'd been discussing in *The Prioress's Tale* seemed similar to the Palestinian press today, emphasizing stories of Jewish cruelty and bloodthirstiness and attempting to justify the destruction of the Jews based upon their evil ways. This sort of analogy works well for them and helps them to understand the text from a more personal perspective, in which case it serves a useful purpose. At the same time, it never forces students out of their own comfort zone or gives them a new point of view. And when I suggest that they might consider looking at an issue from another perspective, they feel as though such a change might go against *halakhah* (accepted Jewish law or observance).

The students frequently check with their rabbis to find out if a certain reading is halakhically acceptable, and the religious and secular aspects of the college frequently clash because of fundamental differences between a liberal arts education and halakhik Jewish teaching. Art history is particularly controversial because students cannot, according to *halakhah*, view nudes, but many art history professors (not only at this institution) insist that nudes are essential to an understanding of artistic movements. As a necessary compromise, students are not required to look at any painting or sculpture that is not appropriately *tznius* (modest), but, even so, a number of the school's rabbis have begun to encourage their students to avoid the study of art history. The problems posed by the religious requirements that supersede secular educational goals should be obvious; certain lines of inquiry simply cannot be pursued. My intellectual prodding is therefore always limited by the knowledge that, at Yeshiva, scholarly curiosity *can* go too far. These limitations are not necessarily set by the school's administration, but by the students themselves, who value their religious ideals so much that they will set their own secular intellectual boundaries. One of my students, for instance, has refused to read the school's newspaper because he was warned by his *shiur* (study group) rabbi that he would find some of the writers' liberalism too disturbing. All of this personal limiting grows from a genuine desire to act as God would have them and to follow, as closely as possible, the rules given to Moses on Mount Sinai. It does not, interestingly, limit their intellectualism in other ways, as they debate for hours the smallest details of Gemara, not merely accepting the great rabbis' interpretations but working to come to terms with the various levels and logics of Talmudic interpretation.

My students have determined that the anti-Semitic aspects of Chaucer do not in any way interfere with *halakhah*, and therefore reading *The Canterbury Tales* is permissible. However, the Wife of Bath's bawdy talk presents the students with other problems. While many of the Yeshiva men are comfortable discussing various aspects of sexuality, particularly since such matters are prominent in biblical writings, they feel decidedly uncomfortable discussing them in front of a woman and in a secular, somewhat lewd context. When I began teaching *The Canterbury Tales* at Yeshiva, I imagined that our greatest problems would come from the anti-Semitic sentiments of *The Prioress' Tale*, or perhaps the Christian-inflected readings of Jewish Scripture in the opening of *The Pardoner's Tale*. Surprisingly, students balk more at having to deal with explicit sexuality than at either anti-Semitism or Christian readings. In our class discussions, students easily dismissed Christianity and all its beliefs, giving no credence or concern to what Christians believe. At the same time, they hesitated to read about female sexuality because such material seems actually to break with *halakhah*, by prompting students to think impure thoughts or, at least, recognize the impure thoughts of others.

To this problem, I fear, there is no solution. The students simply will not read what they fear the rabbis would disallow. My students have been able to discuss, in general terms, the character of the Wife of Bath, but they hesitate to read it aloud or to discuss, for instance, her interactions with her husbands in even the slightest detail. Again, certain students are exceptions to this rule and are willing to discuss all aspects of Chaucer's writing. However, peer pressure tends to prevent those few from speaking out. I *can* stop their classmates from mocking those students outright, but I can't do much to stop the nervous giggling and murmuring in class or the extremely active gossip network outside the classroom, which tells every student on campus that "Moshe said that being gap-toothed seemed to be a sign of being lusty! He said she was lusty!" in an almost surreal "Beavis and Butthead meets Big Brother" way. And when the guys at dinner or in the dorm walk by Moshe and say, "She was lusty, huh?" he knows enough to keep his mouth shut in the future.

The students' jesting comes not merely from immaturity or their almost complete lack of exposure to even the mildest sexual references in popular culture (although those elements do play a part). More pervasive and significant is the sense that secularism means subtly to undermine the Judaism that these students and their families have devoted their lives to preserve. Breaking *halakhah* in any way not only disregards the explicit instructions of God and the great rabbis, as far as these students are concerned, but flies in the face of ancestral traditions. The amazing personal responsibility these young men feel to preserve Judaism in its purest form (despite the debate on what that form might be) necessarily (and rightly, I think) trumps the necessity of reading a medieval text. And while to most Americans the threat of Chaucer seems negligible, to many Yeshiva University students, the hints of promiscuity in his writing stand for a kind of openness and inappropriateness from which Jews must turn if continuity in Jewish life is to be maintained.

Chaucer, like all (or almost all) secular literature, can be taught at Yeshiva University. However, teaching it, in my experience, requires a sensitivity to the background of the students and an acceptance that, in order to retain the respect and attention of the students, certain subjects simply must not be broached. The anti-Semitic insult that some of the tales might offer the

students personally is of less concern than the students' fear that other readers might believe these things of them. And while they may accept that
Chaucer was not an anti-Semite, they cannot let go of the fear of contemporary anti-Semitism based on this literature. Furthermore, a Y.U. instructor
must recognize the nature of Judaism for these students; it is not relegated to
one or several areas of their lives but is present in every thought and action,
making all reading and all learning a "Jewish experience." The problems of
discomfort with and apprehension of secular texts will, I imagine, always
exist at Yeshiva University, where religious and secular thought, old and new
worlds, clash on a daily basis.

Note

1. *Primal Fear* was a film based upon the novel by William Diehl (New York: Vil-
   lard Books, 1993). The film was adapted for the Yeshiva College Dramatics
   Society. [S.D.]

14

Positively Medieval

Teaching as a Missionary Activity

JUDITH S. NEAMAN

Professors belong, at least nominally, to the missionary vocation. In the face of the recent erosion of interest in and familiarity with words, I have become more and more convinced that education really is a process of conversion, since good teachers devote most of their classroom hours to convincing students to abandon their mostly dearly held childhood beliefs about magic and authority.

One such belief is incorporated in the use of the word "medieval" as a term of opprobrium. To denounce actions as brutal or "primitive," people have for several centuries condemned such practices as "positively medieval." To change this attitude toward the Middle Ages requires especially ardent missionary work. This is the intellectual and emotional setting in which all American medievalists teach and it is part of their professional challenge. My preferences and experience lie in old literature, science, art and philosophy, and new (modernist to post-modern) studies in the same areas. I have been fortunate to be able to develop and teach courses in both old and new interdisciplinary studies to students at the women's undergraduate college of an Orthodox Jewish university. Colleagues in city or state universities are inclined to think that students in such a specialized setting are more homogeneous than those in public universities. However, not only are many of the rewards and problems, the enthusiasms and aversions of my students identical to those my colleagues in public universities report about their students, but also my students, like theirs, by no means share a single set of views. However, teaching medieval literature in general and Chaucer in particular to Orthodox Jewish women has continued to stimulate my thoughts about freedom, gender, and education.

This essay is an entirely personal reflection on many years of teaching medieval literature in various colleges and universities, some public and secular, some private and nonsecular. From this wider view, I shall begin, as

Aristotle (whose rhetorical method has never been improved upon) suggested, with the general difficulties and challenges of teaching medieval literature to all kinds of modern students, and then try to differentiate that general case from the particular one of teaching medieval literature to Orthodox Jewish women.

The first and most obvious problem the literature of the Middle Ages poses is that all of it is written in languages both literally and figuratively foreign. Since even medieval English works are written in Anglo-Saxon, Anglo-Norman, Latin, or Middle English, few students can read them in the original language. If even the brightest students frequently ask, "Where can I find a Modern English translation of Shakespeare?", what can they make of Chaucer in Middle English or, worse, *Beowulf* in Anglo-Saxon?

The translation problem only begins with the actual words. Obviously, even familiar-sounding words like "nyce" have period specific meanings that offer the now conventional instruction script: in Chaucer's English, "nyce" means foolish or simplistic. The locus classicus for this kind of translation is Chaucer's well-known description of the Knight's character in the "General Prologue" to the *Canterbury Tales*. How many midterms have asked students to explain what the author meant when he wrote that the knight was " free" (generous or liberal)?

The difficulty of defining individual words masks the larger underlying translation problem: understanding and interpreting the attitudes, presumptions, expectations, beliefs, and experiences that words convey. Teaching *Beowulf*, for example, involves asking students to read and (at least temporarily and partially) to sympathize with epic values. These are the values of a warrior society, one that lived by raiding, hence, one that prized muscular strength and skill at least as highly as ethics or intellect. Combat was waged, not from the distance of a missile site, but hand-to-hand. Women students especially find the epic an unsympathetic type of literature, in part, perhaps, because the epic often excludes female characters or deprives them of active and sympathetic roles. Like their male colleagues, many of whom also deplore the behavior of epic warriors, these women students have been nurtured in a culture that, officially at least, condemns violence and prizes peace. Therefore, the poem of *Beowulf* meets with some resistance in any undergraduate class of any college or university. Male or female students in an Orthodox Jewish university do not seem to dislike war more than Christian or Muslim students in other universities.

It might be argued that knights and other muscular heroes have been especially repugnant to Jews because of a long Jewish tradition favoring the yeshiva *buchur* whose image is that of a gentle, pale, physically helpless scholar who not only deplores force but is also incapable of it. Daniel Boyarin praises what he considers the traditionally anti-physical priorities of Judaism and condemns what he considers the fairly recent creation of the "muscular Jew" by liberal Reform Jews whose assimilationist tendencies are robbing Judaism of its valuable differences from other Western cultures.[1] His logic strikes me as unsound. First, Boyarin claims that modern Jews find medieval knighthood repellent because their culture laudably prizes intellectual, gentle, physically effete men, yet he simultaneously condemns modern Judaism for replacing this model with the assimilationist image of "the muscular Jew" (77). Second, it seems unlikely that Jews predating the nineteenth-century Reform movement or even earlier European assimilation necessarily found violence in medieval literature abhorrent. If they did, why and for what audience were Arthurian and other romances translated into Hebrew during the Middle Ages and later into Yiddish?[2] The truth is that Orthodox Jewish students seem neither more nor less repelled by force than do their Catholic or Protestant counterparts at other universities.

Boyarin's arguments are founded on religious stereotypes. He seeks to combat the female stereotypes of antifeminists and the homophobic stereotypes of gay-bashers, but does so by the very modes of argument and with the identical rhetorical devices that his opponents use. As Boyarin sagely notes, everyone has a bone to pick, so claims of objectivity are invalid. My particular bone here will become immediately clear. While pointing out differences between cultures or religions or literatures, I also consider it important to note individual variations within a category as well as features shared between groups. Although my university, like many others, turns out more doctors, lawyers, accountants, and businessmen than athletes or soldiers, it does not seem to be dominated by giant intellects encased in inadequate bodies. This is a stereotype of the kind I consider it my mission to counter, just as I do the stereotypes of the big, black athletic dope or the brilliant but devious Asian.

But the hero of a battle epic certainly does embody all the strangeness of an alien culture, and the remarkable consistency of the heroic traits in epics of various periods is stereotypic. Like many other epic heroes, Beowulf is skilled in the art of psychological intimidation (the *gab* or bragging contest); he is a raider and great leader who secures the loyalty of his retainers by distributing booty won from ravaging and pillaging. Students find Beowulf's techniques of psychological intimidation repulsive and question whether a true hero could be so "full of himself." Learning that modesty is not a virtue in the Germanic epic does not make them more sympathetic to the poem. And they obviously cannot sanction the raiding life.

Since the poet says Grendel is envious of the happy meadhall fellowship and feels what we call "marginalized," students are inclined to sympathize with the monster. "Why," they often ask, "couldn't Hygelac have saved the lives of his men by inviting the monster to celebrate with them? After all, how much would a cup of mead have cost him?" No arguments about the character of the society, or that Grendel was an offspring of the race of Cain,

can convince them that an invitation for cocktails would not have transformed Grendel into a party animal. This is true not only of students at secular universities but of my present students, who should be more likely to
know from their Torah study who Cain is. But here too their responses are
surprising. As is often the case with students of all persuasions, lifelong
instruction doesn't always take, so that even observant Jews don't know
Torah as well as their years of training might imply. In the case of Grendel,
their very contemporary loyalty to animals and their "politically correct"
sympathy for the underdog triumph over their religious knowledge of evil.
As for the larger field of medieval literature, they find feudalism undemocra-
tic, courtly love deceitful and immoral, trial by combat brutal and barbaric.
They do like the concept of chivalry and the magical aspects of visions,
quests, and treasures. They love the queens and kings of medieval romance
but are less fond of political motivations for marriage. Since, in some Orthodox families and communities, marriages are arranged and some of my students have been matched, one might expect sympathy for the political or
economic matching in medieval society. But these are also modern American
college students, as romantic as their more secular compeers. In their lives,
such arrangements are rare and have little appeal. They tend to ignore the
chivalric training in weaponry, the domination of women, and the violence.

Ultimately, of course, I must share with them my own citizenship in the
modern world. I too do not love war, admire brutality, or naturally incline to
absolute monarchy. But, and here is the difference between my teaching and
more traditional missionary work, perhaps I can show them that my system of
belief is not the only one that ever existed, that it is neither inevitable nor
always superior. The literature itself will demonstrate that medieval people
were capable of self-criticism, insight, compassion, and reason. Examining
the ways in which earlier civilizations merit respect does not mean merely
engaging in moral relativism, but it encourages exploration of real differences
and of some of the possibilities Levi-Strauss pointed out in his analysis of
"hot" and "cold" societies. In such works as *The Raw and The Cooked*, Levi-
Strauss demonstrated that societies and people diametrically opposed to ours
not only solve some problems better than we do, but that they also have their
own admirable minds, products, and systems. Such issues and questions arise
whenever early literature is taught for the first time to contemporary students.

Can there be any further difficulties in the more special circumstance of
teaching medieval literature to Orthodox Jewish women? Of course, there
can. My students are not homogeneous in personality, appearance, cast of
mind, degree of piety, observance, or training. Some wear long skirts and
long sleeves; some wear minis; most wear hats after marriage to cover their
hair; and a few wear very chic *sheitls* (wigs). Still, they do share a history that
makes them suspicious of the largely Christian and West European medieval
literature taught in most curricula.

First, they are from a society perhaps justly wary of missionary religions, among which they count all forms of Christianity. Like most Americans, my students know very little history. What they do know of Jewish history, most of it surrounding World War II, is a chronicle of persecution, exile, annihilation, and even religious martyrdom. Were they to learn medieval English history, they would find similar records in the twelfth-century massacres of the Jews of Oxford and York, and in the expulsion of the Jews from England in 1290. These attacks were often accompanied by promises that the Jews' lives would be spared if they converted to the ruler's religion. It is not a reassuring history. Even their relatively secure lives as American Jews are not untouched by anti-Semitic incidents, Torah burnings, swastikas on synagogues, threatening graffiti on walls and signs, and some instances of real discrimination. I, who had been less sheltered than they, should not have been shocked when, during an oil crisis, I read on the bumper stickers of several cars the slogan, "Oil, not Jews."

Put this history beside the fact that the students who have been educated in Jewish primary and secondary schools have rarely encountered any instruction about religion that was not religious instruction, and you can understand their wariness. Their religious education has been preparation for faith and practice. A simple explanation of an Annunciation image or of the meaning of the words "Holy Ghost"—required to clarify the meaning of a work of medieval fiction—can be mistaken by the more literal-minded for an instruction in faith. I cannot count the occasions on which, while elucidating a doctrine or allusion, I have been asked, "Do you expect us to believe that?"

This question always puzzles me until I remember one further quality my more sheltered students share. They have been taught to respect authority. For them, a professor is an authority and the texts she assigns are also authoritative. The word "rabbi" means teacher, and, while my students know that not all teachers are literally rabbis, there is, nonetheless, a small measure of fluidity in the category. In such a setting, any secular member of the faculty learns that there are both differences of opinion among rabbis and different degrees of independence in the thought and behavior of the students. Because our students learn both secular and religious materials, the students, teachers, and administrators are engaged simultaneously in maintaining tradition and encouraging growth, in being responsible citizens in a modern society and in remaining stable adherents to an ancient heritage. As feminist movements within the religion have publicized, the maintenance of a balance between modernity and tradition may be even more complex for Orthodox Jewish women than it is for the men. A fairly standard proportion of my women students (perhaps thirty to forty percent of every class, about the same as in a secular university) are forthright in their opinions and articulate in their disagreement.

In any group, there are, of course, variations on stereotypic patterns and repetitions of old patterns. Feminist issues present many cases in point. Some students question and disagree less than their classmates or their brothers do, for there is an Orthodox Jewish tradition of male dominance over women at least as pronounced as that in Catholicism, for example. The more passive women are likely to have been trained to respect authority even more than their brothers have been. In this sense, they are like many women in Western society but more so because of their religious orientation. Traditionally, Orthodox Jewish women do not become rabbis and may not study Torah. Our students are justly proud of the fact that they study Torah in this university, though they are not allowed to do so in the presence of men.[3]

When the question of belief arises, I have to establish the fact that I am not trying to tell them what to believe, but what others believe or have believed. This means that I sometimes need longer to earn my students' trust than I might require in a public university, especially since I consider it important to emphasize the idea that religious beliefs different from theirs should not be denigrated. When I teach ancient and medieval literatures, I usually find myself in a position that shows me how narrow contemporary tolerance is. My students are often surprised to find allusions to pantheism and animism in medieval literature. Chaucer's frequent references to Roman and Greek religion provide the most refreshing opportunities for me to rethink religious diversity and ingenuity. For example, in *The Knight's Tale*, when Palemon and Arcite pray to Greek gods, each receives a sign in or near the relevant temple with its cult statue. This scene often provokes questions about heathen idol worship, not at all surprising from adherents to a monotheistic religion that decries realistic representations of God. "Did they really believe that?" they frequently sneer, referring to what they presume is Palemon's or Arcite's or even Chaucer's belief that statues are divine. I can point out that, while Chaucer did not worship the Greek gods, he was able understand his classical sources well enough to sympathize with them temporarily without jeopardizing his own religious faith. Nor, as far as I know, did any of Chaucer's contemporaries question his Christianity or find that classical references tempted his readers or listeners to stray from their faith. Second, but perhaps more important, I can tell my students about pagan beliefs in invisible powers symbolized by or partially represented in the statues of gods. We can discuss pagan concepts of ethics, morals, the immortality of the soul, and a host of other beliefs that twentieth-century smugness often makes us consider too sophisticated or complex for the pagan mind.

This is the ethical, spiritual, and intellectual challenge of teaching medieval literature in general, and Chaucer in particular. Perhaps surprisingly, my students' concern and hesitation about religious doctrine is not the biggest barrier to their study of Chaucer. Far more daunting for them than the Christian theology in Chaucer's works is the frank, deliberately risqué sexuality. *The Miller's Tale*, with its descriptions of Nicholas's seduction of a married woman and her gleeful participation is no less repulsive to them than

Nicholas's fart. They find old January's graphic description of his bride May's sexual dalliance in *The Merchant's Tale* as offensive as they find four letter words. Officially, "good girls" don't use such language.

As far as the administration of the undergraduate colleges is concerned, our institution is largely tolerant of what faculty and administrators consider "worthy" secular study, a category that allows much latitude. Many of the students do not publicly object to the sexual references in literature (which appear, of course, not just in Chaucer, but in Shakespeare, Swift, Whitman, Freud, and so on). Some find they cannot read material that is either highly sexual or that they consider immoral. In such cases, I let them do what they ask; they simply do not read the passage and often are assigned something else instead. In this practice, I adhere to unofficial university policy and follow my own conviction that forcing the issue would be both disrespectful and counterproductive.

Neither, however, do I believe in censoring or banning in advance all materials that might offend my students. I associate the suppression of ideas and information with the worst abuses of human rights and freedom. The students come from the background of a religion whose history is scarred by encounters with intolerance, with intellectual and political dictatorship. It always seems to me that to exercise censorship in an educational institution is to subject those very people whose rights, ideas, beliefs have too often been suppressed to a measure that, in some small way, echoes other tyrannical behavior. The best weapon against the autocracies in which such behavior flourishes seems to me to be an emphasis on individual rights and critical judgment.

This is where the special case of Chaucer comes in, apparently wagging the tail of this dog, but, in fact, just where it belongs, at the heart of all the arguments for and against teaching medieval literature. Chaucer offers both special challenges and special opportunities, first, because he is familiar with many cultures. He puts the reader in a position to sympathize with societies, religions, even attitudes alien to his own. Second, Chaucer is a social critic in complex, many-layered and humorous ways that few medieval fiction writers before him were. When modern students, with all their wariness toward medieval life, religion, morality, and corruption, read Chaucer, they are naturally exposed to an unfamiliar world in a variety of dimensions, tones, and points of view richer than they have ever met before. They encounter otherness in cultures, along with attitudes that are complex and often ambivalent, rather than simply stereotypic or monolithic. In *The Canterbury Tales*, for example, both the characters and the often complex points of view also undercut the social, regional, and professional stereotypes Chaucer manipulates as a sort of template for his observations and analyses of English characters and morals. The complexity of his view always forces the reader to wonder and to question. Is Chaucer, the writer, speaking? Is the narrator whom the critic Talbot Donaldson called "Chaucer the Pilgrim"[4] judging the character? Is the Knight speaking? These varying points of view teach my students that, like their own contemporary views, opinion in earlier societies and religions was not monolithic.

The Prioress, always a crux for my students because of her portrayal of Jews, is clearly charming to the narrator; she is stylish, attractive, and well mannered; qualities all summarized in her lyrical name, Eglantine. But the reader learns that secular virtues can be religious vices: she keeps animals, is sufficiently vain to pluck her forehead, and she expends a *perhaps* inappropriate amount of attention on both her dress and her table manners. Students must learn that she is not just a nun; she is an aristocratic or upper-bourgeois woman whose duty as a leader of one of the more elegant convents is to exercise good rhetoric, cultivated skills in hospitality, and social graces that will advance her convent in the eyes of the ecclesiastical authorities.

Of course, Chaucer's Prioress has traits even more questionable for the modern student. Her fine sensibility shrinks from sick or dead pets, but not from bloody tales of child murder committed by Jews. I am not claiming here that Chaucer sympathized with the Jews, but I do maintain that the Prioress's combined tenderness of heart and bloody-mindedness have all the complexity of human life, whether past or present. Chaucer reveals the inconsistencies. His readers are forced to grapple with them, to form opinions of them, to confront the most extreme consequences of religious debates, conflicts, and rivalries.

Chaucer's voice counters simplistic biases in subtler ways as well. A social and religious critic, who nonetheless defended his society and his religion, Chaucer demonstrated in his work that there are in this imperfect world bribable judges, scheming wives, Epicurean monks, greedy friars, false pardoners, and pedantic authors. It is by now a pedagogical and critical cliché, but an important one for our students to learn, that Chaucer does not recommend destroying the law courts because some judges are corrupt. He does not hate women because the Wife of Bath schemes and Criseyde lacks the conviction to be faithful. He does not condemn Christianity or the Church because some of its minions are far from perfect. Surely the ability to question and to make increasingly fine distinctions, skills Chaucer hones in his readers, makes for a more humane world.

Opinion is still divided about whether Chaucer was a conservative advocate of fourteenth-century attitudes or a liberalizing humanist who provoked his readers to reexamine their beliefs. Were his revelations of corruption in the clergy intended to defend the church as an institution? Was his treatment of women a feminist defense of them, or did he merely wish to enlarge his audience by portraying a range of characters broad enough to include the flirtatious Alisoun of *The Miller's Tale* and the almost unbelievably faithful Constance of *The Clerk's Tale*? Aside from Chaucer's undisputed literary genius, the fact that this debate remains unsettled is a vital reason for teaching Chaucer's works in any modern educational setting, especially a parochial one. The rich variety of opinion and the debatable motives challenge the reader to reject lazy and thoughtless stereotyping. Furthermore, exposure to the medieval world forces students to learn about moral and cultural alternatives that counter the complacent ignorance education is designed to dispel. As usual, Chaucer himself offers the best argument for continuing readership of his works and he does so in one of his typical parodies of medieval rhetoric. In his playful tautology, "Diverse folk, diversely they seyde," Chaucer mocks monolithic views and uncritical generalizations from a vantage point more than seven centuries old.

Notes

1. Daniel Boyarin, *Unheroic Conduct: The Rise of Heterosexuality and the Invention of the Jewish Man* (Berkeley; Los Angeles; London: University of California Press, 1997), 63–65.
2. See Curt Leviant, ed. and trans. *King Artus: A Hebrew Arthurian Romance of 1279* (New York: Ktav, 1969) with extensive cultural and historical commentary. Also, *The Book of the Gests of Alexander of Macedon*, ed. and trans. Israel J. Kazis (Cambridge, MA.: Medieval Academy, 1962), also with an extensive apparatus. For Yiddish translations, see *The Bovo-buch*, trans. Jerry C. Smith (forthcoming from Routledge, 2003); this is the first English translation of the 1509 Yiddish translation that Elias Levita made from an Italian version of the well-known medieval romance *Bevis of Hampton*.
3. More conservative parents who do not wish their daughters to read Torah will not send them to our school.
4. E. Talbot Donaldson, " Chaucer the Pilgrim," in *Chaucer Criticism: the Canterbury Tales*, eds. Richard Schoeck and Jerome Taylor (Notre Dame, IN: University of Notre Dame Press, 1960), 1–13.

Contributors

Anthony P. Bale teaches in the Department of English at Tel Aviv University. He has studied at Oxford University, the University of York, and the Hebrew University of Jerusalem, where he held a Felix Poson Fellowship. He is currently undertaking research on the sixteenth-century historiography of medieval Anglo-Jewry.

Sheila Delany is Professor of English at Simon Fraser University near Vancouver, British Columbia, Canada. She has published widely in medieval and Chaucer studies. Her last book, *Impolitic Bodies: Poetry, Saints, and Society in Fifteenth-Century England* (1998), won the 1999 Canadian Society of Medievalists prize for best book in medieval studies.

Denise L. Despres is Professor of English and Humanities at the University of Puget Sound. She has published articles and reviews in (most recently) *SAC, Speculum, Modern Philology*, and *Jewish History Comparative Literature*. She is coauthor with Kathryn Kerby-Fulton of *Iconography and the Professional Reader* (1999).

Mary Dove is a reader in English at the University of Sussex. She works on medieval interpretation of the Bible, and has published widely on the Song of Songs, including an edition with a translation of the *Glossa Ordinaria in Canticum Canticorum* (1997). She is currently writing a book on the Wycliffite Bible.

Timothy S. Jones is Associate Professor in the Department of English at Augustana College in Sioux Falls, South Dakota. He has published several essays on medieval outlaw narratives and is the editor of *Marvels, Monsters, and Miracles: Studies in Medieval and Early Modern Imaginations* (2001).

WILLIAM CHESTER JORDAN is Professor of History and Director of the Program in Medieval Studies at Princeton University. His most recent book is *Europe in the High Middle Ages* (2001).

JEROME MANDEL, Professor of English at Tel Aviv University, is the author of *Geoffrey Chaucer: Building the Fragments of the Canterbury Tales*, and three other books on medieval literature. He has published numerous articles on Malory, Chrétien de Troyes, and medieval romance, and a collection of short stories, *Nothing Gold Can Stay: 18 Stories of Israeli Experience.*

JUDITH S. NEAMAN is Professor of English at Stern College, Yeshiva University in New York City. She is coauthor with Professor Rhoda B. Nathan of *The American Vision* and with Professor Carole Silver of *Kind Words: A Thesaurus of Euphemisms* and author of *Suggestion of the Devil*, a study of madness in the Middle Ages. Other publications include articles on literature, art, religion, and science. Portions of her recent work on medieval optics appeared in "The Mystery of the Ghent Bird and the Invention of Spectacles," *Viator* (1993), and in the translations of and notes on optical materials in the *Life of Margaret of Ypres*, edited by Margot King (2000).

COLIN RICHMOND is Honorary Research Fellow at the Center for Jewish Studies, University of Manchester. Formerly a professor of medieval history at the University of Keele, he has published several books on Lollardy, the Pastons, and late-medieval England.

CHRISTINE M. ROSE is Professor of English at Portland State University in Oregon. She is the author of numerous articles on Chaucer, medieval women, and late-medieval manuscripts. Her recent publications include *Representing Rape in Medieval and Early Modern Literature*, edited with Elizabeth Robertson (2001). She is currently working on a book about medieval conduct literature for women, and (with Gina Greco) on a new translation of *Le Menagier de Paris.*

GILLIAN STEINBERG is a full-time lecturer in the English department at Yeshiva University. Her current work focuses on the use of classical music theories and structures in Victorian and modern poetry.

SYLVIA TOMASCH, Professor of English and Director of English Graduate Studies at Hunter College (CUNY), is coeditor (with Sealy Gilles) of *Text and Territory: Geographic Imagination in the European Middle Ages* and coeditor (with James J. Paxton and Lawrence M. Clopper) of *The Performance of Middle English Culture: Essays on Chaucer and the Drama.* She has published on Dante, Chaucer, the Pearl-poet, and medieval cartography, and is currently investigating the cultural significance of the work of John Manly and Edith Rickert.

NANCY L. TURNER (Ph.D. University of Iowa) is Assistant Professor of history at the University of Wisconsin–Platteville. Her research focuses upon Christian theologians' attitudes towards Jews in the late Middle Ages.

ELISA NARIN VAN COURT teaches medieval literature at Colby College in Maine. She publishes on late-Middle English literature, and is currently at work on a book about late-medieval English representation of Jews.

Selected Bibliography

Abulafia, Anna Sapir. *Christians and Jews in the Twelfth Century Renaissance.* New York: Routledge, 1995.

Adler, Michael. *Jews of Medieval England.* London: Printed and published for the Jewish Historical Society of England, E. Goldston, 1939.

Alberigo, Joseph et al, eds. *Conciliorum Oecumenicorum Decreta.* Basil: Herder, 1962.

Almog, Shmuel, ed. *AntiSemitism Through the Ages.* New York: Pergamon, 1988.

Ascher, A. et al, eds. *The Mutual Effects of the Islamic and Judeo-Christian Worlds.* Brooklyn, NY: Brooklyn College Press, 1979.

Ashtor, Eliyahu. *The Jews of Moslem Spain,* trans. Aaron Klein and Jenny Machlowitz Klein. 2 vols. Philadelphia: Jewish Publication Society, 1992. [orig. pub. 3 vols., 1973–84].

Baer, Yitzhak. *A History of the Jews in Christian Spain,* trans. Louis Schoffman et al. 2nd ed. 2 vols. Philadelphia and Jerusalem: Jewish Publication Society, 1992 [orig. pub. 1961–66.]

Baron, Salo. *A Social and Religious History of the Jews.* 2nd ed. 18 vols. New York: Columbia University Press, 1952–83.

Berger, David, ed. *The Jewish-Christian Debate in the High Middle Ages: A Critical Edition of the Nizzahon Vetus,* trans. David Berger. Philadelphia: Jewish Publication Society of America, 1979.

Berman, Lawrence V., ed. *Bibliographical Essays in Medieval Jewish Studies.* New York: Ktav for Anti-Defamation League of B'nai B'rith, 1976.

Bolton, Brenda. *Innocent III: Studies on Papal Authority and Pastoral Care.* Aldershot, Great Britain, and Brookfield, VT, USA: Variorum, 1995.

Boyarin, Daniel. *Unheroic Conduct: The Rise of Heterosexuality and the Invention of the Jewish Man.* Berkeley and Los Angeles: University of California Press, 1977.

———. *Carnal Israel: Reading Sex in Talmudic Culture.* Berkeley and Los Angeles: University of California Press, 1993.

Boyd, Beverly, ed. *The Canterbury Tales: Part 20, "The Prioress's Tale."* Norman: University of Oklahoma Press, 1987.

Chazan, Robert. *Medieval Jewry in Northern France: A Political and Social History.* Baltimore and London: Johns Hopkins University Press, 1973.

———. *European Jewry and the First Crusade.* Berkeley and Los Angeles: University of California Press, 1987.

———. *Barcelona and Beyond: The Disputation of 1263 and Its Aftermath.* Berkeley and Los Angeles: University of California Press, 1992.

Cohen, Jeremy. *The Friars and the Jews: The Evolution of Medieval Anti-Judaism.* Ithaca: Cornell University Press, 1982.

———, ed. *Essential Papers on Judaism and Christianity in Conflict from Late Antiquity to the Reformation.* New York: New York University Press, 1991.

———, ed. *From Witness to Witchcraft: Jews and Judaism in Medieval Christian Thought.* Wiesbaden, Germany: Harassowitz Verlag, 1996.

———. *Living Letters of the Law: Ideas of the Jew in Medieval Christianity.* Berkeley and Los Angeles: University of California Press, 1999.

Cohen, Mark R. *Under Crescent and Cross: The Jews in the Middle Ages.* Princeton, NJ: Princeton University Press, 1994.

Cutler, Allan H., and Helen E. Cutler. *The Jew as Ally of the Muslim: Medieval Roots of Anti-Semitism.* Notre Dame, IN: University of Notre Dame Press, 1986.

Dahan, Gilbert, ed. *Les Juifs au regard de l'histoire: mélanges en l'honneur de Bernhard Blumenkranz.* Paris: Picard, 1985.

———. *The Christian Polemic against the Jews in the Middle Ages,* trans. Jody Gladding. Notre Dame, IN: University of Notre Dame Press, 1998.

Deanesly, Margaret. *The Lollard Bible and Other Medieval Biblical Versions.* Cambridge, England: Cambridge University Press, 1920.

Delany, Sheila. *The Naked Text: Chaucer's* Legend of Good Women. Berkeley and Los Angeles: University of California Press, 1994.

———, ed. *"Turn it again": Jewish Medieval Studies and Literary Theory. Exemplaria* 12 (2000) special issue.

Dobson, Richard Barrie. *The Jews of Medieval York and the Massacre of March 1190,* Borthwick Papers 45. York: St. Anthony's Press, 1974.

Duffy, Eamon. *The Stripping of the Altars: Traditional Religion in England 1400–1580.* New Haven, CT: Yale University Press, 1992.

Edwards, John, ed. *Religion and Society in Spain, circa 1492.* Aldershot, England: Variorum, 1996.

Emmerson, Richard. *Antichrist in the Middle Ages.* Seattle: University of Washington Press, 1981.

Epstein, Mark Alan. *The Ottoman Jewish Communities and their Role in Fifteenth and Sixteenth Century Turkey.* Freiburg, Germany: Klaus Schwartz Verlag, 1980.

Evans, M. Carey. *The Legend of St. William Boy-Martyr of Norwich.* Norwich, England: Norwich Cathedral, no date.

Forshall, Josiah, and Frederic Madden, eds. *The Old and the New Testaments, with the Apocryphal Books, in the Earliest English Version Made from the Latin Vulgate by John Wycliffe and His Followers.* 4 vols. Oxford, 1850.

Gilman, Sander L., and Steven T. Katz, eds. *Anti-Semitism in Times of Crisis.* New York: New York University Press, 1991.

Glassman, Bernard. *Anti-Semitic Stereotypes without Jews.* Detroit, MI: Wayne State University Press, 1975.

Grayzel, Solomon. *The Church and the Jews in the XIIIth Century.* New York: Hermon, 1966.

Haverkamp, Alfred, ed. *Juden und Christen zur Zeit der Kreuzzuge.* Sigmaringen: Jan Thorbecke Verlag, 1999.

Hood, John. *Aquinas and the Jews.* Philadelphia: University of Pennsylvania Press, 1995.

Hoving, Thomas. *King of the Confessors.* New York: Simon & Schuster, 1981.

Hudson, Anne. *The Premature Reformatio: Wycliffite Texts and Lollard History.* Oxford: Clarendon Press, 1988.

Jordan, William C. *The French Monarchy and the Jews from Philip Augustus to the Last Capetians.* Philadelphia: University of Pennsylvania Press, 1989.

———. *Women and Credit in Pre-Industrial and Developing Societies.* Philadelphia: University of Pennsylvania, 1993.

Katz, Jacob. *Exclusiveness and Tolerance: Studies in Jewish-Gentile Relations in Medieval and Modern Times.* New York: Schocken, 1961.

Kimhi, Joseph. *The Book of the Covenant of Joseph Kimhi,* trans. Frank Talmage. Toronto: Pontifical Institute of Mediaeval Studies, 1972.

Kölbing, Eugen, and Mabel Day, eds. *The Siege of Jerusalem,* EETS, OS 188. Oxford: University of Oxford Press, 1932.

Krey, Philip D. W., and Lesley Smith, eds. *Nicholas of Lyra: The Senses of Scripture.* Leiden, Netherlands; Boston: Brill, 2000.

Langmuir, Gavin. *Toward a Definition of Anti-Semitism.* Berkeley and Los Angeles: University of California Press, 1990.

———. *History, Religion, and Antisemitism.* Berkeley and Los Angeles: University of California Press, 1990.

Levy, Avigdor. *The Jews of the Ottoman Empire.* Princeton, NJ: Darwin Press, 1994.

Lewis, Bernard. *The Jews of Islam.* Princeton: Princeton University Press, 1984.

Lipman, V. D. *The Jews of Medieval Norwich.* London: Jewish Historical Society, 1967.

Mann, Vivien B., Thomas F. Glick, and Jerrilyn D. Dodds, eds. *Convivencia: Jews, Muslims, and Christians in Medieval Spain.* New York: George Braziller, 1992.

Marcus, Ivan. *Piety and Society: The Jewish Pietists of Medieval Germany.* Leiden, Netherlands: Brill, 1981.

———. *Rituals of Childhood: Jewish Acculturation in Medieval Europe.* New Haven. CT: Yale University Press, 1996.

Mellinkoff, Ruth. *Outcasts: Signs of Otherness in Northern European Art of the Late Middle Ages.* vols. 1 & 2. Berkeley and Los Angeles: University of California Press, 1993.

———. *The Horned Moses in Medieval Art and Thought.* Berkeley and Los Angeles: University of California Press, 1970.

Menocal, Maria. *The Arabic Role in Medieval Literary History: A Forgotten Heritage.* Philadelphia: University of Pennsylvania Press, 1987.

Meredith, Peter, and John E. Tailby, eds. *The Staging of Religious Drama in Europe in the Later Middle Ages: Texts and Documents in English Translation,* trans. Raffaella Ferrari. Early Drama, Art and Music Monograph Series, 4. Kalamazoo, MI: Medieval Institute Publications, Western Michigan University, 1983.

Metlitzki, Dorothée. *The Matter of Araby in Medieval England.* New Haven, CT: Yale University Press, 1977.

Miner, Earl Roy, ed. *Literary Uses of Typology from the Late Middle Ages to the Present.* Princeton, NJ: Princeton University Press, 1977.

Mirrer, Louise. *Women, Jews, and Muslims in the Texts of Reconquest Castile.* Ann Arbor: University of Michigan Press, 1996.

Moore, R. I. *The Formation of a Persecuting Society.* Oxford: Blackwell, 1987.

Morin, Edgar, et al. *Rumour in Orléans,* trans. Peter Green. London: Blond, 1971.

Mundill, Robin R. *England's Jewish Solution: Experiment and Expulsion, 1262–1290.* Cambridge, England: Cambridge University Press, 1998.

Nicholas of Lyra. *Postilla litteralis et moralis in Vetus et Novum Testamentum.* eds. Conradus Sweynheym and Arnoldus Pannartz. 5 vols. Rome, 1471–72.

Nirenberg, David. *Communities of Violence: Persecution of Minorities in the Middle Ages.* Princeton, NJ: Princeton University Press, 1996.

Parkes, James. *The Jew in the Medieval Community.* London: Soncino Press, 1938.

Pearsall, Derek. *John Lydgate.* London, Henly and Boston: Routledge and Kegan Paul, 1970.

Poliakov, Leon. *The History of Anti-Semitism: From the Time of Christ to the Court Jews,* trans. Richard Howard. New York: Schocken, 1974.

Rabinowitz, Louis. *The Social Life of the Jews of Northern France.* 2nd ed. New York: Hermon Press, 1972.

Richardson, H. G. *The English Jewry under Angevin Kings.* London: Methuen, 1960.

Resnick, Irven I. *On Original Sin and a Disputation with the Jew, Leo, Concerning the Advent of Christ, The Son of God.* Philadelphia: University of Philadelphia Press, 1994.

Roth, Cecil. *A History of the Jews in England.* Oxford: Oxford University Press, 1964.

Rubin, Miri. *Corpus Christi: The Eucharist in Late Medieval Culture.* Cambridge, England: Cambridge University Press, 1991.

———. *Gentile Tales: The Narrative Assault on Late Medieval Jews.* New Haven, CT, and London: Yale University Press, 1999.

Ruether, Rosemary Radford. *Faith and Fratricide: The Theological Roots of Anti-Semitism.* New York: Seabury Press, 1974.

Russell, P. E. *The English Intervention in Spain and Portugal in the Time of Edward III and Richard II.* Oxford: Clarendon Press, 1955.

Scase, Wendy, Rita Copeland, and David Lawton, eds. *New Medieval Literatures.* Oxford: Clarendon Press; New York: Oxford University Press, 1997.

Schirmer, Walter F. *John Lydgate: A Study in the Culture of the XVth Century,* trans. Ann E. Keep. Berkeley and Los Angeles: University of California Press, 1961.

Scholem, Gershom G. *Major Trends in Jewish Mysticism.* New York: Schocken Books, 1961 [rpt. 1965].

———. *On the Kabbalah and its Symbolism.* New York: Schocken Books, 1969 [5th printing 1974].

Sebastia, J. Donate, and J. R. Magdalene Nom de Deu. *Three Jewish Communities in Medieval Valencia.* Jerusalem: Magnes Press, 1990.

Seiferth, Wolfgang S. *Synagogue and Church in the Middle Ages: Two Symbols in Art and Literature,* trans. Lee Chadeayne and Paul Gottwald. New York: Frederick Unger, 1970.

Shapiro, James. *Shakespeare and the Jews.* New York: Columbia University Press, 1996.

Shereshevsky, Esra. *Rashi: The Man and His World.* New York: Sepher-Harmon Press, 1982.

Shmuelevitz, Aryeh. *Jews of the Ottoman Empire in the Late Fifteenth and the Sixteenth Century.* Leiden, Netherlands: Brill, 1984.

Simon, Marcel. *Verus Israel,* trans. H. McKeating. Oxford: for the Littman Library by Oxford University Press, 1986.

Simonsohn, Shlomo. *The Jews in the Duchy of Milan.* vol. 1: *1387–1477.* Jerusalem: Israel Academy of Sciences and Humanities, 1982.

———. *The Apostolic See and the Jews: Documents, 492–1404.* Toronto: Pontifical Institute of Mediaeval Studies, 1988.

Smalley, Beryl. *The Study of the Bible in the Middle Ages.* Oxford: Blackwell, 1983.

Spearing, A. C. *Readings in Medieval Poetry.* Cambridge, England: Cambridge University Press, 1987.

Stillman, Norman. *The Jews of Arab Lands: A History and Source Book.* Philadelphia: Jewish Publication Society, 1979.

Stow, Kenneth. *Alienated Minority: The Jews of Medieval Latin Europe.* Cambridge, MA: Harvard University Press, 1992.

Szarmach, Paul, ed. *Aspects of Jewish Culture in the Middle Ages.* Albany, NY: SUNY Press, 1979.

Toaff, Ariel. *Love, Work, and Death: Jewish Life in Medieval Umbria.* London: Littman Library of Jewish Civilization, 1996.

Trachtenberg, Joshua. *Jewish Magic and Superstition: A Study in Folk Religion.* Cleveland and Philadelphia: World Publishing Co. & The Jewish Publication Society, 1961.

———. *The Devil and the Jews: The Medieval Conception of the Jew and its Relation to Modern Anti-Semitism.* Philadelphia: The Jewish Publication Society of America, 1983.

Wallace, David, ed. *The Cambridge History of Medieval English Literature.* Cambridge, England: Cambridge University Press, 1999.

Williams, A. Lukyn. *Adversos Judaeos: A Bird's-Eye View of Christian Apologiae until the Renaissance.* Cambridge, England: Cambridge University Press, 1935.

Wischnitzer, Mark. *A History of Jewish Crafts and Guilds.* New York: Jonathan David, 1965.

Wolfson, Elliot R. *Through the Speculum that Shines: Vision and Imagination in Medieval Mysticism.* Princeton, NJ: Princeton University Press, 1994.

———. *Circle in the Square: Studies in the Use of Gender in Kabbalistic Symbolism.* Albany, NY: SUNY Press, 1995.

Woolf, Rosemary. *The English Mystery Plays.* Berkeley and Los Angeles: University of California Press, 1972.

Wright, J. *The Play of Anti-Christ,* trans. and introd. J. Wright. Toronto: Pontifical Institute of Mediaeval Studies, 1967.

Wright, Stephen K. *The Vengeance of Our Lord: Medieval Dramatizations of the Destruction of Jerusalem.* Toronto: Pontifical Institute of Mediaeval Studies, 1989.

Index